RACE, CLASS, *and* POWER

Raymond W. Mack
Northwestern University

AMERICAN BOOK COMPANY —————————
New York

Preface

This book is intended to provide a theoretically structured view of dominant-minority relations. It is not an attempt to present an eclectic collection of literature on the topic.

What sociologists know about social stratification offers a useful context for the examination of minority status and minority role. I believe it is theoretically productive to explain research data in race relations in a stratification framework. If we look at what are called races in any given society as a culturally accepted definition of the situation, we can explain race relations as part of the distribution of power in the social structure. Dominant-minority interaction can be treated as a class situation or power distribution deemed desirable by privileged groups or categories. Those in power then find it socially convenient and normatively acceptable to explain the *status quo* as a consequence of hereditary differences.

For one example, the so-called "American dilemma" is less a dilemma for the majority if they can justify to themselves the motivations, life chances, and achievements which are a consequence of minority status. The inferior position occupied by minority people can be justified in a competitive society by a belief in hereditary differences. If minorities are innately inferior people, they get what they deserve and deserve what they get.

The linking material at the beginning of each chapter constitutes an attempt to relate the findings of the reprinted articles to this theoretical position—hopefully without doing violence to the intent of the writers. The articles reprinted here are primarily from the professional journals in social science. Selecting articles from the wealth of research material in race relations and social stratification is difficult. The goal is to choose those which are either substantial research contributions or valuable theoretical analyses.

I am grateful to the authors who generously granted permission to reprint their work and appreciate the cooperation of the various publishers. Like any teacher, I have been helped by the many students who have raised questions to which I did not know the answers. I would like especially to thank my associate Troy S. Duster for help in drafting several of the chapters, and even more for helping me to focus on some of the thornier problems in relating race relations data to stratification theory through the concept of definition of the situation. Finally, I am grateful to Mrs. Margaret Walker and Mrs.

iii

Virginia Sandblom for their invaluable secretarial assistance in the preparation of this book. As always, my work was speeded, improved, and made more fun by the help—emotional, secretarial, and editorial—of my wife, Ann Hunter Mack.

Raymond W. Mack
Evanston

Table of Contents

I The Sociology of Minorities

In Deerfield, Illinois, during the troubled months of 1960, native American white Anglo-Saxon Protestants were surprised to hear Jews speak with great venom about "the problem of niggers moving into our town." On the other hand, a few miles away on the South Side of Chicago, an American Jew may be shocked to hear an American Negro complaining that the reason groceries cost too much is "the kikes own everything."

And the surprises keep coming. Some Negroes prefer the association of light-skinned Negroes to dark-skinned Negroes; many Jews deplore the behavior of other Jews who are "loud and vulgar."

Now the Black Muslims have appeared on the scene, preaching black racial superiority. The same people who don't expect to find variations in skin color important to the Negro are surprised by the spread of the Muslim movement.

Isn't there a common theme underlying all this? Social scientists view these events as having definite similarities and exhibiting parallel patterns. They have collected their theories and observations about such things, and now place them in a category called "minorities."

A minority is a set of people who, capable of being distinguished on the basis of some physical or cultural characteristic, are treated collectively as inferior. Since they look or act different from other people, it is possible to identify them as a minority and exclude them from full participation in the society of which they are a part. These people consequently regard themselves as the objects of collective discrimination.

1

The mere existence of a minority means that there is a dominant group in that society with higher status, more rights, and more privileges.

A sociological minority need not be a mathematical one. There are far more Bantu-speaking blacks than European whites in the Union of South Africa, but the whites run the place. Negroes outnumber whites in some counties in southern United States; that is one reason why whites attempt to maintain rigid control of those communities. To be a minority, a number of people need only be identifiable as different and accorded differential access to the rewards of the social structure: less education; lower-quality facilities; exclusion from clubs, theaters, restaurants, neighborhoods; quotas on nominations for public office; segregation of places of worship; or simple categorical rejection in response to overtures of friendship.

Why Study Minorities?: The Sociological Ethic

Sociologists are searching for patterns. It doesn't matter whether they are studying waitresses in restaurants, medical students interning in a large hospital, or influences on voting behavior in a small town—they are always searching for a pattern. The reason for this is very simple. In fact, it is at the base of all scientific endeavor, whether it be natural or social science. Only by searching for the common, uniform, repetitive occurrences can we arrive at any general principles. If we see only the unique and idiosyncratic aspects of events, order escapes us. But order is necessary to the discovery of laws of behavior. If there were no order in the universe, physicists and chemists could discover no formulas. Their formulas refer to events that will occur *repeatedly* under specified conditions.

There are definite similarities between the way an intern addresses his superior and the way a waiter addresses the head waiter. There are patterns of deference. It is the discovery of such patterns that makes it possible to develop general principles and general laws of behavior. The hostility of Jews toward Negroes can no longer be viewed as a unique and peculiar development. It must be cast in a larger framework which allows one to see this as a certain *type* of intergroup relationship.

If we enlarge our perspective, we can see that adolescent delinquent gangs can also be classified in such a manner as to include some elements of minority status: adolescents are a minority in the age structure of society. Adults have more power, and they exclude adolescents from some positions and relationships. Similarly, some of the things that are true of Negroes because they are a racial minority, or true of Italian-Americans because they are an ethnic minority, are also true of women because they are a minority in our society. The attempt to understand the behavior of minorities, then, is much more than an attempt to understand the Negro or the Jew or the Oriental or the Catholic or the recent immigrant. It is an attempt to come to some general principle of intergroup relations which can then be applied across the board to any group, in any society, operating under similar specified conditions.

Why Study Minorities?: The American Dilemma

Perhaps the classic statement on the nature of the relationship between races in the United States is that of the Swedish social scientist Gunnar Myrdal. When Myrdal first came to this country to study its racial situation, he was struck by the continued references to "the Negro problem." He soon concluded that the whole arena had been misnamed. He saw, instead, "the white man's problem." The American creed is one of freedom and equality of opportunity. This is set forth explicitly in the official documents of the land, such as the federal constitution, and unofficially it is part of the folklore which has come down through the years, through the popular literature, and through the various other mass media of communication.

Yet, said Myrdal, the white American does not act in accord with this American creed when it comes to his relations with American Negroes. Instead, he systematically excludes Negroes from equal opportunity, from full participation in the society, and often from equal protection under the law.

This is the American dilemma. This is the white American's dilemma: how to go about reconciling the American creed with the treatment and condition of the American Negro. Supreme Court decisions of the last decade have only intensified the poignant nature of the dilemma. These decisions have disrupted long-standing *patterns* of Negro-white (minority-dominant) relations. Because the whole social order has been infused with a catalyst which is rearranging old patterns and developing new ones, minority group relationships in the United States are of particular interest to social scientists. One of the best ways to understand an occurrence is to watch it develop. Patterns of dominant-minority behavior are being structured all around us. There is no better time than now to study them, to report research findings to other scholars working on similar kinds of problems of process, and to disseminate this information to the public.

Related Readings

Ernest Dunbar provides us with a sociological profile, "The Negro in America Today," an outline of the American dilemma. Here is a detailed report of the consequences of centuries of discrimination.

A theoretical perspective is essential for the analysis of patterns of minority relations. Robert Bierstedt's seminal article, "The Sociology of Majorities," offers such a frame of reference. Bierstedt delineates the role of a majority as a residual locus of social power and a source of sustenance of normative integration for a society. Especially provocative for the student of race relations in the United States is his suggestion that patterned discrimination can be maintained only with the approval of the majority.

—————————Ernest Dunbar

The Negro in America Today

Imagine that you are an American Negro. If you are really not a Negro, this is going to call for all the imagination you can muster. Since I am one, maybe I can help you make the adjustment.

Your ancestors have been in this country for a mighty long time, far longer than the three hundred years that most white folk you bump into believe to be the Negro's length of residence here. That is one of the little ironies of your life in America. Your children's schoolbooks tell them about Christopher Columbus, George Washington, Betsy Ross and Paul Revere. But they will probably never hear of the many heroes of your own race who have figured in this country's development from the very beginning. That is, unless you yourself provide them with the information.

Of course, since you've used the same textbooks, your own information is also scanty. But maybe you know that 30 Negroes accompanied the Spanish explorer Balboa when he discovered the Pacific, that a Spanish Negro called Estevanico blazed a route from Mexico through New Mexico and Arizona to the Northwest and that, in 1526, Negro slaves owned by the Spanish frustrated Spain's attempts to establish a colony in what was to become South Carolina, by deserting the Spanish ranks to join the Indians.

Certainly, you know that Crispus Attucks, for whom your local Elks lodge or boys' club is named, was a Negro sailor who was shot down by British infantry in the "Boston Massacre," among the first Americans to die for this country's independence. But though you know about Betsy Ross, you may not know about Deborah Gannett, a woman of your race who masqueraded as a man and fought with distinction in a Massachusetts regiment during the Revolution.

It was not until 1619, when twenty of your ancestors were shipped

Reprinted from *Look*, April 10, 1962, pp. 25-36. Copyright 1962 by Cowles Magazines & Broadcasting, Inc.

into Virginia as slaves, that the long and unique struggle of your people in America began. The peremptory nature of your ancestors' arrival here had a lot to do with your present outlook.

You don't celebrate St. Patrick's Day or Bastille Day, your mother does not cook the dishes her mother brought over from the "old country," and you don't dress up now and then in the national costume of your former homeland or sing its songs. The roots you possess are sunk deep in the soil of America. The joyful and tragic songs you sing are fashioned from your experiences in America. Although other Americans belong to organizations such as the Sons of Italy, the Sons of Erin or the Japanese-American Association, you tend to fear that joining an organization whose members must be of African descent may be somehow racist, a negation of the long effort of your people to be integrated into American society.

When you visit the United Nations in New York, you see African delegates who look exactly like your Uncle Willie or Cousin Frank, but who perhaps speak French and whose last names are Diop or Diallo, not Johnson or Jones, the names you acquired in the New World. And if they ask you when you are coming "home," you may have difficulty in explaining why "home" is on these shores. Given a map of Africa, you couldn't pick out the spot from which your forebears were wrenched, if your life depended on it.

For better or for worse, America is wedded to you, and you to it, till death do you part. It is this that makes you different from all the other immigrants who are now called Americans.

You are aware that the term "Negro" is an imprecise one and tells little about the human being it designates. Negroes come in all varieties of colors and sizes. They are Baptists, Methodists, Episcopalians, Catholics, Moslems, atheists and agnostics. They can be found on the rolls of the Democratic, Republican, Socialist and Communist parties. They live in Montana and Maine, Alabama and Alaska.

Some Negroes work in the White House. Others are having great difficulty getting any kind of work anywhere.

Income

Today, almost a century after the Emancipation Proclamation and the 13th Amendment, you and 19 million other Negroes are still struggling for rights and privileges that most other Americans take for granted. The Emancipation Proclamation did not say anything about buying a hamburger at a Southern lunch counter or a home in a Northern suburb. And though the U. S. Constitution's 15th Amendment is supposed to guarantee that the Negro citizen should not be denied that basic element of citizenship, the vote, thousands of black Americans live in areas where the 15th Amendment has yet to be recognized.

So you wince inwardly when you hear your white fellow citizens refer to the "free world," and you understand so well why few Negroes employ that phrase. But then this is only one of many split images of life in America—life as you know it and life as the majority group sees it. On some subjects, those images are unified, but on many, they are wide apart, like a picture out of focus.

Probably the most difficult image to focus properly is where you and your 19 million fellow Negroes stand today, 96 years after slavery was formally ended.

You've come a long way. You would agree on that. But *all* Americans have come a long way, so the question more properly is: Where do you stand today in relation to the rest of America?

You know that there are increased opportunities for Negroes in America today. A lot of restrictions that confronted your mother and father when they were growing up are happily now merely the subject of family joking. You are better educated than they were. Negroes are attending colleges and universities in the North and South in increasing numbers, 100,000 in Negro institutions alone. They are moving into professions and skills heretofore closed to members of your race. Pick up a Negro newspaper or magazine, and you may see a picture of a technician with a black skin working on a multistage rocket or a brown-skinned flight surgeon checking instruments electronically linked to a white-skinned astronaut.

Yet, despite the widened horizons and the increased opportunities, there is a mounting sense of frustration in your community, with tensions that threaten to boil over if the pace of advancement is not stepped up. Why? Because of where you stand as compared to other Americans. Many Negroes have seen their income levels rise sharply, their modes of living change in line with their new prosperity. But for many more, getting a job and keeping it are problems of giant proportions.

As a Negro, your chances of being unemployed are about three times as great as they would be if you were white. That fact must be borne in mind when your progress is being considered. In 1939, the median income for Negro families was $489, or 37 per cent of that of white families. Negro wage earners made strides from World War II through the Korean conflict, but they have not shared proportionately in the country's economic advances of the past two decades.

On the contrary, since 1952, Negro income has slipped. In that year, the best yet for the Negro, the median income of Negro families was only 57 per cent of that of white families—$2,338 to $4,114 a year, respectively. The ratio has remained below this level for the past nine years.

When you consider that Negro families have an average of 4.4 members, compared to 3.6 for white families, and thus require more in the way of food, clothing and shelter, the gap in income becomes even more meaningful.

The grim figures for Negro income nationally are heavily influenced by the low income of Negroes in rural areas, most of which are in the

South. Negro males 14 and older in the Northeast, North Central and Western states have a median money income about three fourths that of white males. But in the South, Negro males have only one third of the money income of their white counterparts.

Employment

Discrimination in employment, bias in upgrading and poor education have contributed to the Negro's economic difficulties. Traditionally "last hired and first fired," Negroes must battle the bias of both employers and some unions. Though the race of which you are a member comprises about 11 per cent of the nation's working force, it constituted 21 per cent of the unemployed in the fall of 1961. In Chicago, where the total unemployment rate was 5.7 per cent, the Negro jobless rate was 17.3; in Washington, D. C., where Negroes made up 53.9 per cent of the population, they accounted for 71 per cent of the unemployed; in Detroit, 112,000 of the 185,000 people out of work were Negroes. The fact that Negroes are moving into occupations formerly closed to them does not alter the worsening plight of Negro workers as a whole. That is because the bulk of Negro labor is unskilled, and automation is cutting wide inroads into unskilled labor.

As a Negro, you've got a special kind of problem when it comes to advising your youngsters on the choice of a career. Should you encourage them to prepare themselves for fields in which the doors have long been shut to Negroes, in the hope that they will somehow break through the barriers? Or should you counsel them to stick to the "safe" occupations such as teaching, law or the ministry?

Even if your children do not pursue professional careers, a rocky road awaits them in the crafts. Negro youths are excluded from apprentice training by racial bars in many of the nation's craft unions. Less than 1 per cent of the apprentices in the construction trades are Negroes. In the country's 32 major cities, a survey found only 100 Negro apprentices in all fields. To complete the vicious circle, Negro youths are denied on-the-job training by many employers.

Paradoxically, opportunities are beginning to open up for young Negroes in some fields, but qualified candidates are not available, because past discrimination discouraged them from taking the necessary training for what had seemed to be an unattainable goal. Edwin Berry, executive director of Chicago's Urban League, will tell you, "People call me up with a job. They want a Negro with certain qualifications for a job from which Negroes have always been excluded. *Now* they say, 'Get me a Negro.' It isn't done just like that!"

Perhaps the most militantly articulate battler against bias in labor is A. Philip Randolph, 72-year-old president of the Brotherhood of Sleeping Car Porters and the only Negro vice-president of the AFL-CIO. Randolph says, "Discrimination in employment is the crisis of the Negro American today. With Negroes constituting the major portion of unskilled labor and with no way to get training in skills, Negroes are gradually being replaced with automation. Automation is building up a hard core of unemployables. And when the black worker is in trouble," says Randolph, "the community is in trouble. He can't keep his kids in school, he can't keep his home intact, and, as a result, the morale of the community breaks down."

A veteran in the Negro's long fight for full admission to union ranks, Randolph founded the Negro American Labor Council in 1960 to press for that goal within organized labor. Randolph makes it plain that he is less than happy with the attitude of the AFL-CIO and its leader, George Meany, who once demanded of him, "Who the hell appointed you as guardian of all the Negro members in America?"

"George is a gradualist," says Randolph, "and we Negroes don't want gradualism in this age of automation. It might have been OK ten years ago, but we don't want token-ism today. We've got to have complete integration."

He adds, "The only thing that will deliver the black workingman is his own effort. The leaders of organized labor have taken us for granted for so long they can't understand that the winds of a civil-rights revolution are blowing in the labor movement today."

Housing

As a Negro, housing—or the lack of it—may trouble you even more than employment. The all-Negro ghetto in which you live is like countless others that surround the centers of the nation's cities. From them stem all-Negro schools, all-Negro hospitals and all-Negro churches. In the North, that makes for a segregation in fact that rivals the segregation defined by law in the South.

According to a report of the U. S. Civil Rights Commission, housing ". . . seems to be the one commodity in the American market that is not freely available on equal terms to everyone who can afford to pay." It is estimated that less than two per cent of new housing guaranteed by Federal Housing Authority (FHA) mortgages is available to Negroes. In the case of non-Government-financed housing, the percentage open to Negroes is even smaller.

Since Government-insured or -guaranteed mortgages account for a major portion of all residential housing constructed in the U. S. since World War II, you are likely to view your own Government as one of the chief culprits in limiting your access to better housing.

As a Negro, you know better than to take those bank-mortgage advertisements and television commercials literally. For banks and other leading institutions are the Government's accomplices in closing the door to the Negro homeseeker. No matter what your qualifications, you will generally find it more difficult to obtain a home mortgage than a white person does. If you are trying to buy a home in an all-white area, your chances of getting a mortgage from a commercial lending institution are extremely slim.

While the Federal Government has thrown its weight behind the drive to eliminate racial segregation in schools and employment, its housing policies actually have contributed to the expansion of residential segregation in the nation's cities. Federal money has gone to guarantee mortgages for housing in suburbs that bar Negro buyers, and segregation is prevalent in the Government's own public-housing program. Over 80 per cent of the Federally sponsored housing is segregated racially.

Trapped between Government-assisted discrimination and the bias of private builders and banking institutions, the Negro is squeezed more and more into ghettos. Whites fleeing to the suburbs have left the city to the Negro. The Negro population in the nation's 21 central cities has increased by nearly 2 million, or 50 per cent, in the last 10 years, while the white population has declined by one million. But the increase in the number of Negroes in the cities has not been accompanied by a proportionate increase in the housing available to them. The squeeze has produced an explosive situation that constantly threatens to erupt.

The Greenleigh Report, a 1960 study of aid to dependent children (ADC) in Cook County, reveals some stark insights into the results of deprivations suffered by Negroes in the nation's second largest city. While the Greenleigh study says Chicago "may be the most segregated city in the country, as far as housing is concerned," many of the conditions faced by the 900,000 Negroes there may be found in other communities. Perhaps they may be found in yours.

Chicago spends more than $4.4 million every month on its aid-to-dependent-children program. Of the 100,000 recipients of ADC assistance, 90 per cent are Negro. Since the Federal Government puts up more than half of the funds for the Illinois ADC program, the position of the Negro in Chicago has significance for every taxpayer.

The study points out that, of the job orders placed with private employment agencies in Chicago in 1958, 98 per cent barred non-whites. Yet rents paid by Negro families for poorer housing exceeded considerably those paid by white families, in effect placing a "color tax" on the Negro wage earners. White families paid an average monthly rent of $64.84, while the monthly rent of Negro families averaged $82.77. "This rent differential, a result of discrimination in housing, costs Illinois taxpayers at least $3.4 million a year in Cook County (Chicago) alone," the report says.

The study concludes that discrimination in employment has "a greater direct and indirect impact on the ADC program than almost any other single factor, because it results in desertion, divorce and unwed parenthood, with all their social and economic costs. It has an important causal relationship to unemployment."

Schools, Segregation

Perhaps the school-desegregation struggle in the South has attracted more attention and stirred more emotions than any other issue involving the Negro in the past two decades. As a Negro, you were concerned with this issue long before the 1954 Supreme Court decision, which brought the problem of equal educational opportunity to the attention of the nation as a whole. You remember the long struggles in the courts, some of which dated as far back as the 1930's.

When the Supreme Court finally declared compulsory segregation in public education to be unconstitutional, you also remember, you were filled with expectation. But today, seven years after that decision, only 7.3 per cent of Negroes in the 17 Southern and border states are attending classes with whites. (Aside from the border states and the District of Columbia, no Southern state has as much as 2 per cent of its Negro pupils in classes with white children.)

Out of a total of 2,805 biracial school districts in the Southern and border states, 1,894 have not even *begun* to comply with the Supreme Court ruling, according to the 1961 report of the U. S. Civil Rights Commission. Among them is Clarendon County, S. C., one of the five areas involved in the original 1954 decision.

The cold figures of integrated attendance do not reveal the emotional stress or adjustment problems that may affect the few Negro children admitted to white schools. Last November, an Atlanta couple withdrew their daughter from a previously all-white high school to which she had been admitted, with two other Negroes, in August. Though the girl had been making "A's" and "B's" in her courses, her parents said she sometimes studied as much as ten hours a night and had become nervous and suffered from insomnia. The National Association for the Advancement of Colored People charged that, by admitting only nine of 130 Negro students who applied for transfers to white schools, Atlanta's pupil-placement plan subjected those few who were accepted to undue pressures as "display pieces and guinea pigs." A school administrator contended that the high school involved was one that had higher standards than many of the city's high schools, with more than 90 per cent of its graduates going to college. He added that the girl's parents told him she had encountered no hostility from students there.

Some student pioneers have received warm support from sympathetic teachers. The parent of a first-grader, one of 18 admitted to formerly all-white schools in Dallas last fall, will tell you, "His teachers seem to be extraordinarily nice to him. Often, when my wife or I go to pick him up, one of the teachers has her arm around him, talking to him. There have been no threats and no unpleasantness." For this Dallas parent, his six-year-old's integration meant some changes in his own behavior. "My wife and I decided to stop mentioning color or anything about race around him," he says.

In recent months, a new term—"resegregation"—has emerged to describe a process that is further slowing the already creeping pace of public-school integration. Resegregation occurs as desegregated schools change from all-white to all-Negro, often as whites leave a desegregated school district and move to other areas, and Negroes move in. School desegregation in Washington, D. C., Baltimore and St. Louis has been virtually negated by this condition.

Negroes have now expanded their attack to come to grips with the other axis of the problem: segregated schools in the North. If your child attends public school in one of the major cities of the North or West, the overwhelming majority of his fellow students are likely to be Negroes also, as is every member of the school staff from the principal to the janitor.

New York City has 95 public elementary schools with Negro or Puerto Rican enrollments exceeding 90 per cent. In Chicago, 87 per cent of the Negro elementary-school pupils attend virtually all-Negro schools; Los Angeles has 43 elementary schools with at least 85 per cent Negro enrollment; Philadelphia has 38 such schools that are more than 99 per cent Negro, and 45 per cent of Detroit's Negro public-school pupils attend schools in which Negroes make up more than 80 per cent of the enrollment.

While segregated schools outside the South stem chiefly from segregated neighborhoods, some school officials have come under fire for administrative policies that increase such segregation. A Federal court recently found the New Rochelle, N. Y., school board guilty of deliberately gerrymandering school-zone lines to confine Negro pupils to a predominantly Negro elementary school. The ruling is destined to have wide repercussions in other Northern cities. Already, Negro parents in Philadelphia, Chicago and Englewood, N. J., have brought suits against school officials to alleviate alleged discriminatory school policies in those cities.

If you are a Negro parent, you know that the question of the *quality* of the education dispensed in your child's predominantly Negro school is another sore point in your community. Crowded classrooms, poor library facilities, a high proportion of substitute and inexperienced teachers, outmoded curricula, all serve to increase the handicaps your child and others like him must face. An NAACP survey reported that only 2 per cent of Chicago's predominantly white schools and 19 per cent of its mixed schools were on double shifts, but that 81 per cent of children on double shifts were Negro.

The Armed Forces

It is in the nation's armed forces that the American Negro has made his greatest advances. Indeed, the Negro serviceman has achieved a degree of equality on the base that is considerably ahead of that in the society beyond its gates. President Truman's Executive Order 9981,

issued in 1948, said: ". . . There shall be equality of treatment and opportunity for all persons in the armed services. . . ." With some notable
exceptions, this policy of racial equality has been put into practice.

The number of Negro officers in the services is expanding, although
at a slow rate. Today, 3 per cent of Army officers are Negroes, as compared to .99 per cent at the end of World War II; 1.1 per cent of officers
in the Air Force are Negroes; in the Navy and Marine Corps, which
had no Negro officers at the beginning of World War II, .1 per cent of
the officers are Negroes. At present, 34 of the 8,543 cadets in the Army,
Naval and Air Force academies are Negroes.

The Air Force lists the nation's sole Negro general officer, Maj. Gen.
Benjamin O. Davis, Jr., the fourth Negro to graduate from West Point
and son of the first and only other Negro to gain a general's star, Brig.
Gen. B. O. Davis, Sr., U. S. Army, now retired.

James C. Evans, a Negro, is counselor to the Assistant Secretary of
Defense for Manpower, and his duties include "monitoring" the progress
of integration in the armed forces. If you ask him what the chances are
for the promotion of another Negro to general's rank, he will tell you
that it's not too distant in the Army or Air Force, but that the prospects
are not as bright in the Navy, where no Negro ranks above lieutenant
commander. "It takes 27 years to produce an admiral," says Evans, "and
we just haven't been in the business that long."

The National Guard, military reserve units and the Reserve Officers'
Training Corps still contain significant pockets of resistance to the Federal policy of integration, primarily in the Southern states.

Sports

Another area in which your people have made indisputable progress
is in the sports arena. Perhaps the most spectacular example is baseball.
Since 1947, when Brooklyn's Branch Rickey brought Jackie Robinson to
the Dodgers to break the color bar in baseball, Negro diamond stars have
come into their own. Out of a total of 450 players in both major leagues
during the 1961 season, 80 were Negroes.

In the National League, which has a third again as many Negroes as
the American League, Negro players have almost dominated the game.
Eight of the ten National Leaguers receiving the Most Valuable Player
Award in the past decade have been Negroes, and a Negro was selected
as Rookie of the Year in nine of the past 13 years. Recently, Robinson
became the first of his race to enter baseball's Hall of Fame, while San
Francisco's Willie Mays became the sport's highest-paid player today,
at a salary of $90,000.

In professional football, Negroes are more than holding their own. Of
the 504 players in the National Football League in 1961, 83 were Negroes including seven on the Dallas team.

With the exception of golf, which has been slowest in lowering racial
bars, Negroes have made their mark in all other major sports.

Voting and Justice

A crucial part of your position as a Negro in America is your access to the right to vote, to justice in the nation's courts and to fair treatment from police. The evidence shows you still have a long way to go.

The report of the 1961 U. S. Civil Rights Commission reveals that Negroes are prevented from voting—by outright denial or through fear of physical harm or economic reprisal—in 100 counties in eight Southern states. The report further points out that Negroes "have no real opportunity to serve on a grand or petit jury" in many communities. "A real understanding of the administration of justice in the United States cannot be had," the report goes on, without the knowledge that "Negroes generally do not have fair representation in the agencies of justice . . ." and are the most frequent targets of police brutality in many regions of the country.

Although the obstacles still confronting Negro Americans are formidable, you know many that have overcome racial barriers to win better jobs, more money and a higher standard of living. Fletcher Martin, Louisville-born Negro reporter on the Chicago *Sun Times,* says, "Being a Southern-reared Negro, I am both intrigued and delighted to look out of my office window at the numerous Negroes who have pleasure craft out on Lake Michigan. They certainly don't have them in Jackson, Mississippi!"

Sometimes, the Negro's new affluence has come as a by-product of segregation. Perhaps the wealthiest Negro community in America is to be found in Atlanta, Ga. There, cut off heretofore from many of the services available to whites, Negroes have developed multimillion-dollar banking and insurance firms to meet their own needs.

The Leaders, the Led

Despite its gains, the Negro community in America today is seething with impatience at the rate of its progress—impatience of which the "sit-ins" and "Freedom Riders" are manifestations.

The organization that feels these pressures most keenly is perhaps the 53-year-old National Association for the Advancement of Colored People. If you are not one of the NAACP's 371,060 dues-paying members, you, like most of the other 19 million Negroes in America, probably share its goals. Long damned by white Southerners as a "radical" organization, the NAACP now finds itself under attack by a growing section of Negro opinion, which charges that it is "moving too slowly," that it favors court suits over more direct action such as "sit-ins" and that it is dominated by middle-class intellectuals who are out of touch with Negro masses and youth. Moreover, its civil-rights preserve is being encroached upon by newer groups such as the Congress of Racial Equality (CORE), the Rev. Martin Luther King's Southern Christian Leadership Conference and a number of newly founded student movements.

Roy Wilkins, the association's Minnesota-reared executive secretary, denies this. "The general proposition that the NAACP has law books under one arm and the Supreme Court under the other is a myth," he'll tell you. "Sit-ins? We had sit-ins as long ago as 1929!"

While giving the student protest groups credit for some gains, Wilkins maintains, "The youth bring the fire and drive that's necessary, but it is the adults who do most of the organizing, planning and financing that are the backbone of this fight."

Wilkins says those who accuse the NAACP of being "legalistic" are often "those who want to act 'nonlegally.'" He argues that the groundwork for the Negro's present advancement, including the right to unsegregated interstate travel, was laid by the NAACP in its many court battles.

Wilkins, too, is dissatisfied with the rate of the Negro's progress, but he acknowledges that there *has* been progress. "A couple of years ago," he says, "three Negro engineers at a General Electric plant complained that they would have to apply for a transfer because they couldn't get the kind of homes they wanted in the area where the plant was located. Twenty years ago, the problem would have been getting Negro engineers *into* G.E.!"

"I have infinite good faith in the good sense of the American Negro," Wilkins adds. "He has managed to survive in a society that has erected every bear trap it could, which has hurt him psychologically with constant demeaning, year after year, decade after decade. But, despite job discrimination and other economic disadvantages, he has managed to send his kids to school, to get them an education. He made friends as he went along—he's a hell of a diplomat, you know. He might have made them by a little 'Uncle Tom-ing,' but he made them, and he survived."

Nevertheless, there are many Negroes within the ranks of the NAACP itself who feel that it is not militant enough about combatting the grievances that affect you and other Negroes in your day-to-day activities.

Many of these individuals are young college students and residents of the South. Perhaps typical of this group is Charles Black, a senior at Atlanta's Negro Morehouse College and one of the leaders of a student organization called the Committee on Appeal for Human Rights, whose sit-in demonstrations led to the desegregation of eating facilities of 13 Atlanta drug, department and dime-store firms in 1961.

Like most of the students taking part in demonstrations, Black is a member of the NAACP, but he says, "The NAACP's officers don't seem to like direct-action programs. Their lawyers are usually available if we ask for them, but we try to avoid that. Take this restaurant thing, for instance. It might have taken ten years if we'd tried to push this through the national body."

The cleavage between the student groups and the NAACP is also one between youth and its elders. "We decided to work on these problems with our own organization, because then we don't have to answer to anybody," Black explains. "The older folk in the NAACP have become set in their ways. Litigation is necessary, but it is not the *only* way. I hate to use the word 'conservative,' but they don't do things the way we would."

One of the elders who agrees is Edward Warren, president of the NAACP's Los Angeles adult branch. "The current wave of sit-ins was not started by the NAACP," Warren asserts. "We saw them going, and then said, 'I'm your leader. Where are you going?' The students themselves just got tired of the situation, in city after city."

Warren says, "The old-guard philosophy of the elite leadership of the association does not appeal to the masses," but he concedes that the NAACP is still the organization to which most Negroes in trouble turn. In recent months, the NAACP, CORE and the Martin Luther King forces have moved to consolidate their efforts, with the NAACP contributing legal and financial assistance to CORE and to King's demonstrations.

There is one organization in your community that strives not for integration, but for total separation of the races—the militant Black Muslims. The Muslims demand that "some states" (they never say which or how many) be set aside for exclusive—and independent—occupation by all America's Negroes.

To the Black Muslims, all whites are "devils." Muslim leaders will tell you that white America is headed for the rocks and that you had better separate from it or go down with the ship. An estimated 100,000 Negro Americans have accepted this view and joined the Black Muslim movement. Muslim "temples" are located in more than 60 cities across the nation, North, South, East and West.

The Muslims are a rigidly disciplined group that draws adherents from the most underprivileged sections of America's Negro ghettos. They welcome those who have been ignored or rejected by other Negro groups. The Muslims give their converts a new frame of reference: the glorification of the black man and a total rejection of America's social system.

Muslims also reject the term "Negro" (they say they are "black men"), alcohol, tobacco, pork and all kinds of self-indulgence. Every Black Muslim exchanges "the name given him by his former slavemaster" for the surname "X" as a symbol of his new identity and his break with a society he despises.

The Muslims are especially critical of Negroes who preach non-violence. "Malcolm X," head of Harlem's Muslims, told a Muslim audience, "Everybody defends himself when attacked but us—we are not supposed to fight back. Martin Luther King is like Novocain. The white man is hurting you, and King is going around telling you not to fight back. He's doing their job for them!"

Although Negro leaders privately condemn the racist and separatist aspect of the Muslim movement, few are willing to take a public stand against them, for they are aware of the desperation that spawned the movement.

In the midst of the American Negro's growing dissatisfaction with his rate of advancement, Negro leaders are being forced to make new appraisals of their own people. The economic improvement of urban Negroes has brought insistent demands for the end of Jim Crow in all sectors of their existence, in areas that used to be peripheral to Negro life.

A. P. Tureaud, veteran attorney for the NAACP in New Orleans, says he once took up the complaints of Negroes who were barred from municipally owned New Orleans golf courses with the association's former chief counsel, Thurgood Marshall, now a Federal judge.

Marshall, engulfed in school-desegregation suits and sit-in cases, snorted: "*Golf!* I'm not interested in Negroes playing golf!" "But, Thurgood," Tureaud replied, "you've got to tend to the *whole* Negro, golfers and everybody else, not just the students."

Within your own community, you are often more critical than white people of Negro crime, illegitimacy and civic irresponsibility, although you know well the social and economic facts of life.

A highly placed Negro in the Federal Government says, "When I look in the paper and see there's been a rape or a mugging, and the suspect is a Negro, I'm embarrassed. Some Negroes say, 'To hell with it. It's not *me*.' But I'm afraid it *is* 'me.'" A Negro social worker in Chicago says, "Twenty-five per cent of the Negroes in this city are on some form of relief. It is not a fact of which we are proud."

For the Negro who achieves prominence, success often poses poignantly thorny problems. Such Negroes are idolized by other members of the race and are often trapped between the desire to be themselves and the role they are asked to play as idols. Some reject the special role; others do not.

Singer Barbara McNair, the first Negro woman to have a regularly sponsored television program, will tell you, "Those of us who are in special positions should be especially careful, because we are symbols. We should be good, not bad symbols.

"I'm a relaxed person. When I travel on a plane, I would wear slacks if I were white. Because I'm a Negro, I don't. People would say, 'Ah, HAH! That's a Negro for you!'"

Talk to Judge James B. Parsons of Chicago, first Negro to be appointed to a Federal district-court bench, and he will point out another aspect of this conflict in roles. "My job is to sit on the bench and not know the color of the people who come before me," he says. "I know I run the risk of being misunderstood by Negroes who want to see a sword-in-hand Negro out there fighting for civil rights, but my job involves being incapable of noticing a person's skin color. I'm a natural optimist. Perhaps it is because I did not come from the Deep South. I haven't had the experiences which make me bitter, and perhaps this is best. It helps me to see not just the oppressed Negro, but the oppressed Negro as part of a damnable ethnic system that permeates the Chicago area. It's hard to be an Italian in some Chicago neighborhoods."

Not all Negroes have acquired Judge Parson's detachment. James L. Hicks, editor of Harlem's weekly *Amsterdam News,* says, "I've been fooled and frustrated about racial things so many, many times by white people that I can't help it—most of the time when a white man promises me something racially good, I simply place him on probation. If he does what he says he's going to do, I am happy to have found another one who kept his word with a Negro. If he runs out on his word, I dismiss it by saying, 'That's exactly what I expected.' But I'm never left waiting at the church, because I simply don't get dressed and run to the altar every time a white person says he loves me.

"In short, when it comes to dealing with the white man on racial lines, I follow the Harlem proverb, 'Blessed is he who expects nothing, for he shall not be disappointed.'"

When you talk to some of the Negroes working for access to housing in the suburbs, they will admit there are some wealthy Negroes who would not move to the suburbs if they could. "They find it more congenial in the ghetto where, although segregated, they may have lavish homes," said one. "Moreover, for the Negro politician or businessman, his sources of power or money lie in the Negro community, and he would be cutting his own throat if he moved away from it. Besides, it's more trouble to get to and from the suburbs."

A Northern Negro newspaperman, however, sees suburbia as a welcome form of escape from constant preoccupation with "The Problem." "Man, sometimes I just get tired of talking to Negroes," he says. Many other Negroes reflect this feeling.

As you try to figure out what your position is in America today, you will concede that you have made some rather large strides, but you will know that, from where you sit, the millennium is nowhere in sight. If you are United Nations Under Secretary Ralph Bunche, your son may still be turned away from a tennis club when it is discovered that he is a Negro; if you are Deputy Assistant Secretary of State Carl Rowan, you may have difficulty getting service in a Kansas City nightclub; and though you are Municipal Judge James C. Flanigan of Denver, you may still be refused admission to a local golf course.

After more than three hundred years in America, your people are still climbing a slope named Hope toward a summit named Equality. There are still many crevasses and a lot of climbing ahead.

Unlike America's other ethnic groups, the Negro has not been able to "join" the American people by dint of education and income. His skin is still his prison. But the outcome of the American democratic experiment depends largely on whether all its citizens, regardless of color, can avail themselves of America's opportunities. In that sense, your struggle is America's too.

================ Robert Bierstedt

The Sociology of Majorities

A casual but not uninterested observer of the current sociological scene
could not fail to notice the serious concern within the field for problems
of minorities and minority groups. If he pauses to reflect upon this
phenomenon the thought may occur to him that nowhere is there a
similar or even comparable concern for majorities and majority groups.
Systematic treatments of this latter subject are distinguished by their
scarcity, and this may seem doubly strange in view of the fact that some
of the societies in which sociology has reached its highest development
accept as almost axiomatic the political principle of majority rule.

The proposition that majorities have been neglected requires no more
than negative evidence. Even those sociologists like Simmel,[1] von Wiese,[2]
and MacIver,[3] who have touched upon the subject, have done so largely
in a political rather than a sociological context.[4] Without implying that
political and sociological concerns are mutually exclusive, it may nevertheless be suggested that the latter might be broader in significance than
the former and may present issues which a political emphasis obscures.
Some of these issues we should expect to see treated in sociography.
When we turn to the sociology of groups, however, a subject which has
properly been regarded as of central and indeed of pivotal concern,[5]

[1] "Exkurs über die Überstimmung," in Soziologie, Leipzig: Duncker & Humblot, 1908, pp.
186-197.
[2] Leopold von Wiese and Howard Becker, Systematic Sociology, New York: Wiley, 1932,
pp. 267-268, 431-432, 598.
[3] See Leviathan and the People, Baton Rouge: Louisiana State University Press, 1939; The
Web of Government, New York: Macmillan, 1947; and The Elements of Social Science,
London: Methuen, 1921, pp. 174-176.
[4] Political treatments of the principle of majority rule embrace almost the entire literature
of political philosophy, and particularly the philosophy of democracy. For an excellent
recent discussion, with carefully selected bibliography, see Willmoore Kendall, John Locke
and the Doctrine of Majority Rule, Urbana: University of Illinois Press, 1941. Kendall
suggests that while in one sense no political scientist can avoid the problem of majorities,
in another sense it is the " 'dark continent' of modern political theory" (p. 16). See also
von Gierke, "Über die Geschichte des Majoritätsprinzipes," Schmollers Jahrbuch für
Gezetsbegung Verwaltung und Volkswirtschaft im Deutschen Reiche, 39:565-587, 1915;
and Ladislas Konopczynski, "Majority Rule," Encyclopedia of the Social Sciences, 10:55-
59.
[5] For a comprehensive summary of this subject see Logan Wilson, "The Sociography of
Groups," in Twentieth Century Sociology, Gurvitch and Moore, eds. New York: Philosophical Library, 1945, pp. 139-171. Also Florian Znaniecki, "Social Organization and
Institutions," ibid., pp. 172-217; Wiese-Becker, op. cit., pp. 488-555; G. A. Lunberg,
Foundations of Sociology, New York: Macmillan, 1939, pp. 339-374, and "Some Problems
of Group Classification and Measurement," American Sociological Review, 5:351-360
(June, 1940).

From American Sociological Review, Vol. 13, pp. 700-710. By permission.

we find an almost infinite number of classifications of types of groups, but no mention of majorities. There are open groups and closed groups, organized groups and unorganized groups, primary groups and secondary groups, "A" groups and "B" groups, in-groups and out-groups, "real" groups and "normal" groups, horizontal groups and vertical groups, voluntary groups and involuntary groups, large groups and small groups, long-lived groups and short-lived groups, "unibonded" groups and "multibonded" groups, and many others in terms of sociological form, and others still, such as age, sex, ethnic, occupational, economic, educational, class, religious, linguistic, territorial, and so on,[6] in terms of sociological content.[7] In all these classifications the majority-minority distinction is conspicuous by its absence. If not in sociography at least in the general tests on sociology one would expect the majority-minority distinction to have achieved some prominence, particularly in view of the heavy emphasis upon minorities, but again the distinction fails to appear, and there is no discussion of majorities as such. Finally, one would expect to find treatments of majorities in texts on social control, but once again a cursory examination leaves the expectation unfulfilled.[8] Social control is treated almost exclusively in terms of such cultural factors as folkways, mores, institutions, laws, and so on, rather than in terms of such social factors as the influence of majorities. It is almost as if sociologists had unanimously agreed to leave the subject of majorities to the devices of political scientists.

The subject, however, is worth considering for several reasons. The first of these is that number is a necessary category in sociology and that

[6] For a recent discussion of the problem of group classification see P. A. Sorokin, *Society, Culture, and Personality*, New York: Harper, 1947, pp. 145-255.

[7] In view of the difficulty of finding a *fundamentum divisionis* for a logically rigorous classification of groups, the question arises as to whether a classification can serve any useful purpose, even if an adequate construction could be achieved. Ogburn and Nimkoff, for example, contend with some cogency that all such classifications are of limited usefulness. See *Sociology*, Boston: Houghton Mifflin, 1946, p. 251. In support of this view it may be said that a good deal of so-called formal or structural sociology, whatever its intrinsic merit or logical appeal, has little or nothing to do with sociological theory. Taxonomy is not theory, although the two are often confused. Sociological taxonomy belongs to methodology, sociological theory to sociology itself; taxonomy deals with the logical relations between sociological concepts; sociological theory deals with the spatio-temporal and causal relations between social variables. Logical order is the goal of the former inquiry, scientific truth of the latter; the former issues, ideally, in a modified Tree of Porphyry; the latter in universal propositions. On the other hand, in opposition to the view of Ogburn and Nimkoff, classifications, like nominal definitions, are, if not systematically necessary, at least a desirable propaedeutic to the construction of sociological theories.

[8] On this subject see L. L. Bernard, *Social Control*, New York: Macmillan, 1939; Paul H. Landis, *Social Control*, Philadelphia: Lippincott, 1939; Jerome Doud, *Control in Human Societies*, New York: Appleton-Century, 1936; E. A. Ross, *Social Control*, New York: Macmillan, 1916, (Ross notes, however, that "The prestige of *numbers* gives ascendancy to the crowd," p. 78); and Joseph S. Roucek and Associates, *Social Control*, New York: Van Nostrand, 1947. On the other hand, there is relevant material in William Albig, *Public Opinion*, New York: McGraw-Hill, 1939, although not couched specifically in terms of majorities and minorities. See especially Chapters I, II, and XVI.

phenomena of many different kinds change not only in degree but also in their nature as they vary in size. Certainly small groups, for example, are different from large groups in other ways than that the former are small, the latter large.[9] In like manner, majorities differ from minorities in other ways than that they are larger, and it is these other ways that it is instructive to analyze. Differences of this kind have an intrinsic sociological interest and, difficult as they may be to discern, comprise an integral part of group theory. In this connection von Wiese has the following comment:

> "It is difficult to assign the proper place to the concepts of majority and minority. They are primarily expressions of a purely numerical relation, and they therefore belong among the other colorless terms here discussed [swarm, band, pack, and herd]. The social relationships between majority and minority, however, play an extremely important part in many plurality patterns. . . . The circumstance that these two categories taken in conjunction denote a proportion and not a mere summation makes them sociologically important. Majority and minority are not primarily or usually plurality patterns, but in certain situations they may become groups, and hence should receive attention for this reason as well." [10]

Secondly, it is apparent that the majority-minority distinction differs in principle from distinctions based upon number and size. As von Wiese says in the passage quoted immediately above, a proportion is different from a summation. Groups of whatever size differ from other groups of the same size when the former are majorities and the latter are not. Furthermore, it is obvious that a majority may be relatively small, a minority relatively large, although not, of course, when they are in opposition in the same context. It is also obvious that majorities may vary considerably in size, in relation to their conjoint minorities, without ceasing to be majorities. In a group of 100, 51 and 99 both constitute majorities. For these reasons the majority-minority distinction is not comprehended by any other formal categories of groups and the distinction is, in fact, unique.

In the third place, majorities and minorities are universal in all societies and in all groups, except those which have an even number of members evenly divided and those which are unanimous. In all complex societies, where integration is imperfect and unanimity nonexistent, majorities and minorities are constant phenomena.

A fourth reason for studying majorities has both theoretical and practical consequences, and the latter outweigh the former. For it has often been observed by writers concerned with oppressed minorities

---

[9] On the influence of number and size upon social groups see Simmel, *op. cit.*, pp. 47-133, and Wiese-Becker, *op. cit.*, pp. 498-501.

[10] Wiese-Becker, *op. cit.*, pp. 431-432. These few lines, under the section on "Concepts and Categories: Numerical," are unfortunately all these authors have to say about majorities, with two minor exceptions.

that the problems are essentially not minority problems at all, but majority problems. Writers on the Negro in the United States, for example, and especially Myrdal, have insisted that there is no such thing as a Negro problem, that the problem is actually a "white" problem. In a sense, of course, this is only a manner of speaking, but there can be no doubt that the problem, whether Negro or white, would have a dramatically different impact upon American life if (a) the Negro population were not so large as it is, (b) the Negro population were not so small as it is, (c) the white population comprised not a majority but a dominant minority, (d) the Negro population were the same size but comprised a dominant minority, (e) Northern whites were not a majority and Southern whites not a minority, and so on through many diverse combinations. Whatever the way in which the issue is phrased, it is easy to agree that there is something about majorities which causes and creates minority problems and that a knowledge of the nature and characteristics of the former may contribute to an understanding of the latter. We know, for example, that people become prejudiced not through contact with minority (i.e., oppressed) groups, but through contact with prevailing attitudes toward minority groups.[11] Attitudes "prevail" in a society when they are held by majorities.

Finally, as suggested above, a sociological approach to the subject of majorities may assist in discerning attributes and properties which are not insignificant for the purposes of political science and which tend to be obscured in the latter approach. It may be suggested, for example, that political majorities and what we are unfortunately forced to call societal majorities (i.e., the majority of all the people in a society) do not necessarily coincide, either in personnel or in political predilections. Even under conditions of universal suffrage a political majority may represent only a small societal minority. Of even greater significance, however, is the fact that majorities have so often been conceived of in purely political terms that the broader sociological nature of the subject has suffered neglect. Political majorities are only one kind of majority and, even if they are the most important kind, it does not follow that

[11] There is a vast literature which can be invoked in support of this point. See, for example, Murphy, Murphy, and Newcomb, *Experimental Social Psychology*, New York: Harper, 1937; Murphy and Likert, *Public Opinion and the Individual*, New York, 1938; Theodore M. Newcomb, "The Influence of Attitude Climate upon Some Determinants of Information," *Journal of Abnormal and Social Psychology*, 41:291-302, 1946; Arnold Rose, *Studies in Reduction of Prejudice* (mimeographed), Chicago: American Council on Race Relations, 1947; Robin M. Williams, Jr., "The Reduction of Intergroup Tensions," *Bulletin 57*, Social Science Research Council, 1947; and Robert M. MacIver, *The More Perfect Union*, New York: Macmillan, 1948. For psychological studies of the influence of majorities in the formation of opinion see H. E. Burtt and D. R. Falkenburg, Jr., "The Influence of Majority and Expert Opinion on Religious Attitudes," *Journal of Social Psychology*, 14:269-278 (1941); and C. H. Marple, "The Comparative Suggestibility of Three Age Levels to the Suggestion of Group vs. Expert Opinion," *Journal of Social Psychology*, 4:176-186 (1933). These last two studies, unfortunately, were made with very small groups and are not conclusive. In short, the experimental evidence on the influence of majorities upon opinion is meager.

other kinds are unimportant. Nor does it follow that the nature and characteristics of majorities in general can be discerned in an investigation of political majorities or, for that matter, of any particular kind of majority. In other words, as in most cases affecting the relationships between sociology and the other social sciences, certain phenomena appear which have a more generic and universal significance than can be grasped in any inquiry more specialized than the sociological. It is not inconceivable that a general sociological analysis of majorities may illuminate some of the more special political implications of majorities.[12]

These five reasons, among others, support the opinion that the subject merits attention by sociologists. In the present place it is naturally not possible to inquire into all of the problems presented by majorities, but it is at least desirable to indulge in some preliminary observations of a formal and necessarily hypothetical nature.

A preliminary analysis may begin with the recognition that majorities, like other groups, may be large or small (both absolutely and relative to their conjoint minorities), open or closed, primary or secondary, active or inactive, cohesive through one or many bonds, relatively permanent or relatively impermanent, and so on. Indeed, many additional adjectives of this polar kind may be attached to them. These adjectives will not, however, contribute anything substantial to an investigation of their specific characteristics. One aspect of groups, on the other hand, is significant. This is the aspect which determines whether the group, or the majority, is organized or unorganized. There has been a tendency in sociology, not dominant perhaps but nevertheless discernible, to consider organized groups, often called associations, to be of greater significance than unorganized groups. Attention to majorities may help to dispel the opinion that this is always, or even usually, the case. For majorities, in many situations of interest to sociology, are unorganized, and this absence of organization does not diminish their significance.

The distinction between organized and unorganized groups, however, is insufficiently discriminating when applied to majorities. It is doubtful, in fact, if it is wholly satisfactory when applied to groups. A considera-

CLASSIFICATION OF GROUPS

	Organization	Social Relations between Members	Consciousness of Kind
A. Statistical	No	No	No
B. Societal	No	No	Yes
C. Social	No	Yes	Yes
D. Associational	Yes	Yes	Yes

[12] Kendall, for example, says that Simmel's "Excursus," cited *infra*, note 1, is "a discussion which no student of the social sciences can read without subsequently paying to it the unusual compliment of wishing that it had been many times as long." *Loc. cit.*, p. 27.

tion of majorities illustrates that there are four general kinds, as different one from the other as the kinds of groups of which they are a part. In attempting to delineate these kinds one is embarrassed, as so often in sociology, by the paucity of terms with which to label them and by the consequent necessity of utilizing words already burdened with connotations. In spite of this hazard, we may distinguish four kinds of groups as exhibited in the accompanying somewhat crude "table." These four may be called the statistical, the societal, the social, and the associational. Statistical groups are synonymous with logical classes. They have only an "analytical" existence and are "formed," if one may be permitted the expression, not by people themselves but by people who write about people—in other words by sociologists, statisticians, demographers, and so on. Whether they have members or not is immaterial, and we may accordingly have null groups in sociology in the same sense in which we have null classes in logic. Statistical groups, therefore, have no social organization, they have "members" in a logical but not in a sociological sense; and consciousness of kind, in the absence of a social stimulus to evoke it, is only potential. Similarly, the "members" do not enter into social relations with each other on the basis of the trait in terms of which they constitute a group. They may have one or several traits in common, but they have no interests in common, nor any like interests.[13] Examples of such statistical groups are right-handed persons, red-headed persons, persons fifty years of age, persons who are five feet tall, persons who have had the measles, persons who have died of tuberculosis, persons who prefer soap operas to Italian operas, and so on.

Social groups differ from statistical groups in that they do have members and these members are conscious of their kind, of the similarity or identity of traits they all possess. There are no null groups here and the trait itself may be single or multiple. Here appear external signs by means of which the members recognize each other, such as skin color, language, accent, grammar, response to patriotic symbols, appearance, and so on. The members, in short, are or may easily become "visible" to each other. They have like interests but not common interests. They do not, however, in the absence of a social stimulus, enter into social relations with each other. Examples of societal groups are males, females, Negroes, whites, Southerners, New Yorkers, golfers, the blind, college professors and indeed all occupational groups, and so on.

Social contact and communication appear in the third category. The social group differs from the societal group in that its members have social relations with one another and from the statistical group both in this respect and in that consciousness of kind is present. Social relations are the distinguishing additional characteristic. The members may have like but not common interests, common but not like interests (e.g., an assortment of persons on a life-raft after a shipwreck), or both like and

[13] For a distinction between the like and the common see R. M. MacIver, Society, New York: Farrar & Rinehart, 1937, pp. 28, 30.

common interests. Examples are groups of acquaintances, relatives, cliques, audiences, spectators, crowds, mobs, passengers on board a small ship, and many other unorganized groups discussed in the texts.

When a group has these characteristics and is, in addition, organized, we have the fourth kind of group indicated above, the associational group or, more simply, the association. Examples are a fraternity, a lodge, a club, a team, an orchestra, a committee, and so on. In these groups it is the formal organization which is the prominent characteristic and membership in them in itself confers consciousness of kind and generates social relations in accordance with procedural norms. Here, finally, the members usually have both like and common interests.

Before commenting upon its uses, it is necessary to say that this is not an inclusive classification. Some groups find no place in these categories; for example, groups which involve social relations but no necessary consciousness of kind, and groups comprised not of individuals but of other groups. It should also be recognized that none of these groups is stable, and that in the process of social life they may become transformed into groups in other categories under the impress of events. Red-headed people, a statistical group, would become a societal group with the improbable passage of legislation taxing them, a social group if they entered into social relations on the basis of the color of their hair and attended a meeting, for example, to which only red-headed people were invited, and an associational group if they organized a Red-headed League for the purpose of resisting the legislation. Finally, the classification is a logical but not a temporal continuum; a statistical group may become an association immediately, without passing through the intervening categories; and the reverse could happen on the occasion of the dissolution of an association.

When we return from this digression on group classification in general to the question of majorities in particular, an interesting reflection emerges. For it immediately appears that all four of these groups, the statistical no less than the associational, have sociological significance when they are majorities. And in many cases it is only because they are majorities that they acquire general social significance in the societies in which they occur. This significance can be illustrated by a number of examples. Consider the significance of the majority first of all when it is a statistical group, where no social relations are involved. A society or group in which the majority of the population were of age fifty and above would be a different kind of a society from one in which the majority were fifty and below. Substitute any age categories and the generalization retains its cogency. Similarly, societies differ when or if right-handed persons or left-handed persons are in the majority, urban-dwellers or rural-dwellers, literates or illiterates, and so on. In other words, statistical groups do have sociological significance when they are majorities. They determine to an extensive degree the general characteristics of a society and of a social group. Statistical majorities always have more than a statistical significance. It is therefore a mistake to limit sociology, as formal sociologists are sometimes inclined to do, to a study of social relationships as such, if that term implies social contact and communication between people. For it is apparent that many phenomena of the highest import for sociology, those responsible for the character of an entire society, are determined by the juxtaposition within it of majorities whose members have never met, who do not know each other, and who may, in fact, be unaware of the individual existence of each other.[14]

Comparable observations are relevant to the role of societal majorities. Men's college communities are different from women's college communities, and the differential status of "faculty wives" in the two situations is striking. Of more importance, however, is the fact that minority group problems, problems involving ethnic and national minorities, appear in societies when consciousness of kind and consciousness of difference characterize majority and minority groups. Tension in such situations, in the absence of compensating factors, is directly proportional to the size of the minority and inversely proportional to the size of the majority. That is, majority-minority tension appears to be least when the majority is large, the minority small, and greatest when the minority threatens, by increase in size, to become the majority. Meanwhile, ethnic minorities are oppressed largely in proportion not to their absolute but their relative size. Conversely, a very small minority, again relatively speaking, may suffer the satiric sanction but no specific social disability. This point unfortunately requires more development than can be offered here, but it is noteworthy that it is amenable to empirical research.

The social group also, the group that is unorganized but in which social relations occur, is dependent for its function upon a majority. Whether a group of friends goes to a play or to a musical comedy, to an expensive nightclub or to an inexpensive tavern, drinks coffee or beer on a given occasion, and so on, depends, often unconsciously, upon majority desires. Similarly, in larger groups, a lynching can occur only if it is at least tacitly sanctioned by a majority of those present, and a panic can occur only if a majority of the persons involved in a situation fail to "keep their heads." A clique clearly operates under the influence of the majority of its own members and an elite, although a minority, suffers no discrimination only because it embodies social values of which the majority approves and would like to emulate.

It is in the organized group, the association, in which majorities seem, on the surface, to have the least significance. As social organization

[14] It is similarly a mistake to emphasize the role of organized groups in a society at the expense of the unorganized, and especially of those in the latter category which are only statistical groups, *i.e.*, as defined above, groups the sociologist himself constructs in the process of classifying people in various ways. It may be safe to say, incidentally, that the conslusions of demographers have not been integrated into formal sociology and that chapters on population remain somewhat logically separate from those on social structure, even though frequently bound together in the same book.

introduces an hierarchical structure into a group the significance of numbers, and therefore of majorities, diminishes in proportion. The more
highly organized the association the fewer functions belong to the
majority. Here majority action is, in fact, constrained and limited by
organization, by rules and regulations, and by the creation of authority.
It would be an error to assert that the majority exercises any official influence in a tightly organized, hierarchically ordered association like, for
example, the Roman Catholic Church, the United States Navy, or the
Communist Party, three associations which, whatever their diverse goals,
exhibit a remarkable sociological similarity in internal organization and
structure.[15] There are many more priests than cardinals, seamen than
admirals, and party-workers than members of the Politburo, and it is the
latter, not the former, which possess the power. This, of course, is true in
varying extent of all associations, even the most "democratic." The
power structure is always pyramidal.

But even here majorities play a role. This role appears with the recognition that all associations have two types of organization, a formal organization and an informal organization,[16] and that, while majorities
exercise no formal function whatever—except when they constitute a
legitimate party[17]—they often exercise covert and sometimes even overt
informal control in associations. Utilizing only the most extreme and
rigid cases for illustration, that is associations in which majorities would
seem to have the least influence, it can be demonstrated that they are
not immune from the pressures of majorities. A clear example is afforded
by the Navy during the recent war. Not even the highly inflexible rules
and regulations of the service, enforced by Regular Navy officers in command positions, were impervious to the pressure of the large majority of
Reserve officers who considered some of the niceties of naval etiquette,
particularly with respect to salutes, ceremonies, and relations with en-
listed men, to be more than a little ridiculous. The exodus of Reserve
officers after the war, their declining majority and ultimate minority, con-

[15] One interesting similarity, among others, is that the distinction between "associational"
and "private" statuses of the functionaries tends to disappear and extra-associational
statuses have little importance. Such associations differ in this respect from the "corporate
groups" delineated by Max Weber which exemplify "rational-legal" authority and in
which distinctions between official and private statuses are maintained. On this point see
Max Weber: The Theory of Social and Economic Organization, edited by Talcott Parsons,
New York: Oxford, 1947, pp. 324ff., and especially Parsons' Introductory essay, "The Institutionalization of Authority," pp. 56-77. See also E. T. Hiller on the professions and
on the office, *Social Relations and Structures,* New York, Harper, 1947, pp. 544-596.

[16] Although E. T. Hiller has not used these concepts, his distinctions between intrinsic and
extrinsic valuations of persons and between personal and categoric social relations are
directly relevant. See *ibid.,* pp. 191-213; 631-645. The interrelations between formal and
informal organization represent an important junction of formal sociology and social psychology and require, perhaps, more intensive analysis than they have as yet received.

[17] In sociological terms a party is a device for recruiting a majority and can, as Max Weber
suggests, exist only within an organized group or association (Weber: *Verband;* Parsons:
"corporate group"), even though it operates, as do political parties in the United States,
without specific constitutional sanction. See Max Weber, *loc. cit.,* p. 407. See also R. M.
MacIver, *The Web of Government, op. cit.,* pp. 208-224 and especially p. 213.

tributed increasing conformity to the rules and reduced the discrepancy between the formal and informal organization.[18]

The Roman Catholic Church offers another illustration in a totally different sphere. The long struggle with "modern errors" began in 1543 with the publication of *On the Revolutions of the Celestial Orbs* by Nicolai Copernicus and became intense when Galileo was summoned once in 1616 and five times in 1633 to the bar of the Inquisition. This story is well known. What is not so well known is that a license to print a book espousing the heliocentric hypothesis was refused as late as 1820 and that not until September 11, 1822 was the following decree quietly issued by the Holy Office:

> "There is no reason why the present and future Masters of the Sacred Palace should refuse license for printing and publishing works treating of the mobility of the earth and the immobility of the sun, according to the common opinion of modern astronomers."[19]

What scientific evidence was unable to accomplish, majority and "common" opinion finally did, even though several centuries were consumed in the process.[20] One is tempted to say that no association, no matter how rigidly organized, is able to withstand the permanent pressure of a majority and that an organized majority is the most potent social force on earth. There is a certain authority in a majority which no hierarchy can wholly obliterate.

From these instances and others another principle can be induced. It concerns the nature of formal and informal organization in any association and the role of majorities with respect to these two forms of organization. First, however, it is appropriate to clarify the meaning of these terms which have appeared in preceding paragraphs. The formal organization of an association consists of the formally recognized and established statuses of the members in accordance with the rank of the offices and other positions they occupy, together with the rules and regulations which set out the obligations, duties, privileges, and responsibilities of these positions. The status of non-office holding members, their duties and privileges, is also, of course, a part of the formal organization— formal because formally recognized and concurred in as a condition of membership. Social relations between the members are conducted formally in terms of these statuses, in conformity with explicit norms, and

[18] For an excellent anlysis of formal and informal organization in the Navy see Charles H. Page, "Bureaucracy's Other Face," *Social Forces*, 25:88-94, October, 1946. For an implicit fictional treatment of the same theme see *Mister Roberts*, by Thomas Heggen, Boston: Houghton Mifflin, 1946.

[19] Quoted in Preserved Smith, *A History of Modern Culture*, New York: Henry Holt, 1930, Vol. I, p. 58.

[20] Illustrations for the third example, the Communist Party, are more difficult to exhibit because of lack of information. It is possible, however, that increasing anti-semitism in the high councils of the Party in Russia, as reported in Drew Middleton in articles in the New York *Times* in February, 1948, may be concessions to majority opinion even though in direct opposition to both constitutional and doctrinal orthodoxy.

in accordance with "extrinsic" and "categoric" evaluations of persons. In the formal organization, statuses have differential prestige in independence of the persons who occupy them.

Since this independence is difficult if not impossible to maintain in the dynamics of associational life, however, an informal organization arises to exist coevally with the formal. The informal organization consists of roles rather than statuses, of patterns of dominance and ascendancy, affection, hostility, or indifference of the members in accordance with their intrinsic and personal evaluations of each other. These role patterns may or may not coincide with or conform to the status hierarchy of the formal organization. In the informal organization social relations occur on the basis of the esteem which the members have for one another in independence of their statuses. In short, in formal organization social relations proceed in terms of the prestige of statuses in accordance with explicit associational norms; in informal organization they proceed in terms of the esteem for persons in accordance with implicit societal (*i.e.*, extra-associational) norms. Prestige attaches to statuses; esteem to persons.[21] The former is a component of formal organization, the latter of informal organization.[22]

Now it is apparent that in some associations there may be a close coincidence between the formal and the informal organization and that this coincidence may be relatively permanent. In such cases the statuses which carry the greatest prestige are occupied by the persons who are held in the highest esteem. On the other hand, an association may exhibit a wide discrepancy between its formal and informal organization. In these cases the prestige continues to attach to the status while esteem is withheld from the person who occupies the status and who thereupon becomes a figurehead. The officers then have the formal authority of their positions but not the informal authority sustained by esteem. Now, whether or not offices are filled by "democratic" vote, it is within the power of the majority to confer actual as well as statutory authority upon the officers or to retain authority residually in the informal organization. Similarly, it is within the power of the majority to determine whether social relations in the association shall proceed only in terms of the formal rules and regulations, which are explicit norms, or in terms of informal norms which may or may not coincide with the former. Here then is the principle to which attention is invited, that the discrepancy between the formal and informal organization of any association will be least when the majority gives full support and sanction to the former and greatest when this support is for any reason or in any particular

[21] The writer is indebted to Professor E. T. Hiller for this distinction between prestige and esteem.

[22] It is not altogether clear in what respect it may be appropriate to refer to these informal elements in terms of "structure" or even "organization." In some respects they may be antithetical to organization and in that case the concept "informal organization" becomes an oxymoron. This is particularly true because it is these informal elements which are susceptible to frequent change in contrast to the formal which are, by comparison, relatively stable.

withheld. That this power of determination is a function of the majority rather than of any aspect of social organization itself is clear from the consideration that it is prior to social organization and determines the form which social organization takes. Finally, it is the support of the majority which sustains the association, the absence of this support which moves it in the direction of change or of ultimate dissolution.

We may now inquire whether some of these observations have a similar relevance in the larger society. Here the problem becomes involved in the more general question of the nature and kinds of social power, especially when we attempt to probe the source of the power which the majority exercises. Unfortunately, the subject of social power is not one which has received a comprehensive analysis in the literature, and to discourse on majorities in terms of power is like pronouncing the words of a language one does not fully understand.[23] MacIver defines it variously as "the capacity in any relationship to command the service or the compliance of others,"[24] and "the capacity to control the behavior of others either directly by fiat or indirectly by the manipulation of available means."[25] Among the sources of power MacIver lists property, status, office (apart from status[26]), special knowledge, managerial and executive function, financial resources, artistic, religious or other eminence, publicity, and so on. It is clear from his discussion that social power, whatever its sources and manifestations, is "responsive to the *mores* of the society."[27] And it is the majority which sustains the mores. Here then we find the authority which lies "beyond the realm of government," the authority which community and society retain, which they may or may not confer upon the state, and which, even when it is wrested from the community, wells up again and restrains the actions of governments. Not even an autocrat can remain unresponsive to the will of a majority.[28]

[23] R. M. MacIver observes that "There is no reasonably adequate study of the nature of social power," although he himself contributes some highly pertinent remarks. See *The Web of Government, op. cit.*, p. 458, and especially Chapter 5, "The Pyramid of Power," pp. 82-113. E. A. Ross's discussion, while short, is still suggestive. See *Social Control, op. cit.*, pp. 77-88.

[24] *Ibid.*, p. 82.

[25] *Ibid.*, p. 87.

[26] That is, the power which proceeds from the *possession* of status.

[27] *Ibid.*, p. 98.

[28] In an eloquent passage, MacIver has described this situation as follows: "The authority of government does not create the order over which it presides and does not sustain that order solely by its own fiat or its accredited power. There is authority beyond the authority of government. There is a greater consensus without which the fundamental order of the community would fall apart. This consensus plays a different role under different forms of government. Sometimes it has nothing to do with the processes that make or unmake the princes or potentates who rule the people. Sometimes it has no mode of expression, should the ruler get out of hand and violate the fundamental order he is presumed to protect, save the rare violence of revolution. Sometimes it is alert and sensitive to all that government does and sets its seal of approval or disapproval on the policies that government pursues. But always, whether mainly acquiescent or creatively active, it is the ultimate ground on which the unity and the order of the state repose." *Ibid.*, p. 85.

It would, of course, be highly unrealistic to assert that the power of the majority always manifests itself, or is always successful when it does. Majorities are frequently inert and frequently too have no means of expression. Indeed, it is one of the lessons of history that majorities of one kind or another have long suffered oppression. Nevertheless, it is of sociological significance to note that majorities remain the source of so much residual power, even in these situations, that autocrats and oligarchs bend every effort to prevent them from organizing. It is the power of a majority which gives meaning to the imperial command, "Divide and rule."

We find, thus, in the larger society the same principle which was found in the associtaion. Where there is no organization, the majority determines. In the absence of stratification, likewise, the majority determines. When there is formal organization there is also informal organization, and in the latter the majority plays an important role. Indeed, society itself is an informal organization, the state a formal organization; the laws belong to the formal structure, the mores to the informal. It is the majority which sustains the mores, the minority which initiates changes in them which are then either resisted or finally sanctioned by the majority. In all societies of any complexity there is a discrepancy between the laws and the mores. This discrepancy will be wide or narrow depending upon the position of the majority. Where it is wide it will be found that the majority supports the mores, a minority supports the laws. It is the role that majorities play in societies which gives point to what is one of the most profound and cogent of all sociological principles— "When the mores are adequate, laws are unnecessary, when they are inadequate, laws are useless." The mores are adequate when they are supported by a large majority; they are inadequate when they lack this support. There is a power in the majority which can contravene any law.

It is the majority, in short, which sets the culture pattern and sustains it, which is in fact responsible for whatever pattern or configuration there is in a culture. It is the majority which confers upon folkways, mores, customs, and laws the status of norms and gives them coercive power. It is the majority which guarantees the stability of a society. It is the majority which requires conformity to custom and which penalizes deviation—except in ways which the majority sanctions and approves. It is the majority which is the custodian of the mores and which defends them against innovation. And it is the inertia of majorities, finally, which retards the processes of social change.

Throughout the preceding discussion we have, except for several incidental references, omitted from consideration the question of the size of majorities. Here it is possible to note only one implication of size, one which relates to the general problem of social and cultural integration. Reflection upon majorities enables us to see that cultural integration is a function of the size of the majority which conforms to a single set of patterns, which subscribes to the same myths, and which aspires to attain the same societal goals. When this majority is large, the culture is integrated, no matter how extensively the society is stratified. When it is small the culture lacks integration. When it dissolves into competing minorities all vestiges of integration disappear. A culture is in fact dependent upon the existence in a society of a majority. Without it the society is split into partial and fragmented cultures. Whatever the value of the cultural approach in sociology, when used exclusively it sometimes obscures the *social* factors which create and sustain a society and which determine both its coherence and its cohesion.

What, finally, is the ultimate ground for the power which the majority exercises? The answer is so deceptively simple as to discourage ready acceptance. It rests in the elemental fact, a fact so formidable as to seem incontrovertible, that the majority is stronger than the minority or, in Simmel's words, "dass die Vielen mächtiger sind als die Wenigen." [29] It is certainly incontrovertible that two men can force one man to do what they want, and that ten men can do it even more easily. Given the same organization, the larger number can always control the smaller, can command its service, and secure its compliance. This, incidentally, is a social and not a cultural fact.[30]

In summary, we have noted the neglect of majorities in contemporary sociology and have introduced, in a very preliminary fashion, some hypotheses which a sociology of majorities might subject to further investigation. We have observed that the majority-minority distinction is a distinction *sui generis* which requires inclusion in any comprehensive group theory; that majorities play significant roles in both organized and unorganized social groups, and particularly in the informal aspects of the former; that majorities play a similar role in the larger society; that majorities constitute a residual locus of social power; that they sustain the mores; and that they are responsible for whatever cultural integration a society exhibits. Majorities doubtless have in addition multifarious characteristics and functions which we have neglected to mention. But these will suffice to show that the subject merits sustained sociological analysis.

Supplementary Bibliography

E. Franklin Frazier, *Race and Culture Contacts in the Modern World*. N. Y.: Knopf, 1957.
    A provocative treatment of race relations from a world rather than national perspective, with special attention to the history of colonialism and its consequences.

Oscar Handlin, *Race and Nationality in American Life*. Garden City, N. Y.: Doubleday Anchor Books, 1957.
    A good summary of the American situation by an eminent historian.

[29] *Loc. cit.*, p. 190.
[30] For an expansion of this thesis see John Dollard, "Culture, Society, Impulse, and Socialization," *American Journal of Sociology*, 45:53-56 (July, 1939).

32 The Sociology of Minorities

Charles F. Marden and Gladys Meyer, *Minorities in American Society*, 2nd ed. N. Y.: American Book, 1962.
An excellent textbook, well-grounded in sociological theory.

George Eaton Simpson and J. Milton Yinger, *Racial and Cultural Minorities*, rev. ed. N. Y.: Harper, 1958.
Another fine textbook, with detailed research documentation and an extensive bibliography.

Gunnar Myrdal, *An American Dilemma*. N. Y.: Harper, 1944.
The classic study of the Negro in American society, highlighting the conflict in values between a democratic ideology and a system of racial discrimination.

II Race as a Biological Concept

Nasser speaks frequently of the Arab race. Indeed, much of his success in his attempt to unify the Arabic-speaking peoples has been a result of his talk about racial unity. Meanwhile, on the other side of the border is another group of people, hated as much for their "racial difference" from Arabs as for their religious difference: the Jews.

If the "race hatred" between these two peoples did not involve bloodshed and untold bitterness, it would be amusing. According to the best biological classification we have, not only are most Arabs and most Israelis from the same large racial category (Caucasoid), but most Arabs and most Israelis are also from the same category of *sub*classification (Semitic).

Systems of Classification

The use of biological concepts to classify people on the basis of race is fraught with pitfalls. The ideal system of classification is one in which all the cases can be categorized—the system is exhaustive—and in which there is no overlap in the categories—the categories are mutually exclusive. In such a system all cases are classified, and no one case can legitimately be classified in more than one category. Because all human beings are members of one species and because the various stocks in that species have been mixing with one another for hundreds and thousands of years, biologists have no set of "racial" categories which are both exhaustive and mutually exclusive.

A biologist's classification of race is concerned only with factors of scientific interest to the biologist. Biologists, then, are concerned with genetic relationships, with those things which are hereditary. Religious

33

beliefs do not come through the genes. Nor can you inherit political ideologies, or customs, or beliefs. So the biologist must reject them in making up a classification scheme of the races. He must deal only with those physical properties that may be transmitted through the genes. These include such characteristics as color of eyes, skin, and hair; form of nose, head, and hair; and so on.

It would be very easy for the biologist to categorize men if their head forms came in two distinct shapes: round and square. It would be easy if three distinct nose forms could be found, or distinctly different skin colors of a small number and variety. But nature does not oblige. Head shapes vary along a continuum from round to narrow and cannot be grouped into sharply different categories. Nose form, eye shape, hair type, hair color, and eye color also differ infinitesimally along a gradual scale, and skin coloring is almost infinitely divisible into variation along a color continuum.

And even sharp breaking-off points on these characteristics would not be the total solution. A further problem is introduced by the fact that factors are not associated with each other. A man with a round head may have black skin or white skin. A man with a ruddy complexion may have a flat nose or a sharp one. A man may have dark brown skin, a medium long head, dark eyes, straight hair, and a sharp nose. The combinations and permutations seem virtually infinite.

The point of all this is that the use of biological concepts to classify men into races must be extremely arbitrary. At what point along the continuum of skin color do we make a cut-off, deciding that skin lighter than this will be Caucasoid and skin darker than this Mongoloid?

Human Variation

All human individuals differ from one another in various traits: stature, curl of hair, size of hand, length of toes, and so on. Clusters of similar features can be found distributed among a group of people who have lived together in some region for a long time in relative isolation from other groups. People who live in cool climates generally have lighter skin than those who live in the tropics. Many people in the Far East have coarse black hair. Europeans generally have softer, less tightly curled hair on their bodies than most Asians or Africans. Many of the millions of people in Asia (and some in Eastern Europe) have a skin fold over the inner corner of the eye which gives the eye the appearance of being slanted.

These are minor differences, less notable than, for example, the range of variation among black bears. Human beings are a single species; hence the basic body structure of men is the same all over the world. All human beings have the same kind of lungs, the same kind and number of bones, the same complex nervous systems, the same delicate sensory organs for tasting, smelling, touching, hearing, and seeing. All men have the same blood stream and, while there are slight differences among individuals in blood chemistry, they are not related to skin color: a doctor handed a vial of type "O" blood has no way of ascertaining whether the donor was white or Negro, and no laboratory test of the blood can determine the donor's hair type, eye color, or other external physical traits.

Physical anthropologists and biologists have somewhat arbitrarily divided mankind into three major categories: (1) the whites or Caucasoids, who were inhabitants of Europe, North Africa, and Southwest Asia, but in recent centuries have spread pretty well over the globe; (2) Negroids, black or brown people, often having very curly hair, who originally were mostly Africans but now constitute a goodly proportion of the population of the Western hemisphere; and (3) Mongoloids, yellow to brown people with straight, black hair, originally heavily concentrated in Asia and the islands of the Pacific.

Scientists have also attempted, without notable success, to relate these three large categories based heavily on skin color, hair type, and geographic distribution, to subcategories taking into account eye color, head shape, nose shape, eye form, hair color, and stature. Some scholars list subraces: the North Chinese, the Malays, the red Mongoloids or American Indians, the Nilotic Negroes, the Pygmies, the Nordics, and Alpines, and the Mediterraneans of Europe, and so on.

Weaknesses of Racial Classifications

These categories are neither exhaustive nor mutually exclusive. The Australian aborigines, for example, with Negroid skin and Caucasoid hair, are sometimes classified as a fourth "race." The Mohaves of the American Southwest average nearly six feet in height; their neighbors, the Hopi, average five feet four inches. Both the longest human heads and the roundest are found among American Indian tribes. The tallest and the shortest people in the world, the Watusi and the Pygmy, live within a few miles of each other; both have black skin and kinky hair. But some blond Norwegians also have kinky hair.

In summary, slight differences have grown up between groups living in relative isolation over a considerable period of time in various parts of the earth. But the basic physical structure of all human beings is the same. Furthermore, differences within categories are greater than differences between them; the categories are based on gross averages. There is more difference between the lightest and the darkest Negroid, or between the lightest and the darkest Caucasoid, than between the lightest

Negroid and the darkest Caucasoid. The differences even within a given geographic region are often as marked as the variations among the great groups that are called "races."

Related Readings

The confusion which can arise over the meaning of race is illustrated in Roger Bastide and Pierre van den Berghe's report, "Stereotypes, Norms, and Interracial Behavior in São Paulo, Brazil." Middle-class Brazilians disagree among themselves whether it is better to be a member of an "inferior" race which is "pure," or to mix the "superior" and "inferior" races into a mulatto type which is not "pure."

William W. Howells demonstrates that "The Distribution of Man" is actually a history of the development of racial differences within a single species, Homo sapiens, and that the patterned differences are consequences of geographic isolation and natural selection.

In "The Whippoorwill Cries, The Fox Whimpers," Richard P. Hunt shows us the relevance of a people's cultural values and, by implication, the comparative irrelevance of their physical traits. The Seneca, in their devotion to the land, bear more similarity to contemporary Polish peasants than to Indians of the American Plains. Learned behavior, or the culture of a people, offers more toward understanding them than their biological characteristics.

———————— Roger Bastide and Pierre van den Berghe

Stereotypes, Norms and Interracial Behavior in São Paulo, Brazil

Although the racial situation in Brazil differs markedly from the situation in the United States, there is nevertheless a racial problem in Brazil.[1] Large scale industrialization and urbanization in the great metropolises of the South such as Rio de Janeiro and São Paulo have brought about

[1] For our purposes a "race" is a human grouping socially and subjectively defined in a given society. This grouping considers itself different from other groupings similarly defined by virtue of innate and visible physical characteristics, or, in the extreme case, defined, rightly or wrongly, as biologically separate subgroups.

The same terms such as "Negro" and "white" may, in different societies, cover objectively dissimilar groupings as exemplified by Brazil and the United States. In this research, we shall use the Brazilian definition. "Racial prejudice" is the totality of reciprocal relations of stereotypy, discrimination and segregation existing between human groupings that consider themselves and each other as "races."

From *American Sociological Review*, Vol. 22, pp. 689-694. By permission.

changes in the traditional attitudes and behavior between the various ethnic and racial groups.[2]

Lucila Hermann, from the Faculty of Economics of the University of São Paulo, devised a questionnaire to determine the patterns of race relations in the white middle class of São Paulo.[3] The questionnaire includes four parts:

1. A list of 41 stereotypes derived from the list of Johnson[4] for comparative purposes with the United States, from a content analysis of Brazilian literature, and from oral folklore. For each listed trait (foresight, suggestibility, self-control, intelligence, etc.) the subject was asked whether he considered, first Negroes, then mulattoes, as inferior, equal or superior to whites.
2. A series of 27 questions on social norms of behavior. For example, should white and Negro children play together? Should whites and Negroes exchange courtesy visits? Should they intermarry? etc.
3. A series of 16 questions on actual behavior of the subjects, similar in content to some questions of part 2.
4. A series of 16 questions on hypothetical personal behavior put in the conditional form: Would you marry (fall in love with, go out with) a Negro? A light-skinned mulatto? etc.

The sample is neither random nor proportional. It consists of 580 "white" students from five different teachers' colleges in São Paulo. We have good reason to believe that the questionnaire was applied to whole classes of students in a "captive" class-room situation. The percentage of refusals is unknown, but we think it was very low. We had to reject only one almost blank questionnaire. Most schedules were very conscientiously and completely filled out. The age distribution varies from 15 to 44, but it leans on the young side with a mean age of 19.9 years; 483 subjects are women, 97 are men. Socio-economic data on parents of the subjects are incomplete but they indicate a predominantly lower-middle and upper-middle class background. Seventy-five per cent of the fathers have non-manual occupations. For the 296 subjects who answered the question on family income the mean is 7,000 cruzeiros a month. As con-

[2] On Brazilian racial problems see: Gilberto Freyre, *Casa Grande e Senzala*, Rio de Janeiro, 1934; Gilberto Freyre, *Sobrados e Mucambos*, São Paulo, 1936; Donald Pierson, *Negroes in Brazil*, Chicago, 1942; Charles Wagley, editor, *Races and Class in Rural Brazil*, UNESCO, 1952; Thales de Azevedo, *Les élites de couleur dans une ville brésilienne*, UNESCO, 1953; L. A. Da Costa Pinto, *O Negro no Rio de Janeiro*, São Paulo, 1953; R. Bastide, F. Fernandes, V. Bicudo, A. M. Ginsberg and O. Nogueira, *Relacões Raciais entre Negros e Brancos em São Paulo*, 1955; René Ribeiro, *Religião e Relacões Raciais*, Rio de Janeiro, 1956.
[3] The present study was undertaken under the auspices of the UNESCO but was not included in the final report because of the death of Lucila Hermann. We received the filled-out questionnaires in Paris a few years later.
[4] Guy B. Johnson, "The Stereotype of the American Negro" in O. Klineberg, editor, *Characteristics of the American Negro*, New York: 1944, pp. 1-22. For the complete questionnaire see: R. Bastide, "Stéréotypes et préjugés de couleur," *Sociologia*, 18 (May, 1955).

cerns ethnic origin of parents, 384 subjects are children of Brazilians, 102 have one foreign parent, 85 have both parents foreign. Of the 384 children of nationals 232 have at least one foreign grandparent. This ethnic situation seems representative of the middle class of São Paulo where third generation Brazilians dominate only in the upper and in the lower class.[5] The results of this study hold only for the "white" middle class of São Paulo.

Analysis of the Data—The questionnaire was subjected to a two-fold analysis. First, each question was treated as an entity and the answers of all subjects to each separate question were added together and reduced to percentages. Behind this procedure lies, of course, the assumption that the same answer has the same meaning for all subjects. Although some errors have undoubtedly been introduced, in particular by certain questions intended as "traps," we do not think that the conclusions have been altered.

The second part of the analysis is logically independent of the first and permits a corroboration of the conclusions. Each of the 580 subjects was treated as an entity. An arbitrary score was assigned to each subject for the various parts of the questionnaire, by simple unweighted addition of responses. The two underlying postulates behind this procedure are (1) that qualitative answers may be quantified and (2) that the same score means the same thing for different subjects. From these two postulates there is derived a classification of subjects on six scales treated as unidimensional variables. Four of these variables corresponding to each part of the questionnaire are treated as components of a general prejudice-tolerance continuum. Variable a is a measure of acceptance or rejection of stereotypes. Variable b measures tolerance or prejudice in social norms. Variable c measures actual interracial behavior as reported by the subjects. Variable d measures willingness to enter into specific personal relationships with Negroes or mulattoes. The other two variables are secondary variables on part 1 of the questionnaire. The higher the score on each of the four main variables, the more tolerant is the subject. For the sake of brevity, the great mass of descriptive statistics has been eliminated. The tabular material has likewise been reduced to the bare minimum. Only the salient conclusions have been retained.

Stereotypes against Negroes and mulattoes are widespread. Seventy-five per cent of the sample accept 23 or more stereotypes against Negroes. No one rejects all stereotypes against Negroes. For mulattoes the overall picture is somewhat more favorable, though very similar. Mulattoes are judged inferior or superior to whites on the same traits as Negroes but with somewhat lower percentages. The most widely accepted stereotypes are lack of hygiene (accepted by 91 per cent for

[5] Samuel H. Lowrie, "Origem da populacão de São Paulo e Diferenciação das classes sociais," *Revista do Arquivo Municipal*, 42, São Paulo, pp. 195-212.

Negroes), physical unattractiveness (87 per cent), superstitution (80 per cent), lack of financial foresight (77 per cent), lack of a morality (76 per cent), aggressiveness (73 per cent), laziness (72 per cent), lack of persistence at work (62 per cent), sexual "perversity" (51 per cent), and exhibitionism (50 per cent).

Fifty-five per cent of the sample think that Negroes are intellectually equal to whites (only 43 per cent consider Negroes less intelligent than whites), and only 22 per cent of the sample accept Negroes as musically gifted. The similarities with the North American stereotypes are more numerous than the differences, particularly as concerns the association of racial prejudices with sexuality.

Going back to the comparison between stereotypes against Negroes and stereotypes against mulattoes, one very important difference appears behind the overall similarity. Two hundred sixty-nine subjects judge Negroes as they do mulattoes; 268 subjects are more favorable to mulattoes than to Negroes; finally, a small group of 43 subjects is more favorable to Negroes than to mulattoes. We compared this last group with the 45 subjects having the most extreme differences in the second group of 268. This comparison between the two extreme groups reveals no statistically significant differences for age, sex, nationality of the parents, or family income. But significant differences appear on the means of variables b, c and d ($p < .05$ for each of the three variables). Those differences are further confirmed by the answers to the questions on intermarriage ($p < .05$).

The group more unfavorable to mulattoes shows much more prejudice against *both* Negroes and mulattoes in social norms, in behavior, and in willingness to intermarry, than the group more unfavorable to Negroes.

We may hypothesize that there are two contrasting "schools of thought" in the sample. These two "schools" share a belief in the superiority of the white "race." But the group more favorable to mulattoes considers the latter superior to Negroes because mulattoes are nearer to whites. It is thus less opposed to miscegenation and in general more tolerant. The group more favorable to Negroes expresses a much more virulent form of racism. It judges Negroes superior to mulattoes because the former are a "pure race." Any miscegenation is rejected and the other manifestations of prejudice are likewise stronger. If our hypothesis is correct, there is in Brazil, at least among part of the population, an extreme form of racial prejudice rather than a milder aesthetic prejudice of "physical appearance," which has been propounded by certain students of Brazilian racial relations.[6] There is no indication from our data that this extreme form of racial prejudice where people think in terms of "pure races" has been introduced in Brazil by European immigrants, as

---

[6] Oracy Nogueira, "Preconceito racial de marca e preconceito racial de origem," *Anais do XXXI Congresso International de Americanistas,* São Paulo, 1955, pp. 409-434.

some maintain. A research done in Rio de Janeiro also points to more prejudice against mulattoes than against Negroes, thereby giving partial confirmation to our findings.[7]

The question remains entirely open whether the genesis of such extreme racial prejudice goes back to slavery or to the dynamics of social mobility and of the labor market, where mulattoes might be considered more dangerous competitors than Negroes. Further research on this problem would be highly desirable.

Stereotypes, Norms and Behavior—The ideal norms of behavior contrast in their relative tolerance with the wide acceptance of stereotypes. A theoretical equality of opportunities for whites and Negroes is

TABLE OF INTERCORRELATIONS

Variable a Stereotypes	Var. b Norms	Var. c Behavior	Var. d Hyp. Rel.	
	+.60	+.25	+.37	Variable a Stereotypes
+.60		+.51	+.68	Variable b Norms
+.25	+.51		+.49	Variable c Actual Behavior
+.37	+.68	+.49		Variable d Hypothetical Relationships

accepted by 92 per cent in accordance with the Brazilian democratic ethos. Over 60 per cent accept casual relations between whites and Negroes. The color line is found at the level of closer emotional relationships: 62 per cent are opposed to a degree of intimacy with Negroes beyond that of simple comradeship; 77 per cent are opposed to miscegenation with Negroes, 55 per cent to miscegenation with mulattoes.

In actual behavior as reported, and in hypothetical relationships, the sample leans heavily on the segregation side (although lack of actual contact does not necessarily mean prejudice). One hundred four subjects report no contacts with either Negroes or mulattoes. Ninety-five per cent of the sample would not marry a Negro; 87 per cent would not marry a light skinned mulatto.

The linear correlation coefficients (Pearsonian r) between the four main variables are all positive, which vindicates at least partially our statistical treatment. Particularly noteworthy is the low correlation between stereotypes and actual behavior (+.25).

[7] Costa Pinto, op. cit., pp. 203-208.

A paradox appears in comparing these four variables or dimensions of prejudice. On the one hand, we find a wide adherence to democratic norms, and, on the other hand, a high degree of stereotypy, a great amount of segregation at the intimate personal level, and a practically complete endogamy. This ambivalence constitutes a real "Brazilian Dilemma," different though it may be from the "American Dilemma." [8]

Differences by Sex, Socio-Economic Status and Ethnic Origin— Manifest differences appear between men and women in our sample. Men accept more stereotypes than women but are much more tolerant for the three other variables. The differences between the means are significant at the level $p < .01$. These differences appear for practically all questions taken separately but particularly for the question on inter-marriage. Men are much more ready to marry light-skinned mulattoes than women. This finding is in agreement with the study of Pierson in Bahia,[9] and with Brazilian folklore, which emphasizes the erotic appeal of the "morena." Several hypotheses to be tested empirically may account for these differences. Women are certainly less free in their associations than men. The penalty put on interracial mingling may be greater for women than for men. There may be a sub-conscious fear of sexual aggression by Negroes on the part of some women as indicated by the question on "sensuality": 40 per cent of the women think that Negroes are more sensual than whites as opposed to 4 per cent for men ($p < .01$). On the other hand, as women enter less in economic competition with Negroes than men, there may be less need for women to develop the racial superiority myth as a defense mechanism.

The most tenable hypothesis is perhaps to be found in the Brazilian racial education which rests on two opposite foundations: on the one hand, opposition to miscegenation; on the other hand, avoidance of racial tensions and of open expression of prejudice.[10] As women remain longer than men under the family influence, they absorb more of this racial indoctrination. From the rejection of miscegenation results the greater intolerance of women; from the etiquette of racial "good manners" results the greater self-censorship on the verbal expression of stereotypes.

The criterion of income alone gives a very poor index of socio-economic status. Our conclusions on this point are very tentative. In comparing the two extreme groups on the income distribution (incomes under 4,500 cruzeiros and over 14,500 cruzeiros), the high-income group accepts more stereotypes than the low-income group but is more tolerant in its social norms and actual behavior. Only the first finding on stereotypes is significant at the level $p < .05$.

No definite assertions can be deduced from such uncertain results. The upper-income group is perhaps more "traditional" and paternalistic. In the low-income group there may be developing a more acute "competi-

[8] G. Myrdal, *An American Dilemma*, New York: 1944, pp. 21, 39, 84-89, 460, 614, 899.
[9] D. Pierson, *op. cit.*, pp. 136-137.
[10] R. Bastide, *et al., op. cit.*, p. 126.

tive" type of discrimination and segregation comparable to that of the "poor white" in the post-bellum South in the United States. These historical-dynamic considerations are beyond the scope of our study. In any case, our findings invalidate for São Paulo two conclusions of Pierson in his Bahia study:[11]

(1) That prejudice in Brazil is more a class prejudice than a racial prejudice. Although we have not been able to isolate the effects of class and racial prejudice and although the two are certainly linked together, we can definitely assert that, after having eliminated the effects of class prejudice against colored people, there would remain an important residue of properly racial prejudice. The latent subjective relationship between sexuality and prejudice would among other facts be incomprehensible if there were only a class prejudice.

(2) That prejudice against Negroes is directly proportional to socio-economic status. Our study fails to confirm this statement for the middle class of São Paulo. The relationship between status and prejudice is certainly not as simple and direct as Pierson formulated it.

When the group of first generation Brazilians as a whole is compared with the group of older-stock Brazilians, no significant differences appear. However, mutually canceling differences are found when the various ethnic groups are separated. The group of Japanese descent is much less prejudiced against Negroes than the general sample, perhaps because it suffers itself from some discrimination. The group of descendants of Syrians and Lebanese is much more prejudiced for reasons explained elsewhere.[12] The Italian group responds like the low-income group in the general sample, which is in accordance with the socio-economic level of a majority of its members. The Portuguese group shows the same patterns as the high-income group. This fact may be explained by the common cultural heritage of Portuguese and Brazilians. The "high-income" type of response may come from the more traditional and paternalistic heritage of the past. All these ethnic-group differences cancel each other and are obscured when the descendants of immigrants are lumped together.

Summary and Conclusion—The existence of racial prejudice against Negroes and mulattoes has been established. Opinions vary greatly from relative tolerance to relative intolerance; freedom of attitudes and, to a lesser degree, of behavior is relatively great: social norms are directive rather than compulsive. Equality of opportunities is largely accepted, casual relations are widely tolerated but intimate relationships with colored people are frowned upon. Mulattoes are generally less discriminated

[11] D. Pierson, op. cit., pp. 348-349; and D. Pierson, Bulletin International des Sciences Sociales, vol. IV, n°2, UNESCO, no date, p. 488. For statements more in agreement with our conclusions see: T. de Azevedo, op. cit., pp. 34-45; C. Wagley, op. cit., pp. 147, 150, 159; R. Bastide et al., op. cit., pp. 11, 123-124, 133-139.
[12] R. Bastide et al., op. cit., pp. 128-129.

against than Negroes but a small minority "prefers" Negroes to mulat-toes. This small minority exhibits a much more virulent form of prejudice against both Negroes and mulattoes than does the general sample. Sex is an important determinant of prejudice. So is socio-economic status, although our data are too uncertain and incomplete to determine the exact relationship. Ethnic origin of the parents likewise plays an impor-tant role.

The weaknesses of our study are many and obvious. As we have pointed out, the sample is not random nor proportional; the postulates underlying the analysis are debatable, etc. Our conclusions must be accepted with all caution and we have raised more problems than we have solved. Although our findings largely confirm previous studies, cer-tain revisions of the literature seem in order. Should our study only stimulate criticism, further research, and a few working hypotheses, we should be highly satisfied.

—————————— William W. Howells

The Distribution of Man

Men with chins, relatively small brow ridges and small facial skeletons, and with high, flat-sided skulls, probably appeared on earth in the period between the last two great continental glaciers, say from 150,000 to 50,000 years ago. If the time of their origin is blurred, the place is no less so. The new species doubtless emerged from a number of related populations distributed over a considerable part of the Old World. Thus *Homo sapiens* evolved as a species and began to differentiate into races at the same time.

In any case, our direct ancestor, like his older relatives, was at once product and master of the crude pebble tools that primitive human forms had learned to use hundreds of thousands of years earlier. His inher-itance also included a social organization and some level of verbal com-munication.

Between these hazy beginnings and the agricultural revolution of about 10,000 years ago *Homo sapiens* radiated over most of the earth, and differentiated into clearly distinguishable races. The processes were intimately related. Like the forces that had created man, they reflected both the workings of man's environment and of his own invention. So much can be said with reasonable confidence. The details are another matter. The when, where and how of the origin of races puzzle us not much less than they puzzled Charles Darwin.

A little over a century ago a pleasingly simple explanation of races enjoyed some popularity. The races were separate species, created by God as they are today. The Biblical account of Adam and Eve was meant to apply only to Caucasians. Heretical as the idea might be, it was argued that the Negroes appearing in Egyptian monuments, and the skulls of the ancient Indian mound-builders of Ohio, differed in no way from their living descendants, and so there could have been no important change in the only slightly longer time since the Creation itself, set by Archbishop Ussher at 4004 B.C.

With his *Origin of Species*, Darwin undid all this careful "science" at a stroke. Natural selection and the immense stretch of time provided by the geological time-scale made gradual evolution seem the obvious explanation of racial or species differences. But in his later book, *The Descent of Man*, Darwin turned his back on his own central notion of natural selection as the cause of races. He there preferred sexual selection, or the accentuation of racial features through long-established ideals of beauty in different segments of mankind. This proposition failed to impress anthropologists, and so Darwin's demolishing of the old views left something of a void that has never been satisfactorily filled.

Not for want of trying. Some students continued, until recent years, to insist that races are indeed separate species, or even separate genera, with Whites descended from chimpanzees, Negroes from gorillas and Mongoloids from orangutans. Darwin himself had already argued against such a possibility when a contemporary proposed that these same apes had in turn descended from three different monkey species. Darwin pointed out that so great a degree of convergence in evolution, producing thoroughgoing identities in detail (as opposed to, say, the superficial resemblance of whales and fishes) simply could not be expected. The same objection applies to a milder hypothesis, formulated by the late Franz Weidenreich during the 1940's. Races, he held, descended separately, not from such extremely divergent parents as the several great apes, but from the less-separated lines of fossil men. For example, Peking man led to the Mongoloids, and Rhodesian man to the "Africans." But again there are more marked distinctions between those fossil men than between living races.

Actually the most reasonable—I should say the only reasonable—pattern suggested by animal evolution in general is that of racial divergence within a stock already possessing distinctive features of *Homo sapiens*. As I have indicated, such a stock had appeared at the latest by the beginning of the last glacial advance and almost certainly much earlier, perhaps by the end of the preceding glaciation, which is dated at some 150,000 years ago.

Even if fossil remains were more plentiful than they are, they might not in themselves decide the questions of time and place much more accurately. By the time *Homo sapiens* was common enough to provide a chance of our finding some of his fossil remains, he was probably already sufficiently widespread as to give only a general idea of his "place of origin." Moreover, bones and artifacts may concentrate in misleading places. (Consider the parallel case of the australopithecine "man-apes" known so well from the Lower Pleistocene of South Africa. This area is thought of as their home. In fact the region actually was a geographical *cul-de-sac*, and merely a good fossil trap at that time. It is now clear that such prehumans were widespread not only in Africa but also in Asia. We have no real idea of their first center of dispersion, and we should assume that our earliest knowledge of them is not from the actual dawn of their existence.)

In attempting to fix the emergence of modern races of man somewhat more precisely we can apply something like the chronological reasoning of the pre-Darwinians. The Upper Paleolithic invaders of Europe (*e.g.*, the Cro-Magnons) mark the definite entrance of *Homo sapiens*, and these men were already stamped with a "White" racial nature at about 35,000 B.C. But a recently discovered skull from Liukiang in China, probably of the same order of age, is definitely not Caucasian, whatever else it may be. And the earliest American fossil men, perhaps 20,000 years old, are recognizable as Indians. No other remains are certainly so old; we cannot now say anything about the first Negroes. Thus racial differences are definitely older than 35,000 years. And yet—this is sheer guess —the more successful *Homo sapiens* would probably have overcome the other human types, such as Neanderthal and Rhodesian men, much earlier if he had reached his full development long before. But these types survived well into the last 50,000 years. So we might assume that *Homo sapiens*, and his earliest racial distinctions, is a product of the period between the last two glaciations, coming into his own early during the last glaciation.

When we try to envisage the causes of racial development, we think today of four factors: natural selection, genetic drift, mutation and mixture (interbreeding). With regard to basic divergence at the level of races, the first two are undoubtedly the chief determinants. If forces of any kind favor individuals of one genetic complexion over others, in the sense that they live and reproduce more successfully, the favored individuals will necessarily increase their bequest of genes to the next generation relative to the rest of the population. That is selection; a force with direction.

Genetic drift is a force without direction, an accidental change in the gene proportions of a population. Other things being equal, some parents just have more offspring than others. If such variations can build up, an originally homogeneous population may split into two different ones by chance. It is somewhat as though there were a sack containing 50 red and 50 white billiard balls, each periodically reproducing itself, say by doubling. Suppose you start a new population, drawing out 50 balls without looking. The most likely single result would be 25 of each color, but it is more likely that you would end up with some other combination, perhaps as extreme as 20 reds and 30 whites. After this population divides, you make a new drawing, and so on. Of course at each subsequent step the departure from the then-prevailing proportion is as likely to favor red as white. Nevertheless, once the first drawing has been made with the above result, red has the better chance of vanishing. So it is with genes for hereditary traits.

Both drift and selection should have stronger effects the smaller and more isolated the population. It is easy to imagine them in action among bands of ancient men, living close to nature. (It would be a great mistake, however, to imagine that selection is not also effective in modern populations.) Hence we can look upon racial beginnings as part accident, part design, design meaning any pattern of minor change obedient to natural selection.

Darwin was probably right the first time, then, and natural selection is more important in racial adaptation than he himself later came to think. Curiously, however, it is extremely difficult to find demonstrable, or even logically appealing, adaptive advantages in racial features. The two leading examples of adaptation in human physique are not usually considered racial at all. One is the tendency among warm-blooded animals of the same species to be larger in colder parts of their territory. As an animal of a given shape gets larger, its inner bulk increases faster than its outer surface, so the ratio of heat produced to heat dissipated is higher in larger individuals. It has, indeed, been shown that the average body weight of man goes up as annual mean temperature goes down, speaking very broadly, and considering those populations that have remained where they are a long time. The second example concerns the size of extremities (limbs, ears, muzzles). They are smaller in colder parts of the range and larger in warmer, for the same basic reason—heat conservation and dissipation. Man obeys this rule also, producing lanky, long-limbed populations in hot deserts and dumpy, short-limbed peoples in the Arctic.

This does not carry us far with the major, historic races as we know them. Perhaps the most striking of all racial features is the dark skin of Negroes. The color of Negro skin is due to a concentration of melanin, the universal human pigment that diffuses sunlight and screens out its damaging ultraviolet component. Does it not seem obvious that in the long course of time the Negroes, living astride the Equator in Africa and in the western Pacific, developed their dark skins as a direct response to a strong sun? It makes sense. It would be folly to deny that such an adaptation is present. But a great deal of the present Negro habitat is shade forest and not bright sun, which is in fact strongest in the deserts some distance north of the Equator. The Pygmies are decidedly forest dwellers, not only in Africa but in their several habitats in southeastern Asia as well.

At any rate there is enough doubt to have called forth other suggestions. One is that forest hunters needed protective coloration, both for stalking and for their protection from predators; dark skin would have lowest visibility in the patchy light and shade beneath the trees. Another is that densely pigmented skins may have other qualities—*e.g.*, resistance to infection—of which we are unaware.

A more straightforward way out of the dilemma is to suppose that the Negroes are actually new to the Congo forest, and that they served their racial apprenticeship hunting and fishing in the sunny grasslands of the southern Sahara. If so, their Pygmy relatives might represent the first accommodation of the race to the forest, before agriculture but after dark skin had been acquired. Smaller size certainly makes a chase after game through the undergrowth less exhausting and faster. As for woolly hair, it is easy to see it (still without proof) as an excellent, nonmatting insulation against solar heat. Thick Negro lips? Every suggestion yet made has a zany sound. They may only be a side effect of some properties of heavily pigmented skin (ability to produce thick scar tissue, for example), even as blond hair is doubtless a side effect of the general depigmentation of men that has occurred in northern Europe.

At some remove racially from Negroes and Pygmies are the Bushmen and Hottentots of southern Africa. They are small, or at least lightly built, with distinctive wide, small, flat faces; they are rather infantile looking, and have a five-cornered skull outline that seems to be an ancient inheritance. Their skin is yellowish-brown, not dark. None of this has been clearly interpreted, although the small size is thought to be an accommodation to water and food economy in the arid environment. The light skin, in an open sunny country, contradicts the sun-pigment theory, and has in fact been used in favor of the protective-coloration hypothesis. Bushmen and background blend beautifully for color, at least as human beings see color.

Bushmen, and especially Hottentots, have another dramatic characteristic: steatopygia. If they are well nourished, the adult women accumulate a surprising quantity of fat on their buttocks. This seems to be a simple storehouse mechanism reminiscent of the camel's hump; a storehouse that is not distributed like a blanket over the torso generally, where it would be disadvantageous in a hot climate. The characteristic nicely demonstrates adaptive selection working in a human racial population.

The Caucasians make the best argument for skin color as an ultraviolet screen. They extend from cloudy northern Europe, where the ultraviolet in the little available sunlight is not only acceptable but desirable, down to the fiercely sun-baked Sahara and peninsular India. All the way, the correspondence with skin color is good: blond around the Baltic, swarthy on the Mediterranean, brunet in Africa and Arabia, dark brown in India.

Thus, given a long enough time of occupation, and doubtless some mixture to provide dark-skinned genes in the south, natural selection could well be held responsible.

On the other hand, the Caucasians' straight faces and often prominent noses lack any evident adaptive significance. It is the reverse with the Mongoloids, whose countenances form a coherent pattern that seems consistent with their racial history. From the standpoint of evolution it is Western man, not the Oriental, who is inscrutable. The "almond" eyes of the Mongoloid are deeply set in protective fat-lined lids, the nose and forehead are flattish and the cheeks are broad and fat-padded. In every way, it has been pointed out, this is an ideal mask to protect eyes, nose, and sinuses against bitterly cold weather. Such a face is the pole toward which the peoples of eastern Asia point, and it reaches its most marked and uniform expression in the cold northeastern part of the continent, from Korea north.

Theoretically the Mongoloid face developed under intense natural selection some time during the last glacial advance among peoples trapped north of a ring of mountain glaciers and subjected to fierce cold, which would have weeded out the less adapted, in the most classic Darwinian fashion, through pneumonia and sinus infections. If the picture is accurate, this face type is the latest major human adaptation. It could not be very old. For one thing, the population would have had to reach a stage of advanced skill in hunting and living to survive at all in such cold, a stage probably not attained before the Upper Paleolithic (beginning about 35,000 B.C.). For another, the adaptation must have occurred after the American Indians, who are Mongoloid but without the transformed face, migrated across the Bering Strait. (Only the Eskimos reflect the extension of full-fledged, recent Mongoloids into America.) All this suggests a process taking a relatively small number of generations (about 600) between 25,000 and 10,000 B.C.

The discussion so far has treated human beings as though they were any mammal under the influence of natural selection and the other forces of evolution. It says very little about why man invaded the various environments that have shaped him and how he got himself distributed in the way we find him now. For an understanding of these processes we must take into account man's own peculiar abilities. He has created culture, a milieu for action and development that must be added to the simplicities of sun, snow, forest or plain.

Let us go back to the beginning. Man started as an apelike creature, certainly vegetarian, certainly connected with wooded zones, limited like all other primates to tropical or near-tropical regions. In becoming a walker he had begun to extend his range. Tools, social rules and intelligence all progressed together; he learned to form efficient groups, armed with weapons not provided by nature. He started to eat meat, and later to cook it; the more concentrated diet widened his possibilities for using his time; the hunting of animals beckoned him still farther in various directions.

All this was probably accomplished during the small-brained australopithecine stage. It put man on a new plane, with the potential to reach all parts of the earth, and not only those in which he could find food ready to his hand, or be comfortable in his bare skin. He did not actually reach his limits until the end of the last glaciation, and in fact left large tracts empty for most of the period. By then he had become *Homo sapiens,* with a large brain. He had tools keen enough to give him clothes of animal skin. He had invented projectiles to widen the perimeter of his striking power: bolas, javelins with spear throwers, arrows with bows. He was using dogs to widen the perimeter of his senses in tracking. He had found what could be eaten from the sea and its shores. He could move only slowly, and was probably by no means adventurous. But hunting territory was precious, and the surplus of an expanding population had to stake out new preserves wherever there was freedom ahead. So this pressure, and man's command of nature, primitive though it still was, sent the hunters of the end of the Ice Age throughout the Old World, out into Australia, up into the far north, over the Bering Strait and down the whole length of the Americas to Tierra del Fuego. At the beginning of this dispersion we have brutes barely able to shape a stone tool; at the end, the wily, self-reliant Eskimo, with his complicated traps, weapons and sledges and his clever hunting tricks.

The great racial radiation carried out by migratory hunters culminated in the world as it was about 10,000 years ago. The Whites occupied Europe, northern and eastern Africa and the Near East, and extended far to the east in Central Asia toward the Pacific shore. Negroes occupied the Sahara, better watered then, and Pygmies the African equatorial forest; south, in the open country, were Bushmen only. Other Pygmies, the Negritos, lived in the forests of much of India and southeastern Asia; while in the open country of these areas and in Australia were men like the present Australian aborigines: brown, beetle-browed and wavy-haired. Most of the Pacific was empty. People such as the American Indians stretched from China and Mongolia over Alaska to the Straits of Magellan; the more strongly Mongoloid peoples had not yet attained their domination of the Far East.

During the whole period the human population had depended on the supply of wild game for food, and the accent had been on relative isolation of peoples and groups. Still close to nature (as we think of nature), man was in a good position for rapid small-scale evolution, both through natural selection and through the operation of chance in causing differences among widely separated tribes even if selection was not strong.

Then opened the Neolithic period, the beginning of a great change. Agriculture was invented, at first inefficient and feeble, but in our day able to feed phenomenally large populations while freeing them from looking for food. The limit on local numbers of people was gradually removed, and with it the necessity for the isolation and spacing of groups and the careful observation of boundaries. Now, as there began to be surpluses available for trading, connections between communities became more useful. Later came a spreading of bonds from higher centers of trade and of authority. Isolation gave way to contact, even when contact meant war.

The change was not speedy by our standards, though in comparison with the pace of the Stone Age it seems like a headlong rush. The new economy planted people much more solidly, of course. Farmers have been uprooting and displacing hunters from the time of the first planters to our own day, when Bushman survivors are still losing reservation land to agriculturalists in southwestern Africa. These Bushmen, a scattering of Australian aborigines, the Eskimos and a few other groups are the only representatives of their age still in place. On the other hand, primitive representatives of the Neolithic level of farming still live in many places after the thousands of years since they first became established there.

Nevertheless mobility increased and has increased ever since. Early woodland farmers were partly nomadic, moving every generation following exhaustion of the soil, however solidly fixed they may have been during each sojourn. The Danubians of 6,000 years ago can be traced archeologically as they made the same kind of periodic removes as central Africans, Iroquois Indians and pioneer Yankee farmers. Another side of farming—animal husbandry—gave rise to pastoral nomadism. Herders were much lighter of foot, and historically have tended to be warlike and domineering. With irrigation, villages could settle forever and evolve into the urban centers of high civilizations. Far from immobilizing man, however, these centers served as fixed bases from which contact (and conflict) worked outward.

The rest of the story is written more clearly. New crops or new agricultural methods opened new territories, such as equatorial Africa, and the great plains of the U. S., never successfully farmed by the Indians. New materials such as copper and tin made places once hopeless for habitation desirable as sources of raw material or as way stations for trade. Thus an island like Crete rose from nothing to dominate the eastern Mediterranean for centuries. Well before the earliest historians had made records, big population shifts were taking place. Our mental picture of the aboriginal world is actually a recent one. The Bantu Negroes moved into central and southern Africa, peoples of Mongoloid type went south through China and into Japan, and ancient folk of Negrito and Australoid racial nature were submerged by Caucasians in India. Various interesting but inconsequential trickles also ran hither and yon; for example, the migration of the Polynesians into the far Pacific.

The greatest movement came with the advent of ocean sailing in Europe. (The Polynesians had sailed the high seas earlier, of course, but they had no high culture, nor did Providence interpose a continent across their route at a feasible distance, as it did for Columbus.) The Europeans poured out on the world. From the 15th to the 19th centuries they compelled other civilized peoples to accept contact, and subjected or erased the uncivilized. So today, once again, we have a quite different distribution of mankind from that of 1492.

It seems obvious that we stand at the beginning of still another phase. Contact is immediate, borders are slamming shut and competition is fierce. Biological fitness in races is now hard to trace, and even reproduction is heavily controlled by medicine and by social values. The racial picture of the future will be determined less by natural selection and disease resistances than by success in government and in the adjustment of numbers. The end of direct European dominance in Africa and Asia seems to mean the end of any possibility of the infiltration and expansion of the European variety of man there, on the New World model. History as we know it has been largely the expansion of the European horizon and of European peoples. But the end in China of mere absorption of Occidental invention, and the passionate self-assertion of the African tribes, make it likely that racial lines and territories will again be more sharply drawn than they have been for centuries. What man will make of himself next is a question that lies in the province of prophets, not anthropologists.

────────── Richard P. Hunt

The Whippoorwill Cries, the Fox Whimpers

When the whippoorwill cries in the east, close by the house, some evil will befall the family; when a fox is heard whimpering in the woods, a death will follow. So goes an old tradition of the Seneca Indians.

These days the proud little Seneca Nation is living with one ear cocked for whippoorwills in the east and foxes in the woods. Its Indian face is stoically calm, but its Indian heart winces at a coming evil: the loss of ancestral land. Their brains and bodies will survive, the Senecas know, but the nation flinches at the thought of ultimate death: the loss of its Indian soul.

"The state of the nation," a tribal leader said recently, "is not good." And that, so mildly put, is the way most of the 1,100 Senecas who live here on the Allegany Reservation feel.

The physical threat to them is a dam being built by the Federal Government at Kinzua, Pa., just a few miles down the Allegheny River from

New York Times Magazine, June 10, 1962, pp. 14-15, 59-60.

the southern border of the 30,000-acre reservation. By 1965 the most useful 10,000 acres will be covered by the impounded water, and about 800 Senecas will lose their homes. The remaining tribal land is either too steep for homesites or already occupied.

The threat to the spirit is greater. For the Senecas are struggling with a dilemma often repeated in America, from the pine forests to the asphalt jungles: they want to retain their old traditions, yet make the best of modern life; they want to remain Indian and be American; they want racial integration and cultural segregation.

To the casual eye, there seems to be nothing very special about the Seneca Nation, and it is sometimes difficult for even the most sympathetic whites to understand why the Senecas want to remain just a little bit different.

One can drive through the reservation, forty-four miles long and a mile or less wide along the oxbow of the Allegheny and never know it is Indian land. There is no gate and no sign, except here and there a hand-lettered notice reading, "Souvenirs—tom-toms and beadwork."

Along the flat, fertile shoulders of the river and among the pineclad foothills stand the white farmhouses, the bright bungalows and the unpainted shacks of the Indians, amid the vegetable gardens, cow pastures and henyards of any rural scene in Western New York. The Indian men, in their work boots, khaki jeans and checkered shirts, and the women in their loose cotton housedresses look much like country people anywhere, save for the darkness of their cheeks and the blackness of their hair.

But there are differences that do not show. The Senecas have their own form of government, their own way of life, their own values and their own feelings. Many have their own religion, and all seem to share some indefinable community of the spirit.

Their Government, formally known as the Seneca Nation, is a little democracy with three branches. There is an Executive, with a President, Treasurer and Clerk, an elected Tribal Council of sixteen members—eight from the Allegany Reservation and eight representing the 2,000 Senecas on the nearby Cattaraugus Reservation—and a Judiciary of six judges, called "Peacemakers," and two surrogates.

The Council's law-making powers are few, for the Indians are subject to the civil and criminal laws of New York. But the Council does make tribal policy, especially concerning tribal land, and it decides how to spend the national income.

This is a fund of about $100,000 a year from the rental of land to whites (the entire city of Salamanca is on Allegany Reservation land, and its 8,500 residents pay ground rent to the Senecas), from payments for railroad and utility rights to cross the reservation, from the sale of hunting and fishing licenses to outsiders and from the sale of rights to gravel pits on the reservation.

Most of the money goes to meet the cost of the little Government. But each year every Seneca receives about $1.40 in treaty payments and a yard of unbleached muslin "treaty cloth" from the Federal Government. Seneca housewives use the muslin to make pillow slips.

A Seneca pays no property taxes on reservation land, but he does pay state and Federal income taxes. His education is free, down to the paper and pencils. There are seventy-three youngsters now in the six-grade primary school at Red House; the older children go to integrated junior high and high schools off the reservation.

The "Peacemakers" deal mostly with land disputes and family matters; the surrogates, of course, handle estates and the property of minors. In "Peacemakers' Court," the most common dispute is about land, and who may hold it.

All the land on the reservation belongs to the nation, but plots are assigned to individuals, who may pass them on to their heirs. Disputes arise when a non-Seneca—one whose mother was not a Seneca—claims a plot; then the "Peacemakers" must decide.

There is one other institution, which can be seen, but should be felt. It is the Long House, an unpainted wooden building, sixty feet long and twenty feet wide, that is the center of the ceremonial life of the nation and of much of its religious life.

At the Long House, Seneca elders still retell in the old tongue the legends of the seer and prophet Handsome Lake, whose visions in 1799 cast the spiritual tradition of the tribe into a new and lasting mold. One of these legends tells how Handsome Lake, in a glimpse of life beyond death, saw a wretched Indian crawling along a road with a shovel and a basket. The prophet's guide to the afterworld told him in ghostly tones:

"This is a man who sold his land. Now he must move all the land that he sold and put it in a big pile. You can imagine how long that will take."

That preview of hellish torment strikes to the bones of the Seneca Nation, because it is about the two things that make being a Seneca seem meaningful and important. Without the land and without the teachings of Handsome Lake, the Seneca Nation quite possibly would not exist.

But with their land and their tradition, Senecas have a way that is specially Indian. These are some of the ways it shows in things that Seneca Indians have done within the past few months:

Darla Claflin, a 17-year-old Seneca girl, punched two white boys and a girl who called her a squaw. She did it not because she was ashamed of being an Indian, but because she had been taught to be proud of being one.

Her 15-year-old brother, Butch, learned some Indian dances; he also learned the twist. In Salamanca, Richard Shongo was jailed for the umpteenth time on a charge of public intoxication. Another Seneca tried to borrow money from a bank; he was told to get a white co-signer, "because Indians don't like to pay."

At the Long House, Albert Jones, a 74-year-old leader of the cult of Handsome Lake, appeared in a cornhusk mask and predicted that "the little people"—the leprechauns of Seneca lore—would never let the Kinzua dam be built.

"We Indians got something to protect us. We'll do some little things, and there'll be a lot of people dead down there at the dam, without anybody touching them," he explained afterward.

Serena Pierce and Idabelle Hanson, elderly spinster cousins, made cornhusk dolls for the summer tourist season; some girls they knew went off to hunt sassafras and wild onion; Butch Claflin and his father went hunting. Somebody bought a television set; somebody else won ten dollars at bingo.

And Harry Watt sat on his porch, fifty yards from the place where he was born, and looked at the leafy poplar saplings along the banks of the Allegheny.

"I belong here," he said. "I played over there—my grandmother used to tell me: 'Don't go near the road, or the white man will come and take you away.' I've hunted over all these hills. This is about the only place where I can sit down and really relax. I'm home."

In what all of those Senecas did, there was a lot of being just plain American. But in all of what they did, there was a touch that was only Seneca. "Tell your people they are lost if they follow the ways of the white man," Jesus Christ commands Handsome Lake in the legend. "Tell them to follow their own ways; they are the best."

Most Senecas are poor, but most of them don't mind. Their way of life is noncompetitive, and status-seeking is almost unknown. No one would dare to admit being embarrassed because Dickie Shongo had been jailed again; the man who bought the TV set would never boast about it to his neighbors; the one who won at bingo lent the money to a friend.

"Whites build up a fortune to find contentment or peace of mind," said George Heron, Treasurer of the Seneca Nation. "The Indian doesn't bother building a fortune; his contentment is right here and now." He paused, listening to a cricket chirp in the night. "Hear that? It's worth a lot to me."

Communing with nature is part of the Seneca way of life. Commuting to and from the surrounding white civilization is another. George Heron and his wife, like many other Senecas, drive back and forth daily to jobs miles away. Some go off for years, usually as construction workers, craftsmen or soldiers.

"Those who like a fast buck—no pun intended—are likely to become steelworkers," a Seneca said in talking about how reservation men spend their lives. "A lot of them work on the railroads; some stay here and farm, or just hunt and fish or pick up odd jobs. About twenty of them do a lot of drinking, and the people in Salamanca think that's what all of us do.

"But those who go away always come back to the reservation—unless they become snobs and forget their Indian ways. If they want to think they're better than anybody else, they probably don't belong here anyway. We have no class distinction. The poorest family is accepted as well as the most well-to-do."

Equality, then, is a part of the Indian spirit. A way of speaking and feeling is part of it, too. A Seneca talks slowly, with lots of rumination. He is reserved, and warms up slowly to a stranger. He has a lively wit, and he likes to laugh. When he is serious, there is in him a quality somewhere between stoicism and resignation; he accepts life as it comes.

Serena and Idabelle, plaiting their dolls in a humble house, shed no tears as they talked about losing their land. "It's about 200 acres," gray-haired Idabelle said with a wispy smile. "I've spent most of my life here, and my mother came here at the age of 2. She died at 83." That is the way Senecas talk: description, but not much comment.

But proud of being Indian. "When an application form comes along, and there's a blank for race, I want always to put Indian," said Mrs. Gertrude Claflin, Darla's mother. "And that's what I try to teach my kids, so they'll have something to hang onto."

She and her family are Christians, but they too go to the Long House —along with the seventy-odd followers of Handsome Lake—because there they find that "something to hang onto" that is uniquely Seneca.

Handsome Lake, apart from his religious teaching, was the curator of culture in Seneca history. He inveighed against the witchcraft and spell-casting of the Indian lore that preceded his day, and he would have heartily disapproved of the talk about "little people" interfering with the dam. But he used the old beliefs as a base, teaching the tribe to bend with the conquering whites and still remain Indian.

George S. Snyderman, a Philadelphia anthropologist, has summarized the teaching of Handsome Lake as follows:

"Everything in the universe has a purpose, and was put there by the Creator. No person, plant or animal, no matter how insignificant, is superfluous. Man himself fills only one place in the Creator's scheme, and he must live his life in a good way. The creator's ways are mysterious, and he has spirits to help him."

To that Gertrude Claflin added: "It's not much different from Christianity. It's about the same as the New Testament, in simpler language. But there's one thing different about the Long House people: they never ask favors from God; they only say thank you."

Perhaps no one can come much closer to saying in a few words just what the Seneca spirit is. There remains only to add, in the words of DeForest Billy, a tribal councillor: "All Senecas are followers of Handsome Lake, in a sense. You always have a little of that in you, no matter whether you go to the Baptist Church or not."

So it was that Senecas of many faiths, and a common belief in being Seneca, filed into the Long House last February for the annual midwinter ceremonies. Segregated by sex, they sat on the long narrow benches, listening to the music of the turtle rattle and the water drum, watching the old dances danced and hearing the old tales retold.

That is what Senecas have, and what they are afraid of losing. Handsome Lake taught them to keep their land, and, keeping their land and remaining together, they kept the teachings of Handsome Lake. If they are uprooted and scattered, or divided into small groups, they fear their community life and their common spirit will wither away.

To the people of the Pittsburgh area, the great dam means protection from floods and water storage for their industries. To the Senecas, it threatens disaster. Of course, they will be paid for their land; they may even be given new land. But will life ever be the same?

"You could get along just as well any place else," Gertrude Claflin said, "but you wouldn't be as happy.

"I always want a part of the reservation. It's always home, and you always have that feeling that when you get tired of the rat race, you can go home."

Supplementary Bibliography

Ralph L. Beals and Harry Hoijer, *An Introduction to Anthropology*, 2nd ed. N. Y.: Macmillan, 1959.
    A sound text devoting considerable space to the origins and distribution of races.

Theodosius Dobzhansky, *Evolution, Genetics, and Man*. N. Y.: Wiley, 1955.
    An analysis of the biological development of Homo sapiens.

Clyde Kluckhohn, *Mirror for Man*. N. Y.: McGraw-Hill, 1944. Reprinted as a Premier Book, Greenwich, Conn.: Fawcett Publications, 1960.
    A splendid introduction to anthropology for the layman, with an especially valuable chapter, "Race: A Modern Myth."

William M. Krogman, "The Concept of Race," in *The Science of Man in the World Crisis*, ed. Ralph Linton. N. Y.: Columbia U. Press, 1945.
    A summary of the physical anthropologist's knowledge about human types, including a chart of the physical traits of the three main races.

George Gaylord Simpson, *The Meaning of Evolution*, rev. ed. and abridged. N. Y.: New American Library, 1952.
    A presentation of the role of genetics in modern interpretations of evolutionary theory.

UNESCO, Department of Mass Communication, *What Is Race? Evidence from Scientists.* Paris: United Nations Educational, Scientific and Cultural Organization, 1952.
A simple, readable discussion of genetics and the development of the races of man.

III Race Differences

There is more to this problem than our inability to construct a racial classification system which is exhaustive and the difficulty of defining categories that are mutually exclusive. With the rough and approximate categories we have, is it possible to predict other biological characteristics? Are groupings such as Negroid, Mongoloid, and Caucasoid associated with differences in average intelligence, variations in athletic ability, gradations in musical talent, and meaningful differences in social relationships or culture? In short, does this classification scheme correlate with anything else? If so, approximate and error-laden though it be, it is useful to social scientists in their attempts to classify and understand human behavior.

The only differences we have established among the races are differences by definition. That is, we can say that Negroes *on the average* are darker than whites or Mongoloids; but being darker is only part of what we mean by being Negro. We have used the physical differences to define the racial boundaries. Now we must ask what else is true about people who are darker and curlier-haired than other people.

Biological Classifications of Men: The Lack of Correlates

First, are there systematic differences, by race, in such a basic cultural element as the language with which people communicate? There are not. Any group of human beings can learn to speak any known human language. There is no better evidence of this than the contemporary English-speaking population of the United States. Here we find Negroids, Mongoloids, and Caucasoids from all over the world who have learned in only a few generations to share a common culture and a common language. While many Americans retain a few items from the culture of their grandfathers, whether Chinese-Americans or Hungarian-Americans, all read the labels on the same frozen foods at the supermarket and cheer in the same language at a baseball game.

Nationality and race are also obviously separate matters which bear no necessary relationship to one another. Again, the United States affords an example of a single nation made up of all the major racial stocks. Similarly, the Soviet Union combines in a single nation people ranging from the Mongoloid Eskimos of Eastern Siberia, to the swarthy residents of Turkestan, to the blond Nordic Caucasoids in northwestern Russia.

Can you know a man's race from his religion or predict his religion from his race? No; as with language or any other learned behavior, any normal human beings can learn the belief system of a religion. People sometimes speak of "the Jewish race," but there is no more a Jewish "race" than a Christian one. Judaism arose among Semitic Caucasoids in the Near East, people of the same race—and subrace—as the Arabs, who spread their belief in Mohammed. But there are Chinese Jews, African Jews, European Jews, and American Jews. The American who wonders whether Jews are a race need only look at the blond, blue-eyed American Jews who came from North Germany and the swarthy, dark-haired American Jews who came from Turkey or Spain to be reminded that there are Mongoloid converts to Judaism living half way around the world from him, and that all these believers can hardly be considered a biological race. Islam too has made converts all over the world; and there are Japanese Christians, Nigerian Christians, and English Christians. We can classify people by the color of their skin, the length of their noses, the language they have learned, or the place of worship they choose, but we should remember that these are four separate and distinct methods of grouping human beings, and that the categories have no necessary relationship to one another.

Racial Superiority and the Rise of Civilizations

But white men do seem to be in charge of things. If Caucasoids are not a breed superior to Mongoloids and Negroids, how can we explain the European dominance of Asia and Africa for several centuries? A glance at the patterns of colonial expansion during the seventeenth, eighteenth, and nineteenth centuries seems persuasive evidence of the superiority of the white race.

The answer to this riddle is that one can easily believe in natural racial superiority—he needs only a profound ignorance of history.

Whatever the causes of the rise and fall of civilizations, race, over the span of human history, seems a poor explanation. The ancient Egyptians were a mixture of Negro and Semitic stocks. Kingdoms of Negroid Africans and Mongoloid Asiatics were at the forefront of civilization when Caucasoid Europeans were hunting in forests and living in caves. Even after Europeans had risen to the height represented in Ancient Greece and the Roman Empire, centuries followed during which Caucasoid Europeans were unable to defend themselves against the Mongoloid might of Attila and the Khans.

Various races and subraces have proved capable of expansion and consolidation of power when given fresh ideas in a favorable setting. As the sum of what men know has increased, each society has built on the knowledge of its predecessors and neighbors.

To the extent that various tribes are in touch with one another, knowledge is diffused. There is a pyramiding of learning and skill. The discoveries, social inventions, technology, and organization of one society furnish a foundation for the building of the next. As time goes by, the arts and inventions pioneered by one people become the common property of their neighbors and of far-away tribes with whom they trade, and people of the next civilization are able to devote their imagination and energies to further advances in organization and application.

The power which is the consequence of new knowledge has been the force in the creation of the great civilizations. Therefore, when a people is isolated from the most advanced societies of its time, it is cut off from opportunities for rapid cultural growth. When African civilizations flourished, English and German tribes were unaware of them, and remained relatively primitive. During the period when the Industrial Revolution was changing the social fabric of northwestern Europe and the United States, most Africans and Asians were completely isolated from these developments. The Maya Indians had a decimal system, but no wheel; the Romans had a wheel, but no concept of zero. Hence the Mayas made greater advances than the Romans in astronomy and mathematics; the Romans exceeded the Mayas in transportation and conquest.

Race and Intelligence

People of every race have at one time or another achieved high place, held sway over their neighbors, and advanced in knowledge beyond what was generally known among other races at the time. But the question can still be raised whether, on the average, one race is not superior to the others. A clue to the error in such an assumption can be found where members of several races participate in one society, as in the United States.

Seventy-five years ago, in the heyday of John L. Sullivan, it was widely held that the Irish were "born fighters," innately superior in prize-fighting ability to representatives of other "races." But as time passed and the Irish had time to climb the educational and economic ladders to assimilation in American society, they were replaced in prize-fighting by Italian-American champions and contenders. After a brief period of Italian dominance of the craft, Jews from Eastern Europe used prize-fighting as a route to upward social mobility. (The occupation happens to be a good illustration because it requires a minimum of capital and formal education, and some of what it does require can be readily learned while growing up in the streets of a slum neighborhood.) The Jewish champions and contenders gave way to an era of Negro superiority, and the same phrases were used to describe Negroes that had been assigned to the Irish two generations before: "natural boxers," "hard-headed," "dumb but tough," and even "unfair competition because they're born with less feeling and the ability to take greater physical punishment." Currently, of course, we are seeing American Negroes displaced in the ring by Latin-Americans: Cubans, Mexicans, and Puerto Ricans. Racial differences may seem a good explanation for the behavior of members of a given group at a moment in time. With some historical perspective a better explanation seems to be provided by an examination of the group's position in the social structure.

We have learned a comparable lesson from social scientists' studies of the I.Q. and other measures of ability and achievement. On the average, American Negroes score lower on such tests than American whites. What we need to know is whether this is a racial trait or a difference attributable to the Negroes' position in American society.

In Army tests of aptitude during World War II, Northern soldiers did better than those from the Southern states. We would expect this, because we know that education influences the results of such tests, and schools are, on the average, superior in the North. Northern Negroes excelled Southern Negroes; this would be expected because of the differing quality of the facilities for formal education. But this data poses a challenging question. When we know that (1) rural schools have lower standards and poorer facilities on the average than urban schools and that (2) the quality of formal education in the Southern states is poorer than in the North, and that (3) most American Negroes have been born and reared in the rural South, how should we interpret the finding that Negroes average lower test scores than whites? Is this a consequence of race (heredity) or of social structure (environment)?

It is a more complicated problem than it seems at first, for Negroes and whites in the United States simply do not share a comparable environment, even if we leave region and urban-rural differences out of it. A typical Negro child attending the same school with whites in a Northern city is not in the same environment the whites are in: his parents had less formal education than most of the white parents, and education of inferior quality; he does not have the same things at home as the white children have; he lives in a poorer, more crowded neighborhood than the white children; his teachers treat him with less patience and sympathy than they give their white pupils; his fellow students exclude him from their evening homework sessions, especially if their parents insist. In short, he lives in an environment of discrimination. It is extremely difficult to compare racial abilities in a situation of experimental control.

What we can do is contrast the performance of representatives of the two races in differing environments. Such a contrast casts doubt on any generalizations about race differences. Negro draftees from New York, Ohio, and Illinois averaged much better on Army literacy and aptitude tests than white soldiers from Georgia, Arkansas, and Mississippi. We do not conclude from this that Northern Negroes are a smarter "race" than Southern whites. It simply means that where there are better opportunities, Negroes, like whites, profit from them.

We know that representatives of all races are found throughout the range of intelligence: there are Negroid, Mongoloid, and Caucasoid geniuses, and there are Negroid, Mongoloid, and Caucasoid imbeciles.

From what we have been able to learn from the best tests we have, controlling for regional differences, urban-rural differences, and other cultural influences on opportunity and motivation, we simply cannot conclude that social science research offers us any evidence that there exists any inborn difference in ability between races.

Related Readings

Tom Stacey, in "The Anguish of the White Settlers," quotes both black and white Africans to show that a "culture gap" between groups can be so great that it seems to the participants to be innate, rooted in biological differences.

Actually, as Bernard C. Rosen indicates in "Race, Ethnicity, and the Achievement Syndrome," group differences in performance which are so extreme that an observer might easily conclude they were innate can be traced to a historical tradition. Members of various cultural groups are taught different expectations; young people are socialized into a group-accepted set of aspirations and motivations. To understand the discrepancies in ambition and in social mobility among various groups, a knowledge of their cultural values is more pertinent than information about their racial stock.

=Tom Stacey

The Anguish of the White Settlers

The old Rhodesian stood among the beloved apricot trees and pome-
granates, avocados and lemon trees of his poor, dry acres that bore the
achievement of half his life, and broke our long silence. His vehemence
was startling.

"The munts [Africans] can take over—I'll stay. *They* won't get me
away from here. They'll get me away to bury me, that's all. I've told
everyone, even the Inspector [of police], *they* won't get me away. No-
body's going to take my rifle away, same as they've done in the Congo.
The man that's going to come to take my rifle away is going to take me
with him. If I shot one native—or two—not my brother can come and
catch me. I'd blow his brains out.

"All can go. *I* won't go. Not out of Rhodesia I won't go, boy."

Their land is growing dark for them, and what they are composed of
—the bones of their government and the sinews of their society—is discovered to have the fatal disease. The inexorable agent of destruction of
their body is recognised by the white Africans from the Highlands of
Kenya to the banks of the Limpopo; the terrible desire to survive is confused with the death wish; and those that would fight for their society
and the future they had presumed for their race in Africa would almost
as soon die in the struggle.

People of British stock do not usually like to express anguish by
violence. The brief shadow-life of the so-called Rhodesian Republican
Army cannot earn comparison with the O.A.S. in Algeria. No one can
yet forecast whether one grim day relations between Westminster and
Salisbury might not fatally rupture, and Sir Roy Welensky's jest that the
British government will put him in the Tower for defending Britain's
interests in the depths of Africa might not turn into some kind of agonis-
ing reality. But for the time being, the white Africans can *actively* express
their anguish only by leaving their treasured country.

Last year, 1961, was the first year in which more white men left the
Rhodesian Federation than arrived. In Kenya, the trend is established;
probably more than one in ten of the white farmers have already gone,
and the rate of departure grows. In some areas of Kenya, like Eldoret
where the Afrikaner settlers centred themselves, about three out of ten
have left. Late last year the Kenya 'Convention of Associations'—whose
members comprise all the country's 2,600 white farmers—conducted a
private poll among all their members through the post. The result showed
that 79 per cent. were intending to leave Kenya as soon as they could

The Sunday Times Colour Section, June 3, 1962, pp. 1-13.

dispose of their farms for anything like a fair price—or else were leaving anyway.

Of the 21 per cent. who said they were intending to stay unless compelled to leave, four out of five were over 60. Much the same ratio is considered to apply to that majority of settlers, in business or the professions, or retired, who own their own houses and other property in the towns or suburbs. Virtually all property in Kenya, whether land or houses, is unsaleable. In Nairobi, scores of European houses stand blind and vacant, rank weed and high grasses re-establishing themselves— homes which the absent owners would jump at selling at half their pre-1960 values. Farms, of course, are not abandoned so easily. Even without the existing law of confiscation by the Government of an abandoned farm, there is nature to act as confiscator.

The old 'uns, that 21 per cent. who will stay anyway, possess the fortitude of resignation. They have more to lose of the past than of the future. One couple both about 65 years old, had taught in schools in East Africa for nearly 40 years. When they retired, they bought a creeper-covered cottage and 15 acres at Limuru, a few miles from Nairobi.

Walking home through the evening sunlight of that clean and smiling landscape, "like Somerset," rolling and green and fertile, she said: "After 45 years in Africa we just can't leave now." Inside, the cottage was neat and snug and full of relics of their lifetime in the country. Two armchairs, with their antimacassars, were drawn up before the brick fireplace; and there, in two paper bags beside the arm of each chair, was the only evidence that this was not Somerset but Kenya, where, as independence approaches and security weakens, nocturnal gang attacks on European homes become more frequent, such as that in which an old widow had died a few months before within a mile of their cottage. "Walter had a slight stroke about six months ago, and he doesn't feel he could manage a gun properly. So," she said, amused at herself, "we always have our bags of pepper beside us at night. Mind you, there's nothing unusual about us for you to write about, young man."

The steady deterioration of security is often the reason for leaving Kenya given by young people with small children; yet I always felt it only a fraction of the whole reason, which is too profound, too intricate, for themselves to explain. The white Africans express their anguish in many ways—in terms of love, in terms of hate; in persuasion, and in passion. The feeling floods out in words.

On Kenya's Kinangop plateau at 8,300 feet, Europeans have carved farms out of the cold heathland which the Africans never favoured. The sombre barrier of the Aberdare mountains, barren no less from the parching sun than from the cold, forms the limit on the north, and the steeply falling escarpment of 3,000 feet into the Great Rift Valley is the limit to the south. The third side, to the east, is encircled by the black rim of the forest, secretive and the most silent of all the forests of Africa I know and, all these years after Mau Mau, still the refuge of the hunted and the hunter; for beyond it lies the traditional land of the Kikuyu.

Jim Hughes, though vigorous, fit, and without a grey hair, is 66 this year; and even if he and his wife were not too old to "begin again," he loves his 503 acres against the forest too well not to go on fighting for the Kenya he believed he and his friends and their predecessors had been creating ever since Lord Delamere first staked out a farm in the vacant uplands three generations ago. He had saved most of his life up to 1938 to buy such a farm, and he earns from it what a farmer would earn with half the acreage in Sussex or New England—that is to say, not much. He had served in East Africa with the King's African Rifles and then worked on a sisal estate. The British Colonial governor had signed his 999-year lease in the name of King George VI. But now, talking to me in his isolated home up there on the South Kinangop, he admits he is beaten at last.

"We feel just as anyone would normally feel here—that we've been thoroughly betrayed by a lousy British Government, and that there's no more to it; and that when we can get our chips for the farm we'll go off, and we'll throw in our allegiance with somebody who's not always prepared to pull the bloody flag down. That's all."

Jim Hughes will not mind me describing him as a man of contrasts. When he is speaking of his farm he is gentle and absorbed; the voice, still with its trace of Welsh that survived his father's long service with the British Army in India, is that of a craftsman telling of what he has made. "I came in this Model B Ford, 1933 model. There were no roads. So we went across country and we got here and I bought this piece of land. That's all there was then, a piece of land. And I started to find a means of ploughing it and cultivating it.

"The first thing after I built the bamboo shack we lived in was that house—it's got three rooms, a kitchen and a bathroom . . . We first planted cereals, wheat. It did well until it got susceptible to numerous diseases—black stem rust and others; and then we found this wasn't a suitable place for wheat. But oats and barley, we found, did very well. Oats, barley, pyrethrum, potatoes . . ."

Jim Hughes's small farm is the best-ordered I have seen anywhere in the world. He was offered £35,000 for his 503 acres five years ago: today, with approaching *uhuru*, he could not give it away. He himself makes most of the equipment he uses—from farm wagons to his own perfectly finished padlocks. It was as we were strolling round his farm buildings that the 'other man' unexpectedly came forth. He was saying . . . "then we built this new house. We got the stone from the forest. I taught them how to cut it. I taught them how to use a square—they didn't know what a square was, they went round in a circle with it. We quarried our own stone. We carried our own cement. We carried every single thing; we cut every single mortal thing from the forest and brought it here—there was nothing here. We have done our own doctoring, our own veterinary work."

And then all at once: "Why should I let it go—go to rack and ruin? Do you think the British Government will pay anything for it? Because you never know, there are a few people over here who might create a bit of trouble. And somebody might get hurt." His voice went dry and narrow. "When you leave everything that you've ever had, you might provide for your wife, and after that somebody might get killed. It would be tragic, wouldn't it?"

It was now the voice of an old man who believed he had been fooled into wasting his life; in its bitterness it was savage.

"We don't mean harm," he went on with a sarcastic edge. "We came here—we were invited to come here. 'Here's Crown land. Boys, teach these fellows this, that and the other; help them set up an economy, and help yourselves.' I mean, I'm not a philanthropist; I'm not a missionary; I hate the sight of the bastards. But, I mean, I came here to farm, and look after these fellows [the Africans]. They look up to you as their mother and their father: they come to you in all their trials and their tribulations.

"But these fellows here on occasion have sat on the wrong side of the branch and sawn it off, and wondered why they've fallen down. There are a lot of people who are not tolerant to them. I have a different approach. I teach fellows. I give them the credit of having a certain amount of intelligence. But they're very disappointing—after you've spent a long, long time, they go back, very rapidly.

"It's just the politicians responsible for starting up racial animosity. The African responds to being continually told the land was his. How can we stay after independence? What do you do if cattle are driven across your land and trample down your crops and you telephone the police and they say, 'That's a bloody shame, isn't it, but don't you surely realise, Mr. Hughes, that's independence, that's *uhuru?*' What do you do if they come and squat on your land and you ask them politely to get off and six witnesses go down to the police station and say you insulted some African and it's your word against half a dozen of them? What d'you do?"

After we had visited a neighbour who was leaving for New Zealand that week with his wife and young family, we returned to Jim's home-made bungalow farmhouse. Darkness fell rapidly. With nightfall, it seemed, he gave way completely to his grief and bitterness. In the dim lamplight, his face all at once became a patch of violently contrasting colours—scarlet, and ashen white, his hair and jaw black; and he himself became all gestures and voice in an unstoppable tirade against the British government, against the British people, and the Africans, and the Blundellites, and the police and civil servants . . . "the lousy, stinking British government. The politicians there are like a bunch of bananas—they stick together, they're yellow, and there's not a straight one among 'em.

"Look, you've got to use some of these countries that have got self-government as a sort of looking-glass. And who wants Jomo Kenyatta as member of a coalition? Apart from that, we built this country, as we've paid the highest taxes, as we've subscribed 78 per cent. of the economy. What the hell do they mean, we won't have a voice in affairs? What? Do you think we're going to pay taxes without any voice? Do you think we're going to have our children put up with the standards of hygiene of the African children like in Tanganyika where they've mixed the schools?

"The ——s, they're an elderly couple farming here. They went to Tanganyika for a holiday, three weeks ago. They come down to breakfast in their hotel the first morning. There's an African, union man, at the next table, playing his transistor radio as loud as it can. They ask him to turn it down, politely; and when he doesn't they go out to the verandah for their coffee. And this African follows them, and begins dancing about, snapping his fingers in their faces. They decide to leave, of course. And when they go to their car they find all the windscreen smeared with filth. And they expect us to stay here!"

His wife, grey-haired and heavily built, in a blue print dress, was listening with a kind of agitated awe. He insisted on telling how a sow had torn two fingers off her hand two years before: it was part of the wasted sacrifice. He brought out the gold medal he had been awarded by the Royal Agricultural Society for his farm. "I'd rather burn it down than let anyone take it off me." Then he brought out his pair of Colt .45s, for which he had made the ivory handles. "I'll do anything, I'll murder anyone." He was punching the air, and the colours of his face were so sharp, he looked like an Expressionist puppet.

At this moment I recalled the first time I had seen Jim Hughes. It was about three years before, just after the Lancaster House conference. He had placed himself on a roof at Nairobi airport to proffer abuse at a British Minister passing through. So I said now: "Jim, you don't like the police. But I remember a policeman remarking to me on that occasion, 'Whatever you may think about Jim Hughes, he's one of the best farmers in the country.'"

This silenced Jim. But his wife's chin buckled; and her fingers pressing into her cheek could not stop the momentary tears.

In that dark little living-room, its deep brown furniture made by its owner, the carthorse brasses around the fireplace, and the Kikuyu house-boy lingering over his laying of the dinner-table at the far end of the room, straining to overhear what was said—in that dark brown room without children was the whole story. It was told me in countless ways from the Highlands of Kenya to the southern borders of Rhodesia, but the themes were always the same: the British betrayal; the treachery of liberals; the settlers' struggle in building up the country; the generic backwardness of the native, his uncleanliness, his natural subservience;

fears for security, impending chaos, the imminent collapse of 'standards'; the interference of politics—concocted overseas—into a perfectly contented paternalist relationship between white and black.

Southwards, in Southern Rhodesia, the whites perceive with a horrified incredulity the rapidly approaching threat to their position, but are not yet overwhelmed by it, as in Kenya.

Perhaps the most simple and moving expression of what is regarded as betrayal by Britain was given me by a large, warm-hearted farmer of Afrikaner origin living in Southern Rhodesia. Yapi Jacobs very well exemplifies Churchill's description of the Afrikaner farmer—"an unusual blend of peasant and squire."

"Well, sir, I used to be a very loyal man, so is my father. The old man has fought three wars for Britain, including the South African war. He's lost one of his legs. And I myself, I joined from the beginning until 1945, and I must say all my comrades will think exactly the same, very surprised that Britain wants to sort of sell us. They don't seem to care a demn for what we've done. As far as we're concerned, she'll yust let us go, even if we're cut up, or strangled. As far as I'm concerned, a very, very poor show. It was the white man who fought for the freedom of these people, and now it's the white man who is being given over to them."

Sometimes the 'treachery' is within the family; then it is always painful to hear. The son of a man from Salisbury was a liberal: "Poor old Arthur, my religious son, he went to Oxford and picked up all sorts of ideas. Poor old Arthur, now he wants to go to Cambridge. He has some queer ideas. He doesn't understand that the Africans don't understand weakness, they never will. He is coming up against it day after day but he won't accept it.

"He says: 'God says I must hold out my hand to these chaps, and turn the other cheek,' and all that sort of stuff.

"He's got a car. He drives up the road, and he sees a munt walking with a little bit of a limp, and stops and says, 'Where do you want to go?' 'I'm going to Gwebe' (17 miles away). He drives him to Gwebe, because, you know, he feels he ought to. But now, that munt, the next time he sees Arthur's car, he'll stop it and say, 'Hey, I'm the bloke you took to Gwebe; now come and let's get back there. And Arthur'll say, 'No, I'm in a hurry.' So the munt'll pick up a bloody rock and throw it through his window . . .'"

For a more considered illustration of the implications of the 'culture gap' when Africans have achieved political control, I quote the welfare officer of a Northern Rhodesian copper mine which is run on enlightened principles. The speaker himself was a studiously liberal person.

"If you could do what the Russians do—take all these Africans, take all their parents, and put them in a labour camp and bring up their children in a completely new society, a new cultural background—in one generation you would have a different sort of person; in two generations you would have as good as any in the Western world. But, basically, we have not yet changed their outlook. For example, one of my assistant welfare officers, an African, equivalent of GCE 'o' level in the U.K., came to me the other day to say he was having trouble with his wife because the African who is his immediate superior in the office had put a spell on him. All I could do was to give him two months' leave so that he could go to his village and consult his witch-doctor."

European society in Central and East Africa is the youngest of its kind in the world; and in its youthful lustiness it was quite unaware of its extreme vulnerability. When with great suddenness the realisation of danger struck—in the case of Kenya in a single month, January, 1960, and in the case of Rhodesia over the past two or three swift years—it indeed reacted as might a young man who on the threshold of adulthood was apprised by his parents that he had an incurable disease and not long to live. At once, this strong and outwardly healthy youth recognised the fraudulence of the hopes which his parents (the mother country's government) had encouraged him to entertain; at once, too, he recognised the circumstances of his upbringing had been such as almost to ensure the contraction of his fatal ailment.

I do not believe it is sensible to say to the whites: "You must contentedly accept that this country, which you thought was yours to make, is not yours, but theirs; that these Africans of whom you thought you were the masters and protectors are now *your* masters; that this land, which you believed was yours to possess and render fertile, belongs not to you but to them, on whose sufferance you might perhaps continue to cultivate it; that this wealth you have created, these institutions you have formed, this peace, this justice, this faith, these ideals, this nation you foresaw—a new America, a new Australia—these are not yours, and in them you shall have no significant part. You must accept contentedly that unless your society becomes part of their society, absorbed within it, subject to its control and strange passions and movements, there is no place for you in these territories."

I do not believe it is sensible to expect this of the white settlers of colonial Africa, because in all experience I do not believe it possible.

The Africans have suffered deeply: called upon to exchange an African, tribal *possession* of life for a European, conscious *understanding* of life, they have been haunted by a sense of loss and obsessed by a fear of inherent inferiority. So far as African osmosis within European life is concerned, it has been readily acknowledged that the 'culture gap' has been far too great. It is the same on the white side. I have read arguments to the contrary, based principally on the experience of the Portuguese visitors to West African kingdoms in the pre-slave days of the late 15th and early 16th Centuries.

Far, far from the influence of the Afrikaner churches, or indeed of any white men, I was given among a group of largely pagan Bakonjo, on the wild mountain reaches of the Uganda-Congo border, a theory of racial difference which almost perfectly complies with the Dutch Reformed Churches' pre-Christian doctrine of the Negroes' Hamitic origin, condemned by Jawe to be hewers of wood and drawers of water. We were discussing my immunity from the local spirits which at that time were tormenting the Bakonjo. One Mukonjo explained it was to do with my whiteness. He said: "God made the Europeans better than the Africans in all things. They shall always be so. Because we Africans are to be punished he has made us not clever people, and we must have the spirits."

Perhaps the flaw in that Mukonjo's argument of generic European superiority is indicated by the dependence of Europeans upon their society —a different kind of dependence, it is true, from the tribal submergence in the group and in environment, but nevertheless a reliance which makes any distortion of the corporate image a matter of mental torture for the individual. One of the first things the emergent African learns about the European is that he does not live up to his ideals; and especially "that thou shouldst love thy neighbour as thyself" whether or not you actually feel anything in common with him.

It has been fashionable for us, who are not personally swept up in the situation, to espouse solutions for our fellows in East and Central Africa which we express with a conviction quite undisturbed by our failure to define them: multi-racialism, integration, partnership, and so forth. I do not believe I am expressing an opinion but a fact when I say that *on both sides,* on the spot in Africa, it is accepted that "it is either them or us." That is to say, Kenya and the Rhodesias must each be either a 'white man's country' or a 'black man's country,' in which the white settler will have no permanently tolerated place. The spirit of white Kenya has already been shattered; and it is my conviction—and here I express an opinion—that both Rhodesias are fated before our own infants grow up to become 'black men's countries.'

Some of the modes of expression I have quoted are not attractive. Some even suggest that the minds of the speakers have already become misshapen from the strain of their dilemma. Many—if not most—of the views expressed have little basis in fact: the natural subservience of the African, for example, or his uncleanliness.

I have attempted in this article to perform two things—to describe the mood of the white Africans in East and Central Africa, and to place the reader in a position where he can feel a little of what the white African feels, however unfair and illogical his attitudes might appear. When we know what a man thinks, we may condemn his view; only when we know why he thinks it, may we condemn him.

—————————Bernard C. Rosen

Race, Ethnicity, and the Achievement Syndrome

The upward mobility rates of many racial and ethnic groups in America
have been markedly dissimilar when compared with one another and
with some white Protestant groups. For example, among the "new immigration" groups which settled primarily in the Northeast, the Greeks
and Jews have attained middle class status more rapidly than most of
their fellow immigrants. In general, ethnic groups with Roman Catholic
affiliation have moved up less rapidly than non-Catholic groups. And
the vertical mobility of Negroes, even in the less repressive environment
of the industrial Northeast, has been relatively slow.[1]

The reasons offered to explain these differences vary with the group in
question. Thus, differences in group mobility rates have sometimes been
interpreted as a function of the immigrant's possession of certain skills
which were valuable in a burgeoning industrial society. In this connection, there is some evidence that many Jews came to America with
occupational skills better suited to urban living than did their fellow
immigrants. Social mobility seems also to be related to the ability of
ethnic and racial groups to organize effectively to protect and promote
their interests. Both the Greeks and the Jews were quicker to develop
effective community organizations than were other immigrants who had
not previously faced the problem of adapting as minority groups. For
the Jews, this situation grew out of their experiences with an often
hostile gentile world; for the Greeks, out of their persecutions by the
Turks. The repressiveness of the social structure or the willingness of the
dominant groups to permit others to share in the fruits of a rich, expanding economy has also been given as an explanation of differential
group mobility. This argument has merit in the case of Negroes, but it is
less valid in a comparison of the Jews with Southern Italians or French-
Canadians. Finally, it has been suggested that groups with experiences in
small town or urban environments were more likely to possess the
cultural values appropriate to achievement in American society than
were ethnic and racial groups whose cultures had been formed in rural,
peasant surroundings. Here, again, it has been noted that many Jews
and a small but influential number of Levantine Greeks had come from

[1] Cf. W. L. Warner and L. Srole, *The Social Systems of American Ethnic Groups*, New
Haven: Yale University Press, 1945; F. L. Strodtbeck, "Jewish and Italian Immigration
and Subsequent Status Mobility," in D. McClelland, A. Baldwin, U. Bronfenbrenner and
F. Strodtbeck, *Talent and Society*, Princeton: Van Nostrand, 1958; M. Davie, *World
Migration*, New York: Macmillan, 1936.

Reprinted from *American Sociological Review*, Vol. 24, No. 1, February, 1959, pp. 47-60.
By permission.

small towns or cities, while most of the Roman Catholic immigrants from Eastern and Southern Europe (and Southern Negroes before their migration to the North) came from rural communities.[2]

As valid as these explanations may be—and we believe they have merit—they overlook one important factor: *the individual's psychological and cultural orientation towards achievement;* by which we mean his psychological need to excel, his desire to enter the competitive race for social status, and his initial possession of or willingness to adopt the high valuation placed upon personal achievement and success which foreign observers from Tocqueville to Laski have considered an important factor in the remarkable mobility of individuals in American society.

Three components of this achievement orientation are particularly relevant for any study of social mobility. The first is a psychological factor, *achievement motivation,* which provides the internal impetus to excel in situations involving standards of excellence. The second and third components are cultural factors, one consisting of certain *value orientations* which implement achievement-motivated behavior, the other of culturally influenced *educational-vocational aspiration levels.* All three factors may affect status achievement; one moving the individual to excel, the others organizing and directing his behavior towards high status goals. This motive-value-aspiration complex has been called the *Achievement Syndrome.*[3]

It is the basic hypothesis of this study that many racial and ethnic groups were not, and are not now, alike in their orientation toward achievement, particularly as it is expressed in the striving for status through social mobility, and that this difference in orientation has been an important factor contributing to the dissimilarities in their social mobility rates. Specifically, this paper examines the achievement motivation, values, and aspirations of members of six racial and ethnic groups. Four of these are "new immigration" ethnic groups with similar periods of residence in this country who faced approximately the same economic circumstances upon arrival: the French-Canadians, Southern Italians, Greeks, and East European Jews. The fifth is the Negro group in the Northeast, the section's largest "racial" division. The last, and in some ways the most heterogeneous, is the native-born white Protestant group. Contributing to the fact that these six groups have not been equally mobile, we suggest, are differences in the three components of the

[2] Cf. N. Glazer, "The American Jew and the Attainment of Middle-Class Rank: Some Trends and Explanations," in M. Sklare, editor, *The Jews: Social Patterns of an American Group,* Glencoe, Ill.: Free Press, 1958; W. L. Warner and L. Srole, *op. cit.;* T. Burgess, *Greeks in America,* Boston: Sherman, French, 1913; T. Saloutos, "The Greeks in the U. S.," *The South Atlantic Quarterly,* 4 (January, 1945), pp. 69-82; T. Kalijarvi, "French-Canadians in the United States," *Annals, American Academy of Political and Social Science* (September, 1942); F. L. Strodtbeck, "Family Interactions, Values and Achievement," in D. McClelland, *et al., op. cit.;* G. Myrdal, *An American Dilemma,* New York: Harper, 1944.
[3] B. C. Rosen, "The Achievement Syndrome: A Psychocultural Dimension of Social Stratification," *The American Sociological Review,* 21 (April, 1956), pp. 203-211.

achievement syndrome: their incidence is highest among Jews, Greeks, and white Protestants, lower among Southern Italians and French-Canadians, and lowest among Negroes.

Research Procedure

The data were collected from a purposive sample of 954 subjects residing in 62 communities in four Northeastern states: 51 in Connecticut, seven in New York, three in New Jersey, and one in Massachusetts. The subjects are 427 pairs of mothers and their sons; 62 pairs are French-Canadians, 74 are Italians, 47 are Greeks, 57 are Jews, 65 are Negroes, and 122 are white Protestants. Most subjects were located through the aid of local religious, ethnic, or service organizations, or through their residence in neighborhoods believed to be occupied by certain groups. The subject's group membership was determined ultimately by asking the mothers in personal interviews to designate their religion and land of national origin. The interviewers, all of whom were upper-classmen enrolled in two sociology classes, were instructed to draw respondents from various social strata.[4] The respondent's social class position was determined by a modified version of Hollingshead's Index of Social Position, which uses occupation and education of the main wage-earner, usually the father, as the principal criteria of status. Respondents were classified according to this index into one of five social classes, from the highest status group (Class I) to the lowest (Class V).[5] Most of the mothers and all of the sons are native-born, the sons ranging in age from eight to 14 years (the mean age is about 11 years). There are no significant age differences between the various groups.

Two research instruments were a projective test to measure achievement motivation and a personal interview to obtain information on achievement value orientations and related phenomena. Achievement motivation has been defined by McClelland and his associates as a redintegration of affect aroused by cues in situations involving standards of excellence. Such standards usually are imparted to the individual by his parents, who impart the understanding that they expect him to perform well in relation to these standards of excellence, rewarding him for successful endeavor and punishing him for failure. In time he comes to have similar expectations of himself when exposed to situations involving standards of excellence and re-experiences the affect associated with his earlier efforts to meet these standards. The behavior of people with high achievement motivation is characterized by persistent striving and general competitiveness.

Using a Thematic Apperception Test, McClelland and his associates

---

[4] The interviewers were trained by the writer; efforts were made to control for interviewer biases. It should be remembered that the sample is not random at any point in the selection process. Hence, the reader is cautioned to regard the data presented here as tentative and suggestive.

[5] A. B. Hollingshead and F. C. Redlich, "Social Stratification and Psychiatric Disorders," *American Sociological Review*, 18 (April, 1953), pp. 163-169.

have developed a method of measuring the achievement motive that involves identifying and counting the frequency with which imagery about
evaluated performance in competition with a standard of excellence appears in the thoughts of a person when he tells a brief story under time
pressure. This imagery now can be identified objectively and reliably.
The test assumes that the more the individual shows indications of connections between evaluated performance and affect in his fantasy, the
greater the degree to which achievement motivation is part of his personality.[6] This projective test, which involves showing the subject four ambiguous pictures and asking him to tell a story about each, was given
privately and individually to the sons in their homes. Their imaginative
responses to the pictures were scored by two judges; the Pearson product
moment correlation between the two scorings was .86, an estimate of
reliability similar to those reported in earlier studies using this measure.

Following the boys' testing, their mothers were interviewed privately.
The interview guide included several standardized questions designed to
indicate the mother's achievement value orientations, her educational
and vocational aspirations for her son, and the degree to which she had
trained him to be independent.

Findings and Interpretation

Achievement Motivation—Empirical studies have shown that
achievement motivation is generated by (at least) two kinds of socialization practices: (1) *achievement training*, in which the parents, by imposing standards of excellence upon tasks, by setting high goals for their
child, and by indicating their high evaluation of his competence to do
a task well, communicate to him that they expect evidences of high
achievement; (2) *independence training*, in which the parents indicate
to the child that they expect him to be self-reliant and, at the same time,
grant him relative autonomy in decision-making situations where he is
given both freedom of action and responsibility for success or failure.
Essentially, achievement training is concerned with getting the child
to *do things well*, while independence training seeks to teach him to do
things *on his own*. Although both kinds often occur together and each
contributes to the development of achievement motivation, achievement
training is the more important of the two.[7]

Two bodies of information—ethnographic studies of the "old world"
or non-American culture and recent empirical investigations of the training practices used by Americans of various ethnic backgrounds—strongly
indicate that the six groups examined here, in the past and to some extent

[6] D. C. McClelland, J. Atkinson, R. Clark, and E. Lowell, *The Achievement Motive*, New
York: Appleton-Century-Crofts, 1953.
[7] M. Winterbottom, "The Relation of Need for Achievement to Learning Experiences in
Independence and Mastery," in J. Atkinson, editor, *Motives in Fantasy, Action and Society*,
Princeton: Van Nostrand, 1958; B. C. Rosen, "The Psychosocial Origins of Achievement
Motivation," mimeographed progress report to the National Institute of Mental Health,
1957.

today, differ with respect to the degree to which their members typically emphasize achievement and independence training. Ethnic differences in these matters were first studied by McClelland, who noted that the linkage between independence training and achievement motivation established by recent empirical studies suggests an interesting parallel with Weber's classic description of the characterological consequences of the Protestant Reformation. Weber reasoned, first, concerning salvation, that an important aspect of the Protestant theological position was the shift from reliance on an institution (the Church) to a greater reliance upon self; it seemed reasonable to assume that Protestant parents who prepared their children for increased self-reliance in religious matters would also tend to stress the necessity for the child to be self-reliant in other aspects of his life. Secondly, Weber's description of the personality types produced by the Reformation is strikingly similar to the picture of the person with high achievement motivation; for example, the hard-working, thrifty Protestant working girl, the Protestant entrepreneur who "gets nothing out of his wealth for himself except the irrational sense of having done his job well." [8]

The hypothesis deduced from these observations was put to the test by McClelland, who questioned white Protestant, Irish-Catholic, Italian-Catholic, and Jewish mothers about their independence training practices. He found that Protestants and Jews favored earlier independence training than Irish and Italian Catholics.[9] These findings are supported and enlarged upon by data derived from questioning the 427 mothers in this study about their training practices. The mothers were asked, "At what age do you expect your son to do the following things?" and to note the appropriate items from the following list (taken from the Winterbottom index of training in independence and mastery):[10]

1. To be willing to try things on his own without depending on his mother for help.
2. To be active and energetic in climbing, jumping, and sports.
3. To try hard things for himself without asking for help.
4. To be able to lead other children and assert himself in children's groups.
5. To make his own friends among children of his own age.
6. To do well in school on his own.

[8] D. C. McClelland, "Some Social Consequences of Achievement Motivation," in M. R. Jones, editor, *Nebraska Symposium on Motivation, 1955,* Lincoln: University of Nebraska Press, 1955.

[9] D. C. McClelland, A. Rindlisbacher, and R. C. deCharms, "Religious and Other Sources of Parental Attitudes Towards Independence Training," in D. C. McClelland, editor, *Studies in Motivation,* New York: Appleton-Century-Crofts, 1955.

[10] Winterbottom, *op. cit.* Though primarily a measure of independence training, two items in this index—items 6 and 8—are considered measures of mastery training, a concept akin to our notion of achievement training. The failure to disentangle independence training from mastery (achievement) training has been responsible for some confusion in earlier studies of the origins of achievement motivation. (For an analysis of this confusion, see Rosen, "The Psychosocial Origins of Achievement Motivation," *op. cit.*) The two components were kept in the index in order to maintain comparability between this study and the earlier work on ethnic groups by McClelland reported above.

7. To have interests and hobbies of his own. To be able to entertain himself.
8. To do well in competition with other children. To try hard to come out on top in games and sports.
9. To make decisions like choosing his own clothes or deciding to spend his money by himself.

An index of independence training was derived by summing the ages for each item and taking the mean figure. The data in Table 1 show that the Jews expect earliest evidence of self-reliance from their children (mean age 6.83 years), followed by the Protestants (6.87), Negroes (7.23), Greeks (7.67), French-Canadians (7.99), and Italians (8.03). Both primary sources of variation—ethnicity and social class—are significant at the .01 level.

Data on the relative emphasis which racial and ethnic groups place upon achievement *training* (that is, imposing standards of excellence upon tasks, setting high goals for the child to achieve, and communicating to him a feeling that his parents evaluate highly his task-competence) are much more difficult to obtain. Achievement training as such, in fact, is rarely treated in studies of ethnic socialization practices.

TABLE 1. MEAN AGE OF INDEPENDENCE TRAINING BY
ETHNICITY AND SOCIAL CLASS

| | Social Class* | | | | |
Ethnicity	I-II-III	IV	V	$\bar{\chi}$	N
French-Canadian	8.00	7.69	8.08	7.99	62
Italian	6.79	7.89	8.47	8.03	74
Greek	6.33	8.14	7.52	7.67	47
Jew	6.37	7.29	6.90	6.83	57
Negro	6.64	6.98	7.39	7.23	65
Protestant	5.82	7.44	7.03	6.87	122
$\bar{\chi}$	6.31	7.64	7.59		

Ethnicity: F = 8.55   P < .01
Social Class: F = 21.48 P < .001
Ethnicity × Class: F = 6.25   P < .01

* The three-class breakdown was used in an earlier phase of the analysis. An examination of the means of cells using a four-class breakdown revealed no change in pattern and did not warrant new computations.

Hence, inferences about achievement training were drawn primarily from ethnographic and historical materials, which are usually more informative about achievement as such than about relevant socialization practices.

The groups about which the most is known concerning achievement training, perhaps, are the Protestants, the Jews, and, to a lesser extent, the Greeks. These groups traditionally have stressed excellence and achievement. In the case of the Protestants, this tradition can be located in the Puritan Ethic with its concept of work as a "calling" and the exhortation that a job be done well. Of course, not all Protestants would be equally comfortable with this tradition; it is much more applicable, for example, to Presbyterians and Quakers than to Methodists and Baptists. Nonetheless, the generally longer residence of Protestants in this country makes it probable that they would tend to share the American belief that children should be encouraged to develop their talents and to set high goals, possibly a bit beyond their reach. The observation that Jews stress achievement training is commonplace. Zyborowski and Herzog note the

TABLE 2. MEAN ACHIEVEMENT MOTIVATION SCORES
BY ETHNICITY AND SOCIAL CLASS

| Ethnicity | Social Class | | | | | |
	I-II	III	IV	V	$\bar{x}$	N
French-Canadian	10.00	10.64	8.78	7.75	8.82	62
Italian	8.86	12.81	7.54	10.20	9.65	74
Greek	9.17	12.13	10.40	8.75	10.80	47
Jew	10.05	10.41	10.94	11.20	10.53	57
Negro	11.36	9.00	8.23	6.72	8.40	65
Protestant	11.71	10.94	9.39	7.31	10.11	122
$\bar{x}$	10.55	11.26	9.01	8.32		

Ethnicity: $F = 1.23$ $P > .05$
Social Class: $F = 5.30$ $P < .005$
Ethnicity $\times$ Class: $F = 1.32$ $P > .05$

strong tendency among *shtetyl* Jews to expect and to reward evidences of achievement even among very young children. The image of the Jewish mother as eager for her son to excel in competition and to set ever higher goals for himself is a familiar one in the literature of Jewish family life.[11] Careful attention to standards of excellence in the Greek home is stressed by the parents: children know that a task which is shabbily performed will have to be re-done. In this country, the Greek is exhorted to be "a credit to his group." Failure to meet group norms is quickly perceived and where possible punished; while achievement receives the approbation of the entire Greek community.

Among the Southern Italians (the overwhelming majority of American-Italians are of Southern Italian extraction), French-Canadians, and Negroes the tradition seems to be quite different. More often than not they came from agrarian societies or regions in which opportunities for achievement were strictly curtailed by the social structure and where

[11] M. Zyborowski and E. Herzog, *Life Is With People*, New York: International University Press, 1952.

habits of resignation and fatalism in the face of social and environmental frustrations were psychologically functional. Under such conditions children were not typically exhorted to be achievers or urged to set their sights very high. Of course, children were expected to perform tasks, as they are in most societies, but such tasks were usually farm or self-care-taking chores, from which the notion of competition with standards of excellence is not excluded, but is not ordinarily stressed. As for communicating to the child a sense of confidence in his competence to do a task well, there is some evidence that in the father-dominant Italian and French-Canadian families, pronounced concern with the child's ability might be perceived as a threat to the father.[12]

On the whole, the data indicate that Protestants, Jews, and Greeks place a greater emphasis on independence and achievement training than Southern Italians and French-Canadians. The data on the Negroes are conflicting: they often train children relatively early in self-reliance, but there is little evidence of much stress upon achievement training. No doubt the socialization practices of these groups have been modified somewhat by the acculturating influences of American society since their arrival in the Northeast.[13] But ethnic cultures tend to survive even in the face of strong obliterating forces, and we believe that earlier differences between groups persist—a position supported by the present data on self-reliance training. Hence, the hypothesis that the racial and ethnic groups considered here differ with respect to achievement motivation. We predicted that, on the average, achievement motivation scores would be highest among the Jews, Greeks, and white Protestants, lower among the Italians and French-Canadians, and lowest among the Negroes. Table 2 shows that the data support these predictions, indicated by the following mean scores: Greeks 10.80, Jews 10.53, Protestants 10.11, Italians 9.65, French-Canadians 8.82, and Negroes 8.40.

A series of "t" tests of significance between means (a one-tail test was used in cases where the direction of the difference had been predicted) was computed. The differences between Greeks, Jews, and Protestants are not statistically significant. The Italian score is significantly lower (P < .05) than the score for the Greeks, but not for the Jews and Protestants. The largest differences are between the French-Canadians and Negroes on the one hand and the remaining groups on the other: the French-Canadian mean score is significantly lower (P < .01) than those of all other groups except Italians and Negroes; the mean score for all Negroes is significantly lower (P < .01) than the scores for all other

---

[12] P. H. Williams, *South Italian Folkways in Europe and America,* New Haven: Yale University Press, 1938; H. Miner, *St. Dennis: A French-Canadian Parish,* Chicago: University of Chicago Press, 1939.

[13] It does not necessarily follow that the impact of American culture has reduced the differences between groups. An argument can be made that for some groups life in America has accentuated differences by allowing certain characteristics of the groups to develop. We have in mind particularly the Greeks and Jews whose need to excel could find little avenue for expression through status striving in Europe.

groups except French-Canadians. A "Roman Catholic" score was obtained by combining Italian and French-Canadian scores, and scores for all non-Negro groups were combined to form a "White" score. The differences between group means were tested for significance (by a one-tail "t" test) and it was found that the "Catholic" score is significantly lower than the scores for Protestants, Greek Orthodox, and Jews (P < .01). The Negro mean score is significantly lower than the combined score of all white groups (P < .002).

A comparison of ethnic-racial differences does not tell the whole story. There are also significant differences between the social classes. In fact, analysis of Table 2 indicates that social class accounts for more of the variance than ethnicity: the F ratio for ethnicity is 1.23 (P < .05), for class 5.30 (P < .005). The small number of cases in Classes I and II greatly increases the within-group variance; when these two classes are combined with Class III the variance is decreased and the F ratio for ethnicity increases sharply to 2.13 (P < .06). Social class, however, remains more significantly related to achievement motivation than ethnicity. This finding is especially important in this study since the proportion of subjects in each class varies for the ethnic groups. There are relatively more middle class than lower class subjects among the Jews, Greeks, and Protestants than among Italians, French-Canadians, and Negroes. To control for social class it was necessary to examine the differences between cells as well as between columns and rows. A series of "t" tests of differences between the means of cells revealed that for the most part the earlier pattern established for total ethnic means persists, although in some instances the differences between groups are decreased, in others increased, and in a few cases the direction of the differences is reversed. Neither ethnicity nor social class alone is sufficient to predict an individual's score; both appear to contribute something to the variance between groups, but on the whole social class is a better predictor than ethnicity. Generally, a high status person from an ethnic group with a low mean achievement motivation score is more likely to have a high score than a low status person from a group with a high mean score. Thus, the mean score for Class I-II Negroes is higher than the score for Class IV-V white Protestants: the score for the former is 11.36, for the latter, 7.31; a "t" test revealed that the difference between these two means is significant at the .05 level, using a two-tail test. This relatively high score for Class I-II Negroes, the third highest for any cell in the table, indicates, perhaps, the strong motivation necessary for a Negro to achieve middle class status in a hostile environment. Generally, the scores for each group decrease as the class level declines, except for the Jews whose scores are inversely related to social status—a finding for which we can offer no explanation.

Achievement Value Orientations—Achievement motivation is one part of the achievement syndrome; an equally important component is the achievement value orientation. Value orientations are defined as meaningful and affectively charged modes of organizing behavior—principles that guide human conduct. They establish criteria which influence the individual's preferences and goals. Achievement values and achievement motivation, while related, represent genuinely different components of the achievement syndrome, not only conceptually but also in their origins and, as we have shown elsewhere, in their social correlates.[14] Value orientations, because of their conceptual content, are probably acquired in that stage of the child's cultural training when verbal communication of a fairly complex nature is possible. Achievement motivation or the need to excel, on the other hand, has its origins in parent-child interaction beginning early in the child's life when many of these relations are likely to be emotional and unverbalized. Analytically, then, the learning of achievement oriented values can be independent of the acquisition of the achievement motive, although empirically they often occur together.

Achievement values affect social mobility in that they focus the individual's attention on status improvement and help to shape his behavior so that achievement motivation can be translated into successful action. The achievement motive by itself is not a sufficient condition of social mobility: it provides internal impetus to excel, but it does not impel the individual to take the steps necessary for status achievement. Such steps in our society involve, among other things, a preparedness to plan, work hard, make sacrifices, and be physically mobile. Whether or not the individual will understand their importance and accept them will depend in part upon his values.

Three sets of values (a modification of Kluckhohn's scheme[15]) were identified as elements of the achievement syndrome,[16] as follows:

1. *Activistic-Passivistic Orientation* concerns the extent to which the culture of a group encourages the individual to believe in the possibility of his manipulating the physical and social environment to his advantage. An activistic culture encourages the individual to believe that it is both possible and necessary for him to improve his status, whereas a passivistic culture promotes the acceptance of the notion that individual efforts to achieve mobility are relatively futile.

2. *Individualistic-Collectivistic Orientation* refers to the extent to which the individual is expected to subordinate his needs to the group. This study is specifically concerned with the degree to which the society expects the individual to maintain close physical proximity to his family of orientation, even at the risk of limiting vocational opportunities; and the degree to which the society emphasizes group incentives rather than personal re-

[14] Rosen, "The Achievement Syndrome," *op. cit.*, pp. 208-210.

[15] F. Kluckhohn, "Dominant and Substitute Profiles of Cultural Orientations," *Social Forces*, 28 (May, 1950), pp. 376-393.

[16] For the most part, the value orientations examined in this study, their description, and the items used to index them, are identical with those which appear in Rosen, "The Achievement Syndrome," *op. cit.*

wards. The collectivistic society places a greater stress than the individualistic on group ties and group incentives.

3. *Present-Future Orientation* concerns the society's attitude toward time and its impact upon behavior. A present oriented society stresses the merit of living in the present, emphasizing immediate gratifications; a future oriented society encourages the belief that planning and present sacrifices are worthwhile, or morally obligatory, in order to insure future gains.

Examination of ethnographic and historical materials on the cultures of the six ethnic groups revealed important differences in value orientation—differences antedating their arrival in the Northeast. The cultures of white Protestants, Jews, and Greeks stand out as considerably more individualistic, activistic, and future-oriented than those of the Southern Italians, French-Canadians, and Negroes. Several forces—religious, economic, and national—seem to have long influenced the Protestants in this direction, including, first, the Puritan Ethic with its stress upon individualism and work; then the impact of the liberal economic ethic (Weber's "Spirit of Capitalism") emphasizing competitive activity and achievement; and finally, the challenge of the frontier, with its consequent growth of a national feeling of optimism and manifest destiny. All of these factors tended very early to create a highly activistic, individualistic, future-oriented culture—the picture of American culture held by foreign observers since Tocqueville.[17]

The Jews, who for centuries had lived in more or less hostile environments, have learned that it is not only possible to manipulate their environment to insure survival but even to prosper in it. Jewish tradition stresses the possibility of the individual rationally mastering his world. Man is not helpless against the forces of nature or of his fellow man; God will provide, but only if man does his share. Like Protestantism, Judaism is an intensely individualistic religion and the Jews an intensely individualistic people. While the family was close knit, it was the entire *shtetyl* which was regarded as the inclusive social unit; and in neither case was loyalty to the group considered threatened by physical mobility. The Jews typically have urged their children to leave home if in so doing they faced better opportunities. *Shtetyl* society, from which the vast majority of American Jewry is descended, vigorously stressed the importance of planning and working for the future. A *shtetyl* cultural tradition was that parents save for many years, often at great sacrifice to themselves, in order to improve their son's vocational opportunities or to provide a daughter with a dowry.[18]

In some respects, Greek and Jewish cultures were strikingly similar at the turn of the century. The ethos of the town and city permeated the

---

[17] For a history of the development of the liberal economic ethic and its manifestation on the American scene, see J. H. Randall, *The Making of the Modern Mind*, Boston: Houghton Mifflin, 1926; J. K. Galbraith, *The Affluent Society*, Boston: Houghton Mifflin, 1958.

[18] Zyborowski and Herzog, *op. cit.*; B. C. Rosen, "Cultural Factors in Achievement," mimeographed, 1952; Strodtbeck, "Family Interactions, Values and Achievement," *op. cit.*

Greek more than most other Mediterranean cultures, although only a small proportion of the population was engaged in trade—with the important exception of the Levantine Greeks, who were largely merchants. The image of the Greek in the Eastern Mediterranean area was that of an individualistic, foresighted, competitive trader. Early observers of the Greek in America were impressed by his activistic, future-oriented behavior. E. A. Ross, a rather unfriendly observer, wrote as early as 1914 that "the saving, commercial Greek climbs. From curb to stand, from stand to store, from little store to big store, and from there to branch stores in other cities—such are the stages in his upward path." [19]

Though separated by thousands of miles, French-Canadian and Southern Italian cultures were similar in many respects. Both were primarily peasant cultures, strongly influenced by the Roman Catholic Church. Neither could be described as activistic, individualistic, or future-oriented. In Southern Italian society the closed-class system and grinding poverty fostered a tradition of resignation—a belief that the individual had little control over his life situation and a stress upon the role of fate (*Destino*) in determining success. The living conditions of French-Canadians, although less harsh, were sufficiently severe to sharply limit the individual's sense of mastery over his situation. In neither group was there a strong feeling that the individual could drastically improve his lot; for both groups the future was essentially unpredictable, even capricious. Extended family ties were very strong in both groups: there is the Southern Italian saying, "the family against all others;" the French-Canadian farmer in need of help will travel many miles to hire a kinsman rather than an otherwise convenient neighbor.[20]

Ironically, although Negroes are usually Protestant (however, not ordinarily of the Calvinistic type) and have been exposed to the liberal economic ethic longer than most of the other groups considered here, their culture, it seems, is least likely to accent achievement values. The Negro's history as a slave and depressed farm worker, and the sharp discrepancy between his experiences and the American Creed, would appear to work against the internalization of the achievement values of the dominant white group. Typically, the Negro life-situation does not encourage the belief that one can manipulate his environment or the conviction that one can improve his condition very much by planning and hard work.[21] Generally, family ties have not been strong among Negroes, although

---

[19] Quoted in Saloutos, *op. cit.*, p. 71. The writer is indebted to J. Gregoropoulos, a native of Athens, for many helpful comments on European and American Greek communities.

[20] Miner, *op. cit.* See also Williams, *op. cit.*: Strodtbeck, "Family Interactions, Values and Achievement," *op. cit.*

[21] We recognize that to infer a group's values from its life-situation and then to use these values to explain an aspect of that situation is to reason circularly. However, the temporal sequence between values and mobility has a chicken-egg quality which is difficult to avoid because values and life-situation interact. To some extent, knowledge of ethnic cultures prior to their arrival in the United States helps to establish the priority of values to mobility. In the case of the Negroes, however, relatively little is known about their several cultures before their transportation to this country.

TABLE 3. MEAN VALUE SCORES BY ETHNICITY AND SOCIAL CLASS

Ethnicity	Social Class					
	I-II	III	IV	V	$\bar{x}$	N
French-Canadian	4.00	4.21	4.60	2.46	3.68	62
Italian	5.86	4.00	3.96	3.40	4.17	74
Greek	6.33	5.52	4.80	3.25	5.08	47
Jew	5.94	5.47	5.41	4.80	5.54	57
Negro	6.00	5.00	4.90	4.67	5.03	65
Protestant	5.86	5.50	4.97	3.54	5.16	122
$\bar{x}$	5.91	5.08	4.78	3.49		

Ethnicity: $F = 11.62$ $P < .001$
Social Class: $F = 33.80$ $P < .001$
Ethnicity × Class: $F = 2.43$ $P < .01$

traditionally the mother was an especially important figure and ties between her and her children, particularly sons, may still be very strong.[22]

Another and more direct way of studying ethnic values is to talk with group members themselves; thus our personal interviews with the mothers. (Their sons in many cases were too young to give meaningful answers.) They were asked whether they agreed or disagreed with the following statements, listed here under the appropriate value orientation categories.

(1) *Activistic-Passivistic Orientation.*
    Item 1. "All a man should want out of life in the way of a career is a secure, not too difficult job, with enough pay to afford a nice car and eventually a home of his own."
    Item 2. "When a man is born the success he is going to have is already in the cards, so he might just as well accept it and not fight against it."
    Item 3. "The secret of happiness is not expecting too much out of life and being content with what comes your way."
(2) *Individualistic-Collectivistic Orientation.*
    Item 4. "Nothing is worth the sacrifice of moving away from one's parents."
    Item 5. "The best kind of job to have is one where you are part of an organization all working together even if you don't get individual credit." [23]
(3) *Present-Future Orientation.*
    Item 6. "Planning only makes a person unhappy since your plans hardly ever work out anyway."

[22] E. F. Frazier, *The Negro Family in the United States*, Chicago: University of Chicago Press, 1939; see also Frazier's *The Negro in the United States*, New York: Macmillan, 1957, especially Chapters 13 and 24.

[23] Of course, if Whyte is correct about the growth of the organization man and the importance of the "social ethic," agreement with this statement may indicate an asset rather than a handicap to social mobility. See W. H. Whyte, Jr., *The Organization Man*, New York: Simon and Schuster, 1957.

Item 7. "Nowadays with world conditions the way they are the wise person lives for today and lets tomorrow take care of itself."

Responses indicating an activistic, future-oriented, individualistic point of view (the answer "disagree" to these items) reflect values, we believe, most likely to facilitate achievement and social mobility. These items were used to form a value index, and a score was derived for each subject by giving a point for each achievement-oriented response. In examining the mothers' scores two assumptions were made: (1) that they tend to transmit their values to their sons, and (2) that the present differences between groups are indicative of at least equal, and perhaps even greater, differences in the past.

The ethnographic and historical materials led us to expect higher value scores for Jews, white Protestants, and Greeks than for Italians, French-Canadians, and Negroes. In large measure, these expectations were confirmed. Table 3 shows that Jews have the highest mean score (5.54), followed closely by Protestants (5.16), Greeks (5.08), and Negroes (surprisingly) (5.03). The Italians' score (4.17) is almost a point lower, and the French-Canadian score (3.68) is the lowest for any group. The scores for Jews, Protestants, and Greeks do not significantly differ when the two-tail test is used (we were not able to predict the direction of the differences), but they are all significantly higher than the scores for Italians and French-Canadians. When Italian and French-Canadian scores are combined to form a "Roman Catholic" score, the latter is significantly lower (P < .001) than the scores for Jews, Protestants, or Greeks.

The prediction for the Negroes proved to be entirely wrong. Their mean score (5.03) is significantly higher (P < .001) than the scores for Italians and French-Canadians. Nor is the Negro score significantly different from those for Protestants and Greeks, although it is significantly lower than the Jewish score (P < .05) when the one-tail test is used. The skeptic may regard the relatively high Negro value score as merely lip-service to the liberal economic ethic, but it may in fact reflect, and to some extent be responsible for, the economic gains of Negroes in recent years.[24]

Social class also is significantly related to achievement values and accounts for more of the variance than ethnicity: the F ratio for class is 33.80 (P < .001) for ethnicity 11.62 (P < .001). Almost without exception, the mean score for each ethnic group is reduced with each decline in status. *Social class, however, does not wash out the differences between ethnic groups.* A series of "t" tests between cells across each social class reveals that Greek, Jewish, and Protestant scores remain signifi-

[24] The relatively high value score for Negroes supports our contention that achievement motivation and achievement values are genuinely different components of the achievement syndrome. It will be remembered that the Negroes had the lowest mean motivation score. If achievement motivation and values are conceptually and empirically identical, there should be no difference between the two sets of scores.

cantly higher than Italian and French-Canadian scores. Negro scores also remain among the highest across each social class. Ethnicity and social class interact and each contributes something to the differences between groups: the individual with high social status who also belongs to an ethnic group which stresses achievement values is far more likely to have a high value score than an individual with low status and membership in a group in which achievement is not emphasized. For example, the Class I-II Greek score is 6.33 as compared with the Class V French-Canadian score of 2.46—the difference between them is significant at the .001 level. On the other hand, the score for Class I-II Italians, an ethnic group in which achievement values are not stressed, is 5.86 as compared with 3.25 for Class V Greeks—the difference between them is significant at the .001 level. Neither variable, then, is sufficient to predict an individual's score; and for some groups social class seems to be the more significant factor, for others ethnicity appears to play the greater role. Thus, for Jews and Negroes the mean scores remain relatively high for each social class; in fact, Class V Jews and Negroes have larger mean scores than many French-Canadians and Italians of higher social status.

Aspiration Levels—Achievement motivation and values influence social mobility by affecting the individual's need to excel and his willingness to plan and work hard. But they do not determine the areas in which such excellence and effort take place. Achievement motivation and values can be expressed, as they often are, through many kinds of behavior that are not conducive to social mobility in our society, for example, deviant, recreational, or religious behavior. Unless the individual aims for high vocational goals and prepares himself appropriately, his achievement motivation and values will not pull him up the social ladder. Increasingly, lengthy formal education, often including college and postgraduate study, is needed for movement into prestigeful and lucrative jobs. An educational aspiration level which precludes college training may seriously affect the individual's chances for social mobility.

Their cultures, even before the arrival of the ethnic groups in the Northeast, were markedly different in orientation towards education.[25] The Protestants' stress upon formal education, if only as a means of furthering one's career, is well known. Traditionally, Jews have placed a very high value on educational and intellectual attainment; learning in the *shtetyl* society gave the individual prestige, authority, a chance for a better marriage. Contrariwise, for Southern Italians, school was an upper class institution, not an avenue for social advancement for their children, booklearning was remote from everyday experience, and intellectualism often regarded with distrust. French-Canadians, although not hostile to education and learning, were disinclined to educate their sons beyond the elementary level. Daughters needed more education as preparation

---

[25] For a comparison of ethnic group education and vocational aspirations, see R. M. Williams, Jr., *American Society*, New York: Knopf, 1951, Chapter 8; F. J. Woods, *Cultural Values of American Ethnic Groups*, New York: Harper, 1956, Chapters 5 and 7.

for jobs in the event they did not marry, but sons were destined to be farmers or factory workers, in the parents' view, with the exception at times of one son who would be encouraged to become a priest. Greeks— generally no better educated than Italians or French-Canadians—on the whole were much more favorably disposed towards learning, in large part because of their intense nationalistic identification with the cultural glories of ancient Greece.[26] This identification was strengthened by the relatively hostile reception Greeks met on their arrival in this country, and is in part responsible for the rapid development of private schools supported by the Greek community and devoted to the teaching of Greek culture—an interesting parallel to the Hebrew School among American Jews. Finally, Negroes, who might be expected to share the prevalent American emphasis upon education, face the painfully apparent fact that positions open to educated Negroes are scarce. This fact means that most Negroes, in all likelihood, do not consider high educational aspirations realistic. And the heavy drop-out in high school suggests that the curtailment of educational aspirations begins very early.

To test whether and to what degree these differences between groups persist, the mothers were asked: "How far do you *intend* for your son to go to school?" It was hoped that the term *intend* would structure the question so that the reply would indicate, not merely a mother's pious wish, but also an expression of will to do something about her son's schooling. The data show that 96 per cent of the Jewish, 88 per cent of the Protestant, 85 per cent of the Greek, 83 per cent of the Negro (much higher than was anticipated), 64 per cent of the Italian, and 56 per cent of the French-Canadian mothers said that they expected their sons to go to college. The aspirations of Jews, Protestants, Greeks, and Negroes are not significantly different from one another, but they are significantly higher than the aspirations of Italians and French-Canadians (P < .05).

Social class, once more, is significantly related to educational aspiration. When class is controlled the differences between ethnic groups are diminished—particularly at the Class I-II-III levels—but they are not erased: Jews, Protestants, Greeks, and Negroes tend to have aspirations similar to one another and higher than those of Italians and French-Canadians for each social class. The differences are greatest at the lower class levels: at Class V, 85 per cent of the Protestants, 80 per cent of the Jews, and 78 per cent of the Negroes intend for their sons to go to college as compared with 63 per cent of the Greeks, 50 per cent of the Italians, and 29 per cent of the French-Canadians.

The individual, to be socially mobile, must aspire to the occupations which society esteems and rewards highly. An individual, strongly motivated to excel and willing to plan and work hard, who sets his heart on

[26] Attempts by Mussolini to create a similar bond between his people and ancient Rome, or even the more recent Renaissance, were unsuccessful. French-Canadians for the most part have long refused to be impressed by the "secular" achievement of European anti-clerical French society.

being the best barber will probably be less vertically mobile than an equally endowed person who aspires to become the best surgeon. Moreover, the individual who aspires to a high status occupation is likely to expend more energy in competitive striving—and in so doing improve his chances for social mobility—than someone whose occupational choice demands relatively little from him.

Since many of the boys in this study were too young to appraise occupations realistically, we sought to obtain a measure of ethnic group vocational aspiration by questioning the mothers about their aspirations for their sons, once again assuming that they would tend to communicate their views of status levels and their expectations for their sons. Ten occupations were chosen which can be ranked by social status; seven of our ten occupations (marked below by asterisks) were selected from the N.O.R.C. ranking.[27] The occupations, originally presented in alphabetical order, are given here in the order of status: Lawyer*, Druggist, Jewelry Store Owner, Machinist*, Bank Teller, Insurance Agent*, Bookkeeper*, Mail Carrier*, Department Store Salesman*, and Bus Driver*, The mothers were asked: "If things worked out so that your son were in the following occupations, would you be satisfied or dissatisfied?" To obtain aspiration scores for each mother, her responses were treated in three ways:

1. The number of times the mother answered "satisfied" to the ten occupations was summed to give a single score. In effect this meant giving each occupation of weight of one. Since the subject must inevitably select lower status occupations as she increases her number of choices, the higher the summed score, the lower the aspiration level. The basic limitation of this method is that it is impossible to know from the summed score whether the occupations chosen are of low or high status.

2. To correct for this, a second index was derived by assigning weights to the seven occupations taken from the N.O.R.C. study according to their position in the rank order. Thus the highest status position, lawyer, was given a rank weight of 1.0 and the lowest a weight of 6.5 (store salesman and bus driver were tied for last place). Here again, the higher the score, the lower the aspiration level.

3. A third method of weighting the occupations was devised by taking the percentage of the entire sample of mothers who said that they would be satisfied with a particular occupation, and using the reciprocal of each percentage as the weight for that occupation. (The reciprocal was first multiplied by one thousand to eliminate decimals.) The mothers ranked the occupations somewhat differently than the N.O.R.C. ranking (assigning a higher status to bookkeeper and insurance agent and lower status to machinist and mail carrier). The assumption here is that the higher

[27] National Opinion Research Center, "Jobs and Occupations: A Popular Evaluation," *Opinion News*, 9 (September 1, 1947). We substituted store salesman for store clerk and bus driver for streetcar motorman. The position of the three occupations which did not appear in the N.O.R.C. survey are ranked according to their similarity to occupations in the survey.

TABLE 4. MEAN SCORES AND RANK POSITION OF SIX ETHNIC GROUPS
USING THREE INDEXES OF VOCATIONAL ASPIRATION[*]

Ethnicity	Index of Vocational Aspiration			
	Number Satisfied	Rank Weight	Reciprocal Weight	N
French-Canadian	6.60 (5)	14.43 (5)	119.90 (5)	62
Italian	5.96 (4)	12.66 (4)	104.55 (4)	74
Greek	4.70 (2)	7.78 (2)	73.51 (2)	47
Jew	3.51 (1)	6.02 (1)	59.48 (1)	57
Negro	6.95 (6)	16.18 (6)	138.74 (6)	65
Protestant	5.28 (3)	10.12 (3)	88.19 (3)	122

* Rank positions are shown by figures in parentheses.

the percentage who answered "satisfied," the higher the status of the occupation. A score for each mother was obtained by summing the reciprocal weights for each occupation chosen. With this method, the highest status occupation is lawyer (score of 11.0), the lowest bus driver (48.0). All ten occupations were used in this index. The higher the subject's score, the lower her aspiration level.

Although these indexes differ somewhat, they provide very similar data on ethnic group vocational aspirations. Table 4 shows the same rank ordering of groups for all three indexes, in descending order as follows: Jews, Greeks, Protestants, Italians, French-Canadians, and Negroes. A series of "t" tests of differences between group mean scores revealed differences and similarities much like those found for achievement motivation. Thus the Jews, Greeks, and Protestants show significantly higher mean scores (that is, they tend to be satisfied with fewer occupations and indicate satisfaction with only the higher status positions) than the Roman Catholic Italians and French-Canadians.[28] The mean score for Jews is significantly higher than the scores for Protestants and Greeks, but there are no significant differences between Greeks and Protestants, or between Italians and French-Canadians. The mean score for Negroes is significantly lower than the scores for all other groups except French-Canadians. In examining the aspirations of Negroes it should be remembered that most of these occupations are considered highly desirable by many Negroes, given their severely limited occupational opportunities, so that their aspiration level may appear low only by "white" standards. There are, however, these problems: are the Negro mothers (83 per cent) in earnest in saying that they intend for their sons to go to college? And, if so, how is this to be reconciled with their low vocational aspirations?

[28] Similar Jewish-Italian differences are reported in F. L. Strodtbeck, M. McDonald, and B. C. Rosen, "Evaluation of Occupations: A Reflection of Jewish and Italian Mobility Differences," *American Sociological Review*, 22 (October, 1957), pp. 546-553.

Social class, too, is significantly and directly related to vocational aspiration—a familiar finding—*but it is not as significant as ethnicity.* Analysis of variance of data for each of the three indexes reveals that ethnicity accounts for more of the variance than social class. For example, when the number of occupations with which the mother would be satisfied for her son is used as an index of vocational aspiration, the F ratio for ethnicity is 12.41 (P < .001) as compared with a ratio of 9.92 for social class (P < .001). The same pattern holds for data derived from the other two indexes. Although ethnicity and class interact, each contributing to the differences between groups, the effects of class are more apparent at the middle class (Classes I-II-III) than at the working and lower class (Classes IV-V) levels.

As the question was worded in this study, in one sense it is misleading to speak of the "height" of vocational aspirations. For all groups have "high" aspirations in that most mothers are content to have their sons achieve a high status. The basic difference between groups is in the "floor," so to speak, which they place on their aspirations. For example, at least 80 per cent of the mothers of each ethnic group said that they would be satisfied to have their sons be lawyers, but only two per cent of the Greeks and seven per cent of the Jews were content to have their sons become bus drivers, as compared with 26 per cent of the French-Canadians and 43 per cent of the Negroes. Again, 12 per cent of the Jewish, 22 per cent of the Protestant, and 29 per cent of the Greek mothers said that they would be satisfied to have their sons become department store salesmen, as compared with 48 per cent of the Italians, 51 per cent of the Negro, and 52 per cent of the French-Canadian mothers.

Summary

This paper examines differences in motivation, values, and aspirations of six racial and ethnic groups which may explain in part their dissimilar social mobility rates. Analysis of ethnographic and attitudinal and personality data suggests that these groups differed, and to some extent still differ, in their orientation toward achievement. The data show that the groups place different emphases upon independence and achievement training in the rearing of children. As a consequence, achievement motivation is more characteristic of Greeks, Jews, and white Protestants than of Italians, French-Canadians, and Negroes. The data also indicate that Jews, Greeks, and Protestants are more likely to possess achievement values and higher educational and vocational aspirations than Italians and French-Canadians. The values and educational aspirations of the Negroes are higher than expected, being comparable to those of Jews, Greeks, and white Protestants, and higher than those of the Italians and French-Canadians. Vocational aspirations of Negroes, however, are the lowest of any group in the sample. Social class and ethnicity interact in influencing motivation, values, and aspirations; neither can predict an individual's score. Ethnic differences persist when social class is controlled, but some of the differences between ethnic groups in motivations, values, and aspirations are probably also a function of their class composition.

Supplementary Bibliography

Stuart Chase, *The Proper Study of Mankind*, rev. ed. N. Y.: Harper, 1956.
   A popular introduction to contemporary social science, emphasizing the significance of cultural learning.

F. L. K. Hsu, ed., *Psychological Anthropology*. Homewood, Ill.: The Dorsey Press, 1961.
   A set of papers showing the interrelationship between cultural learning and personality.

Ralph Linton, *The Study of Man*. N.Y.: Appleton-Century-Crofts, 1936.
   A classic work in social science, containing chapters on race and on racial differences.

Robert D. North, "The Intelligence of American Negroes." *Research Reports*, 1955, 3:2-8.
   A summary of data which has been compiled comparing the intelligence of Negroes and whites, including Army test results from World War I.

S. Kirson Weinberg and Henry Arond, "The Occupational Culture of the Boxer." *American Journal of Sociology*, 1952, 57:460-469. Reprinted in Kimball Young and Raymond W. Mack, *Principles of Sociology: A Reader in Theory and Research*, 2nd ed. N. Y.: American Book, 1962, pp. 31-40.
   An analysis demonstrating that ethnic succession in boxing parallels the immigration and assimilation of ethnic minorities.

IV Race as a Social Concept

We have seen that biologists and physical anthropologists can classify mankind into major physical stocks and further divide us into subraces on the basis of physical characteristics. But these physical characteristics do not biologically cause anything else. The combination of a wide nose, kinky hair, and dark skin does not make one innately a prize-fighter; straight hair and a skin fold at the inner eye do not make a man a Buddhist; the prevalence of blond hair and blue eyes in a population does not cause it to industrialize.

But this does not mean that race is unimportant, or that it has no consequences. Race in the biologist's sense has no biologically caused consequences, but what men *believe* about race has social consequences. In other words, most of men's discussions about race are discussions of their beliefs, not of biological fact. Most of men's actions about race are based on what they have been taught to believe about it, not on what scientists know about it. Race is usually not a biological concept. It is a social concept.

The Social Definition of Negroes

All cultures have their myths, and the culture of the United States is no exception. Since the race issue in this country is charged with emotionalism, it is not surprising to find a plethora of myths about racial minorities. One of the most popular of such myths until quite recently was the notion of "Negro blood." If you ask anyone other than a specialist in race relations what defines a man as a Negro, the chances are still very great that the response will be "Anyone with traceable Negro blood." By this it is meant that any person who is known to have a Negro in his ancestry is a Negro. Everyone knows that there are very light-skinned Negroes, some of whom "pass" for white. Since they have no visible physical characteristics which make them look Negroid but are still referred to as "Negroes," these people serve as good examples of the consequences of "Negro blood."

There are four types of blood (A, B, AB, and O). All three major races have all four types. All human blood is exactly the same within each of the four types. What, then, is Negro blood? What is meant is that a Negro is someone with an ancestor who was known to be a Negro. But the ancestor known to be a Negro need not have any of the physical characteristics which scientists use to define Negroid. He, in turn, need only have an ancestor known to be a Negro. Negro blood, then, is a social concept, not a biological one.

Many Negroes in the United States have more Caucasoid ancestry than Negroid, but they are still considered Negro if they are known to have a Negro ancestor. This is pure social definition and pure biological nonsense. In no other area of biology would we reason similarly. Imagine a dog breeder saying, "Most of this pup's forebears were cocker spaniels, but he's really a Doberman pinscher"—meaning that one of his great-grandparents was.

The United States Bureau of the Census takes a realistic cognizance of our social beliefs. Census enumerators are instructed, for example, to count a person as an American Indian if he is considered to be an Indian by most of the people in the community where he lives.

Cross-cultural Differences in Social Definition

One cause of misunderstandings between people from the United States and their Latin-American neighbors is that, though both of us define race socially rather than biologically, we use different definitions. Light mulatto people in some of the islands of the Caribbean who are considered white there would be called Negro by most people in the United States at a glance. On one of these islands is a brother and sister one of whom has run for public office as a Negro, while the other is a member of an exclusively white club! Their mother was mulatto; their father white. Both the brother and sister have relatively Caucasoid features. One has chosen to be white. The other prefers to be colored for the political advantages this offers in a predominantly colored society. People there are aware of their background, and respond to them on the basis of the choices they have made. Obviously, an "exclusively white" club there is working on a different set of social definitions than it would in the United States.

The Social Definition of Jewishness

Another example of social definition can be seen in what Americans mean by "Jew." A man said recently, "I am the only Jew in St. Peter's Episcopal Church." He wasn't trying to be funny, and it was easy to understand what he meant. He was saying that some of his ancestors had believed in Judaism, and that he had therefore been brought up in a culture associated with that faith, and that he was the only Episcopalian with such a background in that church. He was also implying, no doubt correctly, that in the community where he lived, people still thought of him as a Jew despite his religious affiliation.

Jews, while in no sense biologically a race, are, in Europe and the United States, socially defined as a race. Indeed, Jewishness is so completely socially defined that, as we have seen, one is considered a Jew even if he has left the faith which originally defined the concept. The author has tried to illustrate this point in classes in race relations by challenging the students to determine, after they have known him for a month or six weeks, whether or not he is Jewish. He offers to answer any question except one calling for a direct answer to the question "Are you Jewish or not?" After all, the students have been looking at him and hearing him talk daily. If there are characteristics which define Jewishness, they should have had an opportunity to observe whether those characteristics are present or absent. Yet, after an hour's discussion, they are divided: some think he is Jewish; some think he is not; some just don't know what to think. Most of these students are members of social organizations, some of which would not take him as a member if he were Jewish, and others of which would not accept him if he were not.

In such a session, by the end of the hour, the students will have determined through questioning that he knows the difference between Ashkenaz and Sephardic Jews, that he does not attend temple, that he has not changed his name, and a set of other facts. They can see what he looks like, and they have had weeks to listen to his opinions and how he expresses them. Finally someone says plaintively, "There's no way for us to answer your question unless you or someone who knows tells us." And he's right.

You can become Jewish by having a parent who is considered a Jew, or you can have gentile parents and be a convert to Judaism. You can cease to be Jewish, as a Negro with Caucasoid features can "pass," by leaving the community. A Jew who changes his name, leaves the faith and leaves the community where he is known as a Jew is no longer a Jew, because being a Jew is a matter of social definition, not race. You are a Jew if people think you are a Jew.

Group Boundaries

Social definitions of minorities vary from society to society, but the process of social definition is the same everywhere. It consists of establishing group boundaries and identifying individuals as members or nonmembers. Hitler contended that Jews were so different from other Germans that they would subvert the society and weaken the culture, and that since they were so different, they should be required to carry identification cards so that people could tell which Germans were Jewish and which were not.

Related Readings

One should not conclude that a minority status such as Jewishness is of little importance simply because it is socially rather than biologically defined. Social definitions constitute a social reality, and they have social consequences. "A Study of Religious Discrimination by Social Clubs" not only documents the extent of the consequences in voluntary association policies of believing Jews to be different from non-Jews; it also suggests that such beliefs are translated into behaviors which may have far-reaching consequences in the political and economic power structure. One other crucial idea is introduced here: discrimination creates a reaction to itself; institutionalized exclusion spawns a culture of antidiscrimination. The formation of Jewish clubs which exclude Christians is a function of the same process whereby minorities retaliate against rejection by inventing epithets for the dominant population. If a man must bear hearing himself referred to as a "spade" or "nigger," he can at least enjoy sneering about "ghosts" and "ofays."

The student of dominant-minority relations must also guard against glib generalizations about "the prejudiced person," and the concomitant assumption that an individual either discriminates in all compartments of his social life or none of them. John Dollard's "Hostility and Fear in Social Life" explains racial discrimination as a case where the culture of a society grants permission to people to express their aggressions in a socially acceptable channel. One way to define group boundaries is to single out physically or culturally different categories of the population and institutionalize the use of such minorities as scapegoats.

—————— *Rights*

A Study of Religious Discrimination by Social Clubs

Discriminatory practices by social clubs, long recognized as a pervasive pattern among proverbially gregarious Americans, were dramatically and publicly challenged last summer by the U. S. Attorney General and several other important public figures who resigned from the Metropolitan Club, probably the most distinguished club in Washington, D. C.

In the spring of 1959 Dr. Ralph Bunche publicly challenged the action of the West Side Tennis Club in Forest Hills, N. Y. in refusing membership to his son. The club is the scene of the most important national and international tennis matches held in the U. S.

In 1955, Mrs. Eleanor Roosevelt, invited to speak at a community Brotherhood Week function in Lancaster, Pa., cancelled her appearance at the last moment. She found that the club at which the meeting was to be held barred Jews from membership and as guests at all other times.

Why these public challenges? Clubs which discriminate on religious and racial grounds have traditionally taken, and won acceptance for, the position that the social club is an extension of one's own parlor. Since a man has a right to choose whom he will invite into his home, he thus also has the right to choose whom he will admit to his club.

Are these actions then a challenge to the right of privacy or a questioning of the nature of the social or private club? Attorney General Kennedy said it was the latter, explaining that the Metropolitan Club's restrictive policy, because it kept members from inviting certain foreign diplomats into the Club, created international political ramifications.

Dr. Bunche took a similar position. He contended that the West Side Tennis Club, because of its central place in the tennis world, was not merely a private sports club, but had a quasi-public character.

As for Mrs. Roosevelt, she questioned the morality of holding a Brotherhood Week observance in a club that at all other times excluded people whom it was willing to acknowledge as brothers on this one day only.

Are the positions cited here then a challenge to the right of privacy or are they indeed a challenge to those who, by their insistence upon social exclusiveness, seek to obtain or hold economic, political and other power advantages to which they may otherwise not be entitled?

If the latter, social discrimination (i.e., discrimination by clubs) assumes new dimensions. If the seat of power in any community discriminates against Jews, it may sound a note that will be taken up by others in the community. The industrialist will be confirmed in his negative view about Jewish plant managers; the plant managers in turn will find it more expedient not to employ Jewish subordinates. Lower echelon civic groups, ears closely attuned to the note from on high, will find sanction for similar exclusions. The university, upon whose board of trustees sit members of the discriminatory club, will not protest a quota system, the fraternities will mimic their elders in exclusionary practices. Thus may a new generation, while still in its formative years, be schooled in the ways and benefits of social discrimination.

Comparatively few of the exclusionary clubs are strategic elements in the power structure of a community; many more merely foster undesirable and undemocratic social practices. These latter groups may be only minor sources of irritation, singly, but they represent in their totality a formidable expression of anti-Semitic attitudes. They are the result of social and economic forces which have been operating on the American scene for many decades. They represent the attitudes of individual Americans and, in that sense, signify that education for democracy still has far to go.

Obviously, the Anti-Defamation League must be concerned with the irrational exclusion of Jews from clubs which by reasonable test are secular in purpose and program. For such exclusions represent a philosophy of racism. At the same time, ADL is aware that the practices of clubs which bar Jews has had its concomitant in the establishment by Jews of separate club facilities. Some of these, as the statistics on the following pages will show, also adopted exclusionary patterns.

The Sample

To determine the extent of religious discrimination by social clubs in the United States, the Anti-Defamation League surveyed a representative list of such clubs which could be reasonably termed a national cross-section. The criterion for selection was whether the clubs employed professional managers. A list of clubs maintained by a group of professionals in the private club field was used for the sample. The total number of such clubs was 1,332. For purposes of the study 44 Armed Forces clubs on the list were excluded, leaving a balance of 1,288 clubs with essentially civilian memberships.

The 1,288 clubs were situated in 46 states and the District of Columbia. Only four states—Alaska, Maine, New Hampshire and Vermont— were not represented in the survey group which was based on the list. The number of clubs in the other states ranged from one each in North Dakota and Wyoming to 159 in New York State.

The clubs on which information was sought were broadly of two types. First, city clubs which were defined as clubs physically situated within cities or towns; there were 369 such. In terms of distribution among the states, the number of city clubs ranged from one each in seven states to 59 in New York State.

The second major group on which information was sought was country clubs. There were 919 such clubs on the initiation of this survey. Country clubs were defined as those located in suburban and rural areas which had the accoutrements normally associated with country clubs—golf course, tennis courts, swimming pools, and other sport facilities.

The distribution of the country clubs among the states ranged from one in each of four states to 116 in the State of New York.

Aims of the Study

The first step was to obtain an evaluation of the status of each club. Three categories were established: (1) high prestige or power structure clubs; (2) those which enjoyed average acceptance in their community; (3) and those which were considered of little or no importance. This information was obtained by interviewing knowledgeable people and polling a cross-section of community opinion. At the same time, an estimate of each club's membership was sought.

Thereafter, a determination was made for each club as to whether it discriminated on the basis of religion.

An identification of "non-discriminatory" was made if the club accepted Christians and Jews without regard to religion in its membership policy and practice. For any clubs so identified, no further information was sought.

However, if the club were considered discriminatory on grounds of religion, it was studied further. Such clubs would be identified as "Christian" clubs if they either barred Jews or had a quota for Jewish membership. The reporters were asked to distinguish between those clubs that barred Jews absolutely and those that admitted Jews on a limited basis.

In the same way, identification was made of "Jewish" clubs which either barred Christians or had quotas for Christian members.

Finally, wherever a club was identified as a "Christian club" or a "Jewish club," the reporter sought to establish whether the restrictions were official (i.e., in the club's constitution or by-laws) or unofficial (i.e., informal, gentleman's agreements, etc.).

The Final Study Group

Of the 1,288 clubs on which information was sought data was received on 1,152, or almost 90 percent. The remaining 136 included clubs that had gone out of existence, or about which, for a variety of reasons, information was not available.

The 1,152 clubs about which information was obtained were located in 46 states and the District of Columbia. Again, only four states—Alaska, Maine, New Hampshire and Vermont—were not represented. The 1,152 clubs were distributed from a low of one each in Nevada, North Dakota and Wyoming to a high of 149 in New York State.

Of the 1,152 clubs, 349 were city clubs. These city clubs were distributed from a low of one each in Idaho, Mississippi, Montana, New Mexico, North Dakota, Rhode Island and West Virginia to a high of 43 in the State of New York.

Information was obtained on 803 country clubs which were distributed from a low of one each in Idaho, Nevada, South Dakota and Wyoming to a high of 106 in New York State.

National Findings

City & Country Clubs Combined

1. Of the 1,152 clubs on which sufficient information was received for evaluation, 693 (or 60 percent) were deemed to enjoy top status in their communities. 372 clubs in the national group (or almost 33 percent of the total) had average acceptance in their communities. The remaining clubs, numbering 87 (or almost 8 percent of the national survey group), were evaluated as clubs which enjoyed little or no standing in their communities.

2. The total estimated membership of the 1,152 clubs in the survey group was almost 700,000.

3. Of the 1,152 clubs, 371 (or almost 33 percent) were nondiscriminatory, erecting no religious barriers to membership.

4. 781 clubs (or 67 percent) practiced religious discrimination.

5. Of the 781 clubs which practiced religious discrimination, 691 were "Christian clubs" which either barred Jews completely or imposed a limitation upon the number of Jews that could join. These 691 "Christian clubs" represented 88 percent of all the discriminatory clubs and 60 percent of all clubs examined.

6. Of the 781 discriminatory clubs, 90 were "Jewish clubs" which either barred Christian membership or imposed limitations upon Christians. Thus, the "Jewish clubs" represented almost 12 percent of all the discriminatory clubs, and almost 8 percent of all clubs studied.

7. Of the 691 "Christian clubs," 555 (or about 80 percent of the group) barred Jews completely. The remainder, 136 (or about 20 percent), limited Jewish membership to small numbers.

8. Of the 90 "Jewish clubs," 85 (or about 95 percent of the group), barred Christian members completely; the other five admitted Christians in small numbers.

9. Of the 781 discriminatory clubs, 696 (or 90 percent) maintained their restrictions "unofficially"—without religious proscriptions in their constitutions or by-laws. The restrictive practices of these clubs was carried out informally through gentlemen's agreements, etc. The remaining 85 restrictive clubs were said to maintain their restrictions "officially" —by constitution or by-laws.

City Clubs

1. Of the 349 city clubs that were evaluated, 210 (60 percent) enjoyed top status in their cities and towns. 106 (more than 30 percent of the city clubs) had average acceptance in their communities while the remaining city clubs, numbering 33 (almost 10 percent of all the city clubs) were evaluated as groups that enjoyed little or no standing in their communities. It may be noted at this point that the status distribution of the city clubs is almost identical with the status distribution of all *City and Country Clubs Combined*.

2. The total estimated membership of the 349 city clubs was almost 300,000 or slightly less than half of the total estimated membership of *City and Country Clubs Combined*.

3. Of the 349 city clubs surveyed, it was found that 147 (over 40 percent) were non-discriminatory, erecting no religious barriers to membership.

4. 202 city clubs (almost 60 percent) practiced religious discrimination.

5. Of the 202 city clubs that practiced religious discrimination, 186 (or more than 90 percent of all discriminatory city clubs) were "Christian clubs" which either barred Jews completely or imposed limitations on the number of Jews that could join. It may be noted here that discriminatory "Christian clubs" comprised more than 50 percent of all the city clubs examined.

6. Of the 202 discriminatory city clubs, 16 were "Jewish clubs"; 14 of these barred Christians completely while two accepted Christians in small numbers. Thus, "Jewish clubs" represented about 8 percent of all the discriminatory city clubs and about 5 percent of all the city clubs studied.

7. Of the 186 "Christian city clubs," 139 (or about 80 percent) barred Jews completely. The other 47 "Christian city clubs" limited Jewish membership to small numbers.

8. Of the 202 discriminatory city clubs, 183 (or 90 percent) maintained "unofficial" restrictions by means of gentlemen's agreements, etc. The remaining 19 discriminatory city clubs were said to maintain their restrictions "officially."

9. The 202 discriminatory city clubs were analyzed to determine how they were distributed in terms of status. We found that of the 202 discriminatory city clubs, 115 (or 55 percent) were reported as enjoying top prestige in the cities and towns where they were located. 63 of the discriminatory city clubs (32 percent) were identified as having average acceptance in their communities. The remaining discriminatory city clubs, 24 in number (or about 13 percent of the discriminatory group) were identified as being of little or no consequence in their communities. It should be noted that the total estimated membership of the dis-

criminatory city clubs was over 200,000, representing almost a third of the total estimated membership of all the clubs surveyed.

Country Clubs

1. Of the 803 country clubs evaluated, 483 (60 percent) were top status clubs. 266 (33 percent of the country clubs) had average acceptance while the remaining country clubs, 54 (or 7 percent), were evaluated as not having significant standing. Again, it is noteworthy that the status distribution of the country clubs in percentages is virtually identical with the status distribution of all *City and Country Clubs Combined* and with *City Clubs.*

2. The total estimated membership of the 803 country clubs was over 400,000 or more than half of the total estimated membership of all clubs surveyed.

3. Of the 803 country clubs surveyed, 224 (28 percent) were nondiscriminatory, erecting no religious barriers to membership.

4. 579 country clubs (72 percent) practiced religious discrimination It should be noted that this percentage figure is appreciably higher than the proportion of city clubs (60 percent) that used religious criteria.

5. Of the 579 country clubs that discriminate along religious lines, 505 (or 87 percent of all the discriminatory country clubs) were "Christian clubs." It is worthy of note that the "Christian clubs" comprised almost 63 percent of all the country clubs in our study group.

6. Of the 579 discriminatory country clubs, 74 were "Jewish clubs"; 71 barred Christians completely, while three accepted Christians in small numbers. The "Jewish country clubs" represented about 12 percent of all discriminatory country clubs and about 9 percent of all the country clubs studied.

7. Of the 505 "Christian country clubs," 416 (or about 80 percent) barred Jews completely. The other 89 "Christian country clubs" (or about 20 percent) limited the membership of Jews.

8. Of the 579 discriminatory country clubs, 513 (about 90 percent) maintained their restrictions "unofficially." The other 66 country clubs were reported to have restrictions in their constitutions or by-laws.

9. The 579 discriminatory country clubs were analyzed for status distribution. We found that of the 579 country clubs, 352 (60 percent) were top groups. 182 (32 percent) were described as clubs with average acceptance in their communities while the remaining discriminatory country clubs, 45 in number (or 8 percent of the discriminatory group), were of low rank. The total estimated membership of the discriminatory country clubs was about 260,000, or somewhat over a third of the total estimated membership of all the clubs surveyed.

Regional Analysis

As we pointed out in our *National Findings—City and Country Clubs Combined,* our study of 1,152 clubs revealed that 781 (or 67 percent of the national total) practiced religious discrimination. 691 were "Christian clubs" that discriminated against Jews, while 90 were "Jewish clubs" which discriminated against persons of the Christian faith.

In order to determine whether there were any significant regional differences with respect to club discrimination, we analyzed our data in terms of five geographical areas, as follows:

1. *South and Southwest:* Alabama, Arizona, Arkansas, District of Columbia, Florida, Georgia, Kentucky, Louisiana, Mississippi, North Carolina, Oklahoma, South Carolina, Tennessee, Texas, Virginia, West Virginia.

2. *Far West:* California, Colorado, Hawaii, Nevada, New Mexico, Oregon, Utah, Washington, Wyoming.

3. *Mid West:* Idaho, Illinois, Indiana, Iowa, Kansas, Michigan, Minnesota, Missouri, Montana, Nebraska, North Dakota, Ohio, South Dakota, Wisconsin.

4. *North Atlantic:* Delaware, Maryland, New Jersey, New York, Pennsylvania.

5. *New England:* Connecticut, Massachusetts, Rhode Island.

Here follow the findings:

1. The regional percentages of discriminatory clubs are: South and Southwest, 60 percent; Far West, 58 percent; Mid West, 73 percent; North Atlantic, 74 percent; New England, 68 percent. From these data, it appears that discrimination by clubs is significantly higher in the Mid West and North Atlantic states than in the other three regions.

2. Of the discriminatory clubs in the South and Southwest, 91 percent are "Christian clubs." In the Far West the percentage is 95. In the Mid West, the "Christian clubs" comprise 89 percent of all discriminatory clubs. In the North Atlantic states and New England, the proportions were 81 percent and 93 percent respectively.

3. The proportion of "Jewish clubs" among the discriminatory clubs varies little in four regions. In the South and Southwest it is 9 percent; in the Far West, 5 percent; in the Mid West, 11 percent; and in New England, 7 percent. But in the North Atlantic states, 19 percent of all the discriminatory clubs were "Jewish clubs."

The Athletic Clubs

It has long been believed that many major city clubs calling themselves "Athletic Clubs" (usually preceded by the names of their home cities) show a complete disregard for the maxim of fair play. The study provided an opportunity to evaluate the long-held suspicion that "Athletic Clubs" in large American cities frequently set up religious criteria for membership.

The survey group included 19 "Athletic Clubs" situated in 19 great cities. The total membership of these 19 clubs is over 50,000. Fourteen of them are regarded as prestige groups while five are said to have average acceptance in their communities.

Of the 19 "Athletic Clubs," only five are non-discriminatory as between Jews and Christians. However, of the remaining 14 clubs, seven bar Jews completely while seven impose a quota upon Jewish membership.

In short, 75 percent of the city "Athletic Clubs" examined have discriminatory barriers against Jewish members. And, contrary to the courage so commonly associated with athletic activities, these discriminatory clubs universally enforce their restrictions "unofficially"—i.e., by gentlemen's agreements and the blackball.

The Prestige Clubs

In order to understand better the potential impact upon Jews of club discrimination, the data were analyzed with particular attention to clubs that were evaluated as enjoying maximum prestige in their communities.

Of the 1,152 city and country clubs examined, 693 (60 percent) were accorded such distinction. Of these 693 top American clubs, 455 (66 per cent) practice religious discrimination.

Of the 455 discriminatory clubs, 417 (more than 90 percent) discriminate against Jews.

To recapitulate in terms of the total prestige group of 693 clubs included in our study, 60 percent of the prestige group discriminated against Jews; 5 percent discriminated against Christians; and 35 percent were nondiscriminatory in terms of religion.

Conclusions

1. Religious discrimination by clubs in the United States is extensive and pervasive. The fact that 67 percent of all the clubs studied practiced religious discrimination indicates a serious failure on the part of the American community, at the social level, to accept the individual on the basis of individual worth and merit.

2. If the thesis is accepted that many prestige clubs are factors in the power structures which influence greatly the political and economic life of the community, then the fact that 60 percent of the prestige clubs of the United States discriminate against Jews has serious implications for the Jewish group.

3. It would appear that the extent of discrimination against Jews by clubs is far greater than the levels of discrimination against Jews in other areas such as education, employment, housing and public accommodations.

4. A consequence of the development of the institution of the "Christian club" has been the emergence of the "Jewish club." The fact that almost 8 percent of all the clubs studied were "Jewish clubs" that discriminated against Christians is eloquent testimony to the further institutionalization of religious prejudice. When, as and if Jewish community relations agencies conclude that the problem of the "Christian club" merits their attention, they will inevitably have to cope with the other side of the coin—the "Jewish club."

══════════ John Dollard

Hostility and Fear in Social Life

This paper will discuss what is commonly termed "race prejudice." Close analysis of the word reveals at least two distinct situations in which it is used: one where irrational antagonism is vented against other people, and the other where rational, that is intelligible, hostility is aroused in defense of a given status or economic order.[1] The events which common speech indicates as "race prejudice" may perhaps better be denoted in other terms.[2] The first necessity will be to examine the conditions under which animals may make hostile responses in social life and to see "race prejudice" in this context. Prejudice reactions cannot be separated from the responses of the organism to its total environment and can only be seen adequately when the nature of the process of socialization is held clearly in mind. We will begin, therefore, with a series of paragraphs indicating the societal context in which aggression is generated and the types of controls placed on hostility by our moral order.

Society is seen here as a group of cooperating animals, producing goods and services and continuing by procreation within the group.[3] The mode of life of a society is defined by a culture which is for any one generation an arbitrary inheritance of problem solutions.[4] Since aggressive responses of constituent members are a problem to every society, the culture includes patterned ways of dealing with these responses. A society maintains group unity by positive ties between its members based on services mutually rendered, by suppressing in-group aggression and by defensive-aggressive operations against other animal groups.[5] Relatively self-contained societies were easier to define in former days when western European techniques of production had not yet tended to bring the whole world into a specialized and interdependent economic unit. It still seems worth while, however, to speak of such a thing as an "American society,"

[1] Faris indicates a distinction that is apparently analogous in saying that prejudice attitudes are "impermeable to experience." The same imperviousness is characteristic of irrational aggression. See Ellsworth Faris, *The Nature of Human Nature* (New York: McGraw-Hill Book Co., 1937), p. 323.

[2] Dr. A. H. Maslow of Brooklyn College has aided me in clearing up my mind on this score by pointing out the "accretive" nature of the term "race prejudice" and suggesting that, on analysis, it would dissolve into a number of disparate concepts.

[3] W. G. Sumner and A. G. Keller, *The Science of Society* (New Haven: Yale University Press, 1937), pp. 225-246.

[4] An excellent illustration of this view is given by Dr. C. S. Ford. See his "A Sample Comparative Analysis of Material Culture" in G. P. Murdock (ed.), *Studies in the Science of Society* (New Haven: Yale University Press, 1937), pp. 225-246.

[5] W. G. Sumner, *Folkways* (Boston: Ginn & Co., 1906), p. 12.

From *Social Forces*, 1938, XVII, 15-25. Copyright by the University of North Carolina Press, 1938.

albeit it is only relatively an independent economic and procreative unit.

Animals are added to a society one by one and trained individually. Social patterns are transmitted by persons who become the targets of positive and negative feeling from the child as the result of facilitating and frustrating behavior on their parts. Each child develops a positive feeling for its own group members and indirectly for all their traits, such as language, smell, appearance and custom. Since renunciations are invariably imposed on the incoming animal, it develops also hostile attitudes toward these trainers and toward in-group members and symbols; these attitudes include animosity toward parents and siblings and a negative (as well as positive) feeling tone toward the mores, including religion and authoritarian institutions generally. A correct understanding of this process is indispensable to a proper evaluation of in-group and out-group feeling and hence to related phenomena, such as "race prejudice."

The hostility of an animal toward its in-group is a constant threat to the solidarity of the group and therefore to the continuation of economic cooperation, common defensive operations, and the sharing of a common culture. Such hostility in the individual animal is therefore met with a united hostile front by all other members of the group and is, if necessary, forcibly suppressed. Techniques for accomplishing this suppression range from withdrawal of privilege to a disobedient child to the operations of the criminal law. Supernatural sanctions are frequently invoked, as in the taboo, to inhibit countermores tendencies.

Thus the animal coming into the group (by birth) finds that hostile moves toward in-group members are either hopeless, as in the case of the small child against adults, or dangerous, as in the case of a deserter from an army, and they are for the most part abandoned as overt modes of response. Alexander[6] has correctly said that the control of aggressive behavior is one of the chief problems of social life. Sumner[7] has also perceived the underlying fact of hostility between members of society and expressed it in his concept of "antagonistic cooperation." Socialization of the child should be conceived of in one aspect as a battle-ground between the rejection responses[8] of the child and the demands of the existing moral order into which the child is born. Our child psychology is at present so far unrealistic as drastically to underestimate the strength, character and perseverance of these responses. Common experience as well as my own studies of socialization in two children (unpublished) indicate the frustrating character of the limitations imposed on the naive and early acquired reaction tendencies of the child, the aggression which arises in the animal as a result of these frustrations and the social opposition to this aggression which is immediately evident. It is in part the

[6] Franz Alexander, "Psychoanalysis and Social Disorganization," *Am. J. Soc.* 1937; XLII, 806.

[7] *Op. cit.,* p. 16.

[8] Sherman's work indicates that aggressive responses in the newborn are a segment of rejection responses to stimuli. See Mandell Sherman, "A Proposed Theory of the Development of Emotional Responses in Infants," *J. Comp. Psychol.,* 1928, VIII, 385-395.

underestimation of these tendencies which makes "race prejudice" seem so mysterious. Neither child nor adult individual may be seen as a smoothly compacted group of attitudes, perfectly defined by the traditional social order. Rather each person is a record of a battle; he has a rugged history in which frustration, hostility and fear have all played roles. There is further, in our social psychology, an underestimation of the frustrating character of in-group life for its adult participants.[9] These frustrations also arouse antagonism against the cherished in-grouper, an antagonism which is not extinguished by the fact that it is not permitted an expression corresponding to its intensity.

Each animal inducted into the social group finally learns to check hostility toward in-groupers either by self-control or repression. It is this fact which gives acculturated animals such a well accommodated "look" to the outside eye, so that the superficial student will hardly suspect the dynamic nature of the history of the animal or the tension created within its personality by the necessity for suppressing aggressive responses. The fact that animals can repress aggression, as well as other tendencies, is one of their most valuable organic capacities from the standpoint of adjustment in society. Individuals unable to perform this task have to be killed as murderers or rapers or isolated as criminals or mental deviants. Repression[10] takes place either through fear or loss of favor of a valuable group member, such as a parent, or through fear of punishment.

Repressed aggressive tendencies are therefore a standard feature of the life of every well socialized animal. In mature animals the aggression is constantly provoked from at least two sources: first, through continuing demands for satisfactions which had to be tabooed in the course of socialization; such (neurotic) wishes are exemplified by the desire incontinently to master all other people who come within one's ken or to gain control of others by exhibiting constant dependence on them and exciting pity. Second, aggression is aroused through rivalry over the securing of desired goods or values such as high status, sex partners, or satisfactions incident to a standard of living. It is these rivalries, of course, which arouse the aggressions noted by Sumner and which fund the antagonism described in his "antagonistic cooperation." The extent of such frustrations is concealed in many people by a sour-grapes attitude which leads them to affirm grudgingly that they do not want what is actually inaccessible. Deprivation is nevertheless perceived whether it is formally acknowledged or not and from deprivation arise the hostilities toward in-group competitors, hostilities which can never be permitted an expression proportionate to their intensity. As I[11] have elsewhere indicated, it is the underestimation of these two sources of deprivation and

[9] E. S. Bogardus shows awareness of this feature of social life. See his *Immigration and Race Attitudes* (Boston: D. C. Heath & Co., 1928), pp. 21-22.

[10] S. Freud, *Introductory Lectures on Psychoanalysis* (London: 1923), p. 248.

[11] John Dollard, *Caste and Class in a Southern Town* (New Haven: Yale University Press, 1937), p. 442.

antagonism which makes such phenomena as "race prejudice" seem baffling.

The renunciation of aggressive modes of response to in-groupers is not absolute. Each society standardizes its own permissive patterns and differs from the next in the degree to which hostility may be expressed. In our society, we are allowed, for example, a limited right to compete for direct goals as by business manipulations, courtship, or sport. We may, also, kill in war-time, defensively, of course, and we have limited rights to derogate others, such as children by adults, women by men, those who cannot get work by those who cannot give it, and some politicians by other politicians. Those who have carried repression too far, by the way, are not able to make use of these opportunities to compete, and they appear as our neurotic persons.

It seems to be a matter of fact that socially permitted aggression is only rarely adequate to drain off the tensions excited by the limiting conditions of socialization in adult life. As a result, in-group members seem to live in a constant readiness for aggressive responses and are set to take advantage of any break in the barrier of social suppression, as for example, when after an economic depression, a guiltless and helpless President is howled, and aggressively voted, out of public life.

Aggressive responses are apparently powerfully excited by fear. Fear of punishment arouses hostile feelings toward the punishing person and, if strong enough, can lead to direct attack even under circumstances where the response is hopeless as a mode of defense. This is the case of the turning worm and the trapped animal. Intensive studies of individuals have repeatedly demonstrated the existence of the following mechanism: first, wishes to injure other people or the accomplishment of such injury; second, a fear of retaliation based on what has been done or intended; third, the appearance of new aggression against the wronged object. This vicious circle phenomenon is an example of psychological interaction and can lead to apparently reasonless hostile behavior toward those who are guilty only of being the objects of our hostility. The "image" of the ferocious out-grouper, unboundedly hostile toward us, is undoubtedly built up by this process as well as by the reality of damage incurred from such out-groupers.

"Race prejudice" appears as a mixed phenomenon in the context outlined above. It is apparently one of the patterned circumstances under which an animal may kill, injure, exploit, master, scorn, or derogate another animal or group of animals.[12] In examining these circumstances we will ask ourselves three questions: *What type of aggression* is mani-

[12] The presence of aggressive responses in race prejudice has been referred to regularly in one way and another by writers in the field. See, for example, W. I. Thomas, "The Psychology of Race Prejudice," *Am. J. Soc.*, 1904, IX, 609-11; E. B. Reuter, The American Race Problem (New York: T. Y. Crowell Co., 1927), p. 388; H. A. Miller, *Races, Nations and Classes* (Philadelphia: J. B. Lippincott Co., 1924), pp. 35-37; E. Faris, *op. cit.*, p. 320; R. E. Park and E. W. Burgess, *Introduction to the Science of Sociology* (2d ed.; Chicago: University of Chicago, 1924), p. 623.

fested in a variety of events commonly described by the term? *How is social permission* for aggressive behavior obtained? *How* are these animals or groups of animals *identified* which may be hated with impunity from in-group control?

Under the mixed designation "race prejudice" at least two types of aggressive responses can be indicated. The first is *direct aggression.* Here, the animal or group imposing the frustration and inciting the aggressive response is identified, and the aggressive responses are or can be efficient in controlling the frustrating group. The competition in Southern-town for "white man's" jobs is a case in point. Real animosity is manifested against the competing Negro workers, and political and other measures are taken to limit the frustrating competition of such Negroes.[13] Invasion of southern Negroes into northern employment and residence areas, as in East St. Louis and Chicago, has produced similar direct aggressive responses, including riotous attacks.[14] Real competition and frustration lead to real insecurity and out of this insecurity stems the aggression which is designed to restore a balanced situation. Actually in the case of "white man's" jobs, the Negro is pushed out of a "place" which he has formerly occupied and a new and narrower definition of his field of operations is created.

The second type of aggression which appears under the heading "race prejudice" we will call *displaced.* In this case, the inciting cause of the aggressive response is not the object attacked but some in-grouper who can not be attacked because of his value or the danger connected with fighting him. The aggressive response has been restrained or repressed, and it finds a substitute object. Such aggression seems to be the dynamic component of prejudice where the prejudiced individual has had no contact with the object of derogation. The assumption of displaced aggression seems necessary for the cases indicated by Bogardus and Horowitz[15] where groups who could have had no possible direct reason for it, show animosity. It is Freud's[16] indispensable work on the individual human being in our society which has made the knowledge of this mechanism available.

It appears that in the case of direct aggression there is always some displaced aggression accompanying it and adding additional force to the rational attack.[17] Justifiable aggressive responses seem to break the way for irrational and unjustifiable hostilities. This fact is illustrated in any war and probably accounts for the damnable character of the image of the enemy who is hated, and therefore feared, with disproportionate in-

[13] John Dollard, *op. cit.,* p. 127.
[14] Chicago Commission on Race Relations, *The Negro in Chicago* (Chicago: University of Chicago Press, 1922), pp. 1-71.
[15] E. S. Bogardus, *op. cit.,* p. 161; E. L. Horowitz, "The Development of Attitudes Toward the Negro," *Arch. Psychol.,* 1936, No. 194, 34-35.
[16] *Op. cit.,* p. 220.
[17] Dr. Neal E. Miller of The Institute of Human Relations, Yale University, first impressed this point on me during a discussion and suggested the correlative character of direct and displaced aggression.

tensity. The image of the incredibly hostile and amoral out-grouper is built up out of our own real antagonism plus our displaced aggression against him; these heightened aggressive responses raise through fear of retaliation the vision of the unbearably hostile enemy.[18]

In the case of repressed aggression, the covert responses which may accompany such aggressive tensions are worth noting. In dreams and fantasy, which are mildly expressive acts, the sullen in-grouper may reveal his hostilities. Hostile talk in the form of gossip frequently provides a permitted revenge within in-group life. All of these forms of aggression have satisfaction value and tend to reduce aggressive tension even though ever so slightly.[19] When, however, displaced aggression is permitted to overemphasize an attack which has a reality basis it finds its most easing release. This is the case, for instance, when it is just a Jew and not some other competitor who beats one out in a ticket line, smashes into one's automobile, or is the effective rival in love or status situations. The normal resentment toward an in-grouper is decisively overstressed. Probably also in the case of direct aggression toward an out-grouper, the aggressive response is more fully actualized because of the lack of tender ties and inhibitions toward him. This fact would tend to make prejudice responses more vehement even without the admixture of displaced aggression.

A second factor in our analysis is the problem of how social permission to be aggressive is achieved. We must recall the continuous struggle of the in-group to maintain a unified, cooperative life and to suppress disruptive manifestations of hostility. External taboos are internalized in the form of conscience, and these taboos must be escaped whenever aggressive tendencies are to be indulged. There are two situations which make such expression feasible, and one of them is group rivalry.[20]

When there is an actual threat to the dominance of the in-group, socially legitimated hostilities may appear.[21] This actual threat produces conflict, the interfering or invading group is identified, and the mores ratify defensive measures against the invader. An alternative form of rivalry is the attempt of a sub-group to change its defined status. This maneuver also may call out aggression which will be socially approved. The first case is exemplified by the hostile feelings of California farmers toward Japanese immigrants. "Anyone understands" why this type of conflict should lead to physical reprisals, local measures of limitation, and antagonistic feelings toward Japanese.[22] The attempt of Negroes to change their caste status and participate on equal terms in American

[18] See H. D. Lasswell, *Propaganda Technique in the World War* (New York: Alfred A. Knopf, 1927), pp. 77-101.

[19] S. Freud, *The Interpretation of Dreams* (New York: Macmillan Co., 1933), p. 140.

[20] Kimball Young has stressed the factor of economic competition. See his *Social Psychology* (New York: F. S. Crofts & Co., 1930), p. 474.

[21] Brown has a creative discussion of "habitat dominance" which should be related to Sumner's conception of the in-group. See Fred Brown, "A Sociopsychological Analysis of Race Prejudice," *J. Abnorm. & Soc. Psychol.*, 1932, XXVII, 365-367.

[22] J. F. Steiner, *The Japanese Invasion* (Chicago: A. C. McClorg & Co., 1917), pp. 68-92.

life would undoubtedly be greeted by a similar hostility; this phenomenon is most manifest at the present time in the South when the Negroes attempt to claim prerogatives which have not been traditionally assigned to them. Rivalry or conflict occurs, then, over the attempt of an alien or nonprivileged group to claim a share in specific goals or values whether they be economic, prestige or sexual. The in-group accepts rivalry manifestations as legitimate modes of keeping the outsider in his place and of maintaining the undiluted superiority of the prior occupants. In the case of group rivalry, we may note that the object drawing hostility is clearly identified and that this process is one of social conflict.[23] Such conflict processes appear to validate aggressive expression on the part of individuals otherwise bound.

Sheer traditional patterning, without active group rivalry, may also denote a despised group and permit unfriendly manifestations toward its members. This is the case where people are anti-Semitic who have never known any Jews or who "would not like to associate with Negroes," while having no direct conception of what such associations would mean. Such traditional patterning in reference to Negroes may be brought about through books which young children read which present "Little Black Sambo" in a ridiculous light, or through characters in radio sketches which show the Negro as a clown or a superstitious coward. The same thing may happen with reference to Jews, even by terms in common speech, as when people say "I tried to jew him down." Such experiences accumulate into patterned conceptions of Negroes and Jews and seem to offer these figures to living individuals as suitable objects of scorn and targets of hostility. The pattern itself is inherited socially and constitutes a break in the dikes built against individual aggressiveness. Such images of Jews and Negroes are created in a way similar to the "out-group image" that has been discussed earlier, although they are, of course, less highly charged. In the case of current German stereotypes, the image of the Jew, however, closely approximates that of the perennial out-grouper, as the *Sturmer* cartoons of Jews show. We must realize, nevertheless, that these experiences with "social patterns" are actual experiences, even though they do not involve direct contact with the object of the prejudice. We can say only that they do seem to permit hostility to be mobilized against certain groups of people. It is probably also true that inherited patterns are records of ancient rivalries and exist as the detritus of former group conflicts. In the case of current American antagonism against the image of the "Turk," one has no difficulty in surmising that the historical conflicts between Mohammedanism and Christianity have given rise to this image, and that the threatening conception of the Turk has been still more recently reinforced by the wartime propaganda against Turkey.

Either rivalry or traditional patterning creates a stereotyped image[24]

[23] R. E. Park and E. W. Burgess, *op. cit.*, pp. 574-662.
[24] Faris discusses this collective image. *Op. cit.*, p. 321.

in the minds of current members of society of a class of individuals who may be more or less painlessly detested. These images usually denote men who are to some degree released from the moral order which binds us and who are feared because "anything" may be expected of them; because they do not accept our mores, they are also regarded as inhuman beings to whom "anything" may be done. It is an effect of this stereotyping to produce the categorical treatment which is given those against whom prejudice is felt; individual discriminations tend to drop out and the differential treatment accorded to in-groupers is omitted. Within our own group we judge people according to their deserts and not according to standard classifications, but not so with the group against whom prejudiced stereotypes exist.

Our third consideration inquires into the means of identifying the object of "race prejudice." [25] It is highly important to be able to tell an out-grouper on sight so that one may not fall into the error of treating an in-group member with unseemly aggression. In-group taboos must be preserved and hence stigmata must be found which clearly designate those-to-be-hated-with-impunity. The pariah must give his warning cry if the Brahman is to preserve his purity from debasing contact. It has been widely noted that aggression may follow various lines of physical and cultural demarcation. Some of these, I hope the most important, will be indicated here. Among the most secure marks or signs which will expose a group to prejudice demarcations are race marks. These are physical stigmata such as hair form, skin color, eye fold, lip form, and the like. They are easy to identify and offer less possibility of confusing in-group and out-group members. Prejudice reactions based on these signs can be maintained for long periods of time, since it is simple to keep the out-group at arm's length by prohibiting sex contact or defining mixed bloods as belonging to the outcast group. Frequently also a language family structure, religion, standard of living, and work habits accompany these physical stigmata and make clear the reason for rivalry, as in the case of the Japanese in California. Since intermarriage tends to introduce such out-groupers into the circle of family relations and therefore into in-group contact, it is necessary to forbid marriage or sex contact if dominance is to be maintained by the superior group. Around the question of sex contact with "racial inferiors" center also rivalries and hostilities which are displaced from the in-group field.

Nations are also social units in terms of which hostile reactions can be expressed. Aggression seems to flow toward the borders of a nation with special readiness. It would seem that this group is the in-group which is especially designated by Sumner's use of the term. The word "nation" also corresponds closely with our use of the term "society" as

---

[25] This factor is vigorously indicated by Donald Young under the term "visibility." See his *American Minority Peoples* (New York: Harper & Brothers, 1932), p. 588.

a more or less self-contained, procreative group often symbolized in our day and age by tariff walls, passports, and the use of a common form of money. Franco-German rivalry has been in recent times a common symbol of such national rivalry, and there seems a special predisposition in these two groups (based on repeated conflict) to view one another as potential frustrators and to "hate" the enemy accordingly. Both real rivalry resulting from expected attack and displaced aggression serve to vitalize the evil image of the other nation. Language, membership in another state, and various traditional beliefs and aspirations identify the out-grouper. It should be noted that these marks, as compared with race marks, are transitory although they are exceedingly durable if viewed from any short-time perspective.

Nationality serves to distinguish still a further kind of out-group. This is the case where we have a differentiated member group existing in a nation, as just defined. The Irish in Britain, the Poles in old Russia, or the Jews in modern Germany meet these stipulations. Such groups are often marked out by language, sometimes by religion, sometimes by peculiarities of custom or costume, and usually by divergent group memories and aspirations. Hostilities flow across nationality lines also—both in the scorn, derogation and limitation of competition by the superior group and in the resentment and self-admiration of the minorities. If we call the Jews "Kikes," they also have a derogatory name for us, i.e., *Goyim*. If there is the pressure in our society to exclude Jews from recognition and appropriate social reward, they are, perforce, banded into a minority in which the members render mutual assistance to one another. This latter manifestation shocks many persons who do not need the pattern of anti-Semitism, or who need it only a little as a means of expressing their aggression, and such short-sighted individuals may come to believe that this in-group feeling among Jews is the cause and not a result of the antagonistic feeling against them.

Caste stratification is a form of social grouping along which prejudice reactions also form. I cannot agree with other workers[26] who think of the possibility of a caste system so firmly stabilized that no aggressive manifestations are needed to sustain it. What has been correctly analyzed seems to be that high, overt, physical aggression is not needed to maintain caste relations, but if contempt, loathing, scorn, and patronizing attitude are included as manifestations of hostility, I believe we must consider that caste permits of systematic resentment at least toward lower caste groups by their masters. Caste marks may include specialization of work, barriers to legitimate sexual congress, or unalterable lower status accompanied by a degree of social isolation. Sometimes race signs accompany caste, as in the Negro caste in America and to a certain degree in the Hindu caste system, i.e., the lighter the color the higher

---

[26] R. E. Park and E. W. Burgess, *op. cit.*, pp. 623-4; Faris, *op. cit.*, p. 320.

in general the caste.[27] In Hindu caste, also, arbitrary physical signs accompany high caste membership, i.e., the marks on the Brahman forehead.

Class marks too are forms of differentiation around which group hostilities may cluster. Such marks include standard of living, education, occupation, absence or presence of tendencies toward social mobility, location of residence, absence or presence of capital in large or small amounts, influence of distinguished ancestry and family, and the like. These factors can divide people crudely into class divisions. Stereotyped beliefs often exist as to members of other classes than one's own. For instance, middle-class and lower-class people sometimes believe that all upper-class people hold their position by virtue of superior competitive achievement, that upper-class people are happy and free of anxiety, since money brings these values, or that upper-class people are generally wasteful and not worth their social salt. The latter belief, for example, would tend to increase class antagonism and to direct both rational and displaced hostility toward upper-class people. Upper-class individuals, on the other hand, may come to believe that unemployed lower-class people do not want to work, that they are lazy, that they are on relief because they have refused to save their money, or that they are a poor biological stock which has been defeated in the race for social pre-eminence. The latter belief, for instance, would justify severe measures toward unemployed lower-class people such as those initiated in New Jersey last year when State relief was abruptly abandoned, certainly a hostile maneuver based on an incorrect perception of the realities of life for the unemployed. Class antagonism seems to be intrinsic to our society through the necessity of competing for an arbitrarily limited social income. Possibly such antagonisms are inevitable between the leaders and the led in any society; they will certainly be greater the tighter is the economy and the greater is the competition for income and status. Along class lines both direct and displaced aggression may flow; those who picture our industrial leaders as monsters of greed and selfishness are undoubtedly creating a stereotyped image which is engorged with displaced aggression, in addition to the direct aggression earned by their failure to lead our economy along more productive ways.

Slave marks also indicate a group differentiation which invites aggressive expression. These signs include an absence of "rights" on the part of the slaves, that is, of equivalence before the mores. Slaves have a categorical low status, can, like lower-caste members, be arbitrarily and aggressively treated, can be compelled to work, can be limited from intermarriage with the dominant group and may receive a small share of social rewards and status for their work. Race marks often accompany slave status, as in the case of our American Negro slaves, and occasionally class marks, such as relegation to menial occupations. Aggression on the part of slaves which would tend to change their status is vigorously

[27] Personally communicated by Dr. K. T. Behanen of The Institute of Human Relations, Yale University.

combated and exists under constant threat of suppression should it appear.

The physical and group differentiations just cited permit both rational and irrational aggression to be manifested; only in some cases can these manifestations be properly known as "race prejudice." "Race prejudice" seems, then, but a footnote to the wider consideration of the circumstances under which aggression may be expressed within a society. We will now turn to a series of concrete situations and use our analysis of the conditions of social hostility to study these situations.

I

First to be examined will be the case of the employing group in Little Steel against the Steel Workers' Organizing Committee of the CIO. The direct aggression mobilized in this conflict was undoubtedly high and expressed by the employees in striking, picketing, denunciations of their opponents, attempts to prevent strikebreakers from entering a plant, and the use of the "Sit-down." Employers, in turn, engaged in attempts to evict "Sit-down" strikers, denunciations of strike leaders and techniques, arousal of public sentiment against the strikers, injunctions against "Sit-downers," the use of professional strikebreakers, and, in some cases, the invocation of aid from the State with its troops and police to break up picketing. Forces were occasionally joined in riotous manifestations where physical fighting broke out. Undoubtedly irrational aggression was present on both sides. Those who referred to Lewis and other labor leaders as "Reds" were plainly venting irrational hostility on them; on the other hand, "the bosses" and "economic royalists" were decidedly partisan definitions of the hard-pressed employers and plant managers who had to "make profits" or get out.

The aggressive expressions already referred to are obviously not manifested because of social tradition but, on the contrary, as a result of inevitable rivalries between class groups in our society. Aggressions by the laboring group were undoubtedly mobilized due to insecurity states caused by past unemployment and wage cuts.

Identification takes place by means of class marks. The status of employer, manager, or minor administrative personnel identified one group; that of organized worker with his union card, slogans and views identified the other.

II

The Jews in America present a contrasting picture falling within the bounds of what is commonly called "race prejudice." Toward Jews both direct and displaced aggression is expressed. That there is displaced aggression is proved by the increased resentment which is felt when any affront is dealt out by a Jew. The nudge which would remind another passenger on a subway that he is stepping on one's foot may become a push if the offender is a Jew. The difference between the nudge and the push measures the increased hostility that may be expressed toward Jews.

Both ordinary rivalry and permissive tradition conspire to bring about hostile reactions toward Jews. In the first place, Jews compete in all three of our class groups and their competition is keenly felt; special skills acquired in the course of their severe competition for existence in western European society have made them particularly apt at the tasks of an interdependent and specialized economic organization. As traders, bankers, professionals, and intellectual people they are able to be very effective rivals for posts of highest skill, income and distinction. Because of their chronic marginal status in western European society, they have also become exceptionally mobile, feeling that only the highest posts and positions of control will give them even a minimum of security. They have been willing, therefore, by and large to make exceptional sacrifices to achieve pre-eminence, and these sacrifices are the measure of their special effectiveness as rivals. There is also, of course, the permissive tradition for anti-Semitism based on religious grounds. The animosity represented in anti-Semitism is keenly felt in such terms as "Kike" and "Sheeny," and it is not impossible that the term "Christ-killer" may become more familiar to us in this generation than it has been in recent times. It would seem that a rise in anti-Semitism in America is likely because of a steadily shrinking opportunity to earn a living for great numbers of non-Jewish Americans. If the Negroes do not suffice to provide a scapegoat for irrational antagonism, as they have so often in times past, the turn of the Jews may come. It is possible, of course, that a war or series of wars may avert this situation and direct toward an out-group image both the rational and the displaced aggression which is rising against those who seem to be responsible for current straitened conditions of life.

The Jews have maintained to some degree a physical type and are sometimes identifiable by racial signs. However, more common stigmata are those of language and religion. As already noted, Jews often identify themselves by in-group loyalties when they are not especially designated as objects of prejudice.

III

Quite a different problem is presented by the case of American Negro slaves of older time. We have already noted that Park believed race prejudice to be virtually nonexistent under the slave system. In terms of our concepts we would conclude that there was some, although a minimum of physical coercion. The slaves were actually controlled in part by a policing organization which made certain that they did not leave their owners or foregather for antisocial agitation. Even if the whipping of slaves was exceedingly rare, as was apparently the case, there was always the threat of physical punishment in the background, and the possibility even of death for the antisocial Negro. Whether or not we may say that there was "race prejudice" there certainly was some measure of direct aggression applied to the slaves. Displaced aggression seems also to have been present although again in a low degree. There was the humiliating name "nigger," some derogation through obvious patronage and stressing of absolute superiority on the part of the whites and in addition, frequently, the attribution of inhuman or brutish qualities to the slaves. These more subtle items must still be judged as aggression since they tended to damage the self-esteem of individual Negroes and to make Negroes seem in a class apart from the order of human beings. Even the occasional favorable comparison of Negroes with lower-class whites only stressed the implication of white superiority, since it was found so surprising that an individual Negro could turn out to be more acceptable than a white man. We should note here that the slave order is accompanied by a high degree of positive rapport based, of course, on the absolute submission and dependence of Negroes. Affection on the part of the white man necessarily went out to the serviceable, loyal, and self-sacrificing Negro whose works were so great and demands so little. Under these circumstances a minimum of force served to keep the status terraces intact.

Such hostility as existed toward Negroes of course was permitted and ratified by the traditional social order. It was occasionally incited directly by slave revolts, but these were sufficiently infrequent and ineffectual not to play a great role. The threat of status change in the future may be seen as a form of anticipated rivalry which justified the policing and punishing techniques employed. The whole state of affairs, on the basis of which social permission for slavery and aggression toward and derogation of slaves existed, was handed down from a state of group conflict and may be seen as a feature of rivalry between western European and African societies. Here as elsewhere "social permission" is the resultant of actual conflict in the past.

The Negro was, of course, identified by his race marks as well as status marks. Among the latter would be habituation to menial work, imperfect acquisition of American language, morals and customs, and psychological attitudes characteristic of a servile group.

IV

A final case will be that of a group of Germans who invaded a small American industrial town in the early twentieth century. Local whites largely drawn from the surrounding farms manifested considerable direct aggression toward the newcomers. Scornful and derogatory opinions were expressed about these Germans, and the native whites had a satisfying sense of superiority toward them. They were viewed as strangers and their actions suspiciously observed. There was also undoubtedly some displaced hostility. Some of the dissatisfactions which were experienced with the employment system in the town no doubt issued in aggression which was displaced on the foreigners.

The chief element in the permission to be aggressive against the Germans was rivalry for jobs and status in the local woodenware plants. The native whites felt definitely crowded for their jobs by the entering German groups and in case of bad times had a chance to blame the Germans who by their presence provided more competitors for the scarcer jobs. There seemed to be no traditional pattern of prejudice against Germans unless the skeletal suspicion of all out-groupers (always present) be invoked in this place.

The Germans, of course, were clearly recognizable by their nationality marks. They spoke German and attended German Catholic churches: they lived in a single region of the town at first and were more or less isolated from the native Americans, and their language was thought to be funny and was frequently parodied by the English-speaking adults and children in the town. Some of their food preferences, such as their sauerkraut and sausage, were objects of ridicule.

Such marks of identification are transitory as compared with race marks, for instance, but they still do tend to be maintained by the consolidating influence of the language group; singing and athletic societies in this little town testify to this day to the presence of a German cultural stream in the area.

In a previous discussion of "race prejudice" I [28] have offered a theory somewhat similar to the one above except that in the first case I was able to see only the irrational or displaced aggressive components of the reaction. Criticism from other students[29] has compelled me to see the role of actual rivalry in prejudice reactions and to attempt to do it more justice.

At the end, we might ask how such a theory of the role of hostility and fear in social life can be tested. One might indicate the following ways: first, "common experiences" which we have by virtue of the fact that we are participating in a society, are a part of its interactive mechanism and ourselves have felt the surges of affect which are here described. In case reference is made to such experience, however, the events must be specifically recorded. Second, special studies already made in the field are of great aid. Horowitz' work as well as the observations of Bogardus indicate that no mere rational theory of aggressive responses will serve our purpose. Third, the best source of confirmation must inevitably be the detailed, recorded life history, for it is only with the aid of such documents that one can judge disproportionate aggression accurately and distinguish sharply between direct and displaced hostility.

[28] *Op. cit.*, pp. 439-444.
[29] Dr. R. V. Bowers of the University of Rochester has protested most effectively on this score.

The latter studies await a generation of social psychologists better trained and more patient than our own.

Supplementary Bibliography

E. Franklin Frazier, *The Negro in the United States,* rev. ed. N. Y.: Macmillan, 1957.
   A detailed discussion of the history and present institutional structure of the American Negro community.

John Gillin, "Race Relations without Conflict: A Guatemalan Town." *American Journal of Sociology,* 1947, 53:337-343.
   A study of a relatively flexible social definition of race between Indians and Ladinos.

Everett C. Hughes and Helen M. Hughes, *Where Peoples Meet: Racial and Ethnic Frontiers.* Glencoe, Ill.: Free Press, 1952.
   A set of brilliant essays on social definition, status inconsistency, and acculturation.

Melvin M. Tumin, *Caste in a Peasant Society.* Princeton: Princeton U. Press, 1952.
   Another look at Guatemala as an illustration of the cross-cultural variations in caste, class, and race.

Ralph H. Turner and Samuel J. Surace, "Zoot-Suiters and Mexicans: Symbols in Crowd Behavior." *American Journal of Sociology,* 1956, 62:14-20. Reprinted in Kimball Young and Raymond W. Mack, *Principles of Sociology: A Reader in Theory and Research,* 2nd ed. N. Y.: American Book, 1962, pp. 13-20.
   A research report on the process of turning a social definition into an unambiguously unfavorable stereotype.

V Prejudice, Discrimination, and Stereotyping

Being a minority, then, consists of being defined as different and excluded from full participation in the culture. It need have nothing to do with race, or even with physical characteristics, although physical differences are a handy way of establishing and maintaining group boundaries. Let us look now at the process of establishing and maintaining group boundaries through prejudice, discrimination, and stereotyping.

Americans often use the words "prejudice" and "discrimination" interchangeably. However, there is a meaningful distinction which should be made between them. Indeed, the distinction is of such a nature that a person can be prejudiced against a minority without discriminating against that minority, and conversely, can discriminate against a minority without being prejudiced.

"Discrimination" refers to some overt act, some *behavior*, which selects some attribute (in this case, "race") for differential treatment. Thus one can discriminate for or against a minority. Popular usage, however, has come to mean that discrimination is *against* the minority. In any case, there is always some activity involved when there is discrimination. Someone is being excluded from entering a restaurant, or an occupation, or a neighborhood.

Not so with prejudice. Prejudice is an attitude. It is the subjective state of mind of the individual, and need not result in any overt behavior. If we must make arbitrary distinctions between the sciences, the end state of prejudice may be termed a psychological state of affairs, and the end state of discrimination a sociological state of affairs. (The arbitrary nature of this distinction becomes obvious with the confusion resulting from a consideration of the *causes* of prejudice and discrimination. Sociological

118

variables may explain how prejudice comes about, while psychological variables may be able to explain some aspects of discrimination.)

Prejudice, too, can be either positive or negative. But as is the case with discrimination, in popular usage it has come to mean negative attitudes about the out-group.

Now to return to the first point. It should be made clear how it is possible to be prejudiced without discriminating, and to discriminate without being prejudiced.

Prejudice Without Discrimination

There are two kinds of social situation in which the ordinary pattern of human behavior is one of being prejudiced but not discriminating. One occurs when the individual who is prejudiced has no opportunity to discriminate; the other occurs when the punishments for discriminating or the rewards for not doing so outweigh the desire to discriminate.

Under ordinary circumstances, the attitude of prejudice means that one would like to discriminate. But a Wyoming rancher may be anti-Semitic without indulging in any acts against the objects of his prejudice. If there are no Jews in his social environment, the opportunity to discriminate does not arise.

A New York department-store owner may be as anti-Semitic as the Wyoming rancher, have opportunities to discriminate every day against Jewish job applicants and Jewish customers, and choose not to do so. If he is aware that the State Commission Against Discrimination might investigate complaints against him if he discriminated in hiring and that his Jewish customers might take their business elsewhere if he openly expressed his anti-Semitic prejudices by discriminatory behavior, these potential punishments and rewards may lead him to refrain from translating attitude into action. He can remain prejudiced, but he will not discriminate because of the cost to him of doing so.

Discrimination Without Prejudice

A person may, on the other hand, be unprejudiced against a minority but choose to discriminate against them because of the rewards for discriminating or the punishments for failing to do so. Owners of barber-shops may tell you that they are not prejudiced against Negroes but they are afraid that if they allow Negroes to come to the shop for haircuts, white clients will become offended and leave. So they discriminate against Negroes. Undoubtedly there are such barbers, and in this instance we have a case of discrimination without prejudice.

The interesting thing is, however, that you hear the same story from owners of restaurants and motels, bowling alleys and golf courses, bars, and from doctors and dentists. A person's claim that he is free from prejudice while others have it cannot always be accepted at face value as evidence that an unprejudiced person has been pressured into discriminating. We must look to large groups, to the general public, and analyze this behavior within the context of Bierstedt's point about the power of the majority to set normative standards. When a Negro searches for an apartment in a section of town that is not inhabited by other Negroes, the white owner usually says that he himself is not prejudiced, and *would* rent but for the fact that others in the neighborhood would make life miserable for the Negro, and for him, the white owner. The owner is probably correct as to the behavioral consequences. But all the owners say the same thing, that it is not they but the neighbors. It becomes obvious to the outside observer that the range of owners is actually the neighbors. Thus while it is certainly *possible* to discriminate without being prejudiced, it is not often a likely combination. It is far more likely that the two go together. For this reason, perhaps, the terms are often used interchangeably.

Social Types and Stereotypes

Another popular reason landowners give for not selling to Negroes (or for arguing that their neighbors should not sell to Negroes) is that so doing will lessen property values. Sociologists and economists have done a considerable amount of research in this matter in the last decade. The results indicate that the decrease in property values from selling to Negroes is a myth *created by* the panic-stricken white residents. In their mistaken haste to sell "before the value falls any lower," they sell their property immediately at a loss, and move on. The facts now indicate that in nearly half the cases, property values actually *increase* in the long run in all-white residential areas after the sale of property to a Negro and that in most other cases, values remain relatively constant.

How do myths take hold? At least one answer is the process of stereotyping. The stereotype of the Negro in the United States is of one who is lazy, slovenly, happy-go-lucky, and irresponsible. The fact that many Negroes, partly as a consequence of discrimination, live in slum areas of the larger cities adds further credence to the myth of lower property values.

The classification of persons into social types is an everyday occurrence. When strangers first meet, they often try to obtain some clue to the "type" of person they are meeting. We use such terms as *cynic, idealist, bore, agreeable, lazy,* and *intellectual* to describe various social types. We are likely to make the judgment as to the type of person on the basis of the flimsiest evidence. But social typing is extremely important, and often necessary in modern urban society: we associate with so many different people in an ordinary day that we don't have the time to get to know each of them intimately.

Stereotyping is a special form of social typing. It is the classification of a whole category of persons as particular social types. Instead of responding to the individual characteristics of intellectuality or cynicism, American whites see intellectual Negroes and cynical Negroes. In a word, no matter what the Negro does, he is seen first of all as a Negro, and only secondarily as the perpetrator of the deed.

This is stereotyping. It is the use of a category as invariably relevant. How powerful the role of racial stereotyping is is indicated by the fact that whenever a Negro is not seen as conforming to the stereotype, he is still regarded not as a clean, meticulous, erudite, and responsible man but as an "exceptional Negro."

Stereotyping of this sort allows whites to justify, for example, exclusion of all Negroes from "their" residential area on the grounds that, if the "exceptional Negro" is allowed to come in, he will soon be followed by Negroes who are not exceptional, but "typical."

Stereotyping makes the task of discerning social types much easier. Recall that in the ordinary use of social types, the individual first waits for some clues in interaction before making a judgment. One need not wait for such a judgment if he has a ready-made stereotype filed away, to be pulled out at the proper time: Germans are precise, scientific, industrious, and militaristic; the Irish are pugnacious, quick-tempered, and heavy drinkers; etc., etc. These qualities (even if typical) cannot be transmitted through the genes, but are socially acquired. The fact that the stereotypes which help maintain group boundaries are socially learned is what thrusts the problem of minority, race, and ethnic relations into the province of sociological inquiry.

Related Readings

"Prejudice" is a report of a research project by Bruno Bettelheim and Morris Janowitz indicating that racial prejudice is related to frustration and insecurity. This suggests that intolerance may be partly a function of the stratification system; a sharp lowering of social status may intensify frustration and insecurity and hence exacerbate prejudice.

Bierstedt's thesis that majorities have social power is documented in the study of "Situational Patterning in Intergroup Relations," by Melvin L. Kohn and Robin M. Williams, Jr. The hypotheses presented at the end of this article offer an example of the goal of the social scientist which was discussed in Chapter I. One reason for studying minorities (or families, or industry) is to search for propositions or social laws which will hold true in any institutional context, generalizations not just about minorities, but about the human group.

A further example of exactly the point suggested by Kohn and Williams is found in "The Effects of Southern White Workers on Race Relations in Northern Plants," by Lewis M. Killian. When they find themselves in ambiguous circumstances, members of a group will accept the definition of the situation either of the majority or, if there is some group which has more power, of those who wield that power.

=============Bruno Bettelheim and Morris Janowitz

Prejudice

One of the central difficulties facing present-day society is the problem of how to deal with the dissatisfactions and aggressions which seem to be generated by man's close proximity to his fellow men. Since hostility is the force most disruptive to social living, the scientific analysis of group hostility should be one of the chief concerns of social scientists.

This article will report on a recent attempt to study the problem. Of the many tension areas within our society the particular one selected for our investigation was ethnic hostility—a polite term for racial prejudice. To learn whether hostility is actually the result of frustration, we needed a group of subjects with some common life experiences, and this we found in a sample group of Army veterans who had returned to civilian life. Since all had experienced comparable wartime deprivations, they offered an excellent opportunity to examine the hypothesis that the individual who suffers frustrations tries to restore his emotional balance by some form of hostile behavior. Our sample consisted in 150 former G.I.'s who were residents of Chicago and represented all economic classes.

Through intensive interviews in which free association was always encouraged these men were sounded out on their attitudes toward Negroes, Jews and other ethnic minorities. The interviewers were psychiatrically trained social workers experienced in public-opinion surveying. The wide range of personal data sought required long interviews which took from four to seven hours and in several cases were carried on in two sessions. The veterans themselves were offered ample opportunity to express personal views on many issues and to recount their wartime experiences before the matter of ethnic minorities was first mentioned. The extensive contents of these case histories were then subjected to statistical and content analysis, which allowed us to make quantitative statements about the degree and type of ethnic hostility, as well as about feelings of deprivation, anxiety and a range of other psychological and sociological characteristics.

In general the analysis did not bear out the hypothesis that frustration necessarily generates dissatisfaction or hostility. Army experiences which seemed to involve objective hardship (*e.g.*, combat, wounds, long service) did not in themselves appear to heighten dissatisfaction. For example, a 25-year-old infantry private first-class who had fought in North Africa, Italy and Germany, and who claimed, with some justification, that Army life had ruined his health, described his war experience as follows: "I was a teletype operator in Africa for three or four months, and wasn't in combat then, but all the rest of the time I was laying wire in combat areas. We lost 80 per cent of our company. I never thought I had a chance to come out of it alive. I came out lucky. I came out swell on money and passes. I didn't get any breaks, but to come back and be alive today is really swell." Another typical response was that of a 30-year-old staff sergeant who had once been demoted: "In my Army career I got a good break. I was made staff sergeant in 1942, only I was busted. But I made it back in another outfit. And I got to be mess sergeant, and mess sergeants eat good."

On the other hand, a number of veterans whose experiences, objectively speaking, had been relatively free of hardship, felt that they had had bad breaks. A typical response in this group was the following: "I wanted to get somewhere. But somebody else always got it. I deserved a rating and never got it. When they wanted somebody to repair something on a gun, I was always called because the other guy didn't know. That's why I never had no use for the Army. They never gave a rating to a person who should get one."

Thus a man's evaluation of his Army career in retrospect was largely independent of the actual deprivations experienced and depended mainly on his emotional attitude toward this experience in particular, and, one may add, to life experiences in general.

Our main purpose was to find out how all this affected ethnic intolerance. On the basis of an exploratory study we found it possible to classify the veterans in four types according to the degree of intolerance or tolerance toward a specific ethnic group. With respect to their attitude toward Jews, for example, the four types were: 1) the intensely anti-Semitic, who spontaneously expressed a desire for restrictive action against the Jews even before the question was raised; 2) the outspokenly anti-Semitic, whose hostility toward the Jews emerged only on direct question; 3) the stereotyped anti-Semitic, who merely expressed various stereotyped notions about the Jews, some of which were not necessarily unfavorable from the interviewee's point of view; 4) the tolerant, who revealed no elaborately stereotyped beliefs about the Jews.

The attitudes of the 150 veterans toward Jews and Negroes, graded

according to this scale, are summarized in the charts. . . . [See p. 127.]
There was a considerable difference in tolerance toward Jews and Negroes,
and the result showed that true ethnic tolerance, *i.e.*, a tolerance which
also included Negroes, was a rarity among these veterans.

Further analysis revealed that the men's actual Army experiences bore
little relation to their attitude toward ethnic groups, nor was there any
significant correlation between intolerance and age, education, religion,
political affiliation, income, social status or even the subjects' preferences
in newspapers, magazines or radio programs.

There was a close relation, however, between ethnic attitude and social
mobility, *i.e.*, a move up or down on the socio-economic scale, as compared with previous civilian employment, after the veteran was dis-
charged from the Army. Ethnic hostility proved to be most highly concentrated in the downwardly mobile group, while the pattern was significantly reversed for those who had risen in social position. Those who
had experienced no change were "middle-of-the-roaders." Over 70 per
cent of the stereotyped anti-Semites were found in this middle category;
on the other hand, most of the same group were in the outspokenly anti-
Negro category—a reflection of the fact that in this Northern urban industrial community it was "normal" to have stereotyped opinions about
the Jews and to be outspoken in hostility toward the Negro.

It turned out that while the men's actual Army experiences showed
no relation to intolerance, their subjective evaluations of those experiences definitely did. Those who felt they had had bad breaks in the Army
were the most inclined to be hostile toward Jews and Negroes. A further
study was made of the relation between intolerance and a readiness to
submit in general to controls by society. If, by and large, an individual
accepted social institutions, it seemed reasonable to assume that his acceptance implied a willingness to control his aggressive tendencies for
the sake of society. Or, to put it another way, one might say that those
men who felt that society was fulfilling its task in protecting them from
unavoidable frustrations were also the ones who were willing in return
to come to terms with society by controlling their aggressions.

Control, as a psychologist defines it, is the ability to store tension internally or to discharge it in socially constructive action rather than in
unwarranted hostile action. There are three sources from which such
control may come: 1) external or social pressure, 2) the superego, or the
unconscious "conscience," and 3) the ego, or rational self-control.

In actuality the three types of control are nearly always coexistent, and
in any individual control will depend in varying degrees on all three. In
the men studied, wherever control was present it was overwhelmingly
the result of a combination of external and superego control, with the
first dominant. Few men were also motivated significantly by rational
self-control, and in even fewer was this dominant over superego or external control. Hence a study of external (*i.e.*, societal) control was the
only one that promised to allow insight into the correlation between a

man's attitudes toward social control and the extent of his ethnic intolerance.

The analysis indicated that veterans who had stable religious convictions, regardless of the church they belonged to, tended to be the more tolerant. When the political party system was viewed as another norm-setting institution, a similar relationship of at least partial acceptance was found to be associated with tolerance. Whether the veteran was Democratic or Republican was in no way indicative of his attitude toward minorities. But the veteran who rejected or condemned both parties ("they're both crooks") tended to be the most hostile toward minorities.

To explore more fully this relationship between tolerance and control, the responses to other symbols of societal authority which signify external control of the individual also were investigated. The four institutions singled out as being most relevant were: the Veterans Administration, the political party system, the Federal government and the economic system, as defined by the subjects themselves. The analysis showed that only an insignificant percentage of the tolerant men rejected these institutions, while nearly half of the outspoken and intense anti-Semites did so. (This is in marked contrast to studies of certain types of college students, in whom radical rejection of authority is combined with liberalism toward minority groups.) In the case of the attitude toward the Negro, societal controls merely exercise a restraining influence; they do not suppress hostility but only make it less violent. The men who were strongly influenced by external controls were, in the majority, stereotyped and outspoken but not intense in their intolerance toward Negroes.

Thus it appears that in our society intolerance is related first to a lowering of social status, to feelings of frustration and insecurity. Next, the degree to which it finds open expression depends on the degree to which society approves or disapproves its expression. But the question remains: Why is ethnic hostility a favorite channel for discharging aggressive feelings?

Some of the reasons emerged, albeit indirectly, in an analysis of the stereotypes used by the veterans in describing minorities. With respect to the Jews, the composite pattern of stereotypes did not stress personally "obnoxious" characteristics; the members of this sample of veterans, predominantly of the lower class and lower-middle class, did not often characterize Jews as pushy, overbearing or loud. In the main the Jews were represented as a powerful, well-organized group which by inference threatened the subject. The most frequent assertion was that Jews were clannish, and that they helped one another. In the context in which this statement was made it almost invariably indicated that the veteran was decrying what he considered to be the unfair advantage in business and politics which accrued to the Jew who enjoyed greater social solidarity than himself.

On the other hand, the stereotypes used about the Negro stressed personally "offensive" characteristics—his alleged dirtiness and immorality. The intolerant white described the Negro as a threat to the white man's economic and social status, maintaining that the Negro was "forcing out the whites."

This situation differs from that in Germany under the National Socialists. In Germany the National Socialists applied the whole list of stereotypes to the Jews; their anti-Semitic propaganda greatly emphasized the Jews' alleged dirtiness and lack of morality. In the U. S., where more ethnic minorities are available as possible targets, a tendency has emerged to separate the stereotypes into two sets and to assign them to separate minority groups. One set of stereotypes indicates feelings of anxiety over the Jews' supposed power. The other set indicates anxieties aroused by the Negroes' (and the Mexicans') assumed ability to permit themselves the enjoyment of primitive, socially frowned upon forms of indulgence or gratification. The selection and use of stereotypes seems to depend on the needs of the person applying them. It also appears that the minority that shows the greater difference from the majority in physical characteristics, such as skin color, is used for projecting anxieties associated with dirt and sex desires, while the minority that is more like the majority in appearance becomes a symbol for anxieties concerning overpowering control.

Had the veterans' contacts with Jews and Negroes in the Army affected their attitudes? Detailed analysis showed little apparent effect; their stereotypes of Jews they had met in the Army were largely just an extension of civilian concepts. A typical comment: "There were only a few Jews in our outfit. One of them was a master sergeant. They did get up faster in rank and promotion, but we couldn't do anything about that. They would do favors for the officers and get promoted."

Even when the veteran felt a personal attachment and respect for an individual Jew in his outfit, the stereotype remained: "Oh, there was one Jew, Lieutenant Blank . . . almost forgot about him. He took pictures of me and a buddy of mine the day before he was killed. He was really white. At first I didn't like him and he knew it and picked on me at first, too. But then I changed my mind. He took care of his platoon all right. He saw to it that they had things they needed. They had cigarettes all the time when there weren't many around. That's the Jew in him— he was good at getting things like that. He'd do anything for his men and they'd do anything for him."

These and many similar statements support the hypothesis that the individual's stereotypes are not only vitally needed defense mechanisms but are persistent, even under the impact of such immediate and realistic experiences as service with Jews and Negroes under conditions of war. Once a stereotype is formed, it is not easily changed by experience.

It seems reasonable to assume that as long as anxiety and insecurity persists as a root of intolerance, the effort to dispel stereotyped thinking or feelings of ethnic hostility by rational propaganda is at best a half-measure. On an individual level only greater personal integration combined with social and economic security seem to offer hope for better interethnic relations. On the social level a change of climate is necessary. The veterans who accepted social controls and were more tolerant of other minorities were also less tolerant of the Negro, because discrimination against Negroes is more commonly condoned, both publicly and privately. This should lead, among other things, to additional efforts to change social practice in ways that will tangibly demonstrate that ethnic discrimination is contrary to the mores of society—a conviction which was very weak even among the more tolerant veterans.

1. Attitudes toward Jews of the group studied were classified in four categories. The bars indicate the percentage of the group in each category. Numbers on the bars indicate the number of men in each category.
2. Attitudes toward Negroes were similarly classified. There were about the same number of stereotyped anti-Negro as stereotyped anti-Semitic expressions. There was a larger number of outspoken anti-Negro expressions.

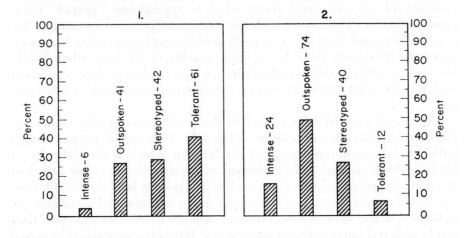

———————— Melvin L. Kohn and Robin M. Williams, Jr.

Situational Patterning in Intergroup Relations

There is now abundant research evidence of situational variability in intergroup behavior: an ever-accumulating body of research demonstrates that allegedly prejudiced persons act in a thoroughly egalitarian manner in situations where that is the socially prescribed mode of behavior, and that allegedly unprejudiced persons discriminate in situa-

Reprinted from *American Sociological Review*, Vol. 21, No. 2, April, 1956, pp. 164-174. By permission.

tions where they feel it is socially appropriate to do so.[1] It is also well known that patterns of "appropriateness" in intergroup behavior have been changing with increasing tempo in recent years. The unthinkable of a short time ago has in many areas of life become the commonplace of today. For a brief period the transition from unthinkable to commonplace arouses extreme emotional fervor; but as the new definition of the situation becomes the socially prescribed, the fervor soon diminishes. What was for the moment an "unpatterned" situation becomes, in Karl Mannheim's terms "built into the framework of the society."[2]

Unpatterned situations, in which definitions of appropriate conduct are in process of change, occur infrequently, and it is even more infrequent that they occur at the convenience of the research observer. Yet their importance for social change is likely to be great. In the multitude of unambiguous, patterned situations we have the raw material for documenting existing patterns of intergroup behavior. In the relatively rare unpatterned situations, however, we may hope to find important information concerning social change. It appears, for instance, that one of the most basic changes in race relations in the South is the growing uncertainty of all concerned about what is appropriate, "proper" intergroup behavior. This, along with the decreased personal interaction between whites and Negroes (especially middle- and upper-class Negroes), is compounded with the relative impersonality of the new urban South, to create an unprecedented situation in which further changes can occur with rapidity that would have been thought impossible only a few years ago.

The social scientist who wishes to study the processes by which unpatterned situations come to be defined by their participants is faced with several major problems, not the least of which is the difficulty of finding situations that can be studied systematically. It is not sufficient to create hypothetical situations and to ask people how they think they would behave in them. People's responses to hypothetical situations are patterned in the same way as ordinary opinion-items—for example, they can be ordered into unidimensional scales. But behavior studied in actual intergroup situations has not proven scalable; such behavior encompasses factors idiosyncratic to the particular situation, that cannot be foreseen by the person asked to predict his probable behavior.

Since hypothetical situations are not adequate, and actual unpatterned

---

[1] We shall define a situation as a series of interactions, located in space and time, and perceived by the participants as an *event:* in this usage "situation" is a delimiting term, cutting out from the flow of experience a particular series of inter-personal actions which are seen by the participants as a describable event, separable from preceding and succeeding events, constraining the participants to act in particular ways, and having its own unique consequences.

[2] "Although situations are in their very nature dynamic and unique, as soon as they become socialized—that is to say, built into the framework of society—they tend to become standardized to a certain extent. Thus we must distinguish between what is called patterned and unpatterned situations." [Karl Mannheim, *Men and Society in an Age of Reconstruction* (London: Kegan Paul, Trench, Trubner, and Co., 1940), p. 301.]

situations occur but rarely, the research worker is left with little choice but to initiate new situations. The procedure must be covert, for if the participants knew that the situations were created for research purposes, their definitions would be radically altered. Many problems are necessarily created, on both ethical and practical levels: the procedure involves a degree of manipulation; it poses a degree of danger to the participant observers and perhaps to other participants as well; it creates barriers to observation and interviewing. In the absence of preferable alternatives, however, we felt justified in initiating a series of forty-three situations in which we could observe and interview in a reasonably systematic fashion.

These situations were initiated in social contexts that were neither so intimate as automatically to exclude Negro participation, nor so functionally specific as to make acceptance of Negroes unproblematic. In particular, we focused on service establishments, such as restaurants and taverns. In white neighborhoods infrequently visited by Negroes, for example, we found many restaurant and tavern managers who had never faced a situation where it was necessary to decide whether or not to serve Negro patrons. Frequently the manager, when confronted by a Negro customer, was caught in a serious dilemma. On the one hand, it is illegal in the communities studied to refuse to serve Negroes. On the other hand, these establishments are often informal neighborhood social centers, and the managers' fears that their customers would object to the presence of Negroes militate against serving. For the manager who has no already established policy, this can be a highly problematic situation.

Within the restricted area in which it was possible to initiate situations —in public service establishments, voluntary organizations, and the like— we attempted to vary the situational conditions to the maximum degree possible. Even so, it must be recognized that our conclusions are based on studies in a very limited range of social institutions; e.g., we could not initiate new situations in industrial organizations or in schools. Thus we cannot assert that the present findings are directly applicable to institutions outside of the range studied. It seems probable, however, that though the processes by which unpatterned situations arise in these institutions are different from those of the present research, the processes by which they come to be defined by participants are similar.

Procedure

Before initiating a situation, we attempted to assess the usual patterns of behavior in the particular setting. The formality of our procedure depended on the social context: in formal organizations we were able to attend meetings, and to interview leaders and a sample of the membership; in service establishments we could only visit frequently enough to establish informal relationships with the staff and a few steady customers. Only after we felt we had some basis for predicting their probable reception, did we introduce Negro "stimulus-participants." White observers, located at strategic positions, observed the reactions of the principal participants.

Immediately after the Negroes withdrew from the scene, these "stimulus-participants" recorded the chronological sequence of events, and in addition filled out recording forms that had been designed to elicit their interpretations of the events. The white observers remained behind long enough to observe after-the-fact reactions, and then recorded their observations and interpretations in similar fashion. Thus we were able to secure the definitions held by non-participant observers and by Negro participants, as well as data on the overt behavior that occurred. In most cases we were also able to secure retrospective reports from white participants (organizational leaders, bartenders, customers) by formal interviewing procedures.

As an example of the procedure followed, let us consider one of these situations in some detail. A Negro couple (members of the research staff) entered a working-class tavern that was believed to discriminate. White observers, some of whom had visited the establishment frequently enough to be able to ask questions without arousing undue suspicion, were seated at strategic spots throughout the tavern. The following are the chronological accounts written by one of the Negro "stimulus participants" and one of the white observers:

The Report of the "Stimulus-Participant"

Entered at 10:15. People looked around, but we strode dauntlessly to table near fire. Most people seemed to look around, notice us, and comment. I needed a match and went to the couple in the first booth. The fellow had a lighter. I asked for a light. He replied eagerly, "Yes sir," and flicked his lighter for me. Testing the afternoon hunch on restrooms, I went to the men's room. As I passed the lady's room, the bartender blocked my way.

Bartender: "What did you say?"

Researcher: "How do you do. I didn't say anything. I'm looking for the men's room."

Bartender: "I'll show you." He leads me to the men's room, stands at the next urinal in a grand rapport gesture, and says confidently, "Now, mind you, I don't have anything against you people. I went to school with you folks and I've got a lot of friends among you. But some of my customers don't like to see you in here. Five or six of them have already complained to me and left. Now I can't have that. I hope you'll understand if I ask you to leave."

Researcher: "It's pretty hard to understand. I went to war for these people."

Bartender: "Yeah, I went to war too. But some of our people are funny. They don't like to see you in here. So I'll have to ask you to go." He leaves, and another young Caucasian enters. I am pretty damn upset.

I: "I suppose you're one of these fine people who wants me to leave."

He: "No, no, everybody's all right with me. What's the matter, you have some trouble?"

I: "You're damned tootin!" I go back to the table. Several people are entering and leaving for no apparent connected reason. No one comes to wait on us. Ten minutes later I go to the cigarette machine.

Bartender (stops me again): "Say, are you going to leave or are we going to have some trouble? Some of the boys are pretty hot. Now I suggest that you get out of here before something happens. We don't want your kind. Remember, I've told you." I go back to the table. L (the Negro girl) is enthusiastic. The waitress comes near to clean off a table and L calls her three times. Waitress tosses her head and leaves. Band returns from intermission and begins to play. After about five danceless numbers, three couples move out on floor. We go to dance. Here comes bartender again.

Bartender: "Now look, I've told you three times. War or no war, now you get out of here. We don't want you. I've got my customers to think of. Come on, get off the floor and get out of here before you have trouble."

I ask him to call the cops if there's trouble, but he demurs and shoves us off dance floor. We leave. Must have been a great side-show to the white customers and observers, but I'm boiling so much I could kill every white face. Decide I'm through with this stunt. As we left, a fellow standing in front of the cigarette machine said, "Hell, we're all Americans. I'm all for you." Bartender was just behind us, shepherding us out, and he stopped and asked, "What did you say?" I didn't hear the rest, but the fellow was evidently championing us in a weak but determined way. Maybe there is some hope for some white folks.

The Report of One of the White Observers

I arrived to find the bar crowded. D and J (observers) arrived, went through barroom to dancehall, just as I was climbing on a recently-vacated stool at the bar. Proprietor was serving a tray of drinks to blonde waitress. The bartender was standing akimbo at north end of the bar, waiting for electric mixer to finish stirring drink for him. Door opened, Negro researchers walked in, going through barroom and into hallway to dance floor. Blonde looked around at them, staring, then looked back at proprietor with her mouth open.

Proprietor (amazed): "Well, how do you like that!"

Bartender (turning): "What?"

Proprietor and Blonde (simultaneously): "Those two jigs that just walked through here." "Two colored people just went in."

Bartender (in surprise): "Where'd they go?"

Blonde: "Into the dance hall."
Enter Jane, a second waitress, from kitchen.

Jane: "I'm not going in there. What can we do? This never happened before. (To proprietor) "What'll we do? (Anguished) Do I *have* to serve them?"

Proprietor (peering through service peephole from bar to dance floor): "Let 'em sit."

Bartender: "Yes, stay away from them. I didn't see them. Where'd they go?"

Blonde: "They're at the table for six. What are we going to do?"

Jane: "I'm not going in there. This is awful."

Proprietor ducks under the lift-up gate at the end of the bar, takes a quick look into dance hall, then back under the gate board to his station behind the bar.

Proprietor: "Just let them sit." For the next several minutes, the proprietor inquired anxiously, from time to time, "What are they doing now? Did they go?" Each time he looked more amazed. Said to me, "Never in my time here did we have any of them at the bar." After a wait of perhaps 15 to 18 minutes:

Proprietor: "Well, I'm going to see that they leave." He took off apron, started to duck under the bar gate again, then said to bartender: "You better go in and get them out of there. I don't think I should go, because my name's on the license . . . if there's any trouble."

Schoolteacher (sitting with husband at the bar): "How can you get them to leave? (then to me) She was an attractive little thing, wasn't she?"

Proprietor (again): "I wish they'd go. (Then to blonde waitress) Are any of your customers leaving?"

Blonde: "A couple, but I think they were leaving anyway. They'd asked for their check. Others are looking around at them, and they're all talking about it . . . it gives me the creeps to have to walk in there, and know they're staring at me, expecting me to come over and wait on them."

Jane (to me): "We never had colored people here. This is the first couple that ever went in there. (Shrugging) I'm just not going in. What a time they picked to come! Saturday night—our busiest time! Why didn't they make it some week night?—there aren't so many people here.

By this time the bartender had taken off his apron, left the barroom, and a few minutes later returned and went directly into the men's room, followed by the Negro researcher.

Proprietor (after a minute or so): "Where did the bartender go?"

Jane: "In the men's room."

Teacher: "They've been in there quite a while."

Proprietor (ducking under gate, apron and all): "I'd better see what's going on. He may have a knife." Goes and peers through four inch opening, as he holds the door ajar. Returns. "They're o.k." Bartender returned to bar, researcher to the dance hall.

Bartender: "He wanted to give me an argument. Said he was a veteran."

Proprietor: "They all have something like that to say, I guess. I want them to get out. What did he say?"

Bartender: "He said yes."

I (turning to man on stool beside me): "This is some situation, isn't it?"

Man (venomously): "It stinks!"

Blonde (watching Negroes through doorway): "He's sitting down. It's a good thing the orchestra is having intermission."

Proprietor: "Yes, I suppose they'd be dancing."

Bartender: "That looks like that Robeson stuff."

Waitress: "I can't think of any time I've seen colored people in here."

Bartender: "Stay away from them. Don't look at them. Don't let them catch your eye." Waitress departs for dance hall again.

Youth (at bar, to proprietor): "Maybe you can get a date." Proprietor snorted, ready to blow his top.

Teacher: "He's getting cigarettes."

Bartender: "Where is he?"

Jane: "At the cigarette machine."

Bartender (apron and all, under the bar gate again): "I'll tell him to get going." Went and spoke to researcher, then back to bar. "They'll leave, I think. I told him there were a couple of fellows were going to see about it, if they didn't." Just about this time the orchestra's intermission was over; they returned to the bandstand.

Proprietor: "There goes the band. I suppose they'll start to dance now. I wish I'd thought to hold up the orchestra until they got out of here. (To blonde) Watch them now. (To Jane) Jane, get me a sandwich, will you?"

Teacher: "You're in a tough spot, aren't you? Are you going to serve them?"

Proprietor: "No."

Bartender: "We'll have to put them out for causing a disturbance."

Blonde: "Four of my couples have left."

Proprietor: "That does it! Go in and get them out of there, NOW!"

Bartender went into dancehall, one man followed him, and three or four other men gathered around. The Negro researchers walked out through the bar. Bartender went back behind the bar and the man resumed his seat.

Proprietor (who had followed, with his eyes, the Negro girl as she left): "Did you see the cute little smile she had on?"

Bartender: "Well, that buck thinks he's tough, I guess. Robeson stuff."

Customer: "You could have served them. They got rights!"

Bartender: "You want to make something of it? Are you with them?"

Customer: "No, I'm not with them. They got a right to have a drink. You all stink."

Bartender (threateningly): "Pick up your change and drift. You want to drink with them? Go on down to the C.D. bar. Lots of them there." Man picked up his change and stalked to door, mumbling.

Proprietor: "What the hell do you suppose is the matter with him? He's not drunk."

Teacher: "Maybe he's one of those people who has Negro friends."

Another customer: "In Germany those black bastards got everything they wanted. Excuse me, ma'm. (To teacher) Two or three of them would come along and take a white soldier's girl right away from him. I hate their guts. They want to stay away from me. I just wish you'd told me, I could have thrown them out. . . ."

Proprietor: "You can if they come back. You can throw out their whole gang. They've probably gone to get the bunch. I don't think they came in just to get a drink."

Teacher's husband: "No, I think they came here deliberately to get served or make trouble. If they dropped in for a drink, they would have left when the bartender talked to him. I think this must be planned somehow."

Bartender: "Yeah, Robeson stuff. Spooks! Little Peekskill, they wanted to make out of this place."

Teacher: "I feel sorry for them. (To me) She looked like a real nice girl. I have to teach my children tolerance and things like that. . . ."

Defining Unpatterned Situations

In these situations, it appeared that the participants attempted to achieve cognitive clarity by striving to assimilate the situation to their past actual or vicarious experience, that is, to categorize it as one of a type of situation with which they knew how to cope. The process, of course, was rarely as rational or as purposive as this formulation would imply. Yet the behavior manifested in these situations can be interpreted as an attempt to see a socially unstructured situation in terms of one or possibly even of several alternative socially acceptable structures. For example, in the illustration above, the bartender and waitress perceived the situation as one that could be categorized in either of two ways:

1. Here are two Negro out-of-towners who do not realize they are not welcome here.
2. Here are a couple of troublemakers who are trying to create another Peekskill riot here.

The importance of being able to categorize the situation is suggested by their dilemma. If the situation were the first type, they could expect the Negroes to leave when asked politely. If the situation were the second type, they could expect resistance to such a request—the Negroes might cause an immediate disturbance, "come back with their gang," or file suit for violation of the State Civil Rights Statute.

In this example two reasonably clear-cut alternative definitions of the situation were possible. At the extreme, even this degree of structure was missing. Here participants reacted by confusion: either the situation was so totally outside the range of their experience, or it partook of so wide a variety of possible definitions, that these participants were initially unable to see any structure to the situation at all.

It seems useful to distinguish these two possible reactions to an un-patterned situation. In one, the individual is confused about what behavior to expect from others and what is appropriate action to take himself. In the other, he has reasonably definite, but contradictory, expectations of how others will act and how he himself should act. These two types of reaction differ in degree only, and it is difficult to distinguish them in some concrete situations. Nevertheless, the distinction is useful because the probable future actions of the person whose orientation is primarily marked by *confusion* are different from the probable future actions of the person whose orientation is primarily marked by *contradiction*.[3]

In the situations studied, the participants who were primarily *confused* actively sought cues from others' behavior that could be useful in clarifying their own definitions of the situation. Where formal leadership roles existed, other participants turned to the presumed leaders for clarification. Members of organizations almost invariably took their cues from the presiding officers—if the club president greeted a Negro lecturer warmly, the members were likely to listen to his speech attentively. Similarly, waitresses and bartenders studied the reactions of owners and managers for hints as to whether or not service to Negro patrons was in order.

But in the nature of the case it most often happened that the people in leadership positions were themselves confused; for them the situation was not structured enough even to suggest where to turn for clarification. In consequence, action on the part of *any* participant became disproportionately important in determining their definitions. Expressions of discomfiture on the part of *any* customer were taken as an index that "the customers" objected to the presence of Negroes. Direct intervention on the part of a customer almost invariably proved decisive. If any white undertook to act as intermediary for a Negro patron, by ordering a drink for him, or buying him a drink, the bartender served the Negro. Even if the white were a disheveled drunk with a friendliness born of liquor, the bartender was likely to take his action as an index that the customers did not object to his serving Negroes. The possibility that the drunk's attitudes were atypical of the attitudes of other customers was for the moment ignored.

Initial behavioral cues, of course, could be variously interpreted. The cues themselves were often ambiguous, allowing of several alternative interpretations even to similarly situated persons. Furthermore, some persons seemed to be more sensitive to nuances of behavior than were others, for reasons that did not seem related to their roles in the situation. However, the most important factor in how participants interpreted be-

[3] We are at the moment concerned only with situations where the individual participants are initially unable to achieve consistent workable definitions of the situation. Situations where two or more participants have *different* definitions of the situation will be considered later. In this latter case each participant has a consistent definition, and the problem is how definitions are *modified,* rather than how unstructured situations become defined.

havioral cues appeared rather clearly to be their prestige-status in the situation. Negro participants were typically far less secure in these situations than were whites. They were more likely to be sensitive to minimal cues, and to interpret cues as indices of prejudice or lack of prejudice. A casual reference by a white to "you people" was frequently taken by Negro participants as an indication that the white was categorizing them as Negroes, and was therefore prejudiced. The white would have no idea that his statement—often made in the form of a testimonial meant to communicate good will—was so interpreted.

Finally, in some situations there were almost literally no appropriate behavioral cues to guide the confused participant. A white woman who taught a theatrical make-up class was thrown into a flurry of aimless excitement for almost ten minutes when a Negro girl who unexpectedly attended the practice session of her class asked her for an appropriate shade of face powder. She knew which shade would be best, but she had no idea of how to react to having a Negro girl attend the class. The reactions of the other members of the class did not help to resolve her confusion, and there were no other adults present. The consequence was that she persisted in her confusion for several minutes.

These interpretations apply only when the impediment to a satisfactory definition of the situation is confusion or ambiguity. Where the problem is that two alternative definitions are applicable to the situation (i.e., where the problem is one of *contradiction* or *conflict*), different behavioral consequences ensue. Usually, in such situations, it is possible to resolve the conflict by *exempting* the particular situation from all but one definition—in effect, by assigning one definition of the situation a higher priority than that accorded to the others. Two forms of exemption were apparent in the observed situations:

1. A particular *type of event* can be exempted from a more general definition: for example, a restaurant-owner, who in other contexts does not discriminate against Negroes, does discriminate against them in his restaurant because he feels that "business" takes precedence over other values.

2. A particular *individual* can be exempted in a range of situations: for example, a white treats a particular Negro as "different from other Negroes" and therefore acceptable in contexts where other Negroes would be unwelcome. One bar-owner served former high school classmates, although he refused to serve other Negroes.[4]

On occasion, however, neither of the alternative definitions can be avoided—the situation constrains the participants to act on the basis of both definitions simultaneously. For example, at a dinner-meeting ten-

---

[4] Calling this behavior exemption does not necessarily mean that the bar-owner perceived his action as making an exception of these particular Negroes; he might have seen it simply as serving friends. Nevertheless the *effect* of his action is exemption, whether he consciously perceives it that way or not, because from the observer's point of view he is acting differently from the way he would act toward other Negroes.

dered to party workers of a major political party, many of the white participants wished to avoid eating with the Negro party-workers, but at the same time did not wish to rebuff them and risk losing Negro votes. Their common mode of behavior was to act in a friendly fashion toward these Negroes, but not to sit at the same tables with them. When all other tables were fully occupied, some of the whites waited for new tables to be set up, rather than sitting at tables already partly occupied by Negroes. This we interpret to be a common mode of behavior by which the whites attempted to act in partial conformity to both definitions of the situation—the definition that this was a solidary group of party members, and the definition that this was an inter-racial situation. They had to eat at tables adjoining the tables at which Negroes were seated, but they did not have to eat with Negroes. Although they rebuffed these Negroes, they did not entirely alienate them. It appears that when an individual is constrained to act on the basis of two or more mutually incompatible definitions of the situation, he will seek a compromise solution by which he deviates as little as possible from the action appropriate to each of these definitions.

Finally, there are situations in which the alternative definitions cannot be reconciled. For example, the dilemma of the bartender who does not know whether or not to serve Negroes and feels: if I serve them, the white customers will object; if I don't, they may create a disturbance. In such a situation, the typical response is withdrawal from the situation, as when the bartender "looks the other way" or the prejudiced club-member leaves upon discovering that the lecturer of the evening is Negro. But withdrawal is not always possible. The bartender may "look the other way" when a Negro patron enters, but he cannot continue to do so when the Negro walks up to the bar directly in front of him. Then the result is usually an inconsistent series of actions, marked by a good deal of wavering. The bartender may begin to serve the Negro quite cordially, then appears to be unwilling to serve the Negro, then once again is quite cordial. If an observer asks him about it, he will be quite frank in stating that he feels impelled first towards one course of behavior, then towards the other. This inconsistent behavior may perseverate for an extraordinarily long time, until the individual is finally able (often for apparent irrelevant reasons) to give one or the other definition a higher priority.

Modification of Definitions

Although these covertly initiated situations enabled us to study the processes by which unpatterned situations are initially defined, they did not provide adequate data on the processes by which initial definitions are modified in interaction. The very conditions required for initiating unpatterned situations precluded our continued observation once the single event had transpired. To study the processes of change, it was necessary to find naturally occurring situations, or series of situations, in which changes of definition were taking place. We wanted to be able to observe a group of people engaged in a continuing series of situations; to interview these people at regular intervals, in order to elicit their interpretations of each situation; and to secure data about their behavior in past situations that might prove useful in interpreting their present behavior. Our procedure was to search for a group that had formed in response to a particular problem in which all were interested. We found the group we sought engaged in a rather dramatic endeavor—a civil rights law suit.

Two Negro men had been refused service in a country tavern, in the presence of Negro waiters. The men left the tavern quietly in spite of the fact that one of the waiters quit his job in protest. Two days later, the wife of one of these men telephoned the president of the local chapter of the National Association for the Advancement of Colored People, who in turn suggested that the men re-visit the tavern in the company of the executive committee of the NAACP chapter.[5] A first visit was, from their point of view, ineffectual: the proprietor was absent, and his son equivocated. A second trip found the proprietor prepared. After protesting his own lack of prejudice, he argued that he could not risk a boycott by white customers. When this argument fell on unresponsive ears —the NAACP president waved a copy of the State Anti-Discrimination Statute in his face—he argued that he didn't care what the law said, he simply was not going to serve Negroes. Then ensued a long debate on whether or not minority groups should insist on service where they were not wanted, ending in an impasse.

The NAACP leaders attempted, without success, to interest the local district attorney in taking court action. Then, with tacit approval by the prospective plaintiffs, they established contact with the state NAACP legal department. Initial plans for court action were made, followed by a delay of several months before the case was tried. The period of quiessence was marked by the plaintiffs' loss of interest in the case.

The weekend preceding the case brought feverish activity on the part of the NAACP lawyer and two members of the executive committee, first in questioning witnesses, and later in detailed "cross-examination" of one waiter who reported that he would testify for the defense. Other members of the executive committee, the second waiter, and another participant-observer were brought in during the last stages of this examination—at a time of open conflict, with the lawyer and NAACP president accusing the dissident waiter of "selling out the race." The incident ended in excited denunciation of the "turncoat" by the waiter who had quit his job in protest against discrimination.

To this point, the plaintiffs had not participated. They, and their wives,

---

[5] Robert B. Johnson, a member of the Cornell research staff, attended these conferences in his role as a member of the NAACP executive committee. Johnson, and others of us who were involved in later situations, filled out detailed research reports after each period of observation.

joined the group at a meeting that evening, called to plan strategy for the trial. The first order of business was a dramatic account of the afternoon's activities. Then the lawyer interrupted abruptly to ask for his clients' minimum demands. He added that cash settlements generally weren't very high in this type of case. The plaintiffs said nothing. But the president jumped in to aver that "these men aren't in this for cash. They're in it for the principle of the thing!" He paid tribute to "men who have the guts to stick it out." A member of the executive committee spoke about the effects that this case would have on the Negro community generally. Others spoke *for* the plaintiffs. One asked that the men be given a chance to speak for themselves—but he too congratulated them "for having the courage to go through with the case *for the principle of it!*"

The lawyer asked the plaintiffs directly: "How do you feel about this?" A long silence. Then one plaintiff answered. He said that he and his friend were fighting for the good of the race. He said that he hoped this action would benefit the Negro community as a whole. He said that he believed in *action* to improve the position of Negroes. He added that he was a poor man.

At once the president exclaimed that he too was a poor man, but that even if it meant losing his job, he would stick it through. There was no further ambiguity about money. The lawyer congratulated the plaintiffs for not seeking monetary retribution, and then asked the group as a whole for a statement of minimal demands. Almost all members of the group spoke up now, including the heretofore-silent plaintiffs and their wives. All agreed to a policy enunciated by the president: the demands were to be a full public apology, together with a statement by the proprietor that he would not discriminate in the future.

Succeeding events need not be described in detail here. The defendant, upon pressure from the judge, settled the case in court on the plaintiffs' terms.

For present purposes, the most striking aspect of this series of events was the radical change in the behavior of the plaintiffs. Their behavior in the discriminatory situation had been passive; upon their return to the community they did nothing to institute action against the bar-owner. Personality studies of the two men, based on detailed life history data, indicate that this passive acceptance of the intergroup relations status-quo was entirely in keeping with their behavior in other situations. In fact, they had but a few weeks before this incident predicted (in response to a questionnaire-interview administered to a cross-section of the Negro community) that in such a situation they would leave the establishment without saying anything, and take no further action. Yet in the course of these situations the positive or negative evaluation of their behavior by a militant group of Negro leaders became important to their own evaluations of their behavior; their self-conceptions changed to those of "race men," or fighters for the good of the Negro community;

their definitions of the discriminatory incident and of their own subsequent behavior were enlarged to include an evaluation of how these actions affected other Negroes in the city; and their passive behavior was transformed into militancy.

In broadest outline, this change can be viewed as the consequence of a long series of successive redefinitions of the situations in which they participated. When the bartender refused to serve them, they quickly developed an initial definition on the basis of which they hurriedly left the tavern. Their definition of this original situation held important consequences for their behavior in subsequent situations. Although each of these, too, contained idiosyncratic elements, there was a significant degree of continuity in their definitions of succeeding situations. The plaintiffs did not define each situation anew, solely on the basis of its idiosyncratic elements, but developed their definitions of particular situations from their definitions of preceding situations. It was as if they tried on their previous definitions for fit, modified them to meet the exigencies of the present, then modified them anew as these exigencies changed. Since new elements entered these situations almost continuously, this process never ceased. In the end, a revolution in definition and in behavior had been produced. But seen as a step-by-step process, this "revolution" was never more than a minor change in a preceding definition, with its appropriate behavioral consequences.[6]

The most readily apparent change in the plaintiffs' orientation was their coming to depend upon the NAACP leaders as referents.[7] But why did the NAACP come to play this role?

It would seem that the plaintiffs must have been predisposed, at least to a limited degree, to see the NAACP definition of the situation as legitimate—even if not the only legitimate definition. It seems further that they must have felt constrained to co-operate with the NAACP leaders, provided that this did not entail a major commitment of time. Otherwise, the president could not have prevailed on them to participate even to the extent of a discussion with the tavern proprietor. Once they were involved in the NAACP activities, several factors conspired to commit

[6] On the basis of one case study, we certainly cannot generalize that this is always the process. One observation can, however, be made: in none of the situations studied (either in this series, or in the situations we initiated for our study of unpatterned situations) did direct and overt conflict bring about a change of definition. Wherever two participants with opposing definitions attempted to argue each other into changing their definitions, an impasse resulted. In fact, overt conflict served only to strengthen the participants' commitment to their original positions. Of course, a participant was on occasion forced to accede to another's demands; but this brought no lasting change in definition, merely resentful compliance.

[7] For purposes of analysis and prediction, it is not necessary that the individual actor be aware of the role his referents play in defining the situation. "Reference group" may be used as an intervening variable in situational analysis if this provides a more adequate explanation of behavior than do alternative methods of analysis. (We may posit that an individual acts as if he used certain referents in defining the situation.) In the present research, however, this was not necessary: the plaintiffs came to be very much aware of the major role played by the NAACP leaders in their definitions of the situations.

them more and more firmly to the NAACP group: the NAACP leaders could and did shame them by holding out the threat that they would be regarded by the community as "quitters"; at the same time, these leaders were able to argue the logic of their philosophy, and to demonstrate by their own action how their philosophy worked in practice; continued group enterprise brought the emotional satisfactions of group *esprit de corps* and of participation in "something important"; finally the plaintiffs' behavior brought approbation from some other members of the Negro community.

At the same time, other pressures generated by the situations served to bring the plaintiffs' definitions into harmony with that of the NAACP leaders. Perhaps the most important event here was the "cross-examination" of the dissident waiter. The NAACP leaders could not have asked for a more compelling demonstration that the point at issue was a moral principle, with all other considerations irrelevant. A clear dichotomy was drawn between those who "sell out the race" and those who "fight for the race." If the dissident waiter stood as the symbol of selling out, his courageous colleague embodied the virtues of the man of principle. In the face of his sacrifice of his job, who could undertake to do less?

Even then, the plaintiffs were not fully committed. Interviews with the major participants indicate that the men hoped to be able to fight for the race and exact some monetary retribution as well. But this was exactly what the NAACP leaders wished to avoid; they did not want it said that the case was merely a matter of Negroes "trying to con a white man out of his money." It had to be a matter of principle, and principle alone! Here the introduction of new information enabled the plaintiffs to redefine the situation: if cash awards were generally not very high in these cases, it was considerably easier to forego the possibility of a windfall. Even so, foregoing cash was not easy. It took some time for a plaintiff to make the offer, and even then his offer was hardly forthright. His statement did, however, allow of slight reinterpretation; once this occurred, the men were hardly in a position to backtrack.

For the plaintiffs, acceptance of the NAACP position brought a change in self-conception: they now thought of themselves as "race men." It also brought a rewriting of history, to bring all past events into line with their present definition. If you ask them now, they will tell you that their orientation has not changed. They are, and always have been, militant. From the very beginning, their one interest has been to fight discrimination. That is why they were so quick to bring the NAACP into the case.

In spite of this, their change in self-conception has not been productive of other militant action. Although they may continue to think of themselves as "race men," and although they may behave like "race men" in any future situation in which they are directly refused service, they have given no evidence that they are likely to carry out the logical implications of the "race man" role and engage in a wider range of interracial activities on behalf of the Negro community. Stated otherwise, it would appear that an individual who uses a particular reference group in defining a particular type of situation will not necessarily use that reference group in defining other types of situations. This is perfectly consistent with the general observation that people do not necessarily behave consistently in different types of situations.

Summary

We have in this report endeavored to interpret the processes by which participants define unpatterned intergroup situations, and the processes by which definitions are in turn modified over the course of time. We recognize that the research has been conducted within a very limited range of institutional contexts; we further recognize that the social constraints operating within other contexts may be quite different. Nevertheless, we believe it likely that the present interpretation is applicable to situations arising in other social contexts; for that reason, we present this summary in the form of hypotheses amenable to testing in a broad range of institutional contexts.

1. Unpatterned Situations

Ambiguous or Confused Definitions. When an individual is constrained to act but feels that he cannot predict the consequences of his own or other participants' behavior, his response to the situation will be to seek cues from other participants' behavior that can be used as indices of their definition of the situation. Where he can turn to persons in formal leadership roles, he will do so; but where this is not possible, the behavior of *any* other participant will be utilized as an index of how "other participants" define the situation. Where there are no appropriate behavioral cues available, the confused participant will tend to perseverate in his confusion until new action intervenes to structure the situation.

Contradiction or Conflict of Definition. When an individual is constrained to act but feels that two or more distinct definitions (each with its appropriate behavioral imperatives) are applicable to the situation, he will first attempt to resolve the conflict by exemption, i.e., by assigning one definition a higher priority than that accorded to others. (This can be done either by exempting a particular type of event or a particular person from a more general definition.) Where this is not possible, he will attempt to achieve a compromise solution by which he can act in partial conformity to both (or all) definitions of the situation. When even this is not possible, he will seek to withdraw from the situation, unless otherwise constrained. If constrained, he will behave inconsistently, wavering between the two alternative definitions, until new action intervenes to structure the situation.

2. Modification of Definitions

Direct, overt interpersonal conflict is not likely to change either party's definition of the situation; its principal effect is likely to be the reinforce-

ment of each combatant's values. Major changes of definition are more
likely to be the result of a series of minor redefinitions, each dependent
upon one or more of the following:

Changed Referents. When an individual's experience in a situation (or
in a series of situations) leads to the reinforcement of particular reference groups, or to the internalization of new reference groups, his ideas
of how he should act in the situation will be modified to conform to his
modified self-conception.

Expectations of Consequences. When an individual's experience in a
situation (or in a series of situations) leads to modification of his expectations of the consequences of his behavior, his ideas of how he
should act in the situation will be modified to meet his new expectations
of these consequences.

Similarly, when an individual's experience in a situation (or in a series
of situations) leads to the modification of his expectations of how other
participants will behave, his ideas of how he should act in the situation
will be modified to meet his new expectations of their behavior.

=========Lewis M. Killian

The Effects of Southern White Workers
on Race Relations in Northern Plants

This analysis of the effects of southern white workers on race relations
in northern industrial plants is part of a larger study of the adjustment
of these migrants to northern, urban ways, as found in Chicago. The relationships of the southern whites to Negroes in the plants, and their
effects on the policies of management, must be viewed in the context of
the position of the so-called "hillbillies" themselves in the community
and in industry.

Prior to the concentration of large numbers of migrants, both white and
Negro, in defense centers during World War II, students of race relations
evinced only a casual interest in the effects of southern white migration
on race relations in other parts of the country. For example, Donald
Young, in his *American Minority Peoples*, dismissed the movement of native white migrants as relatively unimportant, saying:

> "The migrations of the old stock do not seriously concern us, except as
> their movement from the country to the city has brought intolerant pro-
> vincials into contact with minorities whom they cannot understand." [1]

[1] New York: Harper and Brothers, 1932, p. 41.

Reprinted by permission of *American Sociological Review*, Vol. 17, June, 1952, pp. 327-
331. Copyright, 1952, American Sociological Association. All rights reserved.

Erdmann D. Beynon, in a paper on "hillbilly labor" in Michigan, made only passing reference to the attitudes and behavior of the southern whites towards Negroes.[2] His brief comment exemplifies the assumption that the migrant reacts to contacts with Negroes in a new situation in the same manner that he did in the South:

> Migration to northern industrial cities has brought the southern whites into new situations for which they have no cultural definition; therefore, their behavior has been determined largely by life in rural southern regions. For example, race prejudice towards Negroes persists and leads to conflict when they are compelled to work in the same gangs with Negroes.[3]

Little else but conflict could be expected if, indeed, southern white migrants defined interracial situations in the North solely in terms of southern mores and acted accordingly. Gunnar Myrdal made the assumption, based on "a common observation," that the transplanted southern white finds little necessity for accommodation to northern patterns but is more likely to change the situation to conform to his "southern prejudice."[4]

The Detroit race riot of 1943, occurring in a city with a large "hillbilly" element in its population, served to focus attention on the possible effect of southern white migrants on race relations in the North. While no systematic, intensive analysis of the role of the "hillbillies" in the Detroit riot has been reported, even by Humphrey and Lee,[5] the recent migration of large numbers of this group has been singled out repeatedly as one of the most important causes. Witness the dramatic statement of Thomas Sancton, made shortly after the riot:

> During the 'thirties and especially after present armament expansion began, white southerners and other outlanders by the hundreds of thousands came to work in the plants. The old, subdued, muted murderous southern race war was transplanted into a high-speed industrial background.[6]

Thus it has been suggested that, because of the refusal of the southern white in the North to accept a "non-southern" definition of interracial situations, he is both an instigator of racial conflict and an agent for the diffusion of "southern" patterns of Negro-white relations. In the present study, the reactions of southern whites in Chicago to contact with Negroes in a specific situation—work—and their influence on the policies of management were analyzed.

[2] "The Southern White Laborer Migrates to Michigan," *American Sociological Review*, 3, No. 3 (June 1938), pp. 333-343.

[3] *Ibid.*, p. 335.

[4] Gunnar Myrdal, *An American Dilemma*, New York: Harper and Brothers, 1944, p. 79.

[5] Alfred M. Lee and Norman D. Humphrey, *Race Riot*, New York: Dryden Press, 1943.

[6] "The Race Riots," *New Republic*, CIX (1943), pp. 9-13.

The "Hillbillies" as a Group

The southern whites studied were members of many small "clusters" of migrants concentrated in an ethnically heterogeneous portion of the Near West Side of Chicago. The majority of them came from farms and small towns in the South Central States, especially western Tennessee. Although these people were known as "hillbillies" in Chicago, few of them came from mountainous areas and they regarded the name as a misnomer.

In this research, 150 southern white migrants were interviewed, and the actual behavior of these and many other southern whites was observed. Non-southerners and Negroes who were part of the social world of the migrants, including plant managers, foremen, policemen, teachers, bartenders, and other workers, were also interviewed.

Of most significance in the present context is the status of the "hillbillies" in the Near West Side. It was found that a vague, but recognizable, stereotype of the southern white migrant was held by many non-southerners, and that they were regarded as a distinct, cohesive ethnic group. While little hostility toward them was discovered, they were generally regarded by non-southern whites as a culturally inferior group. This was especially true in the case of some employers who consciously avoided hiring "hillbillies." In turn, the southern whites themselves exhibited definite group consciousness.

In Chicago, they found themselves only one group in a mosaic of diverse ethnic groups. The fact that they were white, native-born, and Protestant lost some of its prestige value in an area such as the Near West Side, with its large population of Italian-Americans. Negroes, while subject to many forms of discrimination in Chicago, still possessed far more freedom and power than they could enjoy in the rural South. Comparing their position with those of "foreigners" and Negroes in Chicago and in the South, the southern whites felt a relative loss of status which contributed to the development of a *defensive* group consciousness.

The impersonality and anonymity of many types of social relationships in the northern city stood in sharp contrast to the friendly intimacy of the small southern town. As a result, the "laissez-faire" attitude of the city folk was interpreted by the "hillbillies" as evidence of hostility. The term "hillbilly," even when used in jest, was often perceived as a derogatory group label. To the feeling that they, as southern whites, were a somewhat disadvantaged group was thus added the belief that they were a disliked group.

Their defensive group consciousness did not result in the development of in-group organization of a formal type. But the "hillbillies," preoccupied with "making a living," regarding the South as "home," and, suspicious of non-southerners, constituted a marginal and unstable element in the institutions and associations of the area in which they lived. It may be said that they felt themselves to be in, but not of, Chicago. Visits to the South were frequent, and many families periodically returned to their old homes to live for a year or two. This instability and mobility, more than anything else, caused the "hillbillies" to be regarded by employers as a marginal group of laborers, conveniently available when there was a shortage of other labor, but undesirable as members of a cadre of permanent workers.

Effect on Management Policies

The marginal position in industry of the southern whites themselves explains to a large extent the findings concerning their effect on race relations. The range of policies and practices regarding the hiring of Negroes in fourteen plants which employed southern white workers shows that the presence or absence of "hillbilly" workers had only an indirect and minor effect on the policy of management.

In four of these plants, Negroes were employed on jobs with white workers, and sometimes worked side by side with southern whites on machines or assembly lines. Three of these factories were small plants, employing 55, 110 and 225 workers respectively—the very type of plant in which some managers had said, "You can't have Negroes work with whites in such close quarters without trouble!" Not only did the southern whites in these plants work with the Negroes, but they shared the same rest rooms and dressing rooms. It is true that the proportion of "hillbillies" in these plants was not large. In the two with 225 and 55 workers respectively, the proportion was estimated at between 10 and 15 per cent, but had been higher during the War. The third plant, with 110 workers, had only one southern white because of a definite "anti-hillbilly" employment policy, but during the war the managers had employed both Negroes and a larger number of southern whites.

The fourth plant, which employed not only Negroes—about 15 per cent of the working force—but also southern whites, Mexicans, and a variety of workers of foreign extraction, was a larger establishment. Although the personnel manager regarded "hillbillies" as undesirable workers because of their mobility, the plant was still regarded as a good place to work by the southerners. It had 1,100 workers, slightly less than 10 per cent of them southern white. The personnel manager of this plant felt that the integration of Negroes into the plant had been accomplished without difficulty because of the firm stand taken by management. He stated:

> Having southern white workers hasn't affected our policy at all. When they apply for a job we tell them, "We have Negro workers and they're good workers. If you don't want to work with them, you'd better not take the job." Very few decide that they won't take it. Occasionally we may have complaints about friction with the Negroes, but they may come from northern workers as well as from southern.

Francis J. Haas and G. James Fleming, in an article on "Personnel Practices and Wartime Changes," have said that one of the important steps to "fair employment" is "the taking of a firm position by management once it has decided to adopt the new policy." [7] In these plants, regardless of the presence of southern whites and other white workers who might be equally prejudiced, management had taken such a stand and found that "fair employment" practices could be adopted without difficulty. It may be that the relatively small proportion of southern whites employed in these plants was the result of an aversion by the "hillbillies" to work with Negroes. If so, this does not constitute discrimination in the form of segregation imposed on the Negro minority; instead, it is a form of voluntary self-segregation which hurts no one but the person who imposes it upon himself.

The policies of the ten plants which employed "hillbillies" but had few or no Negroes showed, however, that southern migrants who wished to enjoy such self-segregation could do so without having to spread "southern racist ideas." In all ten plants the policy of excluding Negroes existed before management became aware of the presence of the "hillbillies," and in only one plant was it even suggested that the presence of the southern whites was a deterrent to changes in the policy. Seven of these plants were small, with no more than 200 workers, and with no higher proportion of southern whites than were in some of the plants which did not exclude Negroes. The personnel managers of these plants did not give the fear of "trouble" from the southern whites as a reason for not hiring Negroes; instead, they gave very much the same reasons which Haas and Fleming reported to be "most common" as justification for non-employment. These authors said:

> The National Urban League in 1941-42 found the reasons given for non-employment of Negroes to be of "infinite variety." Most common were the following: Negroes never applied; whites and blacks can't mix on the same job; haven't time or money to build separate toilets; no trained Negroes are available; they are racially unequipped for skilled work; the union won't have them; don't like Negroes and don't want them around; this is a rush job and we haven't time for experiments.[8]

The reasons given by these Chicago employers were very similar, as the following statements indicate:

> This is a small plant and you couldn't mix Negroes with any whites, northern or southern. For one thing, we just don't have room for separate locker and washroom facilities.

> Our policy about hiring Negroes is entirely independent of what the southern whites might think or do. We only hire them for a few "dirty" jobs.

[7] *The Annals* of the American Academy of Political and Social Science, CCXLIV (1946), p. 53.
[8] *Ibid.*, p. 49.

The southerners don't enter into our policy towards hiring Negroes. We base our judgment on what we think the older workers would do, and they're mostly Italians. Anyhow, we don't have too many jobs Negroes could do.

We've just stayed away from hiring Negroes. We've never given what the southern whites might do any thought.

Regardless of the number of "hillbilly" workers being employed, inertia and unwillingness to experiment with a new group of workers, rather than the diffusion of "southern" prejudices, seem to have caused these managers to continue discriminatory policies.

On the other hand, it may be concluded that in the three larger plants with relatively large blocs of "hillbilly" workers—from 20 to 30 per cent of the working force—the presence of the southern whites, but not their actions, had an important indirect effect on the employment policies of the companies. These three plants had opened their doors to "hillbilly labor" during a period when the supply of local white labor was curtailed. The pool of southern white migrant laborers in the West Side constituted for them an alternative to Negro workers as replacements and additions to the working force. Had this alternative not been available, the pressure to hire Negroes would undoubtedly have been much greater. It is highly significant that one of these plants, although engaged in defense production and covered by the wartime Fair Employment Practices Order, hired no Negro workers during the entire period of the War. It was during this same period that the "hillbilly" workers, coming into the plant as replacements for Polish and Italian workers called into the service or attracted by more lucrative jobs, increased to over one quarter of the working force.

The management of this plant, as of the other two with large "hillbilly" blocs, had never hired Negro workers on an equal basis with whites. The standard explanations were given, such as, "We don't have the type of work Negroes can do!" In these three plants, and probably in some of the smaller ones, the southern whites did not cause a policy of discrimination in hiring to be instituted, but they made possible the continuation of an already existing policy.

On the basis of the policies and practices of management in these fourteen plants, it is evident that the presence of southern white workers did not cause an increase in discrimination against Negroes. In plants where management took a firm stand against discrimination, southerners not only failed to incite other white workers to voice protests against the policy, but at least some "hillbillies" accepted the policy themselves by taking employment. In other plants, already existing policies of nonemployment of Negroes, arrived at independently of the influence of southern whites, made it possible for the migrants to enjoy the dubious fruits of racial segregation in employment as fully as they might have in the South. The primary significance of the presence of the "hillbillies" was as we saw in Ernest Dunbar's "The Negro in America Today," we find a preponderance of Negroes in occupations of service, semiskilled, and unskilled labor. Those in the power positions of hiring and firing, of ownership, are generally members of the dominant majority group. As Louis Wirth has said, by definition, the existence of a minority group implies the existence of another group in that society with greater privileges and rights. It is an integral part of the system of social action that the privileged make every attempt to maintain their own position by thwarting the access of the less privileged to these same positions.

Stereotypes and the Self-fulfilling Prophecy

One of the more insightful essays on the sociology of intergroup relations is the "Self-fulfilling Prophecy" of R. K. Merton. This essay is acknowledged as an elaboration and extension of W. I. Thomas' "definition of the situation." Thomas held that, if men define situations as real, they are real in their consequences. Merton fit this concept to the sociological concept of race. If men define racial inferiority as real, it is real in its consequences. In the South especially (although this is often true in the North), the racial inferiority of the Negro is firmly believed. Therefore, say the administrators of funds for Southern schools, it is merely a waste of money to try to educate the Negro to the same level as the whites. Thus, they argue, Negro schools need less money and can get along with inferior curriculums. The vicious circle is closed when the product of this inferior training turns out to score lower on the I.Q. test than the white students. Here is the self-fulfilling prophecy in operation. The end product of the prophecy that Negroes are inferior becomes evidence for the inferiority of Negroes. The prophecy *results* in the condition.

All stereotypes, whether occupational, racial, or whatever, contain the elements of a self-fulfilling prophecy. Most American men know that a standard topic of discussion in barbershops is sports. Part of the occupational stereotype of the barber is that he knows about and is interested in sports. Suppose that a man with neither knowledge of nor interest in sports becomes a barber. If he is to carry on conversations with his customers, the easiest thing for him to do is learn about and cultivate an interest in sports. The belief others hold concerning him exerts social pressure on his behavior.

Similarly, if there is a widely held stereotype of Jews as excessively ambitious or "pushy," one way for people in the dominant category to cope with this undesirable trait which poses a threat to their economic power is to set admissions quotas for Jewish applicants to professional schools. Admissions officers can decide that, no matter how well qualified

that their availability made possible the continuation of previously established discriminatory practices in spite of a shortage of local white labor.

The Reactions of the Migrants

Interviews with 140 "hillbillies" who had worked in Chicago plants corroborated this conclusion that the southern whites were able to make a peaceful accommodation to the norms of the new situation. Of these 140, 59 were working, or had worked, in plants that employed Negroes on the same jobs as whites. Of the 81 who had never worked with Negroes under such conditions, only twelve stated that they had deliberately avoided working in plants with a policy of nondiscrimination. The existence of an uneven pattern of race relations in employment in Chicago made it comparatively easy for the southern whites to retain this part of their racial ideology without making any accommodation in their behavior. As one young worker remarked:

> I guess I've just been lucky, but I ain't never worked in a place where they hired niggers. I would if the job was a good one, but I just never have.

On the other hand, of the 59 persons who had worked with Negroes without protest, all but four were "hillbillies" who expressed unqualified approval of "the way things are in the South." Some of the twelve who had deliberately avoided working with Negroes showed remarkable inconsistency in their actions. One man, who declared that he would "mess up the machine" of any Negro who was put to work in his plant, lived in the same block with Negroes; he also admitted that the first job he had in Chicago was as a waiter in a rastaurant where he had to serve Negroes. The impression of those employers who believed, on the basis of their experience, that most of the "hillbillies" would work with Negroes if confronted by a firm policy was borne out by the actions of the southern whites themselves. In fact, some of the most violently anti-Negro southerners were among those who had worked with Negroes, such as a man who later returned to Tennessee because "he couldn't stand to send his children to school with Negroes," and a former member of the Ku Klux Klan.

To most of the "hillbillies," Chicago was not a place to live but merely a place to make a living. The South continued to be their principal reference group and they followed its practice of racial segregation and exclusion when it was conveniently possible. When confronted with situations in which these ways could not be adhered to without personal sacrifice, however, they tended to make the necessary behavioral adjustments even though changes in atttiudes did not necessarily occur.

Conclusions

This study does not support the hypothesis that the southern white migrant, at least the working class migrant, is likely to change the northern interracial situation to conform to his "southern" prejudice. The southern whites studied here, a marginal group in industry themselves, were found to have little effect in deterring employers from hiring Negroes. Their principal effect in northern industry was to furnish an alternate pool of labor for employers who desired to continue an existing policy of exclusion. When confronted with a firm policy of non-discrimination, however, they tended to accept the situation as defined by management. Yet this did not indicate a radical change in the racial attitudes of the southern whites, but rather an accommodation to the exigencies of a specific situation. At the same time, the prevalence of policies of exclusion of Negroes in Chicago plants made such accommodation unnecessary for many of the "hillbillies."

Supplementary Bibliography

Gordon W. Allport, *The Nature of Prejudice.* Cambridge, Mass.: Addison-Wesley, 1954.
     The outstanding volume on the psychology of prejudice.

Bruno Bettelheim and Morris Janowitz, *Dynamics of Prejudice.* N. Y.: Harper, 1950.
     An insightful analysis of the relationship between social norms and prejudiced attitudes.

Daniel Katz and K. Braly, "Racial Stereotypes of 100 College Students." *Journal of Abnormal and Social Psychology,* 1933, 28:280-290.
     A classical research study of stereotyping.

Luigi Laurenti, *Property Values and Race.* Berkeley and Los Angeles: U. of California Press, 1960.
     A report of research in seven Northern cities on what happens to real-estate values when Negroes move in to white neighborhoods.

Melvin M. Tumin, "Readiness and Resistance to Desegregation: A Social Portrait of the Hard Core." *Social Forces,* 1958, 36:256-263. Reprinted in Kimball Young and Raymond W. Mack, *Principles of Sociology: A Reader in Theory and Research,* 2nd ed. N. Y.: American Book, 1962, pp. 327-337.
     A study of 300 adult white males from Guilford County, North Carolina, showing the correlation between race attitudes and one's position in the social structure.

VI   Class, Power, and Group Boundaries

We have seen that the "racial" distinction between Arabs and Jews is social, not biological. This is clear, and easy enough to accept for those who are not Arabs and Jews. It is a bit more difficult to remember the extent to which the "racial" difference between Chinese and Negroes is social, and not biological. If a Chinese marries a Negro in the United States, the offspring will all be "Negroes." The same marriage in Jamaica, Brazil, Hawaii, or South Africa would produce drastically different perceptions of the racial character of the children.

The Definition of Race and Social Power

It is the *consequences* of the perception of race that sociologists of minorities are concerned with. One such consequence is the difference in access to and use of social power.

Political scientists are vitally concerned with power relationships, while economists are oriented to the interplay of competition and co-operation in the market economy. Sociologists might do well to borrow liberally from these sister social sciences in trying to understand minority relations. In the same manner, economists might be able to obtain some insights into some of the operations of the market by reviewing the findings of sociologists on minority relationships.

The most highly desired jobs in any society are scarcer than the supply of individuals wishing to occupy those jobs. Thus there is competition, and principles of supply and demand from economics may be applied at this level. One may add to this, however, principles of power relationships which elucidate how access to these highly desired positions is controlled. If we look at the occupational structure of the United States, that their availability made possible the continuation of previously established discriminatory practices in spite of a shortage of local white labor.

The Reactions of the Migrants

Interviews with 140 "hillbillies" who had worked in Chicago plants corroborated this conclusion that the southern whites were able to make a peaceful accommodation to the norms of the new situation. Of these 140, 59 were working, or had worked, in plants that employed Negroes on the same jobs as whites. Of the 81 who had never worked with Negroes under such conditions, only twelve stated that they had deliberately avoided working in plants with a policy of nondiscrimination. The existence of an uneven pattern of race relations in employment in Chicago made it comparatively easy for the southern whites to retain this part of their racial ideology without making any accommodation in their behavior. As one young worker remarked:

> I guess I've just been lucky, but I ain't never worked in a place where they hired niggers. I would if the job was a good one, but I just never have.

On the other hand, of the 59 persons who had worked with Negroes without protest, all but four were "hillbillies" who expressed unqualified approval of "the way things are in the South." Some of the twelve who had deliberately avoided working with Negroes showed remarkable inconsistency in their actions. One man, who declared that he would "mess up the machine" of any Negro who was put to work in his plant, lived in the same block with Negroes; he also admitted that the first job he had in Chicago was as a waiter in a rastaurant where he had to serve Negroes. The impression of those employers who believed, on the basis of their experience, that most of the "hillbillies" would work with Negroes if confronted by a firm policy was borne out by the actions of the southern whites themselves. In fact, some of the most violently anti-Negro southerners were among those who had worked with Negroes, such as a man who later returned to Tennessee because "he couldn't stand to send his children to school with Negroes," and a former member of the Ku Klux Klan.

To most of the "hillbillies," Chicago was not a place to live but merely a place to make a living. The South continued to be their principal reference group and they followed its practice of racial segregation and exclusion when it was conveniently possible. When confronted with situations in which these ways could not be adhered to without personal sacrifice, however, they tended to make the necessary behavioral adjustments even though changes in atttiudes did not necessarily occur.

Conclusions

This study does not support the hypothesis that the southern white migrant, at least the working class migrant, is likely to change the northern interracial situation to conform to his "southern" prejudice. The southern whites studied here, a marginal group in industry themselves, were found to have little effect in deterring employers from hiring Negroes. Their principal effect in northern industry was to furnish an alternate pool of labor for employers who desired to continue an existing policy of exclusion. When confronted with a firm policy of non-discrimination, however, they tended to accept the situation as defined by management. Yet this did not indicate a radical change in the racial attitudes of the southern whites, but rather an accommodation to the exigencies of a specific situation. At the same time, the prevalence of policies of exclusion of Negroes in Chicago plants made such accommodation unnecessary for many of the "hillbillies."

Supplementary Bibliography

Gordon W. Allport, *The Nature of Prejudice*. Cambridge, Mass.: Addison-Wesley, 1954.
The outstanding volume on the psychology of prejudice.

Bruno Bettelheim and Morris Janowitz, *Dynamics of Prejudice*. N. Y.: Harper, 1950.
An insightful analysis of the relationship between social norms and prejudiced attitudes.

Daniel Katz and K. Braly, "Racial Stereotypes of 100 College Students." *Journal of Abnormal and Social Psychology*, 1933, 28:280-290.
A classical research study of stereotyping.

Luigi Laurenti, *Property Values and Race*. Berkeley and Los Angeles: U. of California Press, 1960.
A report of research in seven Northern cities on what happens to real-estate values when Negroes move in to white neighborhoods.

Melvin M. Tumin, "Readiness and Resistance to Desegregation: A Social Portrait of the Hard Core." *Social Forces*, 1958, 36:256-263. Reprinted in Kimball Young and Raymond W. Mack, *Principles of Sociology: A Reader in Theory and Research*, 2nd ed. N. Y.: American Book, 1962, pp. 327-337.
A study of 300 adult white males from Guilford County, North Carolina, showing the correlation between race attitudes and one's position in the social structure.

VI Class, Power, and Group Boundaries

We have seen that the "racial" distinction between Arabs and Jews is social, not biological. This is clear, and easy enough to accept for those who are not Arabs and Jews. It is a bit more difficult to remember the extent to which the "racial" difference between Chinese and Negroes is social, and not biological. If a Chinese marries a Negro in the United States, the offspring will all be "Negroes." The same marriage in Jamaica, Brazil, Hawaii, or South Africa would produce drastically different perceptions of the racial character of the children.

The Definition of Race and Social Power

It is the *consequences* of the perception of race that sociologists of minorities are concerned with. One such consequence is the difference in access to and use of social power.

Political scientists are vitally concerned with power relationships, while economists are oriented to the interplay of competition and co-operation in the market economy. Sociologists might do well to borrow liberally from these sister social sciences in trying to understand minority relations. In the same manner, economists might be able to obtain some insights into some of the operations of the market by reviewing the findings of sociologists on minority relationships.

The most highly desired jobs in any society are scarcer than the supply of individuals wishing to occupy those jobs. Thus there is competition, and principles of supply and demand from economics may be applied at this level. One may add to this, however, principles of power relationships which elucidate how access to these highly desired positions is controlled. If we look at the occupational structure of the United States, as we saw in Ernest Dunbar's "The Negro in America Today," we find a preponderance of Negroes in occupations of service, semiskilled, and unskilled labor. Those in the power positions of hiring and firing, of ownership, are generally members of the dominant majority group. As Louis Wirth has said, by definition, the existence of a minority group implies the existence of another group in that society with greater privileges and rights. It is an integral part of the system of social action that the privileged make every attempt to maintain their own position by thwarting the access of the less privileged to these same positions.

Stereotypes and the Self-fulfilling Prophecy

One of the more insightful essays on the sociology of intergroup relations is the "Self-fulfilling Prophecy" of R. K. Merton. This essay is acknowledged as an elaboration and extension of W. I. Thomas' "definition of the situation." Thomas held that, if men define situations as real, they are real in their consequences. Merton fit this concept to the sociological concept of race. If men define racial inferiority as real, it is real in its consequences. In the South especially (although this is often true in the North), the racial inferiority of the Negro is firmly believed. Therefore, say the administrators of funds for Southern schools, it is merely a waste of money to try to educate the Negro to the same level as the whites. Thus, they argue, Negro schools need less money and can get along with inferior curriculums. The vicious circle is closed when the product of this inferior training turns out to score lower on the I.Q. test than the white students. Here is the self-fulfilling prophecy in operation. The end product of the prophecy that Negroes are inferior becomes evidence for the inferiority of Negroes. The prophecy *results* in the condition.

All stereotypes, whether occupational, racial, or whatever, contain the elements of a self-fulfilling prophecy. Most American men know that a standard topic of discussion in barbershops is sports. Part of the occupational stereotype of the barber is that he knows about and is interested in sports. Suppose that a man with neither knowledge of nor interest in sports becomes a barber. If he is to carry on conversations with his customers, the easiest thing for him to do is learn about and cultivate an interest in sports. The belief others hold concerning him exerts social pressure on his behavior.

Similarly, if there is a widely held stereotype of Jews as excessively ambitious or "pushy," one way for people in the dominant category to cope with this undesirable trait which poses a threat to their economic power is to set admissions quotas for Jewish applicants to professional schools. Admissions officers can decide that, no matter how well qualified the Jewish applicants may be, not more than 5 percent will be accepted in any entering class at their medical school. What, then, of the Jewish boy who wants to become a physician? He must be so good that they can't reject him; he must be in that top 5 percent. He had best study extremely hard, argue about every grade point on examinations, check to be sure the admissions board receives and considers his application, and exert every possible pressure to get himself admitted. In short, he is encouraged to be pushy—by policies invented to combat his reputed pushiness.

Minority Subcultures

Some minorities have subcultures somewhat apart from the culture of the dominant majority, while other minorities have virtually no distinctive subcultures. The descendants of most immigrants to the United States belong in the first category; the Negro in the United States belongs in the second.

When immigrants enter a new society, they customarily cluster with others who share their language, religion, tastes, and background. This is partly why large American cities still contain Chinatowns, Little Warsaws, or other ethnic neighborhoods. In Little Italy, for example, the new immigrant can find others who speak his language, help in getting a job, an Italian-speaking priest, and a store which stocks Italian groceries. Hence, over the years, most ethnic immigrants have passed on to their children some traditions, perhaps the celebration of a holiday, a recipe for a dish from the old country, a few words at least from the language.

This does not mean that third- or fourth-generation Italian-Americans are not participants in American society, but that, in addition, they share a subculture composed of selected cultural traits transplanted to and often modified by a new environment.

When the Negro first came to the United States, he was stripped of his native language, his native religion, his family structure and family relationships, his friendships, and his traditions. He was forced to take on the new: English, Christianity, the nuclear family, and so on. He retained few if any elements of his past, and certainly there were insufficient cultural retentions to allow the development of a Negro subculture. His values and his motivations, his likes and dislikes, became the same as that of the rest of the population.

Today the answer to the oft-posed question, "What does the American Negro want?" is that he wants exactly what other Americans want. Perhaps it is a home in the suburbs with a lawn, protection and security for his family, and a well-paying, respectable job. Or perhaps it is a swank and luxurious playboy apartment in the most urban section of the city. In any event, if we address the larger issues of basic values and desires, there is no Negro subculture. The only subculture which the American Negro has is a set of epithets for whites, an in-group humor, some avoidance mechanisms, and other behaviors which have developed as a response to a history of slavery and discrimination.

The Jews, on the other hand, are a genuine subculture. They have largely retained their own religion, their emphasis on familism, and their cultural traditions of scholarly achievement.

The existence of a subculture, then, may help define and designate a particular minority, but it is by no means the most important defining attribute of the existence or boundaries of minority status.

Related Readings

Actually, as George Psathas indicates in "Ethnicity, Social Class, and Adolescent Independence from Parental Control," even differences which seem at first glance to be cultural differences sometimes turn out to be attributable neither to race nor ethnicity, but to values and patterns of behavior which vary according to social class. Within a diversified, multi-group society such as contemporary United States, one's status as urban or rural dweller, as Northerner or Southerner, or one's position in the stratification structure may tell more about him than his racial or ethnic background. The average I.Q. scores of a group of students is more accurately estimated from knowing the school board's average annual expenditure per pupil, or from the median income of parents in the school district, than from the skin color or eye form of the students.

"Evaluation of Occupations: A Reflection of Jewish and Italian Mobility Differences," by Fred L. Strodtbeck, Margaret R. McDonald, and Bernard C. Rosen, should be compared with Rosen's "Race, Ethnicity, and the Achievement Syndrome." Both papers stress, and offer research evidence for, the potency of learned subcultural expectations as an explanation for variations in mobility to high class status among different ethnic groups.

An additional, not necessarily conflicting explanation, is put forward by Daniel Bell in "Crime as an American Way of Life." He contends that the class background of the Italian immigrants was primarily one of rural and unskilled status, unlike that of the Jews. This could account for the findings of Strodtbeck *et al* that Italians in their study were more accepting of low status occupations. Further, Bell's analysis illuminates the role of social power in channeling a minority into the stratification structure: the position achieved by the Irish in politics and the Church had consequences not only for them but for the later Italian immigrants attempting to gain a foothold on the ladders of upward mobility.

————————George Psathas

Ethnicity, Social Class, and Adolescent Independence from Parental Control

During the years of adolescence the individual moves toward independence from parental control. In a society characterized by rapid social change and the lack of explicit norms regarding this transition, there are likely to be variations in the handling of the adolescent. Some families may grant a great degree of independence to the adolescent. Others may continue to supervise and restrict the adolescent much as they do younger children.

In this study the differences between certain ethnic groups and between social classes are investigated with regard to the degree of independence from parental control granted the adolescent. Members of Southern Italian and Eastern European Jewish ethnic groups in New Haven, Connecticut, were selected for study. These groups were similar in their time of arrival and place of settlement in this country but had different cultural backgrounds. Differences could reasonably be attributed to ethnicity only if the groups compared had an approximately equal time in which to become acculturated and assimilated.

No research is reported in the literature contrasting these two ethnic groups with regard to adolescent independence. Studies describing the cultural background of these two groups indicate that both Italian and Jewish children were traditionally subordinated to their parents.[1] Patriarchal authority stressed the duties rather than the rights of the child in Italy. So long as the father lived, the sons owed him a great measure of respect and obedience, whether they were married or not.

This subordination also characterized Jewish culture, but in intellectual matters individuality and independence were highly valued. The

[1] The following sources were helpful in describing Southern Italian culture: Paul J. Campisi, "Ethnic Family Patterns: The Italian Family in the United States," *American Journal of Sociology*, 53 (January, 1948), pp. 443-446; Irving L. Child, *Italian or American? The Second Generation in Conflict*, New Haven: Yale University Press, 1943; Caroline Ware, *Greenwich Village, 1920-1930*, New York: Houghton Mifflin, 1935; and Phyllis H. Williams, *South Italian Folkways in Europe and America*, New Haven: Yale University Press, 1938. For Eastern European Jewish culture: Theodore Bienenstock, "Anti-Authoritarian Attitudes in the Eastern European 'Shtetl' Community," *American Journal of Sociology*, 57 (September, 1951), pp. 150-158; I. Graeber and S. H. Britt, (Eds.), *Jews in a Gentile World*, New York: Macmillan, 1942; Ruth Landes and Mark Zborowski, "Hypotheses Concerning the Eastern European Jewish Family," *Psychiatry*, 13 (November 1950), pp. 447-464; and Mark Zborowski and Elizabeth Herzog, *Life Is With People*, New York: International Universities Press, 1952.

Reprinted from *American Sociological Review*, Vol. 22, No. 4, August, 1957, pp. 415-423. By permission.

contrast between physical and intellectual matters was great in the life of the boy. As soon as he started his studies, sometimes at the age of three, he was treated as an adult in matters of the intellect. But even when physically mature, he was still a "baby" to his mother who never stopped worrying about his health, warmth and safety. The child was taught to respect authority not because of the person who embodied it but because of the matter it pertained to. He was taught to question authority in his schooling, since even the Divine Law is subject to interpretation. Thus, in intellectual matters independence was encouraged while in other activities the Jewish son appears to have received no strikingly different treatment than the Italian boy. The greater encouragement in intellectual matters given the Jewish boy might carry over to other activities, but in Italian culture this possibility did not exist. At any rate, no inference concerning the direction of differences between Italian and Jewish adolescents with regard to independence from parental control seems possible from available evidence.

With regard to social class variations there is little explicit concern in the literature with adolescent independence. An early study by Dimock,[2] using a crude measure labelled "emancipation from parents," found no correlation between socio-economic status and this measure. Nye found that adolescent-parent adjustment is "better" in the higher socio-economic levels where adolescents scored higher on "feeling of being loved and secure, feeling that parents trust and have confidence in them, socialization including disciplinary relationships, attitudes toward the parents' personality, and relationships in interaction affecting the adolescent's contact with groups outside the family."[3] Landis and Stone[4] report that social classes do not differ in terms of whether parental authority patterns are democratic, authoritarian, or intermediate. The democratic authority pattern resembles the definition of independence from parental control used in this study.

Procedure

Twenty-five questionnaire items were compiled, some drawn from studies of adolescents by Nye[5] and Landis and Stone,[6] the others constructed by the writer. Each item was stated in multiple choice form with the answer categories ranging from "high" independence to "low" independence. Some areas of activity such as driving the family car, parties in the home, or holding a job were deliberately omitted since some boys

[2] Helen S. Dimock, *Rediscovering the Adolescent,* New York: Association Press, 1937, pp. 144-145.
[3] Ivan Nye, "Adolescent-Parent Adjustment—Socio-Economic Level as a Variable," *American Sociological Review,* 16 (June, 1951), p. 344.
[4] Paul H. Landis and Carol L. Stone, "The Relationship of Parental Authority Patterns to Teen-Age Adjustments," Bulletin No. 538, Washington Agricultural Experiment Station, Pullman: State College of Washington, 1952.
[5] Nye, *op. cit.*
[6] Landis and Stone, *op. cit.*

might not engage in them. The numbers assigned to the items, which are somewhat abbreviated for presentation here, do not represent the order in which they appeared in the original questionnaire but are arbitrarily assigned for purposes of clarity.

Questionnaire Items

1. Before I go out on dates, parents ask me where I am going: never; seldom; half the time; usually; always
2. Before I go out on dates, parents ask me with whom I am going: never; seldom; half the time; usually; always
3. Do you have to account to parents for way you spend your money: not at all; for some of spending; for almost all spending
4. Are you allowed trips out of town without parents: whenever I want; almost everytime I want; sometimes; rarely, never
5. Do parents check on whether you do your homework: never; seldom; half the time; most of the time; almost always
6. In family discussions do parents encourage your opinion: always; usually; half the time; seldom; never
7. With regard to family problems, parents discuss them with me: always; usually; half the time; seldom; never
8. Do parents give opportunities to share responsibilities: as much as I like; almost as much as I like; yes, but not as much as I like; no, only rarely; no, never
9. Parents respect my opinion and judgment: all of the time; most of the time; half the time; seldom; never
10. In family discussions, parents take my opinion seriously: almost always; usually; sometimes; seldom; never
11. When requiring me to do something, parents explain the reason: always; usually; half the time; seldom; never
12. With regard to whom I go on dates with, parents criticize; never; seldom; half the time; usually; always
13. With regard to where I go on dates, parents criticize: never; seldom; half the time; usually; always
14. When invited to relative's home, parents insist you go with them: never; seldom; half the time; usually; always
15. Do parents try to influence choice of occupation: never; hardly at all; try slightly; try moderately; try very hard
16. Does (Do) parent(s) help you buy your clothes: hardly ever; sometimes; usually; always
17. With regard to evenings out, parents allow: every evening if I wish; all week-end, some school nights; week-end, not school nights; only occasional evening; almost never allowed out
18. Who makes final decision on buying clothes: I do without parents' advice; I do with parents' advice; parents with my advice; parents without my advice
19. Who makes your doctor or dentist appointments: I do myself; I do with parents' agreement; parents do with my agreement; parents without asking me
20. When parents don't approve of a boy you spend a lot of time with what

do they do: they never disapprove; tell me but leave it up to me; tell me to stop seeing him but don't insist; insist I stop seeing him

21. What do parents think of boys you spend a lot of time with: approve all; most; some; very few; none
22. Where do you get most of your spending money: money I earn; a regular allowance; money given as needed but no regular allowance; money earned plus regular allowance; money earned plus money given as needed
23. Considering the family income, my parents, if I need money, are: very generous; fairly generous; average; rather stingy; very stingy
24. Is father unreasonable in his commands: frequently; occasionally; only rarely; never
25. Is mother unreasonable in her commands: frequently; occasionally; only rarely; never

The questionnaire was administered to sophomore boys in public and private high schools in New Haven during regularly scheduled classroom periods.[7] A number of background items were included in the questionnaire to determine the boy's ethnic background and his parents' social class. Persons were classified in the Italian ethnic group if both parents were Italian by country of birth or nationality, and at least three of four grandparents Italian. Jews were so defined if both parents had Jewish religious affiliation. The country of birth of the parents or grandparents was used to distinguish Jews from Eastern Europe (Russia, Poland, Hungary or Rumania) from other Jews. Although it was not possible to distinguish between Northern and Southern Italians, most Italians in New Haven are from Southern Italy and Sicily.[8] The group labelled Other Ethnics is a residual category.

The following additional controls were applied: cases of homes broken by death, separation, or divorce were excluded; only members of the Caucasian race were included; and, from the Italian and Jewish groups, cases of mixed ethnic marriages in the parental generation were excluded.

Almost all boys (92 per cent) were between the ages of 15 and 17, the median age being 15 years and 10 months. In the case of both the Italian and Jewish groups, 56 per cent of the boys were third generation Americans, i.e., parents born in the U.S., and approximately one-third [9] were second generation. Thus, these two groups are roughly comparable in terms of their length of residence in America.

However, they differ considerably when classified according to Hol-

---

[7] Ninety-four per cent of the regularly enrolled sophomore boys in these schools completed the questionnaire.

[8] Jerome K. Meyers, "The Differential Time Factor in Assimilation" (unpublished Ph.D. dissertation, Yale University, 1949), p. 26.

[9] The actual figures are 37 per cent for the Italians and 34 per cent for the Jews. The group labelled Other Ethnic showed a smaller proportion of second generation boys, 15 per cent, approximately the same proportion of third generation, 51 per cent, but a larger proportion of fourth generation, 31 per cent. Thus, the Other Ethnic group includes more of the earlier immigrants.

lingshead's Index of Social Position,[10] a measure of social class based on the father's occupation, education, and ecological area of residence. Table 1 presents a breakdown of the Italian, Jewish and Other Ethnic groups by social class. It will be observed that 88 per cent of the Jews are found in the three highest social classes in contrast to 10 per cent of the Italians.

TABLE 1. ETHNIC GROUPS BY SOCIAL CLASS

Social Class	Italians		Jews		Other Ethnics		Total	
	N	Per Cent	N	Per Cent	N	Per Cent	N	Per Cent
I and II *	2	1.1	23	33.8	40	17.7	65	13.7
III	17	9.3	37	54.4	57	25.2	111	23.3
IV	110	60.4	7	10.3	107	47.3	224	47.0
V	48	26.4	—	—	13	5.8	61	12.8
Unknown†	5	2.7	1	1.5	9	4.0	15	3.2
	182	99.9	68	100.0	226	100.0	476	100.0

* Because of the small number of cases in Class I, Classes I and II are combined.
† Unknown cases are those in which the respondent did not provide sufficient information to permit class assignment.

Constructing a Measure of Independence—Twenty of the original twenty-five items were first submitted to Guttman scale analysis to determine whether the content area was uni-dimensional.[11] The response categories for items included in the scale analysis were dichotomized by determining where a "logical" split could be made between the categories.[12] Scale analysis revealed that more than one dimension existed; the coefficient of reproducibility on the second approximation reached only .84.

In order to establish the number of major dimensions involved in this content area, factor analysis was then employed. For each pair of items

[10] August B. Hollingshead and Fritz C. Redlich, "Social Stratification and Psychiatric Disorders," *American Sociological Review,* 18 (April, 1953), pp. 163-169, present a detailed description of the five classes in the New Haven community this index describes.

The social class distribution of all boys in the present sample was found to compare favorably with the 5 per cent Random Sample of Households in the New Haven community reported by Hollingshead and Redlich. A chi-square test of significance comparing the two samples revealed a p value greater than .05.

[11] Of the five excluded one item revealed no spread of responses (No. 21), one had been designed merely as an introduction to another item which was included (No. 22), and three were judged by inspection to be unrelated to the variable independence from parental control (Nos. 23, 24, and 25). One additional item (No. 20) was included in the scale analysis but eliminated from the factor analysis when it was later discovered that 17 per cent of the respondents had either left it unanswered or checked it as inapplicable.

[12] For example, for No. 9, it seems reasonable to group categories (1) all of the time and (2) most of the time; to also group (4) seldom and (5) never; and to place category (3) half the time, with either of these groups depending on the distribution of responses. Categories (1) and (2) contained 64 per cent of the responses and if category (3) were included with these the percentage would rise to 90. In order to avoid as extreme a split as this, category (3) was placed with the bottom two categories.

Class, Power, and Group Boundaries

a tetrachoric correlation coefficient was computed based on all 476 cases.[13] The matrix of tetrachoric correlations is set out in Table 2. Thurstone's centroid method for factor analysis was then applied.[14] Four factors were extracted and after four orthogonal and five oblique rotations of the axes, a simple structure solution was achieved. Table 3 presents the

TABLE 2. ORIGINAL TETRACHORIC CORRELATION MATRIX
FOR 19 QUESTIONNAIRE ITEMS*

Item Number	1	2	3	4	5	6	7	8	9	10	11	12	13	14	15	16	17	18	19
1	–	742	518	194	280	–172	–115	–168	–207	–104	–156	072	144	246	007	420	347	178	037
2		–	455	106	169	–020	–142	–054	–063	–099	–212	195	208	267	–056	439	338	212	072
3			–	374	265	–162	–135	–021	–085	–084	088	308	217	262	045	137	249	154	–042
4				–	151	001	097	171	183	168	–029	006	063	115	–058	201	348	027	171
5					–	–156	–264	–163	–171	–142	–153	094	–019	200	010	149	315	081	–003
6						–	517	444	474	456	251	–027	–035	–268	021	–002	–132	–037	024
7							–	561	358	374	314	–061	–109	–031	–024	115	–141	–027	014
8								–	510	345	220	152	096	024	073	058	–202	038	041
9									–	548	268	340	118	119	177	023	–008	013	037
10										–	238	006	–087	041	049	069	000	–035	091
11											–	–020	–075	043	–068	083	–084	040	061
12												–	634	226	205	210	246	078	109
13													–	383	195	259	237	117	008
14														–	052	187	330	291	054
15															–	–107	026	–039	–057
16																–	489	646	231
17																	–	295	148
18																		–	142
19																			–

* Decimals, properly preceding each entry, have been omitted for purposes of clarity.

oblique rotated factor matrix. The factor loadings for items included in a particular factor are in bold face type in the column labelled with the name of the factor. Interpretations of the four factors are based on the factor loadings in Table 3 considering only those loadings above .200 as significant.

Interpretations of the Factors

Factor 1, defined by Items 1-5, is concerned with a number of activities that involve parental supervision. These items involve activities that occur outside the home with the possible exception of Item 5 concerning checking on homework. The parents may supervise these activities directly or indirectly and punish the son by withholding permission for his participating or by exercising close supervision of his performance. The adolescent who scores high on this cluster of items may be said to be relatively free from parental supervision in his activities outside the home. For this reason the factor has been labelled Permissiveness in Outside Activities.

Factor 2 includes seven items (Nos. 4 and 6-11) concerning family

[13] It should be cautioned that factor analysis results based on the tetrachoric correlation coefficient are likely to have greater variability than those based on the Pearsonian r. See Raymond B. Cattell, *Factor Analysis*, New York: Harper and Bros., 1952, pp. 326-327.
[14] L. L. Thurstone, *Multiple Factor Analysis*, Chicago: University of Chicago Press, 1947.

discussions and decisions made in the home. Each of these items involves verbal interaction between parents and son and, with the exception of Item 4, concern no specific issue but rather seem to reflect the general regard that the parents have for the son's opinion or judgment. Consequently, this factor is labelled Parental Regard for Judgment.

Factor 3 is a little more heterogeneous. It includes five items (Nos. 9 and 12-15). The activities involved here seem to be those which affect the son's "reputation" or "character." Each of the activities has implications for how others will regard him. His choice of an occupation, his visiting relatives, whom he dates and where he goes on dates may be the object of his parents' concern that he "do the right thing" so that others will have a "good opinion" of him. This factor is labelled Activities with Status Implications.

The activities in Factor 4 (Nos. 14 and 16-19) refer to matters related to the age of the boy. Buying clothes, making doctor and dentist appointments, evenings out, and visiting relatives probably vary more with the age of the boy than the activities in Factor 3. At his present age, making such choices is an indication of his greater freedom from parental control and this factor is called Permissiveness in Age-Related Activities.

TABLE 3. FACTOR LOADINGS* OF 19 ITEMS GROUPED BY EACH OF THE FOUR FACTORS; OBLIQUE ROTATED FACTOR MATRIX V

Item No.	Permissiveness in Outside Activities	Parental Regard for Judgment	Activities with Status Implications	Permissiveness in Age-Related Activities	Communality h^2
1	.644	−.041	−.071	.032	.650
2	.617	−.012	.066	−.015	.611
3	.550	.042	.088	−.036	.464
4	.284	.231	−.090	.183	.218
5	.210	−.187	−.086	.130	.186
6	.071	.698	−.071	−.015	.520
7	.071	.688	−.056	.005	.500
8	.149	.688	.171	−.100	.506
9	−.103	.621	.426	.027	.623
10	−.057	.603	.083	.130	.161
11	−.124	.345	.038	.119	.177
12	.003	.015	.704	.013	.584
13	.016	−.091	.668	.003	.550
14	.051	−.074	.350	.209	.313
15	−.024	.033	.338	−.149	.123
16	.004	.061	−.042	.724	.702
17	.064	−.132	.021	.542	.517
18	−.089	−.029	.055	.522	.349
19	−.094	.046	−.038	.320	.110

* The factor loadings represent the correlation between each item and the factor in question.

Intercorrelations of the Factors

Table 4 presents the intercorrelations of the four factors after the five oblique rotations. Primary Factors 1, 3, and 4 show positive intercorrelations with the highest correlation existing between 1 and 4, Permissiveness in Outside Activities and Permissiveness in Age-Related Activities respectively. Factor 2, Parental Regard for Judgment, is negatively correlated with Factor 1 and shows low negative correlation with Factors 3 and 4.

An examination of the original tetrachoric correlations between items (Table 2) leads to comparable results. For example, the mean (which is here used for summarizing purposes) of the correlation coefficients for every item in Factor 1 with every item in Factor 4 is .197, which is

TABLE 4. CORRELATIONS BETWEEN THE PRIMARY FACTORS
AFTER OBLIQUE ROTATION

	Factors			
Factors	Permissiveness in Outside Activities 1	Parental Regard for Judgment 2	Activities with Status Implications 3	Permissiveness in Age-Related Activities 4
1	1.000	−.307	.325	.499
2		1.000	−.007	−.095
3			1.000	.321
4				1.000

larger than the mean of the inter-item correlations between Factors 1 and 3 (.067), and Factors 3 and 4 (.072). The mean of the coefficients between items in Factors 1 and 2 is negative (−.123), while for Factors 2 and 3 and Factors 2 and 4 it is positive and low (.072 and .033 respectively). The foregoing computations exclude any common items found in the two factors being compared.

By comparison, the intra-factor item by item correlations, i.e. the mean of the coefficients for items within a particular factor, are all positive and larger than the above-mentioned means of the inter-factor item by item coefficients. For Factors 1, 2, 3, and 4 these are .325, .308, .245, and .281 respectively. Computations exclude the correlation between an item and itself which is unity.

We conclude that the factors determined by the factor analysis represent different dimensions of independence from parental control and are only moderately intercorrelated. Factors 1 and 4 come closest to representing a general independence factor. The negative correlation found between Factors 1 and 2 (in Table 4) and also in the interfactor item by item comparison (in Table 2) indicates that Factor 2 bears a qualitatively different relation to the other dimensions of independence. An interpretation of this relation will be advanced below.

Ethnic Groups

The first hypothesis to be tested was stated in null form: There are no differences between Italian and Jewish ethnic groups with regard to the degree of independence from parental control granted the adolescent boy.

A scale score for each individual on each of the four dimensions of independence was computed,[15] and there are thus four tests of the hypothesis. Because of the different social class composition of the two ethnic groups, the analysis of variance[16] was chosen as the most suitable statistical test since it would permit controlling for social class when testing for ethnic differences. Four separate analyses of variance tests were made testing for the difference between ethnic groups holding class constant and four tests of class differences holding ethnicity constant. The latter findings will be discussed below under social class.

TABLE 5. MEAN OF SCALE SCORES FOR ITALIAN AND JEWISH ADOLESCENTS FOR EACH DIMENSION OF INDEPENDENCE BY SOCIAL CLASS

Social Class	Permissiveness in Outside Activities			Parental Regard for Judgment			Activities with Status Implications			Permissiveness in Age-Related Activities			N	
	Ital.	Jews	Ȳ	Ital.	Jews	Ȳ	Ital.	Jews	Ȳ	Ital.	Jews	Ȳ	Ital.	Jews
I and II	80	97	95	137	119	120	134	104	106	89	88	88	2	23
III	103	97	99	113	117	116	101	115	111	92	91	91	17	37
IV	102	90	101	88	107	89	103	102	103	106	96	105	110	7
V	110	—	110	95	—	95	105	—	105	120	—	120	48	—
X̄	104	96		93	117		104	110		108	91		177	67
F between ethnics df 1,236	.80			.47			.59			.35				
F between classes df 3,236	1.09			1.73			.37			5.06°				

° Indicates a statistically significant difference, p < .05.

Table 5 presents the mean scores for Italians and Jews by social class for each of the scales.[17] No statistically significant differences (at the

[15] The procedure used to compute individual scores for each dimension required the calculation of normalized standard scores for the response categories in each questionnaire item. A weight was assigned to each response category in a particular item, this weight being a normalized standard score derived in the manner described by Allen L. Edwards, *Statistical Methods for the Behavioral Sciences*, New York: Rinehart, 1954, pp. 107-111. In order to take into account the factor loading that was determined from the factor analysis, each response category weight was multiplied by the factor loading for the particular item and divided by the standard deviation of the distribution of responses to the particular item. To eliminate negative scores an arbitrary constant of 100 was added to all scores.

[16] In order to correct for disproportionality in the number of Italian and Jewish cases within each class and the absence of any Jewish cases in Class V, the analysis of variance method used is that described by George W. Snedecor, *Statistical Methods*, Ames; Iowa State College Press, 1946, pp. 289-290. This method takes into account disproportionate numbers and requires subtraction of one degree of freedom for the cell with no entry.

[17] Although it would be desirable in the interests of reliability to have more items included in each of the factors, given the design of the research this was not possible. Caution should be exercised in interpreting the results of the F tests reported below since individual scale scores for each factor are based on only a few items.

.05 level) are found between Italian and Jewish adolescents when social class is held constant for any of the four dimensions of independence. Interaction, when tested, was not significant.

It is interesting to note, however, that when a simple t-test is used to compare the means for Italians and Jews on each dimension and social class is not controlled, Jewish boys have significantly higher scores (P < .05) on Parental Regard for Judgment and Italian boys are higher on Permissiveness in Age-Related Activities.

Thus, differences exist between the two ethnic groups (using t-test) with regard to two dimensions of independence but the differences do not exist when social class is controlled. The differential social class distribution of the two groups accounts for this result. It appears, then, that both groups have become assimilated into the class cultures of American society, corroborating Davis' hypothesis that "class cultures are (so strong) that they tend to obliterate differences in the national cultures of foreign-born white groups in this country." [18] To say that there are no cultural differences between the two groups would, however, be erroneous. The differential class distribution of Italians and Jews undoubtedly reflects differences in their cultural backgrounds that operated to produce greater class achievement for Jews. The investigation of such factors is another research problem but the present findings suggest that independence from parental control does not distinguish the two groups. It is probably not capable of explaining the continuation of differences in social class achievement if the Jewish boys follow their fathers' pattern and outstrip Italian boys in class achievement.

Social Classes

The second hypothesis to be tested was stated in the null form: There are no differences between social classes with regard to the degree of independence from parental control granted the adolescent boy.

This hypothesis was tested using all cases, Italian, Jewish and Other Ethnics. The category Other Ethnics was not analyzed by specific ethnic background of the subjects.[19] The analysis of variance, single variable of classification was used to test the differences between social classes. Once again, four separate tests were made, one for each dimension of independence.

Table 6 presents the mean scores for each social class for each scale measuring the dimensions of independence. Significant differences are observed as follows: the *lower* social classes have *higher* scores on Permissiveness in Outside Activities (Factor 1) and Permissiveness in Age-Related Activities (Factor 4). For both of these dimensions there is a gradual progression from low to high mean scores. The *higher* social

---

[18] Allison Davis, "Socialization and Adolescent Personality," in Guy E. Swanson, Theodore M. Newcomb, and Eugene L. Hartley (Editors), *Readings in Social Psychology*, New York: Henry Holt, 1952, p. 522.

[19] Since ethnic background was not determined, cases of mixed ethnic marriages involving persons other than Jews or Italians, are included. Other controls are similar.

classes have significantly *higher* scores on Parental Regard for Judgment (Factor 2).

It is of importance to note that the analysis of variance tests based on data in Table 5 comparing social classes while controlling for Italian and Jewish ethnic background reveal no significant differences for any of the dimensions of independence except Permissivness in Age-Related Activities. When ethnic groups are combined and ethnicity is not controlled, differences between social classes then appear for Permissiveness in Outside Activities and Parental Regard for Judgment as well as for Permissiveness in Age-Related Activities. This finding suggests that comparisons of social classes based on only two ethnic groups, which differ as greatly as do the ones studied here, are not reliable indicators of the true range of class differences in the total population. In addition, it is indicated that ethnic comparisons must always take into account class differences.

TABLE 6. MEAN OF SCALE SCORES FOR ALL ETHNICS COMBINED FOR EACH DIMENSION OF INDEPENDENCE BY SOCIAL CLASS

Social Class	Permissiveness in Outside Activities	Parental Regard for Judgment	Activities with Status Implications	Permissiveness in Age-Related Activities	N †
I and II	90	121	102	86	65
III	98	112	104	92	111
IV	100	91	97	103	224
V	108	94	104	118	61
F between classes df 3,457	4.21 *	9.51 *	1.06	16.89 *	461

* Indicates a statistically significant difference, $p < .05$.
† A total of 15 cases of unknown social class, 1 Jewish, 5 Italian, and 9 Other Ethnics, are omitted from analysis.

Although the findings from research on adolescents have been inconclusive, the present findings with regard to social classes do seem to be comparable to the conclusions of many studies of child rearing practices.[20] Such studies have found that the middle classes are more positively concerned with fostering independence in their children but are less permissive than lower-class parents. They expect the child to assume responsibilities at an earlier age than do lower-class parents. Life in lower-class families, on the other hand, is reportedly "less strictly organized and

[20] Allison Davis and Robert Havighurst, "Social Class and Color Differences in Child Rearing," *American Sociological Review*, 11 (December, 1946) pp. 698-710; Davis, "Socialization and Adolescent Personality," *op. cit.*, pp. 520-531; Martha C. Ericson, "Social Status and Child Rearing Practices," in Theodore Newcomb and Eugene L. Hartley (Eds.), *Readings in Social Psychology*, New York: Henry Holt, 1947, pp. 494-501; and Arnold Green, "The Middle Class Male Child and Neurosis," *American Sociological Review*, 11 (February, 1946), pp. 31-41.

fewer demands are made upon (the children)," according to Ericson.[21]
Our findings show that the less rigid standards in the lower classes lead
to a greater independence, that is, the adolescent boy scores higher on
Permissiveness in Outside Activities and Permissiveness in Age-Related
Activities. These dimensions of independence seem to reflect the relaxa-
tion of controls rather than a positive training for independence.

The lower amount of independence granted by middle-class families in
these two dimensions seems to reflect their deliberate attempts to socialize
anxiety[22] into the adolescent. The maintenance of supervision and the
withdrawal of approval serve to make the adolescent more aware of the
importance of "proper" behavior, i.e. conformity to class standards. In
addition, discussing family problems, explaining the reasons for parental
commands, and asking for his opinion (items included in Parental Regard
for Judgment), may also be instrumental in socializing anxiety. By encouraging, listening to and respecting the son's opinions in discussions
parents not only have the opportunity to establish rules of conduct but
also to test and check the degree of acceptance of these standards by
the son. The higher scores on Parental Regard for Judgment in the middle
classes may indicate that the adolescent son has become sufficiently
socialized to be able to discuss the pros and cons of various decisions
with his parents even though the relaxation of controls over his behavior
has not yet occurred to the same extent that it has in the lower classes.
Parental Regard for Judgment is part of the training for independence
and provides continuing opportunities for the parents to establish and
reinforce rules of conduct. It is perhaps this dimension of independence
that is referred to when it is noted that the middle classes train for
independence.

An additional interpretation is that family discussions serve the function of inducing greater conformity to family norms. In discussions the
son has a chance to voice his opinions and to test his ideas *vis-à-vis* those
of his parents. After discussions are concluded, greater conformity (i.e.
less permissiveness) may result in that the son, by sharing in the decision,
has incorporated it as his own and is more willing to abide by it.

An analogous process has been observed in small group studies. Given
the existence of democratic values in our society, an effective method of
motivating conformity in individuals is to provide them with the opportunity to participate in decisions concerning their activities. The group
dynamics and the human relations in industry approaches stress the idea
that high member participation in decision making leads to high morale
and greater conformity to group norms by individual members.[23]

[21] Ericson, *op. cit.,* p. 501.

[22] Davis, "Socialization and Adolescent Personality," *op. cit.,* describes this process.

[23] Representative of this approach are Ronald Lippitt, *Training in Community Relations,*
New York: Harper and Brothers, 1949; Kurt Lewin, "Group Decision and Social Change,"
in Swanson, Newcomb and Hartley, *op. cit.,* pp. 459-473; and Lester Coch and John R. P.
French, "Overcoming Resistance to Change," *Human Relations,* 1 (August, 1948), pp.
512-532.

The present finding may thus be a specific case of a more general group process. The group in this case is the family and not a work group or laboratory group. High participation on the part of the members, especially the son, leads to greater conformity to family norms. The price for high "independence" in the sense of inclusion in family decisions is having to abide by those family decisions, which may then result in low "independence" in the sense of less permissiveness.

One suggestion that can be made on the basis of the interpretations advanced here is that a revision of the concept of independence is indicated. Independence may involve either permissiveness stemming from few controls being exerted over a person's behavior—or responsibility. Responsibility refers to the individual's inclusion in the decision making process. These two aspects of independence may be negatively correlated in the area of adolescent-parent relationships and either, but perhaps not both, should be used as a measure of "independence from parental control."

Summary

A questionnaire was used to obtain information from a sample of adolescent boys in the New Haven high schools. The Southern Italian and Eastern European Jewish ethnic groups were selected for study.

Factor analysis of 19 questionnaire items revealed four dimensions of the variable independence from parental control, which were not all positively intercorrelated.

When social class was controlled, no significant differences between the scores of Italian and Jewish adolescents on any of the dimensions of independence were observed.

When social classes were compared, adding other ethnic groups to the comparison, significant differences were observed for three of the four dimensions of independence. Lower class families appear to be more permissive as evidenced by the adolescents' higher scores on Permissiveness in Outside Activities and Permissiveness in Age-Related Activities. Adolescents in the middle classes score higher on Parental Regard for Judgment but are nevertheless carefully supervised in other activities.

—Fred L. Strodtbeck–Margaret R. McDonald–Bernard C. Rosen

Evaluation of Occupations: A Reflection of Jewish and Italian Mobility Differences

East European Jews have been more consistently upwardly mobile in America than Southern Italians.[1] There are many alternative explanations for this difference. There is some evidence that Jews came to America with occupational skills better suited to urban living than those of the Italians, even though both groups had approximately the same economic status upon arrival. The cultural tradition of veneration of rational control and learning in the Jewish religion has no parallel in the Catholic beliefs of Southern Italians; and, insofar as this tradition has been transformed into a greater respect and desire for higher education in America, it has probably contributed strongly to Jewish upward mobility. Some may suggest that, among Jews, there is an effective community organization that ethnic groups who had not previously faced the problem of adapting as a minority people did not develop. Such explanations are consistent with one another, but are hard to disentangle and evaluate.

The strategy in the present paper is to focus upon a delimited aspect of mobility in an effort to detect Jewish and Italian cultural differences as they may be present in the perspectives of adolescent boys. The aspect of mobility considered is the evaluation of occupations of different status. The underlying assumption is that boys who find high status occupations more attractive will in later life have a better chance of occupying the higher positions.

The basic technique is quite simple. Twelve occupations were selected that might unequivocally be distributed into six status positions. We were guided by the Hollingshead Index of Social Position (ISP), both in our classification of occupations and in our determination of the socio-economic status of the boys' families. The occupations, originally presented alphabetically, are here arranged by index of social position:

---

[1] This assertion is documented insofar as our knowledge of Italian achievement permits in unpublished paper number 7, "Ethnic Differences in Achievement," prepared by Florence Sultan for the "Cultural Factors" project. For New Haven the data illustrate the heavier concentration of Jews in higher status positions. The median number of parents and grandparents foreign-born for adolescents in our sample is 3.4 for Jews and 3.8 for Italians (out of a possible 6). However, lest the reader believe that recency of arrival might account for the lower status of Italians, we have made comparisons holding the number of parents and grandparents foreign-born constant, and this does not modify the conclusion that Jews as a group are consistently in higher status positions than the Italians. For the Connecticut area a decade ago, see Samuel Koenig, "Ethnic Factors in the Economic Life of Urban Connecticut," *American Sociological Review*, 8 (April, 1943), pp. 193-197.

Reprinted from *American Sociological Review*, Vol. 22, No. 5, October, 1957, pp. 546-553. By permission.

1. Doctor, advertising executive
2. Druggist, jewelry store owner
3. Bankteller, bookkeeper
4. Carpenter, auto mechanic
5. Mail carrier, bus driver
6. Night watchman, furniture mover

The respondent instructions were as follows:

> Maybe you DO and maybe you DON'T know exactly what you would like to be. If things worked out so that you were in the occupations listed below when you are an adult, would you be PLEASED or DISAP-POINTED? Tell us whether you would be pleased or disappointed for each occupation in the column on the left. Now, think how your mother and father would feel if you had these jobs when you are an adult. Tell us whether your parents would be PLEASED or DISAPPOINTED if you had each of the occupations listed in the columns on the right. CIRCLE P TO INDICATE PLEASED. CIRCLE D TO INDICATE DISAP-POINTED.

The subject group comprised somewhat more than 1,000 male students 14 to 17 years of age. To avoid referring to the responses of each occupation, reference will be made to the "slope" of choices. The slope in question is the regression line that describes the percentage of respondents reporting "pleased" to the occupations when they are ordered from lowest status to highest. A steep slope results when the respondents are progressively more pleased with higher status occupations than with lower status occupations; flat slope when the respondents are equally pleased with all occupations; and an inversely tilted slope would result if respondents were progressively more pleased with the lower status occupations than with the higher status occupations.

Hypotheses

Counts demonstrated as early as 1925 that students could rank occupations according to status in a manner that is both realistic, insofar as one may judge by conventional socio-economic indices, and internally consistent.[2] His pioneer work has been applicated many times.[3] While this paper is in the same tradition, something more than a ranking by status is involved. Each boy was asked to indicate which of a set of occupations *he would be pleased to follow*, opening the possibility that his answer could not be explained by the status of the occupation alone. Our inquiry concerning his perception of his parents' perspective was designed to evoke in a non-threatening way what the boy believed to be the dif-

---

[2] G. S. Counts, "The Social Status of Occupations," *School Review*, 33 (January, 1925), pp. 16-27.

[3] For the most convenient description of the studies in this tradition, see D. G. MacRae, "Social Stratification, A Trend Report," *Current Sociology*, 2, number 1 (1953-54), pp. 7-31, particularly bibliographic items 16, 53, 218, 252, 257, 259, 260, 435, 510 and 582.

ference between his own and his parents' perspectives. The most general expectation concerning the responses was that (1) the higher the status of the occupations, the higher the percentage of pleased responses, both for (1a) "self-reports," and (1b) "guesses" (about parents' attitudes). Insofar as there might be a difference between the two, it was expected that (2) the slope of the boy's pleased self-reports would be flatter than the slope of his guesses. That is, in contrast with a boy's perception of his parents' evaluations, he is expected to be less consistently pleased to work in the higher occupations and more pleased to work in the lower occupations.

In making prediction (2) it is assumed that a higher social position than one's father is a social objective perceived by boys as attractive to their parents and in a similar degree attractive to the boys. The prediction of a flatter slope in the boys' responses relates to potential social "costs" that must be borne by the boy and, hence, influence his evaluation. Adolescent anxieties provoked by association with higher status groups, a requirement to apply oneself to school work which is at cross purposes with peer group norms, and the deferring of the attainment of independence from family supervision are examples of costs that might cause a boy to temper his mobility aspirations. A boy's recognition of limited ability, which his parents either do not recognize or do not communicate to him as a basis for lowered expectations for occupational attainment, may also be an important factor in the production of the differing slopes.

With regard to the Jewish-Italian comparison, we expected (3) the slope for the self-reports of Jewish adolescent boys to be steeper than the slope of the self-reports of Italian adolescent boys. Further, with regard to the perception of parents' expectations, it was expected that (4) the slope of guesses for Jewish adolescent boys would be steeper than the slope of guesses for Italian adolescent boys. Finally, with regard to the correspondence between the slopes for self-reports and guesses, we expected Jewish boys to be closer to the perspectives of adults and, therefore, (5) the correspondence between self-reports and guesses to be greater for Jewish adolescents than for Italians. While comment upon the rationale for these hypotheses is included in the discussion of findings, this introductory statement is required so that the reader may anticipate the objectives of the analysis.

Analysis

From each adolescent boy a self-report, a guess for his mother, and a guess for his father on each of twelve positions were obtained. The respondents were classified into the following categories: Italian, Jewish, and Other; and high, medium, and low socio-economic status. Each of the nine main sub-groups contained a set of responses from a differing number of boys. The variation in the number of boys among the sub-groups is large. In order to obtain "per cent pleased" responses of equivalent precision it was necessary to randomly divide the boys in each sub-group into sets of approximately eight, since this was the number of respondents in the smallest cell. From these sets of eight, the per cent pleased values were calculated. The number of sets in each cell is given in Table 1, with the total numbers of respondents involved. The values

TABLE 1. DIVISION OF UNEQUAL CELL FREQUENCIES INTO REPLACED SETS*

Index of Social Position	Italians	Jews	Others
High: owners of large businesses; major and minor professionals	8	24	51
	(1)	(3)	(6)
Medium: owners of small businesses; white collar workers; supervisors	78	64	196
	(10)	(8)	(27)
Low: skilled workers; laborers	177	17	432
	(23)	(2)	(57)

* The number of sets of approximately 8 observations are given in parentheses.

in parentheses represent sets of approximately eight individuals or clusters of 8 x 36 attribute-type responses of pleased or displeased. In Table 2, the per cent pleased for the self-reports and guesses for the entire sample is presented. In the first plotting, the simplest possible metrical assumption that the distance between each index of social position value is unity was used. The observed distribution appeared to be remarkably well described by a linear regression. This assumption was tested in two ways: first, by graphic analysis of sub-samples of the data, and, secondly, by carrying out a factorial analysis of a sample of the groups of eight. From this calculation, it was possible to estimate that 68 per cent of the total variation was accounted for by differences between occupations, and, further, that 94 per cent of the variation due to occupations was attributable to the linear effect. This evidence was suf-

TABLE 2. PER CENT PLEASED BY INDEX OF SOCIAL POSITION
OF TARGET OCCUPATION (ALL RESPONDENTS)

ISP	Self-Reports S-R	Guesses G	Combined
1	52	78	65
2	50	72	61
3	32	59	46
4	39	40	40
5	12	13	12
6	6	6	6

ficent to warrant use of the slope of the per cent pleased linear regression line over the occupations as the response metameter in the remainder of the analysis. The mean per cent pleased values for major sub-classifications are shown in Table 3.

TABLE 3. AVERAGE PER CENT PLEASED*

Index of Social Position		Italians		Jews		Others	
Respondents	Target Occupations	S-R	G	S-R	G	S-R	G
High	1	38	66	60	77	56	72
	2	50	68	44	58	47	59
	3	25	50	6	31	30	37
	4	12	12	12	7	25	16
	5	12	6	4	2	4	1
	6	0	6	2	2	0	0
Low	1	57	81	71	84	55	80
	2	47	75	55	76	49	71
	3	37	66	17	35	31	59
	4	40	40	19	20	38	36
	5	5	6	2	1	11	10
	6	3	4	1	2	3	4
Medium	1	50	76	76	93	47	77
	2	51	72	79	86	48	73
	3	41	67	34	56	33	61
	4	39	45	30	27	46	49
	5	11	8	6	3	17	21
	6	4	4	0	0	10	10

* The n for each cell is given in Table 1.

From each set of twelve per cent pleased values for the 137 groups of eight (see Table 1) for self-reports and guesses, the following linear measure was calculated using the orthogonal polynomials provided in Fisher and Yates.[4] The use of these weights on a group of eight boys' responses is illustrated below:

ISP	Per Cent Pleased	Weights
1	70	−5
2	60	−3
3	50	−1
4	40	1
5	20	3
6	10	5

Per Cent Pleased × Weights = −430

[4] R. A. Fisher and F. Yates, *Statistical Tables*, New York: Hafner Publishing Company (1949), pp. 70-80, especially Table XXIII.

For this case, −430 divided by 35, the divisor which is appropriate for the weights above, gives −12.3, the slope for this particular line. A similar computation (save only the division by the constant) was made for 137 times 2 (for S-R and G) groups.

Four subsequent main analyses of these linear measures were made on (a) the sums, (b) the differences between self-reports and guesses, (c) self-reports, and (d) guesses, separately. After it was apparent that the variances of the nine main sub-groups in Table 1 were homogeneous, an over-all analysis of variance was computed and our hypotheses were tested, using Students' "t" and the relevant residual value.

These analyses provide, for example, the equations for the two lines presented in Figure 1, where y = per cent pleased and x = ISP.

$$y_{(G)} = 44.63 - 15.88 \ (x - 3.5)$$
$$y_{(S\text{-}R)} = 31.85 - 9.72 \ (x - 3.5)$$

To test our expectation (1) we tested the null hypothesis that the slope in each case is equal to or greater than zero. This null hypothesis was rejected;

"t" ratio	Probability
(1a) − 15.88/0.274	<0.001
(1b) − 9.72/0.317	<0.001

and the alternative interpretation is supported. To use this example further, the difference between the slopes may be determined:

$$(-15.88) - (-9.72) = -6.16$$

If it can be shown that this difference between the slopes is negative and significantly different from zero, our expectation (2) will be supported. We tested the hypothesis that the difference is equal to or greater than zero in a parallel manner:

"t" ratio	Probability
(2) −6.16/0.277	<0.001

In this case, our expectation was again strongly supported.

A further advantage of the analysis is that it is possible to replicate the above tests for the three ethnic groups and the three social position groups. The tests in Table 4, based upon sub-classifications of the data, provide in each instance a basis for rejecting the null hypothesis and give further support for expectations (1) and (2).

By a further arrangement of the values given in Table 4, we evaluated hypotheses (3) and (4), which treat the expectation that there will be a steeper slope for Jews than Italians on both self-reports and guesses. Table 5 shows that, while the margin by which the null hypotheses are rejected is somewhat lower, in each case our expectations are clearly supported.

TABLE 4. REGRESSION COEFFICIENTS ARRANGED FOR TESTS
OF HYPOTHESES (1) AND (2)

Ethnicity and Status Grouping		Test of Slope Hypothesis: $b \geq 0$			Test of Difference Between Slopes Hypothesis: $(b_G - b_{S-R}) \geq 0$		
		Value	Error	P(t) df = 128	Value	Error	P(t) df = 128
Italian	S-R [*]	−10.62	±0.637	<0.001	−6.07	±0.556	<0.001
	G	−16.69	±0.551	<0.001			
Jew	S-R	−14.32	±1.030	<0.001	−4.14	±0.900	<0.001
	G	−18.46	±0.891	<0.001			
Other	S-R	− 8.72	±0.391	<0.001	−6.48	±0.342	<0.001
	G	−15.20	±0.339	<0.001			
High	S-R	−11.44	±1.174	<0.001	−4.36	±1.026	<0.001
	G	−15.80	±1.016	<0.001			
Medium	S-R	−11.56	±0.553	<0.001	−5.79	±0.484	<0.001
	G	−17.35	±0.479	<0.001			
Low	S-R	− 8.51	±0.410	<0.001	−6.57	±0.358	<0.001
	G	−15.08	±0.355	<0.001			
Combined Self-Reports		− 9.72	±0.317	<0.001	−6.16	±0.277	<0.001
Guesses		−15.88	±0.274	<0.001			
Total		−12.80	±0.262	<0.001	—	—	—

[*] S-R = Self-reports; G = Guesses.

TABLE 5. REGRESSION COEFFICIENTS ARRANGED FOR TESTS
OF HYPOTHESES (3) AND (4)

Ethnicity and Status Grouping	Slope	Test of Difference Between Slopes			
		Value	Error	df	P(t)
Self-Reports Italian	−10.62	3.70	±1.210	128	<0.01
Jew	−14.32				
Guesses Italian	−16.69	1.77	±1.047	128	<0.05
Jew	−18.46				

Further examination of these differences shows that they are not significant for classes 3 and 4 but are significant for classes 5, 6, and 7 ($P < 0.01$ for S-R, $P < 0.05$ for G). Owing to the single observation in the Italian group, it is not possible to make the Italian-Jewish comparison for the higher-class groups.

This leaves one further matter, the expectation (5) that the angle between the self-reports and guesses would be lower for Jews than Italians. The necessary values are found in the difference column in Table 4—subtracting $(-4.14) - (-6.07) = 1.93$. This difference has a standard error of:

$$(0.900)^2 - (0.556)^2 = \pm 1.055, \text{ and the test}$$

"t" ratio	Probability
(5) 1.93/1.055	<.05

permits us to reject the null hypothesis of no difference.

This result is just barely significant, and the test in this form did not include a correction for the differential class distribution of the two ethnic groups. When such a correction is made (again omitting High comparisons because there is only one set of eight respondents for Italians) significant differences no longer obtain:

	Status	"t" ratio	Probability
(5a)	medium	1.48/1.539	>0.05
(5b)	low	2.48/2.391	>0.05

Thus, although there is some indication of a closer similarity between self-reports and guesses for Jews than for Italians in each of the two status groups, we are *not* warranted in rejecting the null hypothesis of no difference for the individual class groupings.

Repeat Administration

To eliminate the possibility that artificial regularity arising from essentially random questionnaire responses accounted for our results, a stratified subsample of 48 boys was given the same questions again in their homes. The boys gave the same self-report and guess for parents in 81 per cent of the cases. Inspection indicated that the changed responses tended to occur in the mid-status range; therefore it may be concluded that the slopes on which the above analysis was based would not have been greatly influenced by this departure from perfect reliability.

During the home visits required for the repeat administration, evaluations of the target occupations by both parents were obtained. Thus, as a by-product of the reliability check, this further information enabled us to examine the boy's ability to accurately guess his parents' responses: medium status boys guessed more accurately than the other two status groups, and this tendency was more marked for Italians than Jews. In general, Jewish boys were more accurate than Italian and—this was a surprise—boys who were achieving below their ability in school guessed more accurately than boys who were over-achieving.

Discussion

Both the original study and the repeat administration were conducted in New Haven, and the reader is cautioned that there are no grounds for generalizing beyond New Haven. We are encouraged, however, by one recent survey result to believe that adolescents in general have a flatter slope than adults in their evaluations of occupations.[5] The target occupations were selected without previous pilot inquiries; hence the inferences made about status aspirations may be heavily contaminated by the specific occupations that have been used. Particular attention should be given the position 4 self-report value in Figure 1. It may be

FIGURE 1. LINEAR REGRESSION FITTED TO SELF-REPORTS AND GUESSES OF ALL RESPONDENTS

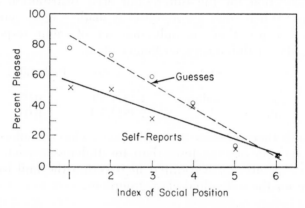

seen that the pleased responses for this occupation fall at 39 per cent— well above the regression value of 27 per cent. This may arise because of the popularity of the auto-mechanic with teen-agers, but it may also arise because we have no adjacent positions in the mechanical and engineering hierarchy. Characteristically, however, the Italian boys were more pleased than Jewish boys by a two to one ratio on their responses to the position 4 occupations.

While Italians have a flatter slope than Jews, they have a steeper slope than the residual category, Other. This difference is not significant for middle-class groups but is a significant ($P < 0.01$) for both self-reports and guesses for lower-class groups. An earlier study by Myers shows most

[5] This statement is supported by our re-analysis of the report, "Attitudes of Adult Civilians Toward the Military Service as a Career," based upon the evaluation of 19 occupations by 1,031 males 16 to 20 and 2,004 adult respondents of both sexes. See Part I of a Study for the Office of Armed Forces Information and Education, Department of Defense, Princeton: Public Opinion Surveys, Inc., 1955; and Graham Du Shane, "Attitudes and Careers," *Science*, Volume 123, Number 3194 (16 March, 1956), p. 1.

conclusively that Italians are continuously improving their position in the New Haven status structure.[6] It is, therefore, to be stressed that while Jews were markedly more mobile than the Italians, other segments of New Haven population (largely old Yankee, Irish Catholic, and French Canadian lower-class groups) have markedly flatter evaluation trace lines and are possibly less mobile. Perhaps these other groups have lost some of the recent immigrants' drive for improvement of status and have become "acclimated" to lower class status.

The stable and pervasive finding that self-reports give a flatter slope than guesses raises a social-psychological question of broad importance. Let us assume that the path of career choices to a particular occupation is perceived to include social costs of the type mentioned earlier as well as economic costs and delayed economic independence. In the face of such difficulties, does the adolescent boy, like La Fontaine's fox, say "Those grapes are sour"? Is the outcome redefined as less attractive, and the intermediate steps that lead to it avoided? Does the outcome thus become less probable? Table 4 demonstrates a constant increase in the disparity between self-reports and guesses as one goes from the highest to the lowest status categories, a fact not inconsistent with this cost hypothesis.

On the other hand, one might reason that a middle-class bias is showing. Probably there are alternative goals of extended family living, leisure for family life, and the like, which lower-class culture, or Italian culture, substitutes for the upward mobility aspirations of the dominant society. From this perspective, the lowered slope of the self-reports may be viewed as a value-directed choice rather than a sour grapes defense. But, if this were the case, how would one account for the slope of the guesses that remains very steep? Does this mean that parents in their role as agents of socialization, consistently represent themselves to their children as favoring mobility notwithstanding the status level at which they may have stopped? In this connection, particular note should be made of the steeper slope in Table 4 of the guesses made by boys from medium status homes. This is consistent with popular conceptions of middle-class culture as achievement oriented.

If the interpersonal relations within a family do not operate to cause a boy to internalize the goals which his parents hold for him, then their expectations may be of little consequence. The correspondence of the self-reports to the guesses is therefore given particular attention. Our data suggest two relationships. First, self-reports and guesses are more nearly parallel in upper than in lower classes (see *High, Medium, and Low Rows of Table 4*) and this class difference accounts to an appreciable degree for the Jewish-Italian differences in (5), which when

[6] Jerome K. Myers, "Assimilation to the Ecological and Social Systems of a Community," *American Sociological Review*, 15 (June, 1950), pp. 367-372; and "Assimilation in the Political Community," *Sociology and Social Research*, 35 (January-February, 1951), pp. 175-182.

corrected in (5a) and (5b) are no longer significant. Therefore, from the analysis of the relatively small number of cases at our disposal (corrected for differential distribution by socio-economic status), there is *no* basis for believing that Jewish socialization practices are any more effective than those of Italian families in causing sons to adopt occupational evaluations similar to those imputed by the son to his parents.

If the socio-cultural aspect of this inquiry had been directed narrowly to a determination of whether there was a different emphasis on education among Jews in contrast with Italians, results that parallel the occupational evaluation material would have been obtained. It is commonplace to speak of emphasis on learning in Jewish culture. While in the larger study from which this paper is drawn attitude expressions toward education have been collected, the use of occupational preferences enabled us to explore perceived toleration by parents for low status positions of a character that could not have been inferred from responses about education. A clear instance of this difference was observed: The parents in an Italian family wanted their son to go to college and to be a doctor; however, at the same time they indicated that they would be satisfied if he became a white-collar worker in the post office. The matched Jewish family also wanted their boy to go to college and to be a doctor, but the occupation of "professor of languages in the university" was the only alternative they expressed themselves as being willing to accept.

Our data indicate that Italian and Jewish boys generally guessed their parents would be satisfied if they achieved the highest positions; but it was predominantly Italian boys who also thought their parents would be pleased with less. It is a fair description of our data to say that the principal source of the difference demonstrated arises because the Italians were (or were perceived to be) more accepting of lower status occupations.

—————————Daniel Bell

Crime as an American Way of Life

In the 1890's, the Reverend Dr. Charles Parkhurst, shocked at the open police protection afforded New York's bordellos, demanded a state inquiry. In the Lexow investigation that followed, the young and dashing William Travers Jerome staged a set of public hearings that created sensation after sensation. He badgered "Clubber" Williams, First Inspector of the Police Department, to account for wealth and property far greater than could have been saved on his salary; it was earned, the Clubber explained laconically, through land speculation "in Japan." Heavy-set Captain Schmittberger, the "collector" for the "Tenderloin

From *The End of Ideology*, pp. 115-136. Reprinted with permission of the publisher from *The End of Ideology*, by Daniel Bell. Copyright 1960 by The Free Press, A Corporation.

precincts"—Broadway's fabulous concentration of hotels, theaters, restaurants, gaming houses, and saloons—related in detail how protection money was distributed among the police force. Crooks, policemen, public officials, businessmen, all paraded across the stage, each adding his chapter to a sordid story of corruption and crime. The upshot of these revelations was reform—the election of William L. Strong, a stalwart businessman, as mayor, and the naming of Theodore Roosevelt as police commissioner.

It did not last, of course, just as previous reform victories had not lasted. Yet the ritual drama was re-enacted. Twenty years ago the Seabury investigation in New York uncovered the tin-box brigade and the thirty-three little MacQuades. Jimmy Walker was ousted as Mayor and in came Fiorello La Guardia. Tom Dewey became district attorney, broke the industrial rackets, sent Lucky Luciano to jail and went to the Governor's chair in Albany. Then reform was again swallowed up in the insatiable maw of corruption until Kefauver and the young and dashing Rudolph Halley threw a new beam of light into the seemingly bottomless pit.

How explain this repetitious cycle? Obviously the simple moralistic distinction between "good guys" and "bad guys," so deep at the root of the reform impulse, bears little relation to the role of organized crime in American society. What, then, does?

II

Americans have had an extraordinary talent for compromise in politics and extremism in morality. The most shameless political deals (and "steals") have been rationalized as expedient and realistically necessary. Yet in no other country have there been such spectacular attempts to curb human appetites and brand them as illicit, and nowhere else such glaring failures. From the start America was at one and the same time a frontier community where "everything goes," and the fair country of the Blue Laws. At the turn of the century the cleavage developed between the Big City and the small-town conscience. Crime as a growing business was fed by the revenues from prostitution, liquor and gambling that a wide-open urban society encouraged and which a middle-class Protestant ethos tried to suppress with a ferocity unmatched in any other civilized country. Catholic cultures rarely have imposed such restrictions, and have rarely suffered such excesses. Even in prim and proper Anglican England, prostitution is a commonplace of Piccadilly night life, and gambling one of the largest and most popular industries. In America the enforcement of public morals has been a continuing feature of our history.

Some truth may lie in Svend Ranulf's generalization that moral indignation is a peculiar fact of middle-class psychology and represents a disguised form of repressed envy. The larger truth lies perhaps in the brawling nature of American development and the social character of crime. Crime, in many ways, is a Coney Island mirror, caricaturing the morals and manners of a society. The jungle quality of the American business community, particularly at the turn of the century, was reflected in the mode of "business" practiced by the coarse gangster elements, most of them from new immigrant families, who were "getting ahead," just as Horatio Alger had urged. In the older, Protestant tradition the intense acquisitiveness, such as that of Daniel Drew, was rationalized by a compulsive moral fervor. But the formal obeisance of the ruthless businessman in the workaday world to the church-going pieties of the Sabbath was one that the gangster could not make. Moreover, for the young criminal, hunting in the asphalt jungle of the crowded city, it was not the businessman with his wily manipulation of numbers but the "man with the gun" who was the American hero. "No amount of commercial prosperity," once wrote Teddy Roosevelt, "can supply the lack of the heroic virtues." The American was "the hunter, cowboy, frontiersman, the soldier, the naval hero." And in the crowded slums, the gangster. He was a man with a gun, acquiring by personal merit what was denied to him by complex orderings of a stratified society. And the duel with the law was the morality play *par excellence:* the gangster, with whom rides our own illicit desires, and the prosecutor, representing final judgment and the force of the law.

Yet all this was acted out in a wider context. The desires satisfied in extra-legal fashion were more than a hunger for the "forbidden fruits" of conventional morality. They also involved, in the complex and ever shifting structure of group, class and ethnic stratification, which is the warp and woof of America's "open" society, such "normal" goals as independence through a business of one's own, and such "moral" aspirations as the desire for social advancement and social prestige. For crime, in the language of the sociologists, has a "functional" role in the society, and the urban rackets—the illicit activity organized for continuing profit rather than individual illegal acts—is one of the queer ladders of social mobility in American life. Indeed, it is not too much to say that the whole question of organized crime in America cannot be understood unless one appreciates (1) the distinctive role of organized gambling as a function of a mass consumption economy; (2) the specific role of various immigrant groups as they one after another became involved in marginal business and crime; and (3) the relation of crime to the changing character of the urban political machines.

III

As a society changes, so does, in lagging fashion, its type of crime. As American society became more "organized," as the American businessman became more "civilized" and less "buccaneering," so did the American racketeer. And just as there were important changes in the structure of business enterprise, so the "institutionalized" criminal enterprise was transformed too.

In the America of the last fifty years the main drift of society has been toward the rationalization of industry, the domestication of the crude self-made captain of industry into the respectable man of manners, and the emergence of a mass-consumption economy. The most significant transformation in the field of "institutionalized" crime was the increasing relative importance of gambling as against other kinds of illegal activity. And, as a multi-billion-dollar business, gambling underwent a transition parallel to the changes in American enterprise as a whole. This parallel was exemplified in many ways: in gambling's industrial organization (e.g., the growth of a complex technology such as the national racing wire service and the minimization of risks by such techniques as lay-off betting); in its respectability, as was evidenced in the opening of smart and popular gambling casinos in resort towns and in "satellite" adjuncts to metropolitan areas; in its functional role in a mass-consumption economy (for sheer volume of money changing hands, nothing has ever surpassed this feverish activity of fifty million American adults); in the social acceptance of the gamblers in the important status world of sport and entertainment, i.e., "café society."

In seeking to "legitimize" itself, gambling had quite often actually become a force against older and more vicious forms of illegal activity. In 1946, for example, when a Chicago mobster, Pat Manno, went down to Dallas, Texas, to take over gambling in the area for the Accardo-Guzik combine, he reassured the sheriff as to his intent as follows: "Something I'm against, that's dope peddlers, pickpockets, hired killers. That's one thing I can't stomach, and that's one thing the fellows up there—the group won't stand for, things like that. They discourage it, they even go to headquarters and ask them why they don't do something about it."

Jimmy Cannon once reported that when the gambling raids started in Chicago, the "combine" protested that, in upsetting existing stable relations, the police were only opening the way for ambitious young punks and hoodlums to start trouble. Nor is there today, as there was twenty or even forty years ago, prostitution of major organized scope in the United States. Aside from the fact that manners and morals have changed, prostitution *as an industry* doesn't pay as well as gambling. Besides, its existence threatened the tacit moral acceptance and quasi-respectability that gamblers and gambling have secured in the American way of life. It was, as any operator in the field might tell you, "bad for business."

The criminal world of the last decade, its tone set by the captains of the gambling industry, is in startling contrast to the state of affairs in the two decades before. If a Kefauver report had been written then, the main "names" would have been Lepke and Gurrah, Dutch Schultz, Jack "Legs" Diamond, Lucky Luciano, and, reaching back a little further, Arnold Rothstein, the czar of the underworld. These men (with the exception of Luciano, who was involved in narcotics and prostitution) were in the main industrial racketeers. Rothstein, it is true, had a larger function: he was, as Frank Costello became later, the financier of the underworld—the pioneer big businessman of crime, who, understanding the logic of co-ordination, sought to *organize* crime as a source of regular income. His main interest in this direction was in industrial racketeering, and his entry was through labor disputes. At one time, employers in the garment trades hired Legs Diamond and his sluggers to break strikes, and the Communists, then in control of the cloakmakers union, hired one Little Orgie to protect the pickets and beat up the scabs; only later did both sides learn that Legs Diamond and Little Orgie were working for the same man, Rothstein.

Rothstein's chief successors, Lepke Buchalter and Gurrah Shapiro, were able, in the early '30's, to dominate sections of the men's and women's clothing industries, of painting, fur dressing, flour trucking, and other fields. In a highly chaotic and cut-throat industry such as clothing, the racketeer, paradoxically, played a stabilizing role by regulating competition and fixing prices. When the NRA came in and assumed this function, the businessman found that what had once been a quasi-economic service was now pure extortion, and he began to demand police action. In other types of racketeering, such as the trucking of perishable foods and water-front loading, where the racketeers entrenched themselves as middlemen—taking up, by default, a service that neither shippers nor truckers wanted to assume—a pattern of accommodation was roughly worked out and the rackets assumed a quasi-legal veneer. On the water-front, old time racketeers perform the necessary function of loading—but at an exorbitant price, and this monopoly was recognized by both the union and the shippers, and tacitly by government. (See my case study "The Last of the Business Rackets," in the June, 1951 issue of *Fortune.*)

But in the last decade and a half, industrial racketeering has not offered much in the way of opportunity. *Like American capitalism itself, crime shifted its emphasis from production to consumption.* The focus of crime became the direct exploitation of the citizen as consumer, largely through gambling. And while the protection of these huge revenues was inextricably linked to politics, the relation between gambling and "the mobs" became more complicated.

IV

Although it never showed up in the gross national product, gambling in the last decade was one of the largest industries in the United States. The Kefauver Committee estimated it as a twenty-billion-dollar business. This figure has been picked up and widely quoted, but in truth no one knows what the gambling "turnover" and "take" actually is, nor how much is bet legally (pari-mutuel, etc.) and how much illegally. In fact, the figure cited by the committee was arbitrary and arrived at quite sloppily. As one staff member said: "We had no real idea of the money spent. . . . The California crime commission said twelve billion. Virgil

Peterson of Chicago estimated thirty billion. We picked twenty billion as a balance between the two."

If comprehensive data are not available, we do know, from specific instances, the magnitude of many of the operations. Some indications can be seen from these items culled at random:

—James Carroll and the M & G syndicate did a 20-million-dollar annual business in St. Louis. This was one of the two large books in the city.

—The S & G syndicate in Miami did a 26-million-dollar volume yearly; the total for all books in the Florida resort reached 40 millions.

—Slot machines were present in 69,786 establishments in 1951 (each paid $100 for a license to the Bureau of Internal Revenue); the usual average is three machines to a license, which would add up to 210,000 slot machines in operation in the United States. In legalized areas, where the betting is higher and more regular, the average gross "take" per machine is $50 a week.

—The largest policy wheel (i.e. "numbers") in Chicago's "Black Belt" reported taxable net profits for the four-year period from 1946 through 1949, after sizable deductions for "overhead," of $3,656,968. One of the large "white" wheels reported in 1947 a gross income of $2,317,000 and a net profit of $205,000. One CIO official estimated that perhaps 15 per cent of his union's lower echelon officials are involved in the numbers racket (a steward, free to roam a plant, is in a perfect situation for organizing bets).

If one considers the amount of betting on sports alone—an estimated six billion on baseball, a billion on football pools, another billion on basketball, six billion on horse racing—then Elmo Roper's judgment that "only the food, steel, auto, chemical, and machine-tool industries have a greater volume of business" does not seem too farfetched.

While gambling has long flourished in the United States, the influx of the big mobsters into the industry—and its expansion—started in the '30's when repeal of Prohibition forced them to look about for new avenues of enterprise. Gambling, which had begun to flower under the nourishment of rising incomes, was the most lucrative field in sight. To a large extent the shift from bootlegging to gambling was a mere transfer of business operations. In the East, Frank Costello went into slot machines and the operation of a number of ritzy gambling casinos. He also became the "banker" for the Erickson "book," which "laid off" bets for other bookies. Joe Adonis, similarly, opened up a number of casinos, principally in New Jersey. Across the country, many other mobsters went into bookmaking. As other rackets diminished, and gambling, particularly horse-race betting, flourished in the '40's, a struggle erupted over the control of racing information.

Horse-race betting requires a peculiar industrial organization. The essential component is time. A bookie can operate only if he can get information on odds up to the very last minute before the race, so that he can "hedge" or "lay off" bets. With racing going on simultaneously on many tracks throughout the country, this information has to be obtained speedily and accurately. Thus, the racing wire is the nerve ganglion of race betting.

The racing-wire news service got started in the '20's through the genius of the late Moe Annenberg, who had made a fearful reputation for himself as Hearst's circulation manager in the rough-and-tumble Chicago newspaper wars. Annenberg conceived the idea of a telegraphic news service which would gather information from tracks and shoot it immediately to scratch sheets, horse parlors, and bookie joints. In some instances, track owners gave Annenberg the rights to send news from tracks; more often, the news was simply "stolen" by crews operating inside or near the tracks. So efficient did this news distribution system become, that in 1942, when a plane knocked out a vital telegraph circuit which served an Air Force Field as well as the gamblers, the Continental Press managed to get its racing wire service for gamblers resumed in fifteen minutes, while it took the Fourth Army, which was responsible for the defense of the entire West Coast, something like three hours.

Annenberg built up a nationwide racing information chain that not only distributed wire news but controlled sub-outlets as well. In 1939, harassed by the Internal Revenue Bureau on income tax, and chivvied by the Justice Department for "monopolistic" control of the wire service, the tired and aging Annenberg simply walked out of the business. He did not sell his interest, or even seek to salvage some profit; he simply gave up. Yet, like any established and thriving institution, the enterprise continued, though on a decentralized basis. James Ragen, Annenberg's operations manager, and likewise a veteran of the old Chicago circulation wars, took over the national wire service through a dummy friend and renamed it the Continental Press Service.

The salient fact is that in the operation of the Annenberg and Ragen wire service, formally illegal as many of its subsidiary operations may have been (i.e. in "stealing" news, supplying information to bookies, etc.) gangsters played no part. It was a business, illicit, true, but primarily a business. The distinction between gamblers and gangsters, as we shall see, is a relevant one.

In 1946, the Chicago mob, whose main interest was in bookmaking rather than gambling casinos, began to move in on the wire monopoly. Following repeal, the Capone lieutenants had turned, like Lepke, to labor racketeering. Murray ("The Camel") Humphries muscled in on the teamsters, the operating engineers, and the cleaning-and-dyeing, laundry, and linen-supply industries. Through a small-time punk, Willie Bioff, and union official George Browne, Capone's chief successors, Frank ("The Enforcer") Nitti and Paul Ricca, came into control of the motion-picture union and proceeded to shake down the movie industry for fabulous sums in order to "avert strikes." In 1943, when the government moved in and smashed the industrial rackets, the remaining big shots, Charley Fishchetti, Jake Guzik, and Tony Accardo decided to concentrate on gambling, and in particular began a drive to take over the racing wire.

In Chicago, the Guzik-Accardo gang, controlling a sub-distributor of the racing news service, began tapping Continental's wires. In Los Angeles, the head of the local distribution agency for Continental was beaten up by hoodlums working for Mickey Cohen and Joe Sica. Out of the blue appeared a new and competitive nationwide racing information and distribution service, known as Trans-American Publishing, the money for which was advanced by the Chicago mobs and Bugsy Siegel, who, at the time, held a monopoly of the bookmaking and wire-news service in Las Vegas. Many books pulled out of Continental and bought information from the new outfit, many hedged by buying from both. At the end of a year, however, the Capone mob's wire had lost about $200,-000. Ragen felt that violence would erupt and went to the Cook County district attorney and told him that his life had been threatened by his rivals. Ragen knew his competitors. In June 1946 he was killed by a blast from a shotgun.

Thereafter, the Capone mob abandoned Trans-American and got a "piece" of Continental. Through their new control of the national racing-wire monopoly, the Capone mob began to muscle in on the lucrative Miami gambling business run by the so-called S & G syndicate. For a long time S & G's monopoly over bookmaking had been so complete that when New York gambler Frank Erickson bought a three months' bookmaking concession at the expensive Roney Plaza Hotel, for $45,000, the local police, in a highly publicized raid, swooped down on the hotel; the next year the Roney Plaza was again using local talent. The Capone group, however, was tougher. They demanded an interest in Miami bookmaking, and, when refused, began organizing a syndicate of their own, persuading some bookies at the big hotels to join them. Florida Governor Warren's crime investigator appeared—a friend, it seemed, of old Chicago dog-track operator William Johnston, who had contributed $100,000 to the Governor's campaign fund—and began raiding bookie joints, but only those that were affiliated with S & G. Then S & G, which had been buying its racing news from the local distributor of Continental Press, found its service abruptly shut off. For a few days the syndicate sought to bootleg information from New Orleans, but found itself limping along. After ten days' war of attrition, the five S & G partners found themselves with a sixth partner, who, for a token "investment" of $20,000 entered a Miami business that grossed $26,000,000 in one year.

V

While Americans made gambling illegal, they did not in their hearts think of it as wicked—even the churches benefited from the bingo and lottery crazes. So they gambled—and gamblers flourished. Against this open canvas, the indignant tones of Senator Wiley and the shocked right-eousness of Senator Tobey during the Kefauver investigation rang oddly. Yet it was probably this very tone of surprise that gave the activity of the Kefauver Committee its piquant quality. Here were some Senators who seemingly did not know the facts of life, as most Americans did. Here, in the person of Senator Tobey, was the old New England Puritan conscience poking around in industrial America, in a world it had made but never seen. Here was old-fashioned moral indignation, at a time when cynicism was rampant in public life.

Commendable as such moralistic fervor was, it did not make for intelli-gent discrimination of fact. Throughout the Kefauver hearings, for ex-ample, there ran the presumption that all gamblers were invariably gang-sters. This was true of Chicago's Accardo-Guzik combine, which in the past had its fingers in many kinds of rackets. It was not nearly so true of many of the large gamblers in America, most of whom had the feeling that they were satisfying a basic American urge for sport and looked upon their calling with no greater sense of guilt than did many bootleg-gers. After all, Sherman Billingsley did start out as a speakeasy pro-prietor, as did the Kreindlers of the "21" Club; and today the Stork Club and the former Jack and Charlie's are the most fashionable night and dining spots in America (one prominent patron of the Stork Club: J. Edgar Hoover).

The S & G syndicate in Miami, for example, led by Harold Salvey, Jules Levitt, Charles Friedman, Sam Cohen, and Edward (Eddie Luckey) Rosenbaum was simply a master pool of some two hundred bookies that arranged for telephone service, handled "protection," acted as bankers for those who needed ready cash on hard-hit books, and, in short, functioned somewhat analogously to the large factoring corpora-tions in the textile field or the credit companies in the auto industry. Yet to Kefauver, these S & G men were "slippery and arrogant characters. . . . Salvey, for instance, was an old-time bookie who told us he had done nothing except engage in bookmaking or finance other bookmakers for twenty years." When, as a result of committee publicity and the newly found purity of the Miami police, the S & G syndicate went out of busi-ness, it was, as the combine's lawyer told Kefauver, because the "boys" were weary of being painted "the worst monsters in the world." "It is true," Cohen acknowledged, "that they had been law violators." But they had never done anything worse than gambling, and "to fight the world isn't worth it."

Most intriguing of all were the opinions of James J. Carroll, the St. Louis "betting commissioner," who for years had been widely quoted on the sports pages of the country as setting odds on the Kentucky Derby winter book and the baseball pennant races. Senator Wiley, speaking like the prosecutor in Camus's novel, The Stranger, became the voice of official morality:

SENATOR WILEY: Have you any children?
MR. CARROLL: Yes, I have a boy.
SENATOR WILEY: How old is he?
MR. CARROLL: Thirty-three.
SENATOR WILEY: Does he gamble?
MR. CARROLL: No.
SENATOR WILEY: Would you like to see him grow up and become a gambler, either professional or amateur?
MR. CARROLL: No . . .
SENATOR WILEY: All right. Is your son interested in your business?
MR. CARROLL: No, he is a manufacturer.
SENATOR WILEY: Why do you not get him into the business?
MR. CARROLL: Well, psychologically a great many people are unsuited for gambling.

Retreating from this gambit, the Senator sought to pin Carroll down on his contributions to political campaigns:

SENATOR WILEY: Now this morning I asked you whether you contributed any money for political candidates or parties, and you said not more than $200 at any one time. I presume that does not indicate the total of your contributions in any one campaign, does it?
MR. CARROLL: Well, it might, might not, Senator. I have been an "againster" in many instances. I am a reader of *The Nation* for fifty years and they have advertisements calling for contributions for different candidates, different causes. . . . They carried an advertisement for George Norris; I contributed, I think, to that, and to the elder LaFollette.

Carroll, who admitted to having been in the betting business since 1899, was the sophisticated—but not immoral!—counterpoint to moralist Wiley. Here was a man without the stigmata of the underworld or underground; he was worldly, cynical of official rhetoric, jaundiced about people's motives, he was—an "againster" who believed that "all gambling legislation originates or stems from some group or some individual seeking special interests for himself or his cause."

Asked why people gamble, Carroll distilled his experiences of fifty years with a remark that deserves a place in American social history: "I really don't know how to answer the question," he said. "I think gambling is a biological necessity for certain types. I think it is the quality that gives substance to their daydreams."

In a sense, the entire Kefauver materials, unintentionally, seem to document that remark. For what the Committee revealed time and time again was a picture of gambling as a basic institution in American life, flourishing openly and accepted widely. In many of the small towns, the gambling joint is as open as a liquor establishment. The town of Havana, in Mason County, Illinois, felt miffed when Governor Adlai Stevenson intervened against local gambling. In 1950, the town had raised $15,000 of its $50,000 budget by making friendly raids on the gambling houses

every month and having the owners pay fines. "With the gambling fines
cut off," grumbled Mayor Clarence Chester, "the next year is going to
be tough."

Apart from the gamblers, there were the mobsters. But what Senator
Kefauver and company failed to understand was that the mobsters, like
the gamblers, and like the entire gangdom generally, were seeking to
become quasi-respectable and establish a place for themselves in American life. For the mobsters, by and large, had immigrant roots, and crime,
as the pattern showed, was a route of social ascent and place in American
life.

VI

The mobsters were able, where they wished, to "muscle in" on the
gambling business because the established gamblers were wholly vulnerable, not being able to call on the law for protection. The Senators, however, refusing to make any distinction between a gambler and a gangster,
found it convenient to talk loosely of a nationwide conspiracy of "illegal"
elements. Senator Kefauver asserted that a "nationwide crime syndicate
does exist in the United States, despite the protestations of a strangely
assorted company of criminals, self-serving politicians, plain blind fools,
and others who may be honestly misguided, that there is no such combine." The Senate Committee report states the matter more dog-
matically: "There is a nationwide crime syndicate known as the Mafia.
. . . Its leaders are usually found in control of the most lucrative rackets
in their cities. There are indications of a centralized direction and control of these rackets. . . . The Mafia is the cement that helps to bind the
Costello-Adonis-Lansky syndicate of New York and the Accardo-Guzik-
Fischetti syndicate of Chicago . . . These groups have kept in touch
with Luciano since his deportation from the country."

Unfortunately for a good story—and the existence of the Mafia would
be a whale of a story—neither the Senate Crime Committee in its testimony, nor Kefauver in his book, presented any real evidence that the
Mafia exists as a functioning organization. One finds police officials
asserting before the Kefauver committee their *belief* in the Mafia; the
Narcotics Bureau *thinks* that a worldwide dope ring allegedly run by
Luciano is part of the Mafia; but the only other "evidence" presented—
aside from the incredulous responses both of Senator Kefauver and
Rudolph Halley when nearly all the Italian gangsters asserted that they
didn't know about the Mafia—is that certain crimes bear "the earmarks
of the Mafia."

The legend of the Mafia has been fostered in recent years largely by
the peephole writing team of Jack Lait and Lee Mortimer. In their *Chicago Confidential*, they rattled off a series of names and titles that made
the organization sound like a rival to an Amos and Andy Kingfish society.
Few serious reporters, however, give it much credence. Burton Turkus,
the Brooklyn prosecutor who broke up the "Murder, Inc." ring, denies

the existence of the Mafia. Nor could Senator Kefauver even make out much of a case for his picture of a national crime syndicate. He is forced to admit that "as it exists today [it] is an elusive and furtive but nonetheless tangible thing," and that "its organization and machinations are not always easy to pinpoint." His "evidence" that many gangsters congregate at certain times of the year in such places as Hot Springs, Arkansas, in itself does not prove much; people "in the trade" usually do, and as the loquacious late Willie Moretti of New Jersey said, in explaining how he had met the late Al Capone at a race track, "Listen, well-charactered people you don't need introductions to; you just meet automatically."

Why did the Senate Crime Committee plump so hard for its theory of the Mafia and a national crime syndicate? In part, they may have been misled by their own hearsay. The Senate Committee was not in the position to do original research, and its staff, both legal and investigative, was incredibly small. Senator Kefauver had begun the investigation with the attitude that with so much smoke there must be a raging fire. But smoke can also mean a smoke screen. Mob activities is a field in which busy gossip and exaggeration flourish even more readily than in a radical political sect.

There is, as well, in the American temper, a feeling that "somewhere," "somebody" is pulling all the complicated strings to which this jumbled world dances. In politics the labor image is "Wall Street," or "Big Business"; while the business stereotype was the "New Dealers." In the field of crime, the side-of-the-mouth low-down was "Costello."

The salient reason, perhaps, why the Kefauver Committee was taken in by its own myth of an omnipotent Mafia and a despotic Costello was its failure to assimilate and understand three of the more relevant sociological facts about institutionalized crime in its relation to the political life of large urban communities in America, namely: (1) the rise of the American Italian community, as part of the inevitable process of ethnic succession, to positions of importance in politics, a process that has been occurring independently but almost simultaneously in most cities with large Italian constituencies—New York, Chicago, Kansas City, Los Angeles; (2) the fact that there are individual Italians who play prominent, often leading roles today in gambling and in the mobs; and (3) the fact that Italian gamblers and mobsters often possessed "status" within the Italian community itself and a "pull" in city politics.[1] These three items are indeed related—but not so as to form a "plot."

[1] Toward the end of his hearings, Senator Kefauver read a telegram from an indignant citizen of Italian descent, protesting against the impression the committee had created that organized crime in America was a distinctly Italian enterprise. The Senator took the occasion to state the obvious: that there are racketeers who are Italian does not mean that Italians are racketeers. However, it may be argued that to the extent the Kefauver Committee fell for the line about crime in America being organized and controlled by the Mafia, it did foster such a misunderstanding. Perhaps this is also the place to point out that insofar as the relation of ethnic groups and ethnic problems to illicit and quasi-legal activities is piously ignored, the field is left open to the kind of vicious sensationalism practiced by Mortimer and Lait.

VII

The Italian community has achieved wealth and political influence much later and in a harder way than previous immigrant groups. Early Jewish wealth, that of the German Jews of the late nineteenth century, was made largely in banking and merchandising. To that extent, the dominant group in the Jewish community was outside of, and independent of, the urban political machines. Later Jewish wealth, among the East European immigrants, was built in the garment trades, though with some involvement with the Jewish gangster, who was typically an industrial racketeer (Arnold Rothstein, Lepke and Gurrah, etc.) Among Jewish lawyers, a small minority, such as the "Tammany lawyer" (like the protagonist of Sam Ornitz's *Haunch, Paunch* and *Jowl*) rose through politics and occasionally touched the fringes of crime. Most of the Jewish lawyers, by and large the communal leaders, climbed rapidly, however, in the opportunities that established and legitimate Jewish wealth provided. Irish immigrant wealth in the northern urban centers, concentrated largely in construction, trucking and the waterfront, has, to a substantial extent, been wealth accumulated in and through political alliance, e.g. favoritism in city contracts.[2] Control of the politics of the city thus has been crucial for the continuance of Irish political wealth. This alliance of Irish immigrant wealth and politics has been reciprocal; many noted Irish political figures lent their names as important window-dressing for business corporations (Al Smith, for example, who helped form the U.S. Trucking Corporation, whose executive head for many years was William J. McCormack, the alleged "Mr. Big" of the New York waterfront) while Irish businessmen have lent their wealth to further the careers of Irish politicians. Irish mobsters have rarely achieved status in the Irish community, but have served as integral arms of the politicians, as strong-arm men on election day.

The Italians found the more obvious big city paths from rags to riches pre-empted. In part this was due to the character of the early Italian immigration. Most of them were unskilled and from rural stock. Jacob Riis could remark in the '90's, "the Italian comes in at the bottom and stays there." These dispossessed agricultural laborers found jobs as ditch-diggers, on the railroads as section hands, along the docks, in the service occupations, as shoemakers, barbers, garment workers, and stayed there. Many were fleeced by the "padrone" system, a few achieved wealth from truck farming, wine growing, and marketing produce; but this "marginal wealth" was not the source of coherent and stable political power.

Significantly, although the number of Italians in the U.S. is about a third as high as the number of Irish, and of the 30,000,000 Catholic com-

---

[2] A fact which should occasion little shock if one recalls that in the nineteenth century American railroads virtually stole 190,000,000 acres of land by bribing Congressmen, and that more recently such scandals as the Teapot Dome oil grabs during the Harding administration, consummated, as the Supreme Court said, "by means of conspiracy, fraud and bribery," reached to the very doors of the White House.

municants in the United States, about half are of Irish descent and a sixth of Italian, there is not one Italian bishop among the hundred Catholic bishops in this country, or one Italian archbishop among the 21 archbishops. The Irish have a virtual monopoly. This is a factor related to the politics of the American church; but the condition also is possible because there is not significant or sufficient wealth among Italian Americans to force some parity.

The children of the immigrants, the second and third generation, became wise in the ways of the urban slums. Excluded from the political ladder—in the early '30's there were almost no Italians on the city payroll in top jobs, nor in books of the period can one find discussion of Italian political leaders—finding few open routes to wealth, some turned to illicit ways. In the children's court statistics of the 1930's, the largest group of delinquents were the Italian; nor were there any Italian communal or social agencies to cope with these problems. Yet it was, oddly enough, the quondam racketeer, seeking to become respectable, who provided one of the major supports for the drive to win a political voice for Italians in the power structure of the urban political machines.

This rise of the Italian political bloc was connected, at least in the major northern urban centers, to another important development which tended to make the traditional relation between the politician and the protected or tolerated illicit operator more close than it had been in the past. This is the fact that the urban political machines had to evolve new forms of fund-raising since the big business contributions, which once went heavily into municipal politics, now—with the shift in the locus of power—go largely into national affairs. (The ensuing corruption in national politics, as recent Congressional investigations show, is no petty matter; the scruples of businessmen do not seem much superior to those of the gamblers.) One way urban political machines raised their money resembled that of the large corporations which are no longer dependent on Wall Street: by self-financing—that is by "taxing" the large number of municipal employees who bargain collectively with City Hall for their wage increases. So the firemen's union contributed money to O'Dwyer's campaign.

A second method was taxing the gamblers. The classic example, as *Life* reported, was Jersey City, where a top lieutenant of the Hague machine spent his full time screening applicants for unofficial bookmaking licenses. If found acceptable, the applicant was given a "location," usually the house or store of a loyal precinct worker, who kicked into the machine treasury a high proportion of the large rent exacted. The one thousand bookies and their one thousand landlords in Jersey City formed the hard core of the political machine that sweated and bled to get out the votes for Hague.

A third source for the financing of these machines was the new, and often illegally earned, Italian wealth. This is well illustrated by the career of Costello and his emergence as a political power in New York. Here the ruling motive has been the search for an entrée—for oneself and one's ethnic group—into the ruling circles of the big city.

Frank Costello made his money originally in bootlegging. After repeal, his big break came when Huey Long, desperate for ready cash to fight the old-line political machines, invited Costello to install slot machines in Louisiana. Costello did, and he flourished. Together with Dandy Phil Kastel, he also opened the Beverly Club, an elegant gambling establishment just outside New Orleans, at which have appeared some of the top entertainers in America. Subsequently, Costello invested his money in New York real estate (including 79 Wall Street, which he later sold), the Copacabana night club, and a leading brand of Scotch whiskey.

Costello's political opportunity came when a money-hungry Tammany, starved by lack of patronage from Roosevelt and La Guardia, turned to him for financial support. The Italian community in New York has for years nursed a grievance against the Irish and, to a lesser extent, the Jewish political groups for monopolizing political power. They complained about the lack of judicial jobs, the small number—usually one—of Italian Congressmen, the lack of representation on the state tickets. But the Italians lacked the means to make their ambitions a reality. Although they formed a large voting bloc, there was rarely sufficient wealth to finance political clubs. Italian immigrants, largely poor peasants from Southern Italy and Sicily, lacked the mercantile experience of the Jews, and the political experience gained in the seventy-five-year history of Irish immigration.

During the Prohibition years, the Italian racketeers had made certain political contacts in order to gain protection. Costello, always the compromiser and fixer rather than the muscle-man, was the first to establish relations with Jimmy Hines, the powerful leader of the West Side in Tammany Hall. But his rival, Lucky Luciano, suspicious of the Irish, and seeking more direct power, backed and elected Al Marinelli for district leader on the Lower West Side. Marinelli in 1932 was the only Italian leader inside Tammany Hall. Later, he was joined by Dr. Paul Sarubbi, a partner of Johnny Torrio in a large, legitimate liquor concern. Certainly, Costello and Luciano represented no "unified" move by the Italians as a whole for power; within the Italian community there are as many divisions as in any other group. What is significant is that different Italians, for different reasons, and in various fashions, were achieving influence for the first time. Marinelli became county clerk of New York and a leading power in Tammany. In 1937, after being blasted by Tom Dewey, then running for district attorney, as a "political ally of thieves . . . and big-shot racketeers," Marinelli was removed from office by Governor Lehman. The subsequent conviction by Dewey of Luciano and Hines, and the election of La Guardia, left most of the Tammany clubs financially weak and foundering. This was the moment Costello made his move. In a few years, by judicious financing, he controlled a block of "Italian" leaders in the Hall—as well as some Irish on the upper West

Side, and some Jewish leaders on the East Side—and was able to influence the selection of a number of Italian judges. The most notable incident, revealed by a wire tap on Costello's phone, was the "Thank you, Francisco" call in 1943 by Supreme Court nominee Thomas Aurelio, who gave Costello full credit for his nomination.

It was not only Tammany that was eager to accept campaign contributions from newly rich Italians, even though some of these *nouveaux riches* had "arrived" through bootlegging and gambling. Fiorello La Guardia, the wiliest mind that Melting Pot politics has ever produced, understood in the early '30's where much of his covert support came from. (So, too, did Vito Marcantonio, an apt pupil of the master: Marcantonio has consistently made deals with the Italian leaders of Tammany Hall—in 1943 he supported Aurelio, and refused to repudiate him even when the Democratic Party formally did.) Joe Adonis, who had built a political following during the late '20's, when he ran a popular speakeasy, aided La Guardia financially to a considerable extent in 1933. "The Democrats haven't recognized the Italians," Adonis told a friend. "There is no reason for the Italians to support anybody but La Guardia; the Jews have played ball with the Democrats and haven't gotten much out of it. They know it now. They will vote for La Guardia. So will the Italians."

Adonis played his cards shrewdly. He supported La Guardia, but also a number of Democrats for local and judicial posts, and became a power in the Brooklyn area. His restaurant was frequented by Kenny Sutherland, the Coney Island Democratic leader; Irwin Steingut, the Democratic minority leader in Albany; Anthony DiGiovanni, later a Councilman; William O'Dwyer, and Jim Moran. But, in 1937, Adonis made the mistake of supporting Royal Copeland against La Guardia and the irate Fiorello finally drove Adonis out of New York.[3]

La Guardia later turned his ire against Costello, too. Yet Costello survived and reached the peak of his influence in 1942, when he was instrumental in electing Michael Kennedy leader of Tammany Hall. Despite the Aurelio fiasco, which first brought Costello into notoriety, he still had sufficient power in the Hall to swing votes for Hugo Rogers as Tammany leader in 1945, and had a tight grip on some districts as late as 1948. In those years many a Tammany leader came hat in hand to Costello's apartment, or sought him out on the golf links, to obtain the nomination for a judicial post.

During this period, other Italian political leaders were also coming to the fore. Generoso Pope, whose Colonial Sand and Stone Company be-

---

[3] Adonis, and associate Willie Moretti, moved across the river to Bergen County, New Jersey, where, together with the quondam racketeer Abner, "Longie" Zwillman, he became one of the political powers in the state. Gambling flourished in Bergen County for almost a decade but after the Kefauver investigation the state was forced to act. A special inquiry in 1953 headed by Nelson Stamler, revealed that Moretti had paid $286,000 to an aide of Governor Driscoll for "protection" and that the Republican state committee had accepted a $25,000 "loan" from gambler Joseph Bozzo, an associate of Zwillman.

gan to prosper through political contacts, became an important political figure, especially when his purchase of the two largest Italian-language dailies (later merged into one), and of a radio station, gave him almost a monopoly of channels to Italian-speaking opinion of the city. Through Generoso Pope, and through Costello, the Italians became a major political force in New York.

That the urban machines, largely Democratic, have financed their heavy campaign costs in this fashion rather than having to turn to the "moneyed interests," explains in some part why these machines were able, in part, to support the New and Fair Deals without suffering the pressures they might have been subjected to had their source of money supply been the business groups. Although he has never publicly revealed his political convictions, it is likely that Frank Costello was a fervent admirer of Franklin D. Roosevelt and his efforts to aid the common man. The basic measures of the New Deal, which most Americans today agree were necessary for the public good, would not have been possible without the support of the "corrupt" big-city machines.

VIII

There is little question that men of Italian origin appeared in most of the leading roles in the high drama of gambling and mobs, just as twenty years ago the children of East European Jews were the most prominent figures in organized crime, and before that individuals of Irish descent were similarly prominent. To some extent statistical accident and the tendency of newspapers to emphasize the few sensational figures gives a greater illusion about the domination of illicit activities by a single ethnic group than all the facts warrant. In many cities, particularly in the South and on the West Coast, the mob and gambling fraternity consisted of many other groups, and often, predominantly, native white Protestants. Yet it is clear that in the major northern urban centers there was a distinct ethnic sequence in the modes of obtaining illicit wealth, and that uniquely in the case of the recent Italian elements, the former bootleggers and gamblers provided considerable leverage for the growth of political influence as well. A substantial number of Italian judges sitting on the bench in New York today are indebted in one fashion or another to Costello; so too are many Italian district leaders—as well as some Jewish and Irish politicians. And the motive in establishing Italian political prestige in New York was generous rather than scheming for personal advantage. For Costello it was largely a case of ethnic pride. As in earlier American eras, organized illegality became a stepladder of social ascent.

To the world at large, the news and pictures of Frank Sinatra, for example, mingling with former Italian mobsters could come somewhat as a shock. Yet to Sinatra, and to many Italians, these were men who had grown up in their neighborhoods, and who were, in some instances, bywords in the community for their helpfulness and their charities. The early Italian gangsters were hoodlums—rough, unlettered, and young (Al Capone was only twenty-nine at the height of his power). Those who survived learned to adapt. By now they are men of middle age or older. They learned to dress conservatively. Their homes are in respectable suburbs. They sent their children to good schools and had sought to avoid publicity.[4] Costello even went to a psychiatrist in his efforts to overcome a painful feeling of inferiority in the world of manners.

As happens with all "new" money in American society, the rough and ready contractors, the construction people, trucking entrepreneurs, as well as racketeers, polished up their manners and sought recognition and respectability in their own ethnic as well as in the general community. The "shanty" Irish became the "lace curtain" Irish, and then moved out for wider recognition.[5] Sometimes acceptance came first in established "American" society, and this was a certificate for later recognition by the ethnic community, a process well illustrated by the belated acceptance in established Negro society of such figures as Sugar Ray Robinson and Joe Louis, as well as leading popular entertainers.

Yet, after all, the foundation of many a distinguished older American fortune was laid by sharp practices and morally reprehensible methods. The pioneers of American capitalism were not graduated from Harvard's School of Business Administration. The early settlers and founding fathers, as well as those who "won the west" and built up cattle, mining and other fortunes, often did so by shady speculations and a not inconsiderable amount of violence. They ignored, circumvented or stretched the law when it stood in the way of America's destiny, and their own—or, were themselves the law when it served their purposes. This has not prevented them and their descendants from feeling proper moral outrage when under the changed circumstances of the crowded urban environments later comers pursued equally ruthless tactics.

IX

Ironically, the social development which made possible the rise to political influence sounds, too, the knell of the Italian gangster. For it is the growing number of Italians with professional training and legitimate business success that both prompts and permits the Italian group to

[4] Except at times by being overly neighborly, like Tony Accardo, who, at Yuletide 1949, in his elegant River Forest home, decorated a 40-foot tree on his lawn and beneath it set a wooden Santa and reindeer, while around the yard, on tracks, electrically operated skating figures zipped merrily around while a loud speaker poured out Christmas carols. The next Christmas, the Accardo lawn was darkened; Tony was on the lam from Kefauver.

[5] The role of ethnic pride in corralling minority group votes is one of the oldest pieces of wisdom in American politics; but what is more remarkable is the persistence of this identification through second and third generation descendants, a fact which, as Samuel Lubell noted in his *Future of American Politics*, was one of the explanatory keys to political behavior in recent elections. Although the Irish bloc as a solid Democratic bloc is beginning to crack, particularly as middle-class status impels individuals to identify more strongly with the G.O.P., the nomination in Massachusetts of Jack Kennedy for the United States Senate created a tremendous solidarity among Irish voters and Kennedy was elected over Lodge although Eisenhower swept the state.

wield increasing political influence; and increasingly it is the professionals and businessmen who provide models for Italian youth today, models that hardly existed twenty years ago. Ironically, the headlines and exposés of "crime" of the Italian "gangsters" came years after the fact. Many of the top "crime" figures long ago had forsworn violence, and even their income, in large part, was derived from legitimate investments (real estate in the case of Costello, motor haulage and auto dealer franchises in the case of Adonis) or from such quasi-legitimate but socially respectable sources as gambling casinos. Hence society's "retribution" in the jail sentences for Costello and Adonis was little more than a trumped-up morality that disguised a social hypocrisy.

Apart from these considerations, what of the larger context of crime and the American way of life? The passing of the Fair Deal signalizes, oddly, the passing of an older pattern of illicit activities. The gambling fever of the past decade and a half was part of the flush and exuberance of rising incomes, and was characteristic largely of new upper-middle class rich having a first fling at conspicuous consumption. This upper-middle class rich, a significant new stratum in American life (not rich in the nineteenth century sense of enormous wealth, but largely middle-sized businessmen and entrepreneurs of the service and luxury trades—the "tertiary economy" in Colin Clark's phrase—who by the tax laws have achieved sizable incomes often much higher than the managers of the super-giant corporations) were the chief patrons of the munificent gambling casinos. During the war decade when travel was difficult, gambling and the lush resorts provided important outlets for this social class. Now they are settling down, learning about Europe and culture. The petty gambling, the betting and bingo which relieve the tedium of small town life, or the expectation among the urban slum dwellers of winning a sizable sum by a "lucky number" or a "lucky horse" goes on. To quote Bernard Baruch: "You can't stop people from gambling on horses. And why should you prohibit a man from backing his own judgment? It's another form of personal initiative." But the lush profits are passing from gambling, as the costs of coordination rise. And in the future it is likely that gambling, like prostitution, winning tacit acceptance as a necessary fact, will continue on a decentralized, small entrepreneur basis.

But passing, too, is a political pattern, the system of political "bosses" which in its reciprocal relation provided "protection" for and was fed revenue from crime. The collapse of the "boss" system was a product of the Roosevelt era. Twenty years ago Jim Farley's task was simple; he had to work only on some key state bosses. Now there is no longer such an animal. New Jersey Democracy was once ruled by Frank Hague; now there are five or six men, each top dog, for the moment, in his part of the state or faction of the party. Within the urban centers, the old Irish-dominated political machines in New York, Boston, Newark, and Chicago have fallen apart. The decentralization of the metropolitan centers, the growth of suburbs and satellite towns, the break-up of the old ecological patterns of slum and transient belts, the rise of functional groups, the increasing middle-class character of American life, all contribute to this decline.

With the rationalization and absorption of some illicit activities into the structure of the economy, the passing of an older generation that had established a hegemony over crime, the general rise of minority groups to social position, and the break-up of the urban boss system, the pattern of crime we have discussed is passing as well. Crime, of course, remains as long as passion and the desire for gain remain. But big, organized city crime, as we have known it for the past seventy-five years, was based on more than these universal motives. It was based on certain characteristics of the American economy, American ethnic groups, and American politics. The changes in all these areas means that it too, in the form we have known it, is at an end.

Supplementary Bibliography

Joseph A. Kahl, *The American Class Structure*. N. Y.: Rinehart, 1957.
    An excellent discussion of stratification in the United States, with especially valuable sections on minorities and on style of life.

Wallace E. Lambert and Otto Klineberg, "A Pilot Study of the Origin and Development of National Stereotypes." *International Social Science Journal,* 1959, 11:221-238.
    A provocative piece of research with implications for students of nationalism and of ethnic minority stereotypes.

Kurt B. Mayer, *Class and Society*. N. Y.: Random House, 1955.
    A fine brief analysis of social stratification.

Robert K. Merton, *Social Theory and Social Structure*, rev. ed. Glencoe, Ill.: Free Press, 1957.
    Chapter II, "The Self-fulfilling Prophecy," is a fascinating discussion of the process by which "social beliefs father social reality."

Sister Frances Jerome Woods, *Cultural Values of American Ethnic Groups*. N. Y.: Harper, 1956.
    A useful introduction to minority subcultures.

VII The Appearance and Disappearance of Minorities

We have seen that some minorities are defined partially by the ethnic subculture which they bring to and maintain in a new society, while other minority peoples have virtually no subculture except the by-products of discrimination. Obviously, one factor affecting the position and prospects of a minority is the process by which it achieved its minority status.

Patterns of Minority Emergence

To become a racial or ethnic minority, a set of people must share some characteristic different from the dominant people in the society (a different language, religion, eye form, or even a different history); the characteristic must be socially defined as relevant by the dominant people, and the minority therefore treated as different. Such a situation can arise through colonialism, annexation, voluntary migration, or involuntary migration.

Colonialism is a pattern of behavior in which people become dominant in a society other than their own by gaining power over the resource base through organization, investment capital, or force of arms. The typical colonial situation serves as a good example of the fact that the opposite of *minority* is *dominant*, not *majority*. That is, by *minority* we mean people having less social power; they need not be a mathematical minority. There are far more Indians in India than there ever were British, but during the colonial regime the British had more power, and so the Indians were a minority.

When the boundaries of a society change suddenly through warfare or diplomatic settlement, people can be dominant in their own society one day and find themselves a minority in a different society the next. When

198

boundaries change frequently by annexation, as they have between Greece and Turkey or in central Europe or the Balkans, an individual may experience the shift from dominant to minority status and back on several occasions during his lifetime.

Voluntary migrants, seeking new opportunities or fleeing persecution, ordinarily enter the new society of their choice as members of a minority. Whether or not physically or racially different, immigrants usually are unfamiliar with the language, monetary system, and other customs, and hence can be quickly socially defined as inferior. Occasionally voluntary migrants bring some prized skill which exempts them from all or most discrimination in their new home, but Albert Einstein, Enrico Fermi, and Arturo Toscanini are not typical cases.

Involuntary migrants always enter a new society in minority status. Since, as slaves, they are brought in against their will, the situation of dominance and power inferiority is clearly defined at the beginning.

The United States as a Laboratory

For the student interested in minority problems, the United States offers fascinating opportunities for observation. Not only have we created minorities by each of the four means described above, we are a society entirely composed of minorities and descendants of minorities.

The first settlers in the New World were voluntary migrants who had to make their peace with the far more numerous Indians and learn some of the native culture from them, such as the use of corn. Soon the European settlers were able to exercise superior power and convert the Indians into a colonial minority. Then slaves were imported from Africa as involuntary migrants. The country was expanded through a series of annexations, picking up, among others, a French-speaking minority with the Louisiana Purchase and a Spanish-speaking minority with acquisitions in the Southwest. It continues to grow through voluntary migration; indeed, during some years around the turn of the century, the United States experienced more growth from immigration than from the birth rate.

As a result of the country's having been built in this way, everyone in it is either a minority group member or is descended from people who were at one time a part of minorities. The corollary of this is that every person in the United States is able to be a part-time member of the dominant group. Jews and Protestants can worry together over whether one should vote for a Catholic for President. Negro and white Protestants can unite in opposition to the expansion of Catholic power. Catholics and Protestants, Negro and white, can join in deploring the ways of the Jew. Jews can band together with their white gentile neighbors to keep Negroes out of the neighborhood. Because everyone has been part of a minority, everyone gets part-time access to dominant status.

However, some of these Americans whose ancestors were minority people are no longer, at least for most purposes, minorities themselves. How did this occur?

Factors Affecting Rate of Assimilation

The more recent a group's entry into the social structure, the more resistance there is to its assimilation. When the dominant people are unfamiliar with persons who speak Italian and attend the Catholic Church, the newcomers seem a dangerously foreign menace. When, after a few generations, it has been demonstrated that such people can learn American ways and become part of the society, they seem less threatening. An Irishman who arrives in the United States today is viewed with considerably less suspicion and alarm than his great-grandfather encountered a century ago.

In addition to recency of arrival, cultural dissimilarity is a factor in rate of assimilation. The more there is to learn, the slower the process of absorption of a group will be. It is easier for an Englishman to learn to become like an American than for a Turk, because the Englishman has an enormous head start over the Turk in what he must learn. The Englishman's cultural background is similar to the American's in language, religion, diet, political traditions, and many other features in which the Turk's differs drastically.

The rate of assimilation is further affected by the concentration of minority people in the population. For an American community to absorb a Swedish family is one thing; for it to experience the influx of several thousand Swedish families over a period of a few years is another. For one thing, such a concentration of people with foreign ways makes them noticeable, and may crystallize resistance to their acceptance. For another, it retards their rate of learning of the new culture. If they live in "Swedetown" in the center of a metropolitan area, they can continue to speak Swedish with their neighbors and not be forced to learn English as a single immigrant family would be; they can retain many of their old country ways without much pressure to participate in the culture of their adopted homeland.

Finally, any marked physiognomic difference serves to deter total assimilation. A difference in physical appearance from the dominant population means that one is noticeable even when he has learned the ways of the society. One may be a Protestant office worker, a college graduate, and speak flawless English, but if dominant people can glance at his skin color and hair type and say, "We don't hire Negroes," he has not been assimilated.

All four of these factors which affect the rate of assimilation of a minority—recency of arrival, cultural dissimilarity, concentration, and physiognomic difference—are fundamentally matters of visibility. If a group can be *seen* as different, it can be socially defined as different and discriminated against.

But the first three pass with time. Minority people can learn the new ways. When one no longer speaks Rumanian and wears a babushka, some of the visibility is lessened. It is possible to learn one's way out of being visible and socially defined as a minority on the grounds of behavioral or cultural differences, but racial minorities cannot escape their physical differences. Well-educated Chinese-Americans cannot work their way up to Caucasoid. Physical attributes are more permanent definers and maintainers of group boundaries than are culture traits.

Related Readings

"Park Forest: Birth of a Jewish Community," by Herbert J. Gans, describes a process of development of group cohesiveness in many ways similar to that characteristic of a newly arrived immigrant group. In addition, it illustrates the manner in which concentration in the population and self-consciousness about cultural dissimilarity can define group boundaries and deter assimilation.

Several of the factors affecting rate of assimilation can be seen at work in S. N. Eisenstadt's report, "The Process of Absorption of New Immigrants in Israel." Especially valuable are his descriptions of the impact of cultural dissimilarity and of the vastly different situations facing the "pioneers" as opposed to the more recent arrivals.

Stanley Lieberson, in "A Societal Theory of Race and Ethnic Relations," uses social organization as the variable to account for some of the range of observable minority situations. He argues that there are sociologically significant differences between the structure of a colonial society and that of a society with an immigrant minority where the dominant population is indigenous.

—————————Herbert J. Gans

Park Forest: Birth of a Jewish Community
A Documentary

In November 1949, the author of this article completed a study of the Jews of Park Forest, Illinois. The study had one especially intriguing

Reprinted by permission of *Commentary*, Vol. II, April, 1951, pp. 330-339. Copyright, 1951, American Jewish Committee. All rights reserved.

aspect: under its very eyes—in the midst of answering questionnaires, as it were—Park Forest's Jews gave birth to a young, awkward, but unmistakable Jewish community. It was an entirely natural birth, and the witnessing of it was an illuminating introduction to some of the whys and wherefores of Jewish life and of present-day Judaism in America.

Obviously Park Forest is not Flatbush or Scarsdale or Detroit—so undoubtedly there are limitations in what it has to teach us. On the other hand, when we think of the present composition of American Jewry—which is by and large second generation, mostly business and professional in occupation, and overwhelmingly middle class—perhaps Park Forest is not so atypical after all. What we can see happening there may be chiefly different from what is occurring in other locales only in being more visible and accessible to the student. Park Forest may thus turn out to be a by-no-means unrepresentative Jewish neighborhood in today's rapidly changing American scene. Here, in any case, is what happened, and how.

Park Forest is a garden-apartment housing project located thirty miles south of Chicago. The project, privately developed, was started in 1947, when the Chicago housing shortage was at its height. The first tenants moved in on August 30, 1948, and for two years they continued to come in as new sections of the village were completed. By November 1949, there were 2,000 families—nearly 8,000 people—renting garden apartments at $75 to $100 per month. One hundred and forty-one of these families were Jewish. Of these, about thirty had not been in the village long enough to have relations with the other Jewish families; another fifteen were "mixed marriages," with both husband and wife having rejected any identification as Jews; and the remainder, approximately one hundred families (including a few mixed marriages), 5 per cent of the project, formed a fledgling "Jewish community."

In Park Forest the accent is on youth; the project naturally attracted the people most sorely pressed for housing: veterans with children. The men average thirty to thirty-five years of age, the women somewhat less (anyone over forty is generally considered old). Most of the men are at the beginning of their careers, in professional, sales, administrative, and other business fields. (Only four of the men interviewed owned their own businesses.) Although not long removed from the GI Bill of Rights, they were in 1949 already earning from $4,000 to $10,000 a year—most of them perhaps around $5,000. Few of the men, and few of the wives even, are without some college experience, and educationally the Jews as a whole stand even higher than the rest of the Park Forest community. Ninety per cent of the Jewish men interviewed have college training, 60 per cent hold degrees, and no less than 36 per cent have graduate degrees.

The Jews of Park Forest dress as do the other Park Foresters, enjoy similar leisure-time activities, read the same newspapers, look at the same movies, hear the same radio programs—in short they participate with other Park Foresters in American middle-class culture. They observe few traditional Jewish religious practices; the village's isolation from synagogues and kosher food shops has probably discouraged observant Jews from becoming tenants, and brought problems to those few who did.

Not only do Park Forest Jews live like other Park Foresters, they live with them. Whereas most American cities have "neighborhoods" dominated by one ethnic group or another—in atmosphere and institutions if not in numbers—this is not true of Park Forest. Most Park Foresters live in what are called "courts"—*culs de sac* surrounded in circular fashion by twenty to forty two-story garden apartments. Each "apartment" is actually a house, built together with five or seven others into a single unit. Privacy is at a minimum and each court is almost an independent social unit. Many of the Park Foresters find all their friends in their own court—but this is not the case with the Jews. The Jewish families are scattered all over the village, and only rarely are two Jewish families to be found in adjacent apartments. Yet in just one year, a Jewish community consisting of informal groups of friends, a B'nai B'rith lodge, a National Council of Jewish Women chapter, a Sunday school, and even a Board of Jewish Education had emerged.

How did this happen?

From the very beginning it seemed to be important to Jewish Park Foresters to "recognize" whether or not any of their neighbors were Jewish. And the widespread labeling, in America and Europe, of certain Mediterranean-Armenoid facial features as "Jewish," plus the monopolization of certain surnames by Jews, has resulted in a stereotypical formula of recognition, used by Jews and non-Jews, which is accurate more often than not.

One early resident related: "I saw Mrs. F. in the court a couple of times. . . . I thought she looked Jewish. With me, there's no mistaking it. Then someone told me her name, and I went up to talk to her. Finally we talked about something Jewish, and that was it."

"Jewish mannerisms" were also used to establish, or at least guess at, the other person's Jewishness. "The woman across the street, her actions were typical New York, so we recognized them as Jewish immediately. . . ." People very skillfully explored each other through conversations, attempting to discover whether the other person was Jewish or not, and offering clues to their own Jewishness. "She's been told I'm Jewish, and I know she's Jewish, we haven't discussed it, but she uses Jewish expressions she wouldn't use in front of other people." Others turned the conversation to favorite foods: "It was a slow process, we told them what kind of food we like, corned beef, lox. . . ." Sometimes there are no symbols or formulas which can be applied, and people find out by accident: "I asked before Passover if they wanted macaroons, and we found out."

Many Jewish Park Foresters had known each other previously, had mutual friends or acquaintances elsewhere, or bore introductions from mutual friends to "go look up so-and-so when you get to Park Forest." The people with such previous contacts, however loose these may have been, quickly established friendships and often became "charter members" of social circles which then attracted strangers. In this respect, the Jews differ sharply from other Park Foresters, most of whom knew no one and had no "introduction" to anyone when they arrived in the village. (Even in cities as large as New York and Chicago a surprisingly large number of Jews know or know of each other, because there are relatively few groups which they join, few temples which they can belong to, and few neighborhoods in which they choose to live.)

Barely had this informal network of friendships and acquaintances sprung up among the first Jews moving into Park Forest (it did not, of course, preclude friendships with non-Jewish neighbors—though these, as we shall see later, were rather different in quality from the friendships with Jews), when two formal Jewish organizations were set up—a chapter of the B'nai B'rith and a chapter of the National Council of Jewish Women. Both enrolled only about forty members—those who, for various motives and reasons, were "organization-minded," and those, especially women, who had no Jewish neighbors and wanted to meet Jews from other parts of the village.

Both almost immediately found a purpose: "doing something" about the Jewish children of the growing Park Forest community. And through them steps were soon taken to establish the single most important Jewish institution in Park Forest: the Sunday school.

By June 1949, less than a year after the first resident moved in, the chapters of the B'nai B'rith and National Council of Jewish Women were already fairly well established. Eighty-six Jewish families were now living in the rapidly growing project. Passover had come and gone; the handful of Jewish people who observed it in the traditional way had banded together to order *matzos* and all the trimmings from Chicago. The men who had organized the B'nai B'rith lodge and now formed its ruling clique had begun to talk of a congregation. Some of them were "Jewish professionals," men who make their careers within the American Jewish community; others were men who had been active in big-city Jewish affairs and whose social life had been oriented around a congregation and its activities. But it was generally agreed that Park Forest's prime problem was a Sunday school for the forty-odd eligible children then in the village, and for the others who were to come.

The B'nai B'rith leadership met one evening and sketched out the organization of a Sunday school as part of a congregation—Reform or Conservative, it was not yet clear—to be established in the village. At a meeting with a delegation of women from the Council, however, the latter refused to help organize a congregation, insisting that what Park Forest needed was a Sunday school now, and a congregation later, perhaps. One man said of the women: "They don't care for Jewish values, but they recognize that they are Jewish and they need a Sunday school because the kids ask for it. . . . They want a nonsectarian school." The women, on the other hand, accused the men of trying to take over the community for their own political ambitions, of wanting a "Jewish Community Incorporated."

Eventually a steering committee of four men and four women was formed to proceed with the organization of a Sunday school. While the administrative organization and the budget were being prepared, largely by the men, the school's curriculum was left to a young Chicago rabbi who had become interested in Park Forest. Quite unexpectedly to some, he supported the women in their rejection of a congregation, and formulated instead a Sunday school that would involve the parents in their children's Jewish education: "As we train the children," he told the parents, "you will have to train yourselves. . . . You'll have to move toward a community center and a synagogue eventually. . . ." The parents' major contribution would be to prevent such inconsistencies as would be apt to arise from not practicing at home the content of the Sunday school curriculum.

At a meeting of parents there was a sharp reaction to the rabbi's plans. A large number of those present objected to the curriculum proposed; they wanted a "secular" Sunday school, one which would teach the child *about* Jewish traditions, but which would not put pressure on the parents to *observe* these traditions in the home. For the reasons that they did not want a congregation, they did not want a school that would involve them either. The committee resigned and a new committee was formed.

But exactly what type of "Jewish content" should be brought into the school, and how? The new committee did not have sufficient Jewish background to set up any kind of Jewish curriculum, secular or otherwise, and called for aid from a Jewish professional family that lived in Park Forest, the husband a group worker, and his wife a trained Sunday school principal. The group worker was finally successful in devising a formula that reconciled the two sides, and the basis of the reconciliation is revealing: "The children will not be taught that parents have to light candles; the children will be informed of the background of candles. . . . We're teaching the child not that he must do these things, we just teach him the customs. . . . Why, we even teach them the customs of the Negro Jews . . . and that the customs have been observed for many years, and are being modified."

In "Yankee City's" Jewish community[1] the conflict over the synagogue was between generations, the foreign-born and the first-generation

[1] W. Lloyd Warner and Leo Srole, *The Social Systems of American Ethnic Groups* (Yale University Press, 1945).

American. In Park Forest, where almost everyone is native-born, the conflict over the Sunday school was of a different nature: it was between those who wanted what may be called an *adult-oriented* community and those who wanted a *child-oriented* one.

The adult-oriented community is the traditional (but not necessarily Orthodox) one whose activities are focused around its congregation of adults, and in which the role of the children is to become Jewish adults and assume an adult role. The men who wanted a congregation, with its Sunday school, were thinking of such an adult Jewish community, training its children for eventual membership in the organized Jewish group. In a child-oriented community, the community's energy is focused almost exclusively around the children, around their problems and needs as Jewish children—but, of course, as the adults see these needs. Thus, the women wanted a school for the children and, as became clear, not one that would involve the adults in Jewish community life.

The focus of Park Forest's problem—and conflicts—lies in the family. The Sunday school, much as other Jewish institutions, is recognizably an ethnic rather than a religious institution—more correctly, an American reaction to an ethnic situation—which transmits ethnic behavior and identity; the Jewish home, however, is run by American middle-class behavior patterns. The women feared that the contradictions between the traditional Jewish home, whose features are now incorporated in the Sunday school curriculum, and the American home, which embodies their primary present-day values, would lead to family tensions. So, although they wanted their children to learn about traditional Jewish life, they did not want it brought home.

The situation in Park Forest, then, is that many parents reject involvement in the cultural-religious aspects of the Jewish tradition for themselves as adults, while they demand that their children involve themselves to the extent of learning about this tradition, without, however, getting so involved as to wish to practice it. The fruit of this might well be a Judaism that ends rather than begins with Bar Mitzvah.

Why, however, did the parents want the children to go to Sunday school at all?

First, and quite important, was the fact that the children, in contrast to the parents of Park Forest, having found their friends within the court without concern for ethnic origin, would see their non-Jewish friends leave for school on Sunday mornings. As one mother explained: "Our kids want to get dressed up and go to church too. The Sunday school [the Jewish one] will give them something to do." A few children were actually sent to the Protestant Sunday school a couple of times, but the overwhelming majority of the parents found this intolerable, so the pressure from the children was translated into parental demand for a Jewish Sunday school.

Second, and this is perhaps the more important reason, the parents wanted to send their children to Sunday school because they wanted to make them aware of their ethnic identity, to acquaint them with Jewishness through Jewish history and customs. (Quite frequently, this explanation was complemented by the qualification, ". . . so that later he can choose what he wants to be." The notion that the Jewish child would have a choice between being Jewish or not Jewish, a decision he would make in adolescence or early adulthood, was voiced even by parents who admitted their own continuing confusion as to how to act, and as to the identity they had and wanted to have.)

But why become aware of ethnic identity and of "Jewish customs"? Because parents want their Jewish identity explained to their children, often as a *defense* against hardships they might run into because they are Jews. Representative of this rather widespread sentiment was the comment: "A Jewish child, he's something different, he's never one of the boys in a Gentile group, even if he's the best guy, he's one of the outsiders, the first to get abused, and if he doesn't know why, it's going to be a shock. It's part of his training, the Sunday school, he needs it."

A number of parents of six- and seven-year-olds were particularly clear in their hopeful expectation that Sunday school would supply the children with answers about their identity. It seems to be at that age that questions first develop in the children's play groups as to what they are, in terms of religion or nationality. Sometimes the children are stimulated by a remark made in school or kindergarten, sometimes by something overheard in parents' conversation. One child may thus discover that he is Protestant, and that there are also Catholics and Jews. He brings this information to the group, which then tries to apply these newly discovered categories to its members. Soon the children come home and ask their parents what they are, and are they Jewish, and perhaps even "Papa, why do I have to be Jewish?" Here the Sunday school is asked to come to the rescue. One father reported of his son now in Sunday school: "He can probably tell me more than I can tell him."

It is not only the Sunday school that is child-oriented. The entire community shows itself child-oriented: during the first fourteen months of existence, the largest part of its organized adult activities was for the children. B'nai B'rith nearly collapsed because its leadership was drawn off into the task of establishing the Sunday school; and after the school had been set up, the lodge immediately went to work on a Chanukah party which it hoped to make an annual event. Even among those who wished to found a congregation, a goodly portion explained they wanted it exclusively for the sake of the children: "I don't believe in praying . . . in God . . . I want it for my son and daughter. I want them to know what it's like. I have had the background . . . I remember I enjoyed it at the time."

The Jewish holidays have become perhaps the chief mechanism of teaching and reinforcing Jewish identity. All the "happy" holidays—

Pesach, Purim, Sukkoth, and Chanukah, especially the last—are emphasized and made into children's festivals. At Chanukah time 1948, when
the Park Forest Jewish community consisted of less than twenty families,
the problem of Chanukah versus Christmas first presented itself to Jewish parents. A year later, the problem loomed so large in everyone's mind
that people discussed it wherever they gathered. The women's Council
devoted its November meeting to "Techniques of Chanukah Celebration," that is, techniques of competing with Christmas.

By late November, the non-Jewish friends of the Jewish children are
eagerly awaiting Christmas and Santa Claus. Naturally, the Jewish children are inclined to join in these expectations, and ask their parents
for Christmas trees. In 1948 and 1949, the parents acted quickly. One
mother explained: "The F.'s had a big menorah in their window, that
was very fine, maybe I'll do the same next year. . . . I could put my
little menorah up there, I could wire it, is that O.K., we could have different color lights—no that's too much like Christmas." Another parent
said: "My child wanted a Christmas tree and we talked her out of it.
. . . I make a fuss about Chanukah to combat Christmas, I build up
Chanukah and she appreciates it just as much."

Other parents told how they decorated the menorah, and even the
entire house, and used electric candles instead of wax ones. They tried
hard to emphasize and advertise Chanukah to the child, and at the same
time to exclude the Christmas tree and its related symbols from his
environment. Parents were very bitter about the Jewish families who
displayed Christmas trees. "In our house we do certain things, and in
other Jewish houses they don't, and the children ask questions. . . . It's
very confusing. . . ."

In the process of making a children's holiday in December (or sometimes in November) just as good as the Christian one, the parents' adult
participation in the holiday is forgotten, and Chanukah, more than any
other holiday, becomes completely child-oriented. In this, ironically,
the fate of Chanukah closely resembles that of the American Christmas,
which has tended to be transformed from a solemn religious festival to
a day of delights for children.

Meanwhile, the adults were not nearly so lavish in providing for their
own needs as Jews.

Park Forest has a number of families, either Reform or mildly Conservative, whose social life before moving to Park Forest took place
largely in or near the congregation of their choice. Some of these people
did not hesitate long before joining a wealthy congregation in Chicago
Heights—especially those whose own income and social position were
more or less equal to that of the Heights community. In addition there
are a number of families, probably less than ten, who have maintained
enough of the traditional system of religious attitudes and ritual practices

to be called Orthodox or Conservative. They favor the establishment of a congregation, preferably Orthodox or Conservative, in the village.

But for the remainder, the large majority of the Jews, religious institutions and practices play no role. Of forty-odd families interviewed, more than half reported that they observed no customs or holidays, and had not attended synagogues or temples "for years." Ten reported attending High Holiday services only; seven attended on High Holidays, some other holidays, and a few Friday evenings during the year.

For the majority of Park Foresters, the problems of traditional observance (such as the kosher home) or of attending religious services simply do not exist. They spend Friday nights as others do in Park Forest, entertaining, or going out occasionally when Saturday is not a workday for the man of the house, or staying at home if it is. Saturdays are reserved for work around the house, shopping, visiting, and taking care of the little things suburbanites have no time for during the week.

There are, however, two religious patterns which are still being observed, not universally but by many. First, as has been indicated, there are those holidays and traditions that concern the children. Second are those aspects of death and birth that relate the Jew to his parents. Several of the men remarked matter-of-factly that they were not interested in religious observances, but added just as matter-of-factly, "except of course *Yortzeit*" (anniversary of the death of a parent). Another said: "The only thing we did—at my son's birth we had a rabbi at the circumcision, mostly for my wife's parents, they would have felt bad." (Circumcision is probably all but universal. As for Bar Mitzvah, as yet there are almost no children as old as thirteen.)

Some people celebrate the Jewish holidays by spending them with parents or in-laws, not as religious holidays but as family get-togethers. One woman explained, jokingly: "I believe Rosh Hashanah should be two days, Passover too, for practical purposes. One day we go to his family, the other to mine."

There have been some attempts to establish the beginnings of a religious institutional system in Park Forest. In January 1949, when the Jewish population did not exceed twenty-five families, the group already had a rabbi-substitute, a gregarious "Jewish professional" who roamed through the Jewish community and from his Conservative background ministered to occasional religious needs. "Someone needed Hebrew writing on a tombstone, they were told to call me, someone else wanted *Yizkor* [prayer for the dead] or *Yortzeit* services, they called me. . . ."

Before Rosh Hashanah 1949, two men, one an early comer, the other just arrived, tried independently to set up a *minyan* (minimal group of ten) for the High Holidays. Since communication between Jewish tenants in the older courts and the newer ones had not yet been established, these men never knew of each other's attempts. Both were unsuccessful. Various groups have talked sporadically about setting up a regular congregation.[2] Most interesting in this demand for a congregation is the reason given by many supporters: "They'll have more respect for us, to show that we have arrived, that we're not merely a bunch of individuals."

The "they" referred, of course, to the non-Jewish neighbors. This congregation movement was thus born not entirely of a religious impulse, but of one which attempted to demonstrate the solidarity and respectability of the Jewish community to the rest of Park Forest. Significantly enough, the area of Park Forest in which this congregation movement sprang up was populated by a large number of small-towners and Southerners who from the first indicated that they did not think favorably of Jews.

Uninterested as Park Foresters may be in "the Jewish heritage," they are nevertheless very much Jews. Clearly and unmistakably, that is, they remain both matter-of-factly and by conscious design, members of identifiably Jewish groups. This Jewish group may be another Jewish couple with whom they spend much of their time; it may be a regular and more or less stable group which gathers, in full or in part, almost every weekend and on special occasions. These groups make up the informal Jewish community, the "spontaneous" community that did not require professionals and organizers to be created.

For the most part, this informal community exists at night. In the daytime, when only housewives and the children inhabit Park Forest, the Jewish housewife participates in the general court social life. She interrupts her household duties to chat with a neighbor, while "visiting" over a morning cup of coffee or while watching the children in the afternoon. In most cases, there is no distinction here between the Jewish and the non-Jewish housewife; they belong together to the bridge and sewing clubs that have been established in many courts. There are a few courts in which religious or ethnic cliques of women have formed, and where "visiting" is restricted to such groups. In most courts, however, there are few ethnic distinctions in daytime social life. This applies even more to the men when they participate with other men in court life on weekends (and occasional evenings) through athletic teams and poker clubs. As one of the women observed: "The boys are real friendly. I imagine they don't think about it [ethnic distinctions] but the women have different feelings. Women have little to do; they talk about it in the afternoons."

At night, however, in the social relations among "couples," the Jewish husband and wife turn to other Jews for friendship and recreational partnership. As one person summarized it: "My real close friends, my after-dark friends, are mostly Jewish; my daytime friends are Gentile." Of thirty Jewish residents who listed the names of Park Foresters they see regularly, ten named only Jews; ten named mostly Jews, and one or

[2] In November 1950, after the completion of this study, a congregation was finally organized.

two non-Jews; ten named a majority of non-Jews or only non-Jews. And many of the people who named both Jews and non-Jews pointed out, like the person quoted above, that their most intimate friends were Jewish.

There are, of course, all types of friendship circles in this informal Jewish community. One of the largest groups is made up predominantly of older, well-to-do Park Foresters, many of them previously active in big-city Jewish congregations and groups. Most of these men are employed by business or industry, or in the non-academic professions (medicine, dentistry, law, engineering). A second group consists largely of young academic intellectuals (research scientists, teachers, writers) and their wives. A third is made up of people who have only recently emerged from lower-middle-class Jewish neighborhoods, and are just exploring, with occasional distaste, the life of the middle- or upper-middle-class American Jew. And there are many others.

It is easy to explain the tendency to find friends in one's own group, even when this takes one from one's own front door, as it does in Park Forest. As the Park Foresters say, "It's easier being with Jews"—it is psychologically more accommodating, and there is less strain in achieving an informal, relaxed relationship with other Jews: "You can give vent to your feelings. If you talk to a Christian and say you don't believe in this, you are doing it as a Jew; with Jewish friends you can tell them point blank what you feel."

The in-group attitude, and the anti-out-group feeling that often goes with it, are expressed most frequently at the informal parties and gatherings where the intimate atmosphere and the absence of non-Jews create a suitable environment. Often these feelings are verbalized through the Jewish joke—which generally expresses aspects of the Jew's attitude toward himself, his group, and the out-group—or through remarks about the *goyim*. At parties that are predominantly Jewish, it is of course necessary to find out if everyone is Jewish before such attitudes can become overt.

One man, who had been converted to Judaism in his twenties, when he was married to a Jewish girl, became disturbed, at an informal party, over a discussion of how to inculcate Judaism into the children, "and keep them away from the *goyim*," and felt it time to announce that he had been until a number of years ago a member of a Christian denomination. The declaration broke up the party, and upset many people. After that he felt: "From now on, they'll be on their guard with me, they've lost their liberty of expression, they don't express themselves without restriction now. At a party, if anybody says something, everybody looks to see if I've been offended and people are taken into a corner and told about me." This man has adopted the Jewish religion, is bringing up his children as Jews, and has been more active than the average person in Jewish community life. Yet he is no longer a member of the Jewish in-group, although he remains a member both of the Jewish community and his smaller Jewish group. In his presence, the group sheds the informality and intimacy of the in-group, and is "on guard."

There are many Jewish Park Foresters who reject these in-group attitudes as "chauvinistic," and when asked about their friends, are quick to reply that they do not distinguish between Jews and non-Jews in choosing friends. Yet as one said: "The funny thing is, most of our friends are Jewish even though we say we don't care." And to quote another: "I think we should try to have friends that aren't Jewish. I don't like the fact that all my friends are Jewish."

But these Jewish Park Foresters, too, feel that they differ from the majority of the non-Jewish Park Foresters—and not only because their friends are Jews. The focus of these feelings of difference was summarized by one person: "I have a friend who is not Jewish who told me how fortunate I was in being born Jewish. Otherwise I might be one of the sixteen to eighteen out of twenty Gentiles without a social conscience and liberal tendencies; he is cruel and apathetic. . . . Being Jewish, most of the Jews, nine out of ten, are sympathetic with other problems, they sympathize, have more culture and a better education; strictly from the social and cultural standpoint a man is lucky to be born a Jew."

These feelings have a basis in Park Forest reality. The Jews are distinguished by a feeling of "social consciousness," by concern over political and social problems, by a tendency toward a humanistic agnosticism, and by an interest in more "highbrow" leisure activities: foreign films, classical music, the fine arts, and in general the liberal intellectual-aesthetic leisure culture of America, and perhaps the Western world. There seem to be proportionately more Jews than non-Jews in Park Forest who participate in this culture. Jews who seek other people with whom they can share these attitudes and interests tend to find other Jews. This culture—which includes an important proportion of Park Forest's Jews—itself is largely devoid of Jewish content, and the Jews who come together in it would seem to do so not primarily because they are Jews but because they share a culture. When Jewish problems are discussed by these people (and they are discussed), they are seen from a generalized world view, rather than from an in-group perspective.

Just as Jews form a large proportion of those interested in "culture," they form a large proportion of those interested in the self-government of Park Forest, and in other local activities. Although in November 1949 the Jews made up only 9 per cent of Park Forest's population, eleven of thirty-seven candidates in the first two village elections were Jewish. All but one member of the first Board of Education, and half of the original six-man Board of Trustees that runs the village, are Jewish. The community newspaper was started by a group of women many of whom were Jewish; the American Veterans Committee and the local affiliate of the Democratic party were organized with the help of a number of Jewish men.

If for a moment we take a broader view and consider non-Jewish Park Forest, we discover that the Jewish community is only one of three quite similar organized ethnic-religious groups. Both the large Catholic group (close to 25 per cent of the village population is Catholic) and the smaller Lutheran one also consist of a religious body, men's and women's social organizations, and a more or less extensive informal community. The two Christian groups, unlike the Jewish one, are organized primarily for adult activities, but also emphasize the Sunday school. Both communities developed much more quickly than the Jewish one—largely because there was much less internal disagreement as to what to do and how to proceed—and both were in 1949 already engaged in building programs. The Catholic and Lutheran groups are primarily religious bodies (although they are in part ethnic groups), and have fewer members who reject the group culture. Those who do reject it can quite easily "resign" and become part of the large amorphous body of Americans not strongly identified by religious or ethnic group, something that is much more difficult for the Jew.

In its first year, the Jewish community was very sensitive to the problem of anti-Semitism. Just as every newly arrived tenant would try to recognize other Jews, he would also try to discover the attitudes of non-Jewish neighbors toward Jews. This led quickly to the sprouting of a grapevine which transmitted actual cases, suspicions, and imagined occurrences of anti-Semitism throughout the Jewish community, and sometimes dominated conversation among Jews. A number of people complained strongly that there was a great deal too much talk about anti-Semitism.

Actually, there has probably been very little anti-Semitism in Park Forest. In the interviewing, which covered thirty-five of the fifty-five courts occupied by November 1949, only seven people from seven different courts mentioned incidents they considered to be anti-Semitic. For the most part, these were cases of exclusion, Jewish women (and sometimes children) being left out of some formal and informal activities of the Christian members of the court. There are a number of courts where Jewish and non-Jewish women have split off into separate cliques. It would perhaps be surprising to expect these rather traditional forms of segregation to be absent, especially since Park Forest harbors so many people from different parts of the country, including small-town people from regions generally not friendly to Jews. And one must always ask how much this segregation results from the tendency, described above, of Jews to seek each other out as friends. And it seems certainly true that if anti-Semitism played any role in the formation of the community, it was the fear and expectation of anti-Semitism rather than actual experience of anti-Semitism in Park Forest, on the part of either children or parents.

On the other hand, there are many "liberals" in Park Forest, so that friendly and unquestioned social mixing of Jews and non-Jews is perhaps more common here than elsewhere. This spirit is perhaps typified by an incident that occurred early in the life of the village. A door-to-door salesman asked a non-Jewish resident to point out the Jews in the court because he did not want to sell to Jews. The next day the company was requested not to send any more salesmen to the village.

Park Forest is a new and growing community; it has changed since this study was made, and will continue to change in the future as its present tenants are replaced by others or decide to stay and settle down. Nevertheless, the Jewish community has already become oriented around a number of elements which are not likely to change.

Whereas their parents were not only socially "clannish" but culturally different from their non-Jewish neighbors, the adult Jews of Park Forest are "clannish" but culturally not very different. (Or, rather, their cultural distinctiveness, when it exists, is not along Jewish lines.) Their adjustment to American society and their present status can be described as one of cultural assimilation and continued social distinctiveness. Thus, the Jews of Park Forest remain an ethnic group, albeit different from the parental one.

It is this feeling of Jewish togetherness, to sum up, which provides the impetus for child-orientation, for the parents' insistence on a Sunday school, their transformation and use of the Chanukah holiday, and the unending attempt to indoctrinate the child with a sense of Jewishness.

It is noteworthy that whereas in most cultures the transmission of the group's *esprit de corps* is carried out unconsciously through the children's imitation of, and partial participation in, adult activities, in Park Forest this transmission has become conscious, has become indoctrination— without the parents accepting for themselves the things they are passing on. This no doubt affects the very process of transmission, the thing transmitted, as well as the way the child receives it. Nevertheless, the transmission does take place. Child-orientation is the mechanism that would seem to guarantee the existence of the ethnic group for another generation, even when the adult carriers of the group's culture are ambivalent about it, or have rejected it. So long as Judaism is the curriculum for teaching and transmitting Jewishness, the traditional behavior patterns will be studied, discussed, and taught. However, the high cultural assimilation of the group makes improbable the incorporation of traditional Jewish elements into the rules of daily life.

A major force in the development of the Park Forest Jewish community has been the "Jewish professional," who so far has been the spearhead, "the catalytic agent," as one called himself, in the process of community formation. It was Jewish professionals who helped bring the Jews together, ministered to their early religious needs, started the men's social organization, tried to organize a congregation, helped in forming the Sunday school, resolved the crisis that resulted, and have since supervised Jewish education in the village.

The Jewish professional is a new man on the Jewish scene. He is not a rabbi, but a leader of adults, a youth worker, a teacher, a fund-raiser, a social worker, a contact man, a community relations director, etc. The Jewish professional may not have special training in how to start a Jewish community, but he is expert as being Jewish, something other Park Forest Jews are not. Sometimes this expert Jewishness is a part of his background, and his reason for becoming a professional; sometimes it is the result of a desire to work in the Jewish community, among Jews rather than non-Jews. Sometimes the expert's Jewishness may be only a career, and the professional's activities in these organizations are for him a means of advancing in his career. Whatever his motives, however, the Jewish professional, rather than the rabbi, would seem to have taken over the initiatory role and the largest part of the work of creating the formal Jewish community. In the informal community, his influence is much smaller.

A final factor for an understanding of the Park Forest Jewish community is the sexual division of social labor that takes place within it. The Jewish informal community is based on the Jewish woman. It is she who generally inaugurates and stimulates acquaintances and friendships, who founds the social circles and sets their pattern and content. She has in addition the opportunity of establishing all-female groups which reinforce the groups of couples. Most of the men seem to lay less emphasis on ethnic association, and although there are some all-Jewish male groups, male activities are more likely to take place in groups which more or less ignore ethnic distinctions. Perhaps that is why the B'nai B'rith lodge has been less successful than the women's group in uniting its membership into an active and developing organization. The larger concern of the women with Jewish education, and their more intense interest in the Sunday school, obviously arise from the fact that the women generally have the major role in bringing up the child. In general, the women live a greater part of their life within the Jewish group, and are more concerned with it and about it than the men. In Park Forest, and presumably in communities like it, they seem to be the most influential element in determining the nature of "Jewish" activities. At a somewhat later stage these activities may be handed over to the men.

As to how representative the events and processes that took place in this one Jewish community are, the writer would not be able to hazard a guess, and certainly his study, of a single community and not comparative, would throw little light on this question. But his impression is that it is very unlikely that they are unique to Park Forest. Perhaps in other American Jewish communities these developments are masked by the fact that the group is not so distinctively limited to young married couples with one or two children as it is in Park Forest. In all of them, however, it would seem reasonable to suppose that developments such as have been described must play an increasingly important role in the future Jewish community life in America. Certainly, it would not be claiming too much to suggest that the Park Forest Jewish community offers much illustrative and prophetic material as to the next major stage in the process of Jewish adjustment to American society: the stage in which it is the relations between the second and third generations, both American-born, not the relations between a foreign-born first and a native-born second generation, that are the crucial ones.

—————— S. N. Eisenstadt

The Process of Absorption of New Immigrants in Israel

Predisposition to Change Among Immigrants

The research which is reported here has been undertaken by the Research Seminar in Sociology of the Hebrew University.[1] Its main purpose is to investigate in an objective and systematic way the processes of absorption of new immigrants in Israel (i.e., those who have arrived since the establishment of the State of Israel), specifically of Oriental Jews.

The field work on which this material is based has been carried on in ten centres of new immigrants' settlements—three urban quarters, three semi-urban quarters, and four cooperative agricultural settlements. The field work was carried out from October 1949 to November 1950, and dealt mainly with "new" immigrants—those who arrived after the establishment of the State of Israel. The average length of stay of the immigrant in Israel was, at the end of the field work, about 19 months. The field work was executed in the following way: In each location a field worker, or—in the urban centres—a group of two-three field workers, established themselves as students of the problems of new immigrants. They worked in three directions: 1. Continuous, systematic observation of the behaviour of the new immigrants in various typical social situations—work, school, public life, religious life, relief agencies, and, to some degree, also in their homes. 2. Intensive "free," "open-ended" interviewing of a selected sample in each location—usually a random sample within each main "ethnic" group—according to prearranged

---

[1] The research was done under the auspices of the Department of Oriental Jews of the Jewish Agency and the Hebrew University, under a grant for sociological research from Mr. G. Wise of New York.

schedules, which were not, however, shown during the interviews. These interviews took place either in the immigrants' homes or in informal walks and like situations, and usually included the adult and adolescent members of the family. The schedule dealt with a variety of topics, namely, their general background, motives for immigration, general interest, levels of aspiration in different spheres, social participation and identification, and so on. This sample served also as a panel for repeated interviewing on different problems of attitudes and behaviour, such as identification with the new country and participation in the new social setting, in regard to which changes may have taken place during the year. The interviews were undertaken only after the field workers established themselves in the locations. They were extended in time, and on many topics repeated three or four times, according to changing conditions and situations. 3. More extensive and freer conversations and interviews with a larger sample of immigrants, usually with a great part of the inhabitants of a given quarter. These were used for obtaining more general background information and for investigation of various points raised during the interviews. All these interviews varied in the degree of their intensity.

The research has comprised in all about 1,000 families, investigated in a systematic way (not taking into account those "background" families touched upon during the research), the ethnic distribution of which was as follows:

TABLE I. THE DISTRIBUTION OF OUR SAMPLE ACCORDING
TO COUNTRIES OF ORIGIN

Country	Number of Families
Yemen	102
Turkey	91
North-Africa:	
Tunisia	58
Morocco	123
Algiers	58
Tripoli	78
Bulgaria	125
Yugoslavia	95
Eastern and Central Europe:	
Poland	72
Czechoslovakia	43
Hungary	45
Rumania	64
	Total: 954

These families do not constitute a representative sample of the whole country at any given point of time, although they did constitute samples

of most of their specific ecological settings. Consequently we have restricted ourselves to the analysis of those elements about which definite
correlations could be found within the limits of our sample and its different types.

The series of papers of which this is the first constitute an extension
and reformulation of the original English summary of the full Hebrew
report. These papers analyse only some of the most important problems
of the research, and in every case we have indicated the limitations of
our analysis and possible further developments. Some of the further reports will break down some of the factors reported here in greater detail,
while others will deal with specific topics, such as an analysis of development of different agricultural settlements, and conditions of group tension. All of the quoted material is from interviews in the files of the
Research Seminar in Sociology.

The General Problem of the Research

The most general problem with which this research was concerned
was the conditions under which successful adaptation of immigrants took
place. Adaptation was broadly defined as the immigrants' effective
capacity to perform successfully those basic roles inherent in the main
institutional spheres (family, economic, political, etc.) of the social
structure of the absorbing country.[2] This effective capacity can be subdivided into three main spheres: 1. The actual learning of new social
roles and their performance in different spheres; 2. the extent of stable
social participation with old inhabitants, either in existing or in new
types of groups, and 3. the evolution and maintenance of positive identification with the new social structure and its values, and the minimization of aggressive behaviour oriented against it. It is, of course, obvious
that the achievement of maximal adaptation is a slow, gradual, and
uneven process which can be attained, if at all, only under specific conditions. Broadly speaking, two main sets of such conditions can be
distinguished: (a) those relating to the immigrants' own motivations and
predispositions to action in the new social field, and (b) those relating to
the conditions existing within the new social field, which define the
opportunities available to the new immigrants and the attitudes existing
towards them. In this paper we shall concentrate mainly on some aspects
of the first set of conditions.

Some Social Characteristics of Immigration and Adaptation

The process of immigration is a process of physical transition from one
society to another. Through it the immigrant is taken out of a more or
less stable social system and transplanted into another.

This process of transplantation involves considerable frustrations and

[2] A general outline of this problem has been given by the writer in, "A Proposal for International Research on Absorption of Immigrants," *International Social Science Bulletin*,
July 1951.

gives rise to many social problems among the immigrants. The initial immigration is usually motivated by some feelings of inadequacy and insecurity within the old social system, and by the hope to resolve this insecurity in the new one. In the first stages of transplantation, the immigrant encounters, however, an additional element of insecurity, caused by two interdependent factors: First, the mere necessity to act in a new, relatively strange social field may increase the feeling of insecurity; and second, the process of immigration and transplantation involves a considerable shrinking of the immigrants' social life and participation. Immigration usually takes place in groups which do not encompass all the social spheres of the people, and for some time at least the immigrant is confined to such smaller groups as his mainstay of social participation and identification. Thus throughout this period the immigrant can perform adequately only some of his roles, as only in these smaller groups are his role-expectations more or less institutionalized. In other, wider spheres the immigrant lives in an unstable, unstructured field, with only minimal institutionalization of role-expectations.[3]

The immigrants' integration within the new country may, then, be visualized as a process of extension of the immigrants' field of social participation through mutual adaptation of their role-expectations and the institutionalized norms of the absorbing society. Through this process the immigrants may find solutions to the double social and psychological insecurity in which they are involved.

It should be emphasized that, despite the shrinkage of their social field, the immigrants have some "idea" or "image" of the new country, and some more or less definite role-expectations with regard to the wider social field. These role-expectations are usually determined by the nature of the motives for immigration, the nature of the immigrants' insecurity within the old social system, and the type of solution of this insecurity to which they aspire. These role-expectations are among the most important determinants of the immigrants' perception of the new social structure, its institutional norms, and their own place within it.

The Problem of Predisposition to Change

Among these expectations are attitudes of crucial importance, namely, the extent to which the immigrant expects and is prepared to change his behaviour and undertake the performance of new roles. Some such changes are always expected from him in the new situation. This necessity may, however, run counter to the immigrant's expectations and aspirations. In this respect there exists wide variation between immigrants— from total acceptance of this necessity (positive predisposition to change) to total rejection (negative predisposition to change). As this predisposi-

---

[3] The concept of an "unstructured social field" has been developed by the writer in a paper, "Unstructured Social Behaviour in a Situation of Culture Contact," read at the 12th International Congress of Psychology (Edinburgh, 1948).

tion determines to a very large extent, the direction and tempo of the immigrants' activities and adaptation, and the extent to which their absorption will change the institutional structure of the absorbing country, it is one of the most important variables to be investigated. Its importance is enhanced in the situation of "mass-absorption" in Israel, as here the conditions of absorption have been very difficult from the outset and have involved many hardships—in getting housing accommodations, and in giving, for the majority, little choice other than manual labour.

In the first part of our research, which is reported in this paper, we have set out to investigate the main manifestations of positive (and negative) predisposition to change, the conditions under which they develop, and their general bearing on the structure of the absorbing country.

The Nature and Manifestations of Predisposition to Change

Our first task is to set out a set of indices (or attributes) of these (positive) predispositions. The mere undertaking or performance of new roles could not constitute such an index, as almost every immigrant has to perform some of the roles, especially in the occupational field. It is the immigrant's definition of, and attitude toward, this change that is of interest to us and which should be indicated by these indices.

The most general attribute of a positive predisposition to change is *a high level of frustration-toleration.* Such factors as the exigencies of the absorbing situation and the necessity for reorientation constitute definite frustrations,[4] and an attitude which accepts these conditions as inescapable necessarily entails a high level of frustration-toleration. The main concrete manifestations of this attribute are the following:

1. *Ego-integrity* in face of frustrations imposed by the new situation, which can be seen in (a) a low degree of personal apathy and/or aggression as a reaction to these frustrations; (b) the maintenance of personal initiative within the new situation—a high degree of selective activity in the exploration of the new environment, in utilization of different opportunities, etc.; and (c) a general "experimental" attitude towards the new environment, which is closely related to (b), and which also manifests itself in a low incidence of complaining and bitterness and in a preparedness to "try out" the new roles and to perform them faithfully.

2. *Flexibility of levels of aspirations,* which manifests itself in (a) the readiness to change aspirations if found to be unrealizable in the existing situation, and to adjust them to present possibilities, and (b) "open-mindedness" with regard to aspirations oriented to the future and preparedness to "experiment" with alternative future possibilities.

Both ego-integrity and flexibility of levels of aspirations were also manifested in a strong positive future-perspective, i.e., the evaluation of

---

[4] Almost all of the immigrants investigated by us (90%) spontaneously emphasized this feeling of frustration.

the present as a preparatory stage for the future, making possible the endurance of present hardships, as opposed to "fixation" on the present and evaluation of the future in terms of present difficulties only.

The non-existence of these attributes constitutes the negative predisposition to change (i.e., the lack of readiness to undertake and perform new roles). In the analysis of our material it was found that the existence (or non-existence) of all these attributes was interconnected among 82-85% of our sample. In about 7-8% no consensus of evaluation could be found among the investigators, and in about 10% it was found that this total interconnection did not exist.

Predisposition to Change and Ego-strength

From the extent of these empirical interrelations, it can be adduced that a high level of frustration-toleration constitutes an important unitary personality trait, i.e., it is closely connected with the personality's integrative mechanisms and their functioning. It seems to be most closely connected with—or even to be a manifestation of—"ego-strength," and the inverse manifestations (negative predisposition to change) indicate a weak ego-structure. In our sample, the difference between strong and weak ego-structures is most easily discerned through the extent to which the individual is dependent for his psychological security on the continued reception of various expressive symbols of evaluation inherent in a stable, coherent social field. It is, of course, obvious that everyone is to some extent dependent on such evaluation for the maintenance of his psychological security. The precise extent of this dependence varies, however, and is of special importance in those situations, such as situations of culture-contact—immigration among them—in which one is put within an unstructured social field where the possibility of reception and maintenance of these symbols is minimized. In these instances, only those people can maintain some degree of stability in their activities and personalities whose dependence on these symbols is minimal. For such people their own self-evaluation and perception constitute an important basis of psychological security which assures the integrations, i.e., the strength of their ego-structure.

This difference between ego-strength and ego-weakness may be related to a psychological characteristic recently investigated by Fraenkel-Brunswick and Rokeach—namely, the "tolerance of ambiguity." [5] The initial absorbing situation is, we think, highly ambiguous for the immigrants, both because of its novelty and because of the almost always present discrepancy between their hopes and the existing reality. It seems that those with a positive predisposition to change have a high level of ambiguity-toleration and can resolve this ambiguity (and give some

[5] Fraenkel-Brunswick, W., "Intolerance of Ambiguity as an Emotional and Perceptual Personality Variable," *Journal of Personality* (1949, *18*, pp. 108-43); Rokeach, M., "Generalized Mental Rigidity as a Factor in Ethnocentrism," *Journal of Abnormal and Social Psychology* (1948, 43, pp. 259-78).

positive meaning to their situation) through their own self-integrative principles; while those with a negative predisposition to change lack these principles and this strength and consequently cannot resolve and tolerate the existing ambiguity.

Ego-strength and Evaluation of Status-symbols

In our sample, this characteristic can best be seen in the different ways of self-evaluation of status and occupational standing. The necessity for change of roles is, as we have seen, most pressing in this sphere, and it may involve forgoing many of the amenities, patterns of behaviour, and expressive symbols, such as standard of living, style of dress, dwelling, occupational choice, etc., that are either closely interwoven with social status or constitute its main symbols. The attitude towards this necessity differs markedly as between those with positive and those with negative predisposition to change. Those with positive predisposition to change are quite prepared to forgo some of these symbols and the expressive gratifications inherent in them, as long as they feel they can achieve *through* their present activities—even if only in a future time—some basic economic and social security. They do not renounce any aspirations of achieving some high social status in the future—but their image of this status is not bound to any of the "symbolic" patterns of behaviour, and they are quite prepared to experiment with many different possibilities and avenues of achievement, and to vary them according to the necessities and demands of the situation. Throughout this process of "experimentation" and change their self-evaluation does not suffer to any great extent because of the necessary changes, and is not dependent on their clinging to these various amenities and symbols. In the present stage their evaluation of all these symbols and amenities is essentially an "instrumental" one, e.g., as a means to social and economic security.

The interpretation of status is entirely different among those with a negative predisposition. Here we find a definitely "ritualistic" attitude which makes their self-esteem dependent on the acquisition and holding of these different symbols and amenities, which become, as it were, ends in themselves, and necessary symbols of self.

The following excerpts from interviews with new immigrants may illustrate this difference:

"Yes, it really is difficult here, and it has not been easy to accustom ourselves to these new conditions. In Europe we lived in a five-roomed flat, and here we have only one-and-a-half rooms. There I had an easy and important occupation—that of a lawyer—while here I have to learn to hew rocks and do other physical labour. And my wife's lot is perhaps even more difficult, with all this housework and without any help. But I know that one must adapt, must really change one's ways here, and that we must be patient. Now the most important thing is to be sure of one's roof and bread—and then slowly we shall build a new life— either for us or for our children . . . No, I do not think that we shall have in the future the same type of life that we had in Europe . . . and it is not really important. One does not have to be a lawyer to be a good man and a respected person. This can be achieved here in a different way, even now, in my situation. I do not think that I really am a worse man than I was before. I miss many things, of course, but those who think that without these things one is not worth anything are fools . . . One must have much patience and hope, and believe in himself."

Another man, from Yemen, in this same vein: "In Yemen only the rich and the learned were the good people. I always wanted to be rich, and to have houses and to study Torah (the Law)—but I think here it is otherwise. One must forget many things one had there, and do new things, and still be a good man. I do not know exactly what it is I must do, but I shall learn . . . Yes, it is difficult, but I shall try . . . the most important thing is that one is a Jew, not what one has . . ."

And some contrary examples: "I have not come through all the hardships of the war to endure more hardships. I must demand what is due a man in my position—all the nice and important things—a flat, the same occupation and living standard I had in Europe. All these things are very important to me—if I had them there, among Gentiles, why should I not have them here . . . without them I may become like one of the rabble, the worst people—I already feel that way here . . . what a disappointment!" From North Africa: "At home all this work was done by Arabs, by the lowest and worst of them. A Jew would be ashamed to do such work, and here we have to do it . . . it is a shame . . . I have many friends here, but we do not want to meet and see one another, because we are so ashamed of ourselves . . . we are no longer human beings."

Although we could not inquire explicitly into the correlation between these different types of self-evaluation and predisposition to change in our sample, whenever it was inquired into (in about 65% of the sample) such a correlation was found to exist.

These different evaluations of self and own status were also found to be very highly correlated with different types of identification with the Jewish nation (or the State of Israel). We have seen earlier that the type of orientation that the immigrant has toward his new country is of great importance for the process of adaptation, and here we could find a definite correlation between this orientation and those attributes which make for differential-tempo and direction of adaptation, viz., the predisposition to change. Among those with positive predisposition, it was found that belonging to the Jewish community and coming to Israel were defined, in themselves, as sources of security, strength and "feeling of belongingness." It was non-conditional identification, evaluated mainly in terms of "living together"; "among own people"; "without disturbances"; "being at home." Among those with a negative predisposition this identification was mainly conditional on the possibility of their maintaining—or, usually, acquiring—within this community symbols of status which had for them the above-mentioned ritual quality. Belonging to the Jewish community as such does not constitute for them a source of security. Characteristically enough, among them the identification with the Jewish community is to a very large extent "power-oriented," [6] i.e., it is evaluated in terms of strength and power *vis-à-vis* other communities or nations. This is generally so among large sectors of North-African and Oriental Jews, in their relation to their former Arab neighbours (and oppressors).

We may, then, sum up by saying that the immigrant with a positive predisposition to change is usually one with considerable ego-strength, which enables him not to cling "ritually" to various status characteristics as prerequisites for self-esteem and social acceptance, and whose ego-strength is, at least to some degree, connected with his positive, non-conditional identification with the Jewish community as a source of security and belongingness.

It is this "ego-strength" and self-assurance which enable those with positive predisposition to change to participate actively in the structuring and "rebuilding" of the social field in which they are placed through the process of immigration, and to contribute to their own social re-integration. The flexibility of their role-expectations enables them to adapt them to the institutional norms of the absorbing society, and to achieve full institutionalization of their role-expectations. On those with negative predisposition the forces of the social field impinge sharply without their being able to reinterpret and reintegrate them actively in their social field. For them the social field remains unstructured, and their situation mainly "anomic."

Conditions of Predisposition to Change: Sources of Ego-strength

Our next step was the analysis of the social conditions under which positive and negative predisposition to change develop among different types of immigrants.

First, we tried to see whether any significant correlations existed between the predisposition to change and some "usual" objective, socio-economic variables—such as country of origin, occupation, economic status, education level, and age at time of marriage.

Among these it was found that the positive predisposition is relatively higher among unmarried people within the age-groups of 15-22 than in other comparable groups, and that no significant correlations exist with the other variables. It was found, however, that the distribution of these two types is not the same among immigrants of different countries of origin, as shown by the table overleaf.

The exact sociological meaning of the difference between the various countries of origin could not be understood through these different socio-economic variables, and we had to find some "intervening" variables

---

[6] This term is used here according to the definition by the Oslo Seminar in Sociology on Nationalism.

which would, on the one hand, be within our initial framework, and, on the other, would account for differences within countries of origin. At this stage of inquiry we have focussed our analysis on two interdependent factors closely related to the problem of sources of personal security within the process of immigration.

This focus is in line with the general exposition of our problem as outlined above. If the existence of a positive predisposition to change can be more or less equated with "ego-strength," then in looking into conditions giving rise to it we should look into possible sources of such

TABLE II. THE DISTRIBUTION OF POSITIVE AND NEGATIVE PREDISPOSITION TO CHANGE AMONG IMMIGRANTS OF DIFFERENT COUNTRIES OF ORIGIN

Countries of Origin	Heads of Families with Positive Predisposition to Change		Heads of Families with Negative Predisposition to Change	
	Number	Per cent	Number	Per cent
Yemen	86	85	16	15
Turkey	55	65	36	35
North Africa:				
Tunisia	24	40	34	60
Morocco	41	33	82	67
Algiers	20	35	38	65
Tripoli	32	40	46	60
Bulgaria	100	80	25	20
Yugoslavia	62	65	33	35
Central and Eastern Europe:				
Poland	18	25	54	75
Czechoslovakia	11	25	32	75
Hungary	12	27	33	73
Rumania	13	20	51	80
Total:	474		480	

strength (or weakness) within the immigrants' social groups and settings. Although ego-strength has been defined as relative independence from "external" evaluation, it is obvious that (a) ego-strength is acquired through distinct types of social interaction, in which psychological security is assured, and that (b) for its maintenance it is dependent on the continuity of some such relations. The problem, then, could be restated in terms of which groups, relations, and identifications provide the immigrant with enough emotional support to enable him not to be dependent on the expressive symbols of status and to withstand the ambiguity and lack of structuring of the absorbing situation.

Family Solidarity

It was assumed that the greatest importance should be attributed here to those basic groups which continued to exist throughout the process of immigration and which constituted the immigrants' mainstay and the centre of their most continuous and effective social relations. Among these, the family stood out clearly as of greatest importance, and we have focused our analysis on some aspects of family structure related to our problem.

Two main types of families could be distinguished in their ways of facing the difficulties inherent in immigration: the solidary and the non-solidary types. The main distinction between the two types of families is based on the extent of their internal cohesion and collectivity-orientation. The solidary family is a cohesive group, the existence of which is perceived by its members as an end in itself. Their activities and relations are oriented towards the maintenance and perpetuation of the collectivity, with its common goals and norms; and the mutual relations of its members are to a very large extent evaluated accordingly. Every member of the group is highly valued as such because of his belonging to the group. The non-solidary family, on the other hand, does not evince any high degree of cohesion, of sharing goals and ends, and its existence is mainly perceived as a means for attaining the discreet goals of its members. The same holds true, of course, of the mutual relations of its members.

This distinction was empirically established through the following manifestations:

1. *Type of attitude and interaction of various members of the family.*
   (a). The extent to which constant demands on and complaints about one another were made by members in relation to the fulfilment of various needs (lowest in solidary type—highest in non-solidary type).
   (b). The extent to which members (particularly husbands and fathers) suffered loss of respect and affection if they did not fare well in the outside world, did not maintain their status, and could not bring their families the amenities to which they were accustomed (lowest in solidary type, highest in non-solidary type).

2. *Type of family organization and communication.*
   (a). The extent of cooperation and consultation in difficult, "critical" situations (highest in solidary type, lowest in non-solidary type).
   (b). The extent of preparedness of different members of the family (particularly husband, wife) to exchange some of their roles (both intra-familial and external, e.g., occupational) when the necessity arises (highest in solidary type, lowest in non-solidary type).

3. The extent to which the maintenance of mutual affection is dependent on the vicissitudes of the outer world—this is clearly related to 1 (b)— (highest in non-solidary type, lowest in solidary type).

These different characteristics were ascertained both through direct observation of behaviour and through the intensive interviews. The consistency of evaluation and interrelation was very high—about 88% of the cases in the sample. The following excerpts from interviews may serve as illustrations of the two types:

". . . whenever I am in difficulty I go to my wife and oldest daughter and tell them about it and ask how to solve it. When I was promised some work on condition that I spend three months learning the trade, we decided that my wife should go to work temporarily, and also that my daughter should contribute something—but only on the condition that it would not interfere too much with her studies. She took her mother's place in caring for the smaller children. The children's future and studies are very important and we are all prepared to sacrifice . . . It is really a very good feeling to know that the family is together . . . it makes everything so much easier and nicer . . ." And the contrary attitude: "No, . . . I do not find much comfort from my family. My wife does not want to help me—she just wants to live as we were accustomed to living in Europe . . . and perhaps she is right . . . She is always nagging me about money, about my lack of success, about my lack of interest in the future of the children. I am quite often ashamed to come home . . . when I am out of work or when something goes wrong . . . they would only laugh at me and my ineptitude . . . And I myself would not really like my wife to work . . . it is not done . . . but I do not know what will happen to us here . . . our house is no home, really . . ."

A very high correlation has been found between positive predisposition to change and membership in a solidary family, and negative predisposition and unsolidary types, as can be seen in the following table:

TABLE III. DISTRIBUTION OF SOLIDARY AND NON-SOLIDARY FAMILIES ACCORDING TO PREDISPOSITION TO CHANGE AND REGIONS OF ORIGIN

Region of Origin	Positive Predisposition to Change		Negative Predisposition to Change	
	Solidary Families	Non-Solidary Families	Solidary Families	Non-Solidary Families
Yemen	70	16	5	11
North Africa	102	15	25	170
Turkey	45	10	16	20
Bulgaria				
Yugoslavia	149	13	13	45
Central and Eastern Europe	48	6	78	92
Total:	414	60	137	338
Total percentage:	87%	13%	23%	77%

It should be emphasized that these two types of families to a large extent cut through cultural and structural differences, although they are unequally distributed among the different countries of origin. Both types can be found, however, within the traditional patriarchal, extended family of the Balkan Jews, and within the conjugal, individualistic, small, "modern" family of Central and Eastern European Jews. Our typology refers not to the formal structure and distribution of power within the family, but to the internal processes of the family as a functioning unit. It seems that these processes may sometimes even run

counter to the formal structure, or are at least to some extent independent of it. What the exact limits of this independence are, and to
what extent structural and cultural differences facilitate the existence of
these types, has (except as to what follows) not been investigated by
us at this stage, as it was considered of relatively little concern for our
immediate purposes. From our point of view the most important fact is
that membership in each of these types of families affects the immigrant's
behaviour (predisposition to change) in the same way, irrespective of
such conditions as his country of origin or cultural tradition.

How can this correlation between predisposition to change and family-
type be explained? Our research bears out that the focal point is the
extent of affectional and social security which the immigrant can receive
in his family. In so far as he (or she) is accepted within the family in
his own right, and not as a means for ends outside the scope of the
family group, and in so far as he is, consequently, assured of a constant
flow of affection and mutual protection, he acts within a relatively secure
social field which strengthens—or maintains the strength of—his ego
and his self-esteem. However, in so far as the family does not act as a
solidary primary group, and the relationships between the members are
more in the nature of means to outside ends, one's acceptance within the
family and receipt of affection is conditional to his achievement of these
ends. Consequently the family does not constitute a "base of security"
in times of stress, its members tend to cling to those symbols (and
amenities) which alone can assure them acceptance within the family,
and their predisposition to change is mainly negative. (Our investigation
could not bring out whether or not personality type determines the type
of family one establishes, i.e., whether people with initially strong ego
tend to establish "solidary" families, or whether solidary families
strengthen the ego. Probably the relation is—both genetically and struc-
turally—circular, but more specific investigation must be carried out in
order to analyse this problem.) In other words, the solidary family does
not foster a strong status-anxiety, and consequently does not compel its
members to cling "ritually" to various status symbols; while the opposite
holds true to a large extent in the non-solidary family.

Jewish Identification

The importance of family solidarity to the predisposition to change is
not, however, in itself sufficient to account for all the sources of security
and ego-strength of the immigrants. Although the family constituted the
main stable social unit throughout the process of immigration, this very
process, its motivation and course, are interwoven within wider social
settings. It is the insecurity felt within the society of origin which gives
rise to migration, and it is within the entire social fabric of the new
country that the immigrant hopes to resolve this insecurity. Therefore it
is important to investigate what security and strength the immigrant
can derive from this wider orientation, and under what conditions this

orientation hampers the achievement of this security. In our sample, the importance of this problem was accentuated by the specific Jewish element. Most of the immigrants came to Israel because they felt insecure as Jews in their countries of origin, and because they hoped to be able to overcome this insecurity in Israel—as a new, independent, Jewish society. From the outset it was some sort of Jewish identification that motivated them to immigrate to Israel. The exact nature of this Jewish insecurity and identification varies, however, from country to country; and we have already seen that positive and negative predisposition to change is closely connected with different types of Jewish identification. Thus our problem here is to investigate to what extent specific types of Jewish social structure serve as bases of personal security or insecurity for the immigrant. We therefore classified and analysed the different Jewish communities according to those elements and aspects of their social structure most closely related to our problem.

The most important characteristic of Jewish social structure in the Diaspora, from this point of view, is the ambivalence of the Jews with regard to the wider, Gentile society. The Jewish community in the more or less traditional countries of the Diaspora lives within the ecological and political orbit of the general society, in a situation of (formal or informal) discrimination, segregation, and social inferiority, at the same time maintaining its own tradition, regarded by its members as of higher value than that of the surrounding society. This inferiority-superiority role necessarily gives rise to a feeling of insecurity on the one hand, and of ambivalence (based on tension between actual inferiority and evaluative cultural superiority) towards the Gentile society, on the other. This ambivalence is usually centred around problems of acceptance within the Gentile society. The structuring and resolution of this ambivalence vary from one Jewish community to another according to the possibilities of (a) segregating the relative spheres of superiority and inferiority; (b) limiting the bestowal of status effective within the community to those spheres in which cultural superiority can be maintained; (c) orienting the aggressive tendencies accruing from ambivalence towards the out-group, while at the same time maintaining a high degree of in-group cohesion and solidarity.

These characteristics can be maintained only under specific conditions, among which the extent of social autonomy, self-regulation and "autarchy" of the different Jewish communities is most important.

The Main Types of Jewish Communities

From this point of view we have been able to distinguish in our sample the following main types of Jewish communities:

1. The traditional sector, which comprises the Yemenite Jews and some sectors of North African Jewry. This sector is characterized by a relatively wide extent of social autonomy and orientation towards particularistic Jewish values and traditions (although the degree of intensity

of this orientation and of the activities of specifically Jewish *élites* varies greatly from place to place). Cultural orientation towards the out-group is mainly negative, and the Jewish community succeeds in maintaining independent, autonomous status criteria not directly related to or dependent on the parallel criteria of the Gentile society. This community therefore evinces a very high degree of solidarity and cohesion in relation to the out-group, and insecurity within the surrounding Gentile society is resolved, or overcome, through this in-group solidarity. Segregation of the relative spheres of superiority-inferiority is achieved, and serves to enhance the solidarity.

2. The "insecure" transitional sector, which comprises great parts (especially urban) of the North African Jewish communities, and most of the Central and Eastern European communities which remained intact after the war. Its main characteristics are the following: (a) A very small extent of social autonomy; (b) relatively strong aspirations towards entrance into the Gentile society and identification with it; (c) social and occupational mobility towards the Gentile society; and (d) a feeling that belongingness to a Jewish community usually constitutes an impediment for the achievement of status and successful mobility towards the Gentile society. (In our sample, the transitional sector which achieves social and economic security was very poorly represented, and could not be fully taken into account.) Among the North African Jews this mobility aspiration towards the Gentile (French or Italian) society was hampered, not only by that society, but also by the rising tide of semi-modern Arab nationalism, between the two of which most Jewish communities were caught.

Within this sector ambivalence towards the Gentile society could not be resolved through segregation of the relative spheres of superiority-inferiority, and the in-group could not develop cohesion and solidarity oriented against the out-group. These sectors live in a constant state of tension, status-anxiety, and insecurity, which does not find any permanent solution in the structure of their societies.

3. The secure, transitional sector, which comprises Jewish communities settled within Gentile society and approved by it. This group, in our sample, is confined mainly to Serbian and Bulgarian Jewries, which constituted, it seems, a unique type of Jewish society. Their most important characteristics are the following: (a) Small degree of social autonomy, mainly confined to family traditions and religious worship; (b) strong primary identification with the general community and secondary, associational identification with the Jewish community; (c) acceptance of their Jewishness by the Gentile community as a sub-system within the general social structure, and, consequently, their Jewishness usually fostering, or emphasizing, their social status. It is very important and characteristic that only in these countries was the social crisis which prompted them to immigrate to Israel not a specifically Jewish one, i.e., they were not deported, etc., because of being Jews but mainly because

of general social and political upheavals, and, for them, belonging to the Jewish community proved to be a source of a specifically strong feeling of security.

4. The sector of ex-inmates of D.P. camps, survivors of the destroyed Jewish communities in Eastern Europe, for whom the experience of destruction and camp-life overshadowed any other social traditions and feeling in their self-consciousness as Jews. (In our further analysis we shall subsume the fourth sector under the second, and the third sector will be called the "insecure transitional sector.")

The different types of predisposition to change (both positive and negative) were unquestionably connected with these characteristics of Jewish communities and their crises. Positive predisposition took place mostly among those coming from countries where belongingness to the Jewish community constituted an approval of social status and/or a source of group cohesion against the outside world, namely, in the first and third sectors. Negative predisposition took place mostly among those for whom belongingness to the Jewish nation was a factor of insecurity and status-anxiety—the second and fourth sectors. In the first case, un-conditional identification with the Jewish community develops because belongingness to it is a positive factor of morale and of social security. In the second case, the Jewish self-consciousness of the immigrants is of a most ambivalent type, and their immigration to Israel was, to put it metaphorically, motivated by the desire to resolve this ambivalence—by achieving in Israel all those symbols and emoluments of social status which were denied to them, as Jews, in their countries of origin—hence their "ritual" clinging to these symbols of status and their conditional identification with the Jewish Nation in Israel. Their peculiar situation within the pluralistic European-Arab society explains also the strong power-orientation of their national identification.

This connection between predisposition to change and the different types of Jewish identification can be very clearly illustrated from some of our interview material:

"It is much easier to be here, to know that you are among your own brothers. It is really a wonderful feeling, and even I myself, who am far from being enthusiastic about anything, can feel it. And it makes you feel that many other things are not so very important . . . I am pre-pared to endure here many hardships which I would never agree to in Bulgaria . . . here it is different. It is not so important how much money you have, or whether the work is difficult . . . after all you know that you are really at home . . . Oh yes, I got along all right in Bulgaria, I did not encounter any anti-semitism—but here it is somehow different— it makes you see things in a different way."

"Here we are all Jews, all one family. And we should help one another in whatever way we can. In Yemen we could not do anything we liked, we were surrounded by Arabs who ruled over us, and we had to observe many customs which were really unimportant . . . and we had to distinguish ourselves from them . . . but here, with our own people, it is already not so important . . . you can do any work you want, it is no shame here—just as within the family it is no shame" (a young Yemenite).

"I do not want to do here all the things that only the Arab riff-raff did in Morocco. I did not come to Israel to become like one of them. We are better than they, we are stronger—why should I do all this manual labour . . . At home they would laugh at us for this . . ."

The importance of the different types of Jewish life stands out clearly also in the social organization of the immigration movement itself. We have already emphasized the importance of the "small," basic group which remains intact throughout the process of immigration. The attitudes and identifications evolved in these groups influence to a very great extent the immigrants' perception and role-expectations. It is in these groups that the immigrants' orientation towards the new country is moulded and articulated. It is therefore interesting to note that the structure of these groups differed to a very great extent in the sectors of Jewish society enumerated above: In the first and third sectors, immigration to Israel has brought whole communities together and either emphasized or intensified Jewish identification and solidarity. The process of immigration here gave rise to a stronger group cohesion—based on the immigrants' Jewish identification and aspirations towards Israel. Within the other sectors the process of immigration did not usually give rise to new groups,[7] nor enhance the solidarity of the existing one through the immigrants' orientation to Israel. Immigration here took place in small, non-cohesive groups (mostly family groups), which were "taken out" of their setting without showing any high ability of organization and initiative.

Family Solidarity and Jewish Identification

Our next problem was to see whether any relation exists between the two main conditions of predisposition to change—family structure and the type of crisis of Jewish societies, i.e., whether the degree of family solidarity is related to these broader structures of Jewish social life. The following table shows us the extent of overlapping of the two factors.

From this table we see that although there exists no full overlapping between these two factors, it still exists to a very large extent, especially within the first three sectors. Our material bears out the fact that this relation is not accidental. While it would be futile to assert that all the personality characteristics associated with family solidarity can be accounted for by "structural" or cultural factors, there still exists a strong relation between these two. These relationships stand out most clearly in

[7] Almost nowhere among the new immigrants did we find the type of new primary group (a "pioneering" group) formed and dedicated specially to immigration to Israel—the type which was prevalent in the first stages of the development of the Yishuv. The new mass immigration usually took place within previously existing groups (families, neighbourhoods, communities, etc.). The extent of their internal organization and reorientation, however, differed, as outlined above.

TABLE IV. THE DISTRIBUTION OF PREDISPOSITION TO CHANGE AND FAMILY SOLIDARITY AMONG THE DIFFERENT SECTORS OF THE JEWISH COMMUNITY

	Positive Predisposition to Change		Negative Predisposition to Change	
	Solidary Families	Non-Solidary Families	Solidary Families	Non-Solidary Families
North Africa:	87	10	10	15
1. Traditional Sector				
2. Transitional Sector with Status-anxiety	—	5	15	155
3. Secure Transitional Sector	15	—	—	—
Central and Eastern Europe:				
1. Traditional Sector	18	2	23	12
2. Transitional Sector with Status-anxiety	5	2	10	52
2a. Ex-D.P. Camp Inmates	—	2	45	28
3. Secure Transitional Sector	25	—	—	—
Turkey:				
1. Traditional Sector	40	5	6	2
2. Transitional Sector with Status-anxiety	5	5	10	18
Bulgaria and Yugoslavia:				
1. Transitional Sector with Status-anxiety	5	6	8	38
2. Secure Transitional Sector	144	7	5	7
Yemen:				
1. Traditional Sector	70	16	5	11
Total	414	60	137	338

TABLE IV(B). THE DISTRIBUTION OF PREDISPOSITION TO CHANGE AMONG THE DIFFERENT SECTORS OF THE JEWISH COMMUNITY

	Summary		
	Positive Predisposition to Change	Negative Predisposition to Change	Total
1. Traditional Sector	248 (68%)	84 (32%)	100%
2. Transitional Sector with Status-anxiety	35 (8%)	379 (92%)	100%
3. Secure Transitional Sector	189 (94%)	12 (6%)	100%

TABLE IV(C). THE DISTRIBUTION OF FAMILY SOLIDARITY AMONG THE DIFFERENT SECTORS OF THE JEWISH COMMUNITY

	Summary		
	Solidary Families	Non-Solidary Families	Total
1. Traditional Sector	259 (72%)	73 (28%)	100%
2. Transitional Sector with Status-anxiety	103 (23%)	311 (77%)	100%
3. Secure Transitional Sector	187 (93%)	14 (7%)	100%

TABLE IV(D). THE DISTRIBUTION OF SOLIDARY FAMILIES WITH
A NEGATIVE PREDISPOSITION TO CHANGE

1. Traditional Sector	44 (32%)
2. Transitional Sector with Status-anxiety	88 (64%)
3. Secure Transitional Sector	5 (4%)
Total	100%

TABLE IV(E). THE DISTRIBUTION OF NON-SOLIDARY FAMILIES WITH
A POSITIVE PREDISPOSITION TO CHANGE

1. Traditional Sector	33 (48%)
2. Transitional Sector with Status-anxiety	30 (42%)
3. Secure Transitional Sector	7 (10%)
Total	100%

the "transitional" sector. Within this sector we quite often find that marriage and establishment of family life is a factor of "regression" from the point of view of social mobility towards the Gentile society. This is because the women have usually undergone a much slower process of assimilation, since Jewish tradition is most strongly evinced in family rituals, and intermarriage with Gentiles is blocked to a very large extent. This feeling of "regression" has been expressed quite often by the immigrants in their life histories[8] and it has no doubt hampered the establishment of full cooperation and primary relations and identifications within the family. The lack of cooperation can be seen most clearly in the Oriental sectors in the fact that the social spheres of the men and of the women were entirely different, that the "home" did not serve as a basis of wider social relations, and that people were sometimes "ashamed" of their family life before those whose society they valued most highly. The great intensity of status-anxiety has operated more or less in the same direction. This status anxiety would intensify the propensity to evaluate the members of the family—and the family unit as such—in the light of their contributions to (or impediment to) advancement of such status, and not on their own merits. The family's ability to render affection and security was then secondary, conditional and not primary. There is also some indication that the ambivalent attitude towards women, developed through transition from the traditional sector to the more "free" modern sector, does not always facilitate the harmonious functioning of the family unit. It is interesting to note that while negative predisposition to change exists equally among men and women within the European

[8] An excerpt from an interview may serve to illustrate this point: "I had a gay life until I married . . . I had many French friends and we used to spend our time together outside of the Jewish quarter . . . There I felt like a real man . . . But it all changed after marriage . . . My wife does not speak any French and was not interested in all these things . . . I couldn't bring my friends home . . ."

families, within the Oriental families the women evince a more positive predisposition. This can be accounted for mainly by the fact that, being much more immersed in the traditional sector than the men, their orientation towards the general society, and, consequently, their status-anxiety, is much smaller.

It should be clear, of course, that this explanation is only a partial and preliminary one, and does not account for the different degrees of overlapping between the two factors. Among the different exceptions only one group is of immediate interest to us, namely, those solidary families who come from the fourth sector and whose predisposition to change is mainly negative. It seems that this can be explained to some extent by the fact that these families were established in D.P. camps, etc., and although evincing a very high degree of solidarity born out of the difficult experiences there, they lack any strong orientation toward the general social structure and have no specific status-aspirations beyond the achievement of peace and security.

From this analysis and discussion of the conditions under which different types of predispositions to change develop, some general conclusions relating to the process of adaptation can be stated.

The type of the immigrant's predisposition to change is important with respect to the extension of his social field from the small group in which immigration takes place to the new social setting, i.e., the bridging over by him of the "unstructured" parts of this field. The higher the positive predisposition, the quicker the achievement of stable relations within this field and, consequently, the tempo of adaptation as well. This predisposition is dependent mainly on the extent of basic psychological security provided by (a) the primary family unit in which immigration usually takes place; and (b) the immigrant's orientation to the new country and his identification with it. In so far as this security is provided both by the small group and by the *general* social framework towards which the immigrant is oriented, the bridging over of the unstructured field which exists between the two is relatively easy. In so far as this security is not provided, the predisposition to change is usually negative, and the "bridging over" is hampered, delayed, and sometimes not achieved at all.

"Open Flexibility"

In our former discussion we have not differentiated between various degrees of predisposition and have dealt with "negative" and "positive" types only. The nature of our material and methods of investigation would make any such differentiation at this stage very artificial. It is only with respect to one element that some differentiation could be made, a differentiation which was also connected—even if in a tentative way only—with some important social factors. This element is the flexibility of the levels of aspiration. Here a differentiation can be made between those whose flexibility was limited to the present only, i.e., those who were prepared to accept any situation in the present as a preparatory stage for the future, but had very fixed aspirations for the future—usually connected with their former occupational status. On the other hand, there were those whose flexibility extended to the future also, and who maintained throughout the "instrumental" approach to social status. We shall refer to the latter as those with "open" flexibility.

It was found that women in the traditional and transitional (Oriental) sector have a more "open" flexibility than men; adolescents and unmarried young adults more than married adults, and that, within the traditional sector, members of the Jewish *élite* have more "closed" flexibility than other non-*élites*. There was no difference between women and men in non-traditional sectors, and between members of different occupational and social "strata" outside the traditional sectors. The table overleaf shows us the extent of these correlations.

The data at our disposal do not allow any definite explanation, but a tentative one may be suggested at this stage. It seems that within the scope of solidary families and positive, unconditional community-identification, it is those who have least "vested interest" in high social positions and roles who can show the greatest "openness" and flexibility in their levels of aspiration, as change cannot affect their privileged positions. They enjoy, as it were, the benefits of social and psychological security inherent in these groups without being tied to any special positions within them. While this explanation accounts for our data, it does not show why the difference between *élites* and non-*élites* existed only within the traditional sector. The tentative explanation of this may be that the

TABLE V. THE DISTRIBUTION IN PERCENTAGE OF "OPEN" LEVELS OF FUTURE
ASPIRATIONS AMONG MEN, WOMEN AND ADOLESCENTS (YOUTH)—
WITHIN THE SECTOR WITH POSITIVE PREDISPOSITION
TO CHANGE—BY REGIONS OF ORIGIN

Regions of Origin	Men	Women	Adolescents (Youth)
Yemen	55	80	85
North Africa	45	70	85
Turkey	60	65	75
Bulgaria and Yugoslavia	85	85	90
Central and Eastern Europe	55	50	65

difference holds only in those groups which have maintained themselves and their cultural identifications intact through the process of immigration, and who could have hoped to maintain their old patterns of life in the new social setting. This holds true only for the more active parts of the traditional sector, while in all other sectors the process of immigration has involved a thorough reshuffling of social groups emergence of new *élites*.

The Problem of Direction of Change

In our report we have not, until now, indicated the *direction* of the immigrants' predisposition to change—either from an occupational or from a cultural point of view. We have inquired into the immigrants' *general* predisposition to undertake new social roles, but not into their occupational preferences or the specific cultural patterns which they were willing to change. It seems to us that such an inquiry would be entirely premature at this stage. Because of the specific economic limitations of the first periods of absorption, the present occupational distribution cannot give us any information as to the immigrants' ultimate preferences or the exact influence of cultural differences on the occupational distribution of the immigrants at the present time.

Because of the nature of the absorbing situation and the cultural heterogeneity of the immigrants, it would be futile to ask them specific questions about their (professed) occupational preferences, as it would be impossible to evaluate the relation of these preferences to actual behaviour in any situation. As for the general trend of cultural change and assimilation, the short period of the immigrants' residence in Israel does not allow any long-term conclusions. Only one problem bearing on the trend of occupational change may be briefly investigated at this stage— namely, the relation between occupational aspirations and changes and the specific identification with the Jewish nation evolved through the process of immigration to Israel. This problem is of special importance because of the part it played in the establishment of the Yishuv in its initial, pioneering stage. At that stage occupational change and "normalization" constituted a very important element in the new national identification and aspirations of the immigrants, and, hence, there developed great emphasis on agriculture and industrial labour as "basic" occupations. Occupational standing was to a very large extent evaluated in terms of its contribution to the normalization of the economic structure of the Yishuv; not only on purely economic terms. This trend has greatly influenced the occupational distribution of the Yishuv, and it has been of great interest whether or not the same complex of motivations exists within the new immigration. From the material at our disposal the answer seems to be rather negative. It seems that occupational aspirations are not directly connected with national identification. The immigrants' evaluation of occupational possibilities is usually defined either in "ritual" terms of status (among those with a negative predisposition) or in intrinsically occupational terms, and mainly in those of social and economic security.

The strong emphasis on belongingness to the Jewish nation as a source of social security among the immigrants tends to direct their occupational aspirations within the same pattern of motivation. They accept the Jewish community in Israel as a given datum, and seek security within the orbit of its social structure, not through changing or establishing a new social structure. The conscious ideal of establishing a new social structure, which was predominant among the pioneers, does not exist to any large extent among the new immigrants.

It seems that the main explanation of this difference in attitude between the former and the contemporary immigrations can be understood mainly in terms of the different types of crises of Jewish society in the Diaspora which originated these movements. The "pioneers" usually came from sectors of Jewish society which were undergoing a process of social and economic ascendance, and the "pioneers" formed new intensive primary groups which dissociated themselves from their communities and social settings. They established a new, intensive, universal Jewish identification, oriented towards the establishment of a new, modern Jewish nation. Among most of the new immigrants the "social" crises have encompassed entire Jewish communities, whose members were looking for security, and who more or less perpetuated their social groupings throughout the process of migration, and maintained their particular types of Jewish identification. Hence their orientation in Israel was mainly in terms of achieving social and political security, and not of social change.

―――――――――― Stanley Lieberson

A Societal Theory of Race and Ethnic Relations

"In the relations of races there is a cycle of events which tends everywhere to repeat itself." [1] Park's assertion served as a prologue to the now classical cycle of competition, conflict, accommodation, and assimilation. A number of other attempts have been made to formulate phases or stages ensuing from the initial contacts between racial and ethnic groups.[2] However, the sharp contrasts between relatively harmonious race relations in Brazil and Hawaii and the current racial turmoil in

[1] Robert E. Park, *Race and Culture*, Glencoe, Ill.: The Free Press, 1950, p. 150.
[2] For example, Emory S. Bogardus, "A Race-Relations Cycle," *American Journal of Sociology*, 35 (January, 1930), pp. 612-617; W. O. Brown, "Culture Contact and Race Conflict" in E. B. Reuter, editor, *Race and Culture Contacts*, New York: McGraw-Hill, 1934, pp. 34-47; E. Franklin Frazier, *Race and Culture Contacts in the Modern World*, New York: Alfred A. Knopf, 1957, pp. 32 ff.; Clarence E. Glick, "Social Roles and Types in Race Relations" in Andrew W. Lind, editor, *Race Relations in World Perspective*, Honolulu: University of Hawaii Press, 1955, pp. 243-262; Edward Nelson Palmer, "Culture Contacts and Population Growth" in Joseph J. Spengler and Otis Dudley Duncan, editors, *Population Theory and Policy*, Glencoe, Ill.: The Free Press, 1956, pp. 410-415; A. Grenfell Price, *White Settlers and Native Peoples*, Melbourne: Georgian House, 1950. For summaries of several of these cycles, see Brewton Berry, *Race and Ethnic Relations*, Boston: Houghton Mifflin, 1958, Chapter 6.

Reprinted from *American Sociological Review*, Vol. 26, No. 6, December, 1961, pp. 902-910. By permission.

South Africa and Indonesia serve to illustrate the difficulty in stating—to say nothing of interpreting—an inevitable "natural history" of race and ethnic relations.

Many earlier race and ethnic cycles were, in fact, narrowly confined to a rather specific set of groups or contact situations. Bogardus, for example, explicitly limited his synthesis to Mexican and Oriental immigrant groups on the west coast of the United States and suggested that this is but one of many different cycles of relations between immigrants and native Americans.[3] Similarly, the Australian anthropologist Price developed three phases that appear to account for the relationships between white English-speaking migrants and the aborigines of Australia, Maoris in New Zealand, and Indians of the United States and Canada.[4]

This paper seeks to present a rudimentary theory of the development of race and ethnic relations that systematically accounts for differences between societies in such divergent consequences of contact as racial nationalism and warfare, assimilation and fusion, and extinction. It postulates that the critical problem on a societal level in racial or ethnic contact is initially each population's maintenance and development of a social order compatible with its ways of life prior to contact. The crux of any cycle must, therefore, deal with political, social, and economic institutions. The emphasis given in earlier cycles to one group's dominance of another in these areas is therefore hardly surprising.[5]

Although we accept this institutional approach, the thesis presented here is that knowledge of the nature of one group's domination over another in the political, social, and economic spheres is a necessary but insufficient prerequisite for predicting or interpreting the final and intermediate stages of racial and ethnic contact. Rather, institutional factors are considered in terms of a distinction between two major types of contact situations: contacts involving subordination of an indigenous population by a migrant group, for example, Negro-white relations in South Africa; and contacts involving subordination of a migrant population by an indigenous racial or ethnic group, for example, Japanese migrants to the United States.

After considering the societal issues inherent in racial and ethnic contact, the distinction developed between migrant and indigenous superordination will be utilized in examining each of the following dimensions of race relations: political and economic control, multiple ethnic contacts, conflict and assimilation. The terms "race" and "ethnic" are used interchangeably.

Differences Inherent in Contact

Most situations of ethnic contact involve at least one indigenous group and at least one group migrating to the area. The only exception at the

---

[3] Bogardus, *op. cit.*, p. 612.
[4] Price, *op. cit.*
[5] Intra-urban stages of contact are not considered here.

initial point in contact would be the settlement of an uninhabited area by two or more groups. By "indigenous" is meant not necessarily the aborigines, but rather a population sufficiently established in an area so as to possess the institutions and demographic capacity for maintaining some minimal form of social order through generations. Thus a given spatial area may have different indigenous groups through time. For example, the indigenous population of Australia is presently largely white and primarily of British origin, although the Tasmanoids and Australoids were once in possession of the area.[6] A similar racial shift may be observed in the populations indigenous to the United States.

Restricting discussion to the simplest of contact situations, i.e., involving one migrant and one established population, we can generally observe sharp differences in their social organization at the time of contact. The indigenous population has an established and presumably stable organization prior to the arrival of migrants, i.e., government, economic activities adapted to the environment and the existing techniques of resource utilization, kinship, stratification, and religious systems.[7] On the basis of a long series of migration studies, we may be reasonably certain that the social order of a migrant population's homeland is not wholly transferred to their new settlement.[8] Migrants are required to make at least some institutional adaptations and innovations in view of the presence of an indigenous population, the demographic selectivity of migration, and differences in habitat.

For example, recent post-war migrations from Italy and the Netherlands indicate considerable selectivity in age and sex from the total populations of these countries. Nearly half of 30,000 males leaving the Netherlands in 1955 were between 20 and 39 years of age whereas only one quarter of the male population was of these ages.[9] Similarly, over 40,000 males in this age range accounted for somewhat more than half of Italy's male emigrants in 1951, although they comprise roughly 30 per cent of the male population of Italy.[10] In both countries, male emigrants exceed females in absolute numbers as well as in comparison with the sex ratios of their nation. That these cases are far from extreme can be illustrated with Oriental migration data. In 1920, for example, there were 38,000 foreign born Chinese adult males in the United States, but only 2,000 females of the same group.[11]

In addition to these demographic shifts, the new physical and biological conditions of existence require the revision and creation of social institutions if the social order known in the old country is to be approxi-

[6] Price, op. cit., Chapters 6 and 7.

[7] Glick, op. cit., p. 244.

[8] See, for example, Brinley Thomas, "International Migration" in Philip M. Hauser and Otis Dudley Duncan, editors, The Study of Population, Chicago: University of Chicago Press, 1959, pp. 523-526.

[9] United Nations, Demographic Yearbook, 1957, pp. 147, 645.

[10] United Nations, Demographic Yearbook, 1954, pp. 131, 669.

[11] R. D. McKenzie, Oriental Exclusion, Chicago: University of Chicago Press, 1928, p. 83.

mated and if the migrants are to survive. The migration of eastern and southern European peasants around the turn of the century to urban industrial centers of the United States provides a well-documented case of radical changes in occupational pursuits as well as the creation of a number of institutions in response to the new conditions of urban life, e.g., mutual aid societies, national churches, and financial institutions.

In short, when two populations begin to occupy the same habitat but do not share a single order, each group endeavors to maintain the political and economic conditions that are at least compatible with the institutions existing before contact. These conditions for the maintenance of institutions can not only differ for the two groups in contact, but are often conflicting. European contacts with the American Indian, for example, led to the decimation of the latter's sources of sustenance and disrupted religious and tribal forms of organization. With respect to a population's efforts to maintain its social institutions, we may therefore assume that the presence of another ethnic group is an important part of the environment. Further, if groups in contact differ in their capacity to impose changes on the other group, then we may expect to find one group "superordinate" and the other population "subordinate" in maintaining or developing a suitable environment.

It is here that efforts at a single cycle of race and ethnic relations must fail. For it is necessary to introduce a distinction in the nature or form of subordination before attempting to predict whether conflict or relatively harmonious assimilation will develop. As we shall shortly show, the race relations cycle in areas where the migrant group is superordinate and indigenous group subordinate differs sharply from the stage in societies composed of a superordinate indigenous group and subordinate migrants.[12]

Political and Economic Control

Emphasis is placed herein on economic and political dominance since it is assumed that control of these institutions will be instrumental in establishing a suitable milieu for at least the population's own social institutions, e.g., educational, religious, and kinship, as well as control of such major cultural artifacts as language.

Migrant Superordination—When the population migrating to a new contact situation is superior in technology (particularly weapons) and more tightly organized than the indigenous group, the necessary conditions for maintaining the migrants' political and economic institutions are usually imposed on the indigenous population. Warfare, under such circumstances, often occurs early in the contacts between the two groups as the migrants begin to interfere with the natives' established order. There is frequently conflict even if the initial contact was friendly. Price,

[12] See, for example, Reuter's distinction between two types of direct contact in E. B. Reuter, editor, *op. cit.,* pp. 4-7.

for example, has observed the following consequences of white invasion and subordination of the indigenous populations of Australia, Canada, New Zealand, and the United States:

> During an opening period of pioneer invasion on moving frontiers the whites decimated the natives with their diseases; occupied their lands by seizure or by pseudo-purchase; slaughtered those who resisted; intensified tribal warfare by supplying white weapons; ridiculed and disrupted native religions, society and culture, and generally reduced the unhappy peoples to a state of despondency under which they neither desired to live, nor to have children to undergo similar conditions.[13]

The numerical decline of indigenous populations after their initial subordination to a migrant group, whether caused by warfare, introduction of venereal and other diseases, or disruption of sustenance activities, has been documented for a number of contact situations in addition to those discussed by Price.[14]

In addition to bringing about these demographic and economic upheavals, the superordinate migrants frequently create political entities that are not at all coterminous with the boundaries existing during the indigenous populations' supremacy prior to contact. For example, the British and Boers in southern Africa carved out political states that included areas previously under the control of separate and often warring groups.[15] Indeed, European alliances with feuding tribes were often used as a fulcrum for the territorial expansion of whites into southern Africa.[16] The bifurcation of tribes into two nations and the migrations of groups across newly created national boundaries are both consequences of the somewhat arbitrary nature of the political entities created in regions of migrant superordination.[17] This incorporation of diverse indigenous populations into a single territorial unit under the dominance of a migrant group has considerable importance for later developments in this type of racial and ethnic contact.

Indigenous Superordination—When a population migrates to a subordinate position considerably less conflict occurs in the early stages. The movements of many European and Oriental populations to political, economic, and social subordination in the United States were not converted into warfare, nationalism, or long-term conflict. Clearly, the occasional labor and racial strife marking the history of immigration of the United

[13] Price, op. cit., p. 1.
[14] Stephen Roberts, Population Problems of the Pacific, London: George Routledge & Sons, 1927.
[15] John A. Barnes, "Race Relations in the Development of Southern Africa" in Lind, editor, op. cit.
[16] Ibid.
[17] Witness the current controversies between tribes in the newly created Congo Republic. Also, for a list of tribes living on both sides of the border of the Republic of Sudan, see Karol Józef Krótki, "Demographic Survey of Sudan" in The Population of Sudan, report on the sixth annual conference, Khartoum: Philosophical Society of Sudan, 1958, p. 35.

States is not on the same level as the efforts to expel or revolutionize the social order. American Negroes, one of the most persistently subordinated migrant groups in the country, never responded in significant numbers to the encouragement of migration to Liberia. The single important large-scale nationalistic effort, Marcus Garvey's Universal Negro Improvement Association, never actually led to mass emigration of Negroes.[18] By contrast, the indigenous American Indians fought long and hard to preserve control over their habitat.

In interpreting differences in the effects of migrant and indigenous subordination, the migrants must be considered in the context of the options available to the group. Irish migrants to the United States in the 1840's, for example, although clearly subordinate to native whites of other origins, fared better economically than if they had remained in their mother country.[19] Further, the option of returning to the homeland often exists for populations migrating to subordinate situations. Jerome reports that net migration to the United States between the midyears of 1907 and 1923 equalled roughly 65 per cent of gross immigration.[20] This indicates that immigrant dissatisfaction with subordination or other conditions of contact can often be resolved by withdrawal from the area. Recently subordinated indigenous groups, by contrast, are perhaps less apt to leave their habitat so readily.

Finally, when contacts between racial and ethnic groups are under the control of the indigenous population, threats of demographic and institutional imbalance are reduced since the superordinate populations can limit the numbers and groups entering. For example, when Oriental migration to the United States threatened whites, sharp cuts were executed in the quotas.[21] Similar events may be noted with respect to the decline of immigration from the so-called "new" sources of eastern and southern Europe. Whether a group exercises its control over immigration far before it is actually under threat is, of course, not germane to the point that immigrant restriction provides a mechanism whereby potential conflict is prevented.

In summary, groups differ in the conditions necessary for maintaining their respective social orders. In areas where the migrant group is dominant, frequently the indigenous population suffers sharp numerical declines and their economic and political institutions are seriously undermined. Conflict often accompanies the establishment of migrant superordination. Subordinate indigenous populations generally have no alternative location and do not control the numbers of new ethnic popu-

---

[18] John Hope Franklin, *From Slavery to Freedom*, second edition, New York: Alfred Knopf, 1956, pp. 234-238, 481-483.

[19] Oscar Handlin, *Boston's Immigrants*, revised edition, Cambridge, Mass.: The Belknap Press of Harvard University Press, 1959, Chapter 2.

[20] Harry Jerome, *Migration and Business Cycles*, New York: National Bureau of Economic Research, 1926, pp. 43-44.

[21] See, George Eaton Simpson and J. Milton Yinger, *Racial and Cultural Minorities*, revised edition, New York: Harper & Brothers, 1958, pp. 126-132.

lations admitted into their area. By contrast, when the indigenous population dominates the political and economic conditions, the migrant group is introduced into the economy of the indigenous population. Although subordinate in their new habitat, the migrants may fare better than if they remained in their homeland. Hence their subordination occurs without great conflict. In addition, the migrants usually have the option of returning to their homeland and the indigenous population controls the number of new immigrants in the area.

Multiple Ethnic Contacts

Although the introduction of a third major ethnic or racial group frequently occurs in both types of societies distinguished here, there are significant differences between conditions in habitats under indigenous domination and areas where a migrant population is superordinate. Chinese and Indian migrants, for example, were often welcomed by whites in areas where large indigenous populations were suppressed, but these migrants were restricted in the white mother country. Consideration of the causes and consequences of multi-ethnic contacts is therefore made in terms of the two types of racial and ethnic contact.

Migrant Superordination—In societies where the migrant population is superordinate, it is often necessary to introduce new immigrant groups to fill the niches created in the revised economy of the area. The subordinate indigenous population frequently fails, at first, to participate in the new economic and political order introduced by migrants. For example, because of the numerical decline of Fijians after contact with whites and their unsatisfactory work habits, approximately 60,000 persons migrated from India to the sugar plantations of Fiji under the indenture system between 1879 and 1916.[22] For similar reasons, as well as the demise of slavery, large numbers of Indians were also introduced to such area of indigenous subordination as Mauritius, British Guiana, Trinidad, and Natal.[23] The descendants of these migrants comprise the largest single ethnic group in several of these areas.

McKenzie, after observing the negligible participation of the subordinated indigenous populations of Alaska, Hawaii, and Malaya in contrast to the large numbers of Chinese, Indian, and other Oriental immigrants, offers the following interpretation:

> The indigenous peoples of many of the frontier zones of modern industrialism are surrounded by their own web of culture and their own economic structure. Consequently they are slow to take part in the new economy especially as unskilled laborers. It is the individual who is widely removed from his native habitat that is most adaptable to the conditions imposed by cap-

---

[22] K. L. Gillion, "The Sources of Indian Emigration to Fiji," *Population Studies*, 10 (November, 1956), p. 139; I. M. Cumpston, "A Survey of Indian Immigration to British Tropical Colonies to 1910," *ibid.*, pp. 158-159.

[23] Cumpston, *op. cit.*, pp. 158-165.

italism in frontier regions. Imported labor cannot so easily escape to its
home village when conditions are distasteful as can the local population.[24]

Similarly, the Indians of the United States played a minor role in the
new economic activities introduced by white settlers and, further, were
not used successfully as slaves.[25] Frazier reports that Negro slaves were
utilized in the West Indies and Brazil after unsuccessful efforts to enslave
the indigenous Indian populations.[26] Large numbers of Asiatic Indians
were brought to South Africa as indentured laborers to work in the rail-
ways, mines, and plantations introduced by whites.[27]

This migration of workers into areas where the indigenous population
was either unable or insufficient to work in the newly created economic
activities was also marked by a considerable flow back to the home
country. For example, nearly 3.5 million Indians left the Madras Presi-
dency for overseas between 1903 and 1912, but close to 3 million returned during this same period.[28] However, as we observed earlier, large
numbers remained overseas and formed major ethnic populations in a
number of countries. Current difficulties of the ten million Chinese in
Southeast Asia are in large part due to their settlement in societies
where the indigenous populations were subordinate.

Indigenous Superordination—We have observed that in situations
of indigenous superordination the call for new immigrants from other
ethnic and racial populations is limited in a manner that prevents the
indigenous group's loss of political and economic control. Under such
conditions, no single different ethnic or racial population is sufficiently
large in number or strength to challenge the supremacy of the indigenous
population.

After whites attained dominance in Hawaii, that land provided a
classic case of the substitution of one ethnic group after another during
a period when large numbers of immigrants were needed for the newly
created and expanding plantation economy. According to Lind, the shifts
from Chinese to Japanese and Portuguese immigrants and the later shifts
to Puerto Rican, Korean, Spanish, Russian, and Philippine sources for the
plantation laborers were due to conscious efforts to prevent any single
group from obtaining too much power.[29] Similarly, the exclusion of
Chinese from the United States mainland stimulated the migration of the
Japanese and, in turn, the later exclusion of Japanese led to increased
migration from Mexico.[30]

[24] R. D. McKenzie, "Cultural and Racial Differences as Bases of Human Symbiosis" in
Kimball Young, editor, Social Attitudes, New York: Henry Holt, 1931, p. 157.
[25] Franklin, op. cit., p. 47.
[26] Frazier, op. cit., pp. 107-108.
[27] Leo Kuper, Hilstan Watts, and Ronald Davies, Durban: A Study in Racial Ecology, London: Jonathan Cape, 1958, p. 25.
[28] Gillion, op. cit., p. 149.
[29] Andrew W. Lind, An Island Community, Chicago: University of Chicago Press, 1938, pp.
218-229.
[30] McKenzie, Oriental Exclusion, op. cit., p. 181.

In brief, groups migrating to situations of multiple ethnic contact are thus subordinate in both types of contact situations. However, in societies where whites are superordinate but do not settle as an indigenous population, other racial and ethnic groups are admitted in large numbers and largely in accordance with economic needs of the revised economy of the habitat. By contrast, when a dominant migrant group later becomes indigenous, in the sense that the area becomes one of permanent settlement through generations for the group, migrant populations from new racial and ethnic stocks are restricted in number and source.

Conflict and Assimilation

From a comparison of the surge of racial nationalism and open warfare in parts of Africa and Asia or the retreat of superordinate migrants from the former Dutch East Indies and French Indo-China, on the one hand, with the fusion of populations in many nations of western Europe or the "cultural pluralism" of the United States and Switzerland, on the other, one must conclude that neither conflict nor assimilation is an inevitable outcome of racial and ethnic contact. Our distinction, however, between two classes of race and ethnic relations is directly relevant to consideration of which of these alternatives different populations in contact will take. In societies where the indigenous population at the initial contact is subordinate, warfare and nationalism often—although not always—develops later in the cycle of relations. By contrast, relations between migrants and indigenous populations that are subordinate and superordinate, respectively, are generally without long-term conflict.

Migrant Superordination—Through time, the subordinated indigenous population begins to participate in the economy introduced by the migrant group and, frequently, a concomitant disruption of previous forms of social and economic organization takes place. This, in turn, has significant implications for the development of both nationalism and a greater sense of racial unity. In many African states, where Negroes were subdivided into ethnic groups prior to contact with whites, the racial unity of the African was created by the occupation of their habitat by white invaders.[31] The categorical subordination of Africans by whites as well as the dissolution and decay of previous tribal and ethnic forms of organization are responsible for the creation of racial consciousness among the indigenous populations.[32] As the indigenous group becomes increasingly incorporated within the larger system, both the saliency of their subordinate position and its significance increase. No alternative exists for the bulk of the native population other than the destruction

---

[31] For a discussion of territorial and tribal movements, see James S. Coleman, "Current Political Movements in Africa," *The Annals of the American Academy of Political and Social Science*, 298 (March, 1955), pp. 95-108.

[32] For a broader discussion of emergent nationalism, see Thomas Hodgkin, *Nationalism in Colonial Africa*, New York: New York University Press, 1957; Everett C. Hughes, "New Peoples" in Lind, editor, *op. cit.*, pp. 95-115.

or revision of the institutions of political, economic, and social subordination.

Further, it appears that considerable conflict occurs in those areas where the migrants are not simply superordinate, but where they themselves have also become, in a sense, indigenous by maintaining an established population through generations. In Table 1, for example, one can observe how sharply the white populations of Algeria and the Union of South Africa differ from those in nine other African countries with respect to the per cent born in the country of settlement. Thus, two among the eleven African countries for which such data were available[33] are outstanding with respect to both racial turmoil and the high proportion

TABLE 1. NATIVITY OF THE WHITE POPULATIONS
OF SELECTED AFRICAN COUNTRIES, CIRCA 1950

Country	Per Cent of Whites Born in Country
Algeria	79.8
Basutoland	37.4
Bechuanaland	39.5
Morocco[a]	37.1 [c]
Northern Rhodesia	17.7
Southern Rhodesia	31.5
South West Africa[b]	45.1
Swaziland	41.2
Tanganyika	47.6
Uganda	43.8
Union of South Africa	89.7

Source: United Nations, *Demographic Yearbook,* 1956, Table 5.
[a] Former French zone.
[b] Excluding Walvis Bay.
[c] Persons born in former Spanish zone or in Tangier are included as native.
Note: Other non-indigenous groups included when necessary breakdown by race is not given.

of whites born in the country. To be sure, other factors operate to influence the nature of racial and ethnic relations. However, these data strongly support our suggestions with respect to the significance of differences between indigenous and migrant forms of contact. Thus where the migrant population becomes established in the new area, it is all the more difficult for the indigenous subordinate group to change the social order.

Additionally, where the formerly subordinate indigenous population has become dominant through the expulsion of the superordinate group, the situation faced by nationalities introduced to the area under earlier

[33] United Nations, *Demographic Yearbook, 1956,* Table 5.

conditions of migrant superordination changes radically. For example, as we noted earlier, Chinese were welcomed in many parts of Southeast Asia where the newly subordinated indigenous populations were unable or unwilling to fill the economic niches created by the white invaders. However, after whites were expelled and the indigenous populations obtained political mastery, the gates to further Chinese immigration were fairly well closed and there has been increasing interference with the Chinese already present. In Indonesia, where Chinese immigration had been encouraged under Dutch domain, the newly created indigenous government allows only token immigration and has formulated a series of laws and measures designed to interfere with and reduce Chinese commercial activities.[34] Thompson and Adloff observe that,

> Since the war, the Chinese have been subjected to increasingly restrictive measures throughout Southeast Asia, but the severity and effectiveness of these has varied with the degree to which the native nationalists are in control of their countries and feel their national existence threatened by the Chinese.[35]

Indigenous Superordination—By contrast, difficulties between subordinate migrants and an already dominant indigenous population occur within the context of a consensual form of government, economy, and social institutions. However confused and uncertain may be the concept of assimilation and its application in operational terms,[36] it is important to note that assimilation is essentially a very different phenomenon in the two types of societies distinguished here.

Where populations migrate to situations of subordination, the issue has generally been with respect to the migrants' capacity and willingness to become an integral part of the on-going social order. For example, this has largely been the case in the United States where the issue of "new" vs. "old" immigrant groups hinged on the alleged inferiorities of the former.[37] The occasional flurries of violence under this form of contact have been generally initiated by the dominant indigenous group and with respect to such threats against the social order as the cheap labor competition of Orientals on the west coast,[38] the nativist fears of Irish Catholic political domination of Boston in the nineteenth century,[39] or

[34] B. H. M. Vlekke, *Indonesia in 1956*, The Hague: Netherlands Institute of International Affairs, 1957, p. 88.
[35] Virginia Thompson and Richard Adloff, *Minority Problems in Southeast Asia*, Stanford, California: Stanford University Press, 1955, p. 3.
[36] See, for example, International Union for the Scientific Study of Population, "Cultural Assimilation of Immigrants," *Population Studies, supplement*, March, 1950.
[37] Oscar Handlin, *Race and Nationality in American Life*, Garden City, New York: Doubleday Anchor Books, 1957, Chapter 5.
[38] Simpson and Yinger, *op. cit.*
[39] Oscar Handlin, *Boston's Immigrants, op. cit.*, Chapter 7.

the desecration of sacred principles by Mexican "zoot-suiters" in Los Angeles.[40]

The conditions faced by subordinate migrants in Australia and Canada after the creation of indigenous white societies in these areas are similar to that of the United States; that is, limited and sporadic conflict, and great emphasis on the assimilation of migrants. Striking and significant contrasts to the general pattern of subordinate immigrant assimilation in those societies, however, are provided by the differences between the assimilation of Italian and German immigrants in Australia as well as the position of French Canadians in eastern Canada.

French Canadians have maintained their language and other major cultural and social attributes whereas nineteenth and twentieth century immigrants are in process of merging into the predominantly English-speaking Canadian society. Although broader problems of territorial segregation are involved,[41] the critical difference between French Canadians and later groups is that the former had an established society in the new habitat prior to the British conquest of Canada and were thus largely able to maintain their social and cultural unity without significant additional migration from France.[42]

Similarly, in finding twentieth century Italian immigrants in Australia more prone to cultural assimilation than were German migrants to that nation in the 1800's, Borrie emphasized the fact that Italian migration occurred after Australia had become an independent nation-state. By contrast, Germans settled in what was a pioneer colony without an established general social order and institutions. Thus, for example, Italian children were required to attend Australian schools and learn English, whereas the German immigrants were forced to establish their own educational program.[43]

Thus the consequences of racial and ethnic contact may also be examined in terms of the two types of superordinate-subordinate contact situations considered. For the most part, subordinate migrants appear to be more rapidly assimilated than are subordinate indigenous populations. Further, the subordinate migrant group is generally under greater pressure to assimilate, at least in the gross sense of "assimilation" such as language, than are subordinate indigenous populations. In addition, warfare or racial nationalism—when it does occur—tends to be in societies where the indigenous population is subordinate. If the indigenous move-

---

[40] Ralph Turner and Samuel J. Surace, "Zoot-Suiters and Mexicans: Symbols in Crowd Behavior," *American Journal of Sociology*, 62 (July, 1956), pp. 14-20.

[41] It is, however, suggestive to consider whether the isolated settlement of an area by a racial, religious, or ethnic group would be permitted in other than frontier conditions. Consider, for example, the difficulties faced by Mormons until they reached Utah.

[42] See Everett C. Hughes, *French Canada in Transition*, Chicago: University of Chicago Press, 1943.

[43] W. D. Borrie assisted by D. R. G. Packer, *Italians and Germans in Australia*, Melbourne: F. W. Cheshire, 1954, *passim*.

ment succeeds, the economic and political position of racial and ethnic populations introduced to the area under migrant dominance may become tenuous.

A Final Note

It is suggested that interest be revived in the conditions accounting for societal variations in the process of relations between racial and ethnic groups. A societal theory of race relations, based on the migrant-indigenous and superordinate-subordinate distinctions developed above, has been found to offer an orderly interpretation of differences in the nature of race and ethnic relations in the contact situations considered. Since, however, systematic empirical investigation provides a far more rigorous test of the theory's merits and limitations, comparative cross-societal studies are needed.

Supplementary Bibliography

Brewton Berry, *Race and Ethnic Relations,* rev. ed. Boston: Houghton Mifflin, 1958.
A good textbook, containing in Chapter 6 a summary of the idea of race relations cycles.

Leonard Broom and John I. Kitsuse, "The Validation of Acculturation: A Condition to Ethnic Assimilation." *American Anthropologist,* 1955, 57:44-48. Reprinted in Kimball Young and Raymond W. Mack, *Principles of Sociology: A Reader in Theory and Research,* 2nd ed. N. Y.: American Book, 1962, pp. 117-120.
A study of access to participation in the dominant institutions as a precondition for the assimilation of minorities.

William M. Kephart, "Negro Visibility." *American Sociological Review,* 1954, 19:462-467. Reprinted in Young and Mack, *op. cit.,* pp. 161-165.
A research project relating minority population concentration, visibility, and law enforcement.

Seymour M. Lipset and Reinhard Bendix, *Social Mobility in Industrial Society.* Berkeley and Los Angeles: U. of California Press, 1960.
A discussion of the mobility ethic in American society and a comprehensive, well-documented comparative analysis of the rates of social mobility in industrial societies.

Raymond W. Mack, Linton Freeman, and Seymour Yellin, *Social Mobility: Thirty Years of Research and Theory.* Syracuse: Syracuse U. Press, 1957.
An annotated bibliography of scholarly work on social mobility.

VIII   Class, Minority Status, and Minority Role

As it happened, the pattern of European immigration to the United States was one in which recency of arrival and cultural dissimilarity reinforced each other. The voluntary migrants from Europe had no marked physiognomic differences to deter their assimilation. The first to arrive in large numbers were the English, and white Anglo-Saxon Protestants still retain the highest status in this country. Then the waves from Western Europe and then from other countries of Great Britain followed. These Western Europeans were culturally quite similar to the early English settlers; they spoke somewhat different languages, but they were North European Caucasoids, Nordic or Alpine, and Protestant. Then came the Irish, not drastically different culturally, but Catholic. Then came wave after wave of Southern and Eastern Europeans during the decades around the turn of the century. Again, the most recent arrivals were the least similar culturally to those already here: Italy and Poland are less like England than Scotland and Germany, and most of these newcomers were Catholic or Jewish.

The Process of Assimilation

If we examine the history of minority status of European ethnic groups, we find that the most recently arrived ethnic group occupied the lowest status. As time went by, they assimilated into the dominant society and lost most of their minority status. The next wave of immigrants would take up the low-status occupations. The Germans were the minority group occupying the lower stratum before the Irish arrived; then the Germans moved upward. The Poles arrived, pushing the Irish to a higher status. Some of this can be explained by the kinds of job skills which newcomers to a society possess. Those who leave a country in droves are not usually the well-off, highly trained professionals. They are far more likely to be of the disgruntled peasant class, whose major skill has been in agriculture. They come not only to a new country, but to the city. Therefore, they are forced to go to the bottom of the occupational structure, to unskilled occupations in a factory. The rate of assimilation into the culture, for these groups, is related to the amount of time it takes them to learn the language, to acquire technical training and skills, and to learn the acceptable ways of the new culture. However, since their visible difference from dominant people is behavioral rather than physical, they can learn their way out of minority status.

The Peculiar Status of the Negro

The Negro was a slave until the latter half of the nineteenth century. As such, he was forced to remain at the base of the social structure. Nonetheless, he was freed from slavery, and one might expect that at this point the Negro would follow the same pattern of assimilation as the waves of immigrants. But the Negro was to be an exception for two major reasons. First of all, the condition of slavery had an effect on the way the dominant majority regarded Negroes. Many whites found it difficult to endure the idea that they were subjecting their fellow man to the degradation of slavery. They began to salve their consciences by asserting that the Negro was subhuman. As is often the case, many began to believe their own assertions, and to transmit this belief to succeeding generations.

Thus freedom from slavery could not be regarded as a single act which wiped away all concomitants of slavery. The nation could not forget that the Negro had been a slave.

Vitally related to this, as we have seen, is the second reason for the inability of the Negro to assimilate into the social structure with the same rapidity as the European immigrants: visibility. Obviously, visibility alone would not explain this unassimilatability. Redheads are visible, and they assimilated. Yet if all redheads had been slaves, their visibility would take on a social meaning that would have precluded their rapid assimilation. It is the social definition and stereotype associated with the visible features which make them important. This is of critical importance to the physically different or racial minorities, such as Negroes, Indians, and Chinese- and Japanese-Americans. As long as their visibly physical difference is socially defined as relevant, they are precluded from learning their way out of minority status and assimilating.

Self-awareness and Minority Role

One of the defining characteristics of minority status is the self-awareness of minority group members. This would be quite similar to the notion of "consciousness-of-kind" for members of the same social class. Many sociologists of stratification hold that the working "class" is not really a class until its members develop (1) an explicit awareness of their class position and (2) the feeling of awareness that others around them share the same condition.

At the point where this awareness of minority status becomes poignant and relevant to the members, the alternative social roles become quite distinct. For purposes of this discussion, we can ignore those who are so enmeshed in the daily activities of living that they are seldom if ever directly confronted with their minority status—for whom, that is, this minority condition has no direct role relevance. One minority role is that of the militant member, who fights for the elimination of the minority status. Another role is that of the proud member, who basks in the accomplishments of members of his group and sees many positive effects of minority group status. (These two roles, of course, can be combined empirically and are in such militant minority organizations as the Black Muslims.) A third role is that of the minority person who accepts minority status as his just lot—the kind of response characterized in the Negro community as that of an "Uncle Tom" or a "hankie-head." Another possible minority role is one of avoidance, or simply trying to stay out of situations that are reminders of dominant-minority differences. The most effective way of doing this is to avoid any interaction with members of the dominant category, a policy followed by some self-segregating religious groups. Finally, there is the minority group member who casts aside all traces of his affiliation with the minority and chooses to "pass" as a member of the dominant category, to assimilate.

Related Readings

The Negro heroin addict described by Harold Finestone in "Cats, Kicks, and Color" represents one extreme role adjustment to minority status. Like the Italian-American hoodlums in Bell's "Crime as an American Way of Life," the "cats" are to some extent a product of a social stratification system which demands upward mobility even of members of minority groups blocked by the culture from achieving it.

The analysis, "Social Stratification in Georgia Town," by Mozell C. Hill and Bevode C. McCall contrasts the caste-like structure of a Southern community with the stratification systems of towns in New England and the Midwest. In addition, it demonstrates the skewed class distribution by race which is a product of a segregated economy. Finally, the impact of the standards of the dominant white community and the significance of visibility are demonstrated by the association among Negroes of light skin color and high class status.

As in Psathas' "Ethnicity, Social Class, and Adolescent Independence from Parental Control," we see in Frank R. Westie and David H. Howard's "Social Status Differentials and the Race Attitudes of Negroes" that we cannot generalize with accuracy about the attitudes of ethnic groups without specifying the class status of the members. High-status Negroes are less categorical in their attitudes toward whites than low-status Negroes, and the responses of Negroes to whites vary according to the class status of whites and the area of social interaction. Class is an important determiner of expectations, values, and attitudes.

—————————Harold Finestone

Cats, Kicks, and Color

Growing recognition that the most recent manifestation of the use of opiates in this country has been predominantly a young peoples' problem has resulted in some speculation as to the nature of this generation of drug users. Is it possible to form an accurate conception as to what "manner of man" is represented by the current species of young drug addict? Intensive interviews between 1951 and 1953 with over fifty male colored users of heroin in their late teens and early twenties selected from several of the areas of highest incidence of drug use in Chicago served to elicit from them the expression of many common attitudes, values, schemes of behavior, and general social orientation. Moreover, since there was every reason to believe that such similarities had preceded their introduction to heroin, it appeared that it was by virtue of such shared features that they had been unusually receptive to the spread of opiate use. Methodologically, their common patterns of behavior suggested the heuristic value of the construction of a social type. The task of this paper is to depict this social type, and to present a hypothetical formulation to account for the form it has taken.

No special justification appears to be necessary for concentrating in this paper on the social type of the young colored drug user. One of the distinctive properties of the distribution of drug use as a social problem, at least in Chicago, is its high degree of both spatial and racial concentration. In fact, it is a problem which in this city can be pinpointed with great accuracy as having its incidence preponderantly among the young male colored persons in a comparatively few local community areas. The following delineation of the generic characteristics of young colored drug users constitutes in many respects an ideal type. No single drug addict

Reprinted from Social Problems, Vol. V, No. 1, July 1957, pp. 3-13.

exemplified all of the traits to be depicted but all of them revealed several of them to a marked degree.

The young drug user was a creature of contrasts. Playing the role of the fugitive and pariah as he was inevitably forced to do, he turned up for interviews in a uniformly ragged and dirty condition. And yet he talked with an air of superiority derived from his identification with an elite group, the society of "cats." He came in wearing a non-functional tie clip attached to his sport shirt and an expensive hat as the only indications that he was concerned with his appearance and yet displayed in his conversation a highly developed sense of taste in men's clothing and a high valuation upon dressing well. He came from what were externally the drabbest, most overcrowded, and physically deteriorated sections of the city and yet discussed his pattern of living as though it were a consciously cultivated work of art.

Despite the location of his social world in the "asphalt jungle" of the "Blackbelt" he strictly eschewed the use of force and violence as a technique for achieving his ends or for the settling of problematic situations. He achieved his goals by indirection, relying, rather, on persuasion and on a repertoire of manipulative techniques. To deal with a variety of challenging situations, such as those arising out of his contacts with the police, with his past or potential victims, and with jilted "chicks," etc., he used his wits and his conversational ability. To be able to confront such contingencies with adequacy and without resort to violence was to be "cool." His idea was to get what he wanted through persuasion and ingratiation; to use the other fellow by deliberately outwitting him. Indeed, he regarded himself as immeasurably superior to the "gorilla," a person who resorted to force.

The image of himself as "operator" was projected onto the whole world about him and led to a complete scepticism as to other persons' motives. He could relate to people by outsmarting them, or through open-handed and often ruinous generosity, but his world seemed to preclude any relationship which was not part of the "scheme" or did not lend itself to an "angle." The most difficult puzzle for him to solve was the "square," the honest man. On the one hand the "square" was the hard-working plodder who lived by routine and who took honesty and the other virtues at their face value. As such he constituted the prize victim for the cat. On the other hand the cat harbored the sneaking suspicion that some squares were smarter than he, because they could enjoy all the forbidden pleasures which were his stock in trade and maintain a reputation for respectability in the bargain.

The cat had a large, colorful, and discriminating vocabulary which dealt with all phases of his experience with drugs. In addition, he never seemed to content himself with the conventional word for even the most commonplace objects. Thus he used "pad" for house, "pecks" for food, "flicks" for movies, "stick hall" for pool hall, "dig the scene" for observe, "box" for record player, "bread" for money, etc. In each instance the word he used was more concrete or earthier than the conventional word and such as to reveal an attitude of subtle ridicule towards the dignity and conventionality inherent in the common usage.

His soft convincing manner of speaking, the shocking earthiness and fancifulness of his vocabulary, together with the formidable gifts of charm and ingratiation which he deployed, all contributed to the dominant impression which the young drug user made as a person. Such traits would seem to have fitted naturally into a role which some cats had already played or aspired to play, that of the pimp. To be supported in idleness and luxury through the labors of one or more attractive "chicks" who shoplifted or engaged in prostitution or both and dutifully handed over the proceeds was one of his favorite fantasies. In contrast with the milieu of the white underworld, the pimp was not an object of opprobrium but of prestige.

The theme of the exploitation of the woman goes close to the heart of the cat's orientation to life, that is, his attitude towards work. Part of the cat's sense of superiority stems from his aristocratic disdain for work and for the subordination of self to superiors and to the repetitive daily routine entailed by work, which he regards as intolerable. The "square" is a person who toils for regular wages and who takes orders from his superiors without complaint.

In contrast with the "square," the cat gets by without working. Instead he keeps himself in "bread" by a set of ingenious variations on "begging, borrowing, or stealing." Each cat has his "hustle," [1] and a "hustle" is any non-violent means of "making some bread" which does not require work. One of the legendary heroes of the cat is the man who is such a skillful con-man that he can sell "State Street" to his victim. Concretely, the cat is a petty thief, pickpocket, or pool shark, or is engaged in a variety of other illegal activities of the "conning" variety. A very few cats are actually living off the proceeds of their women "on the hustle."

The main purpose of life for the cat is to experience the "kick." Just as every cat takes pride in his "hustle," so every cat cultivates his "kick." A "kick" is any act tabooed by "squares" that heightens and intensifies the present moment of experience and differentiates it as much as possible from the humdrum routine of daily life. Sex in any of its conventional expressions is not a "kick" since this would not serve to distinguish the cat from the "square," but orgies of sex behavior and a dabbling in the various perversions and byways of sex pass muster as "kicks." Some "cats" are on an alcohol "kick," others on a marihuana "kick," and others on a heroin "kick." There is some interchangeability among these various "kicks" but the tendency is to select your "kick" and stay with it. Many of these young drug users, however, had progressed from the alcohol to the mari-

---

[1] Finestone, Harold, "Narcotics and Criminality," *Law and Contemporary Problems*, 22 (Winter, 1957), 60-85.

huana to the heroin "kick." Each "kick" has its own lore of appreciation and connoisseurship into which only its devotees are initiated.

In addition to his "kick" the cat sets great store on the enjoyment of music and on proper dress. To enjoy one's "kick" without a background of popular music is inconceivable. The cat's world of music has a distinctive galaxy of stars, and the brightest luminaries in his firmament are performers such as "Yardbird" (the late Charlie Parker) and disc jockeys such as Al Benson. Almost every cat is a frustrated musician who hopes some day to get his "horn" out of pawn, take lessons, and earn fame and fortune in the field of "progressive music."

The cat places a great deal of emphasis upon clothing and exercises his sartorial talents upon a skeletal base of suit, sport shirt, and hat. The suit itself must be conservative in color. Gaiety is introduced through the selection of the sport shirt and the various accessories, all so chosen and harmonized as to reveal an exquisite sense of taste. When the cat was not talking about getting his clothes out of pawn, he talked about getting them out of the cleaners. With nonchalant pride one drug user insisted that the most expensive sport shirts and hats in the city of Chicago were sold in a certain haberdashery on the South Side. The ideal cat would always appear in public impeccably dressed and be able to sport a complete change of outfit several times a day.

The cat seeks through a harmonious combination of charm, ingratiating speech, dress, music, the proper dedication to his "kick," and unrestrained generosity to make of his day to day life itself a gracious work of art. Everything is to be pleasant and everything he does and values is to contribute to a cultivated aesthetic approach to living. The "cool cat" exemplifies all of these elements in proper balance. He demonstrates his ability to "play it cool" in his unruffled manner of dealing with outsiders such as the police, and in the self-assurance with which he confronts emergencies in the society of "cats." Moreover, the "cat" feels himto be any man's equal. He is convinced that he can go anywhere and mingle easily with anyone. For example, he rejects the type of music designated "the blues" because for him it symbolizes attitudes of submission and resignation which are repugnant and alien to his customary frame of mind.

It can be seen now why heroin use should make such a powerful appeal to the cat. It was the ultimate "kick." No substance was more profoundly tabooed by conventional middle-class society. Regular heroin use provides a sense of maximal social differentiation from the "square." The cat was at last engaged, he felt, in an activity completely beyond the comprehension of the "square." No other "kick" offered such an instantaneous intensification of the immediate moment of experience and set it apart from everyday experience in such spectacular fashion. Any words used by the cat to apply to the "kick," the experience of "being high," he applied to heroin in the superlative. It was the "greatest kick of them all."

In the formulation now to be presented the cat as a social type is viewed as a manifestation of a process of social change in which a new type of self-conception has been emerging among the adolescents of the lower socio-economic levels of the colored population in large urban centers. It is a self-conception rooted in the types of accommodation to a subordinate status achieved historically by the colored race in this country, a self-conception which has become increasingly articulated as it responded to and selected various themes from the many available to it in the milieu of the modern metropolis. Blumer's classification of social movements into general, specific, or expressive, appears to provide a useful framework for the analysis of the social type of the cat.[2]

In terms of these categories the cat as a social type is the personal counterpart of an expressive social movement. The context for such a movement must include the broader community, which, by its policies of social segregation and discrimination, has withheld from individuals of the colored population the opportunity to achieve or to identify with status positions in the larger society. The social type of the cat is an expression of one possible type of adaptation to such blocking and frustration, in which a segment of the population turns in upon itself and attempts to develop within itself criteria for the achievement of social status and the rudiments of a satisfactory social life. Within his own isolated social world the cat attempts to give form and purpose to dispositions derived from but denied an outlet within the dominant social order.

What are these dispositions and in what sense may they be said to be derived from the dominant social order? Among the various interrelated facets of the life of the cat two themes are central, those of the "hustle" and the "kick." It is to be noted that they are in direct antithesis to two of the central values of the dominant culture, the "hustle" versus the paramount importance of the occupation for the male in our society, and the "kick" versus the importance of regulating conduct in terms of its future consequences. Thus, there appears to be a relationship of conflict between the central themes of the social type of the cat and those of the dominant social order. As a form of expressive behavior, however, the social type of the cat represents an indirect rather than a direct attack against central conventional values.

It is interesting to speculate on the reasons why a type such as the cat should emerge rather than a social movement with the objective of changing the social order. The forces coercing the selective process among colored male adolescents in the direction of expressive social movements are probably to be traced to the long tradition of accommodation to a subordinate status on the part of the Negro as well as to the social climate since the Second World War, which does not seem to have been favorable to the formation of specific social movements.

The themes of the "hustle" and "kick" in the social orientation of the

[2] Blumer, Herbert, "Social Movements," in Robert E. Park, ed., *An Outline of the Principles of Sociology* (New York: Barnes & Noble, 1939), pp. 255-278.

cat are facts which appear to be overdetermined. For example, to grasp the meaning of the "hustle" to the cat one must understand it as a rejection of the obligation of the adult male to work. When asked for the reasons underlying his rejection of work the cat did not refer to the uncongenial and relatively unskilled and low paid jobs which, in large part, were the sole types of employment available to him. He emphasized rather that the routine of a job and the demand that he should apply himself continuously to his work task were the features that made work intolerable for him. The self-constraint required by work was construed as an unwarranted damper upon his love of spontaneity. The other undesirable element from his point of view was the authoritarian setting of most types of work with which he was familiar.

There are undoubtedly many reasons for the cat's rejection of work but the reasons he actually verbalized are particularly significant when interpreted as devices for sustaining his self-conception. The cat's feeling of superiority would be openly challenged were he to confront certain of the social realities of his situation, such as the discrimination exercised against colored persons looking for work and the fact that only the lowest status jobs are available to him. He avoided any mention of these factors which would have forced him to confront his true position in society and thus posed a threat to his carefully cherished sense of superiority.

In emphasizing as he does the importance of the "kick" the cat is attacking the value our society places upon planning for the future and the responsibility of the individual for such planning. Planning always requires some subordination and disciplining of present behavior in the interest of future rewards. The individual plans to go to college, plans for his career, plans for his family and children, etc. Such an orientation on the part of the individual is merely the personal and subjective counterpart of a stable social order and of stable social institutions, which not only permit but sanction an orderly progression of expectations with reference to others and to one's self. Where such stable institutions are absent or in the inchoate stages of development, there is little social sanction for such planning in the experience of the individual. Whatever studies are available strongly suggest that such are the conditions which tend to prevail in the lower socio-economic levels of the Negro urban community.[3] Stable family and community organization is lacking in those areas of the city where drug use is concentrated. A social milieu which does not encourage the subordination and disciplining of present conduct in the interests of future rewards tends by default to enhance the present. The "kick" appears to be a logical culmination of this emphasis.

Accepting the emergence of the self-conception of the cat as evidence of a developing expressive social movement, we may phrase the central

[3] Drake, St. Clair and Horace R. Cayton, "Lower Class: Sex and Family," *Black Metropolis* (New York: Harcourt, Brace & Co., 1945), pp. 564-599.

theoretical problem as follows: What are the distinctive and generic features of the cat's social orientation? Taking a cue from the work of Huizinga as developed in *Homo Ludens*,[4] we propose that the generic characteristics of the social type of the cat are those of play. In what follows, Huizinga's conception of play as a distinctive type of human activity will be presented and then applied as a tool of analysis for rendering intelligible the various facets of the social orientation of the cat. It is believed that the concept of play indicates accurately the type of expressive social movement which receives its embodiment in the cat.

According to Huizinga the concept of play is a primary element of human experience and as such is not susceptible to exact definition. "The *fun* of playing resists all analysis, all logical interpretation . . . Nevertheless it is precisely this fun-element that characterizes the essence of play." [5] The common image of the young colored drug addict pictures him as a pitiful figure, a trapped unfortunate. There is a certain amount of truth in this image but it does not correspond to the conception which the young colored addict has of himself or to the impression that he tries to communicate to others. If it were entirely true it would be difficult to square with the fact that substantial numbers of young colored persons continue to become drug users. The cat experiences and manifests a certain zest in his mode of life which is far from self-pity. This fun element seemed to come particularly to the fore as the cat recounted his search for "kicks," the adventure of his life on the streets, and the intensity of his contest against the whole world to maintain his supply of drugs. Early in the cycle of heroin use itself there was invariably a "honeymoon" stage when the cat abandoned himself most completely to the experience of the drug. For some cats this "honeymoon" stage, in terms of their ecstatic preoccupation with the drug, was perpetual. For others it passed, but the exigencies of an insatiable habit never seemed to destroy completely the cat's sense of excitement in his way of life.

While Huizinga declines to define play, he does enumerate three characteristics which he considers to be proper to play. Each one of them when applied to the cat serves to indicate a generic feature of his social orientation.

(a) "First and foremost . . . all play is a voluntary activity." [6] "Here we have the first main characteristic of play: that it is free, is in fact freedom." [7] The concept of an expressive social movement assumes a social situation where existing social arrangements are frustrating and are no longer accepted as legitimate and yet where collective activity directed towards the modification of these limitations is not possible. The cat is "free" in the sense that he is a pre-eminent candidate for new

---

[4] Huizinga, Johan, *Homo Ludens, A Study of the Play Element in Culture* (Boston: Beacon Press, 1955).
[5] *Ibid.*, p. 3.
[6] *Ibid.*, p. 7.
[7] *Ibid.*, p. 8.

forms of social organization and novel social practices. He is attempting to escape from certain features of the historical traditions of the Negro which he regards as humiliating. As an adolescent or young adult he is not only fully assimilated into such social institutions as the family, school, church, or industry which may be available to him. Moreover, the social institutions which the Negroes brought with them when they migrated to the city have not as yet achieved stability or an adequate functioning relationship to the urban environment. As a Negro, and particularly as a Negro of low socio-economic status, he is excluded from many socializing experiences which adolescents in more advantaged sectors of the society take for granted. He lives in communities where the capacity of the population for effective collective action is extremely limited, and consequently there are few effective controls on his conduct besides that exercised by his peer group itself. He is fascinated by the varied "scenes" which the big city spreads out before him. Granted this setting, the cat adopts an adventurous attitude to life and is free to give his allegiance to new forms of activity.

(b) . . . . A second characteristic is closely connected with this (that is, the first characteristic of freedom), namely, that play is not "ordinary" or "real" life. It is rather a stepping out of "real" life into a temporary sphere of activity with a disposition all of its own. Every child knows perfectly well that he is "only pretending," or that it was "only for fun." . . . . This "only pretending" quality of play betrays a consciousness of the inferiority of play compared with "seriousness," a feeling that seems to be something as primary as play itself. Nevertheless . . . the consciousness of play being "only a pretend" does not by any means prevent it from proceeding with the utmost seriousness, with an absorption, a devotion that passes into rapture and, temporarily at least, completely abolishes that troublesome "only" feeling.[8]

It is implicit in the notion of an expressive social movement that, since direct collective action to modify the sources of dissatisfaction and restlessness is not possible, all such movements should appear under one guise, as forms of "escape." Persons viewing the problem of addiction from the perspective of the established social structure have been prone to make this interpretation. It is a gross oversimplification, however, as considered from the perspective of the young drug addict himself. The emergence of the self-conception of the cat is an attempt to deal with the problems of status and identity in a situation where participation in the life of the broader community is denied, but where the colored adolescent is becoming increasingly sensitive to the values, the goals, and the notions of success which obtain in the dominant social order.

The caste pressures thus make it exceedingly difficult for an American Negro to preserve a true perspective of himself and his own group in relation to the larger white society. The increasing abstract knowledge of the

[8] *Ibid.*

world outside—of its opportunities, its rewards, its different norms of competition and cooperation—which results from the proceeding acculturation
at the same time as there is increasing group isolation, only increases the
tensions.[9]

Such conditions of group isolation would appear to be fairly uniform
throughout the Negro group. Although this isolation may be experienced
differently at different social levels of the Negro community, certain
features of the adaptations arrived at in response to this problem will
tend to reveal similarities. Since the struggle for status takes place on a
stage where there is acute sensitivity to the values and status criteria of
the dominant white group, but where access to the means through which
such values may be achieved is prohibited, the status struggle turning in
on itself will assume a variety of distorted forms. Exclusion from the
"serious" concerns of the broader community will result in such adaptations manifesting a strong element of "play."

Frazier in *Black Bourgeoisie* discusses the social adaptation of the
Negro middle class as "The World of Make-Believe." [10]

> The emphasis upon "social" life or "society" is one of the main props of
> the world of make-believe into which the black bourgeoisie has sought an
> escape from its inferiority and frustrations in American society. This world
> of make-believe, to be sure, is a reflection of the values of American society,
> but it lacks the economic basis that would give it roots in the world of
> reality.[11]

In the Negro lower classes the effects of frustrations deriving from
subordination to the whites may not be experienced as personally or as
directly as it is by the Negro middle class, but the massive effects of
residential segregation and the lack of stable social institutions and community organization are such as to reinforce strong feelings of group
isolation even at the lowest levels of the society.

It is here suggested that the function performed by the emergence of
the social type of the cat among Negro lower class adolescents is analogous to that performed by "The World of Make-Believe" in the Negro
middle class. The development of a social type such as that of the cat
is only possible in a situation where there is isolation from the broader
community but great sensitivity to its goals, where the peer group
pressures are extremely powerful, where institutional structures are weak,
where models of success in the illegitimate world have strong appeals,
where specific social movements are not possible, and where novel forms
of behavior have great prestige. To give significance to his experience,
the young male addict has developed the conception of a heroic figure,
the "ideal cat," a person who is completely adequate to all situations,

[9] Myrdal, Gunnar, *An American Dilemma* (New York: Harper & Brothers, 1944), p. 760.
[10] Frazier, E. Franklin, *Black Bourgeoisie* (Glencoe, Illinois: Free Press, 1957).
[11] *Ibid.*, p. 237.

who controls his "kick" rather than letting it control him, who has a lucrative "hustle," who has no illusions as to what makes the world "tick," who is any man's equal, who basks in the admiration of his brother cats and associated "chicks," who hob-nobs with "celebs" of the musical world, and who in time himself may become a celebrity.

The cat throws himself into his way of life with a great deal of intensity but he cannot escape completely from the perspective, the judgments, and the sanctions of the dominant social order. He has to make place in his scheme of life for police, lockups, jails, and penitentiaries, to say nothing of the agonies of withdrawal distress. He is forced eventually to confront the fact that his role as a cat with its associated attitudes is largely a pose, a form of fantasy with little basis in fact. With the realization that he is addicted he comes only too well to know that he is a "junky," and he is fully aware of the conventional attitudes towards addicts as well as of the counter-rationalizations provided by his peer group. It is possible that the cat's vacillation with regard to seeking a cure for his addiction is due to a conflict of perspectives, whether to view his habit from the cat's or the dominant social order's point of view.

(c) Play is distinct from "ordinary" life both as to locality and duration. This is the third main characteristic of play: its secludedness, its limitedness. It is "played out" within certain limits of time and place. It contains its own course and meaning.[12]

It is this limited, esoteric character of heroin use which gives to the cat the feeling of belonging to an elite. It is the restricted extent of the distribution of drug use, the scheming and intrigue associated with underground "connections" through which drugs are obtained, the secret lore of the appreciation of the drug's effects, which give the cat the exhilaration of participating in a conspiracy. Contrary to popular conception most drug users were not anxious to proselyte new users. Of course, spreading the habit would have the function of increasing the possible sources of supply. But an equally strong disposition was to keep the knowledge of drug use secret, to impress and dazzle the audience with one's knowledge of being "in the know." When proselyting did occur, as in jails or lockups, it was proselyting on the part of a devotee who condescended to share with the uninitiated a highly prized practice and set of attitudes.

As he elaborates his analysis of play Huizinga brings to the fore additional aspects of the concept which also have their apt counterpart in the way of life of the cat. For instance, as was discussed earlier, the cat's appreciation of "progressive music" is an essential part of his social orientation. About this topic Huizinga remarks, "Music, as we have hinted before, is the highest and purest expression of the *facultas ludendi*."[13]

[12] Huizinga, p. 9.
[13] P. 187.

The cat's attitude toward music has a sacred, almost mystical quality. "Progressive music" opens doors to a type of highly valued experience which for him can be had in no other way. It is more important to him than eating and is second only to the "kick." He may have to give up his hope of dressing according to his standards but he never gives up music.

Huizinga also observes, "Many and close are the links that connect play with beauty." [14] He refers to the "profoundly aesthetic quality of play." [15] The aesthetic emphasis which seems so central to the style of living of the cat is a subtle elusive accent permeating his whole outlook but coming to clearest expression in a constellation of interests, the "kick," clothing, and music. And it certainly reaches a level of awareness in their language. Language is utilized by the cat with a conscious relish, with many variations and individual turns of phrase indicating the value placed upon creative expression in this medium.

It is to be noted that much of the description of the cat's attributes did not deal exclusively with elements unique to him. Many of the features mentioned are prevalent among adolescents in all reaches of the status scale. Dress, music, language, and the search for pleasure are all familiar themes of the adolescent world. For instance, in his description of the adolescent "youth culture" Talcott Parsons would appear to be presenting the generic traits of a "play-form" with particular reference to its expression in the middle class.

> It is at the point of emergence into adolescence that there first begins to develop a set of patterns and behavior phenomena which involve a highly complex combination of age grading and sex role elements. These may be referred to together as the phenomena of the "youth culture." . . .
>
> Perhaps the best single point of reference for characterizing the youth culture lies in its contrast with the dominant pattern of the adult male role. By contrast with the emphasis on responsibility in this role, the orientation of the youth culture is more or less specifically irresponsible. One of its dominant roles is "having a good time." . . . It is very definitely a rounded humanistic pattern rather than one of competence in the performance of specified functions. [16]

Such significant similarities between this description and the themes of the social type of the cat only tend to reinforce the notion that the recent spread of heroin use was a problem of adolescence. The cat is an adolescent sharing many of the interests of his age-mates everywhere but confronted by a special set of problems of color, tradition, and identity.

The social orientation of the cat, with its emphasis on non-violence,

[14] P. 7.
[15] P. 2.
[16] Parsons, Talcott, "Age and Sex in the Social Structure," *Essays in Sociological Theory Pure and Applied* (Glencoe, Illinois: Free Press, 1949), pp. 220-221.

was quite in contrast to the orientation of the smaller group of young white drug users who were interviewed in the course of this study. The latter's type of adjustment placed a heavy stress upon violence. Their crimes tended to represent direct attacks against persons and property. The general disposition they manifested was one of "nerve" and brashness rather than one of "playing it cool." They did not cultivate the amenities of language, music, or dress to nearly the same extent as the cat. Their social orientation was expressed as a direct rather than an indirect attack on the dominant values of our society. This indicates that the "youth culture" despite its generic features may vary significantly in different social settings.

In his paper, "Some Jewish Types of Personality," Louis Wirth made the following suggestive comments about the relationship between the social type and its setting.

> A detailed analysis of the crucial personality types in any given area or cultural group shows that they depend upon a set of habits and attitudes in the group for their existence and are the direct expressions of the values of the group. As the life of the group changes there appears a host of new social types, mainly outgrowths and transformations of previous patterns which have become fixed through experience.[17]

What are some of the sources of the various elements going to make up the social type of the cat which may be sought in his traditions? The following suggestions are offered as little more than speculation at the present time. The emphasis upon non-violence on the part of the cat, upon manipulative techniques rather than overt attack, is a stress upon the indirect rather than the direct way towards one's goal. May not the cat in this emphasis be betraying his debt to the "Uncle Tom" type of adjustment, despite his wish to dissociate himself from earlier patterns of accommodation to the dominant white society? May not the "kick" itself be a cultural lineal descendant of the ecstatic moment of religious possession so dear to revivalist and store-front religion? Similarly, may not the emphasis upon the exploitation of the woman have its origin in the traditionally greater economic stability of the colored woman?

W. I. Thomas in one of his references to the problems raised by the city environment stated, "Evidently the chief problem is the young American person." [18] In discussing the type of inquiry that would be desirable in this area he states that it should

> . . . lead to a more critical discrimination between that type of disorganization in the youth which is a real but frustrated tendency to organize on a higher plane, or one more correspondent with the moving environment,

[17] Wirth, Louis, "Some Jewish Types of Personality," in Ernest W. Burgess, ed., *The Urban Community* (Chicago: University of Chicago Press, 1926), p. 112.

[18] Thomas, William I., "The Problem of Personality in the Urban Environment," in Ernest W. Burgess, ed., *The Urban Community* (Chicago: University of Chicago Press, 1926), p. 46.

and that type of disorganization which is simply the abandonment of standards. It is also along this line . . . that we shall gain light on the relation of
fantastic phantasying to realistic phantasying. . . .[19]

Posed in this way the problem becomes one of evaluating the social
type of the cat in relation to the processes of social change. This social
type is difficult to judge according to the criterion suggested by Thomas.
Since many of the cat's interests are merely an extreme form of the
adolescent "youth culture," in part the problem becomes one of determining how functional the period of adolescence is as preparation for subsequent adult status. However, the central phases of the social orientation
of the cat, the "hustle" and the "kick," do represent a kind of disorganization which indicates the abandonment of conventional standards. The
young addicted cat is "going nowhere." With advancing age he cannot
shed his addiction the way he can many of the other trappings of adolescence. He faces only the bleak prospect, as time goes on, of increasing
demoralization. Although the plight of the young colored addict is intimately tied to the conditions and fate of his racial group, his social
orientation seems to represent a dead-end type of adjustment. Just as
Handlin in *The Uprooted* suggests that the first generation of immigrant
peoples to our society tends to be a sacrificed generation,[20] it may be
that the unique problems of Negro migrants to our metropolitan areas
will lead to a few or several sacrificed generations in the course of the
tortuous process of urbanization.

The discussion of the social type of the cat leads inevitably to the issue
of social control. Any attempt to intervene or modify the social processes
producing the "cat" as a social type must have the objective of reducing
his group isolation. For instance, because of such isolation and because
of the cat's sensitivity to the gestures of his peers, the most significant
role models of a given generation of cats tend to be the cats of the
preceding age group. Where, in a period of rapid change, the schemes
of behavior of the role models no longer correspond to the possibilities
in the actual situation, it is possible for attitudes to be transmitted to a
younger generation which evidence a kind of "cultural lag." Thus the
condition of the labor market in Chicago is such as to suggest the existence of plentiful employment opportunities for the Negro in a variety of
fields. But because such openings are not mediated to him through role
models it is possible that the cat is unable to take advantage of these
opportunities or of the facilities available for training for such positions.

The social type of the cat is a product of social change. The type of
social orientation which it has elaborated indicates an all too acute
awareness of the values of the broader social order. In an open class
society where upward mobility is positively sanctioned, an awareness
and sensitivity to the dominant values is the first stage in their eventual

---

[19] *Ibid.*, p. 47.
[20] Handlin, Oscar, *The Uprooted* (New York: Grosset and Dunlap, 1951), p. 243.

assimilation. Insofar as the social type of the cat represents a reaction to a feeling of exclusion from access to the means towards the goals of our society, all measures such as improved educational opportunities which put these means within his grasp will hasten the extinction of this social type. Just as the "hoodlum" and "gangster" types tend to disappear as the various more recently arrived white ethnic groups tend to move up in the status scale of the community,[21] so it can confidently be expected that the cat as a social type will tend to disappear as such opportunities become more prevalent among the colored population.

[21] Bell, Daniel, "Crime as an American Way of Life," *Antioch Review*, 13 (June, 1953), 131-154.

———————Mozell C. Hill and Bevode C. McCall

Social Stratification in "Georgia Town" *

During 1949 we were engaged in the study of the social life of a biracially structured modern community, "Georgia Town." Among other problems, we set for ourselves the task of securing data which might serve as independent measures of validity of the "Index of Status Characteristics" (I.S.C.) developed by W. Lloyd Warner and his research associates at the University of Chicago.[1] We began with the assumption that the I.S.C. has validity as a measure of social status, in that it distinguishes clearly the various social levels within a community. In addition to selecting a contemporary community as a laboratory for testing our assumption, we wanted to view its status structure comparatively; that is, we thought it significant to compare the social organization of a "Georgia Town" through the employment of the I.S.C., with those of "Yankee City," [2] "Jonesville," [3] "Old City," [4] and the "All-Negro Society of Oklahoma." [5]

[1] Warner established the validity of the I.S.C. by correlating the scores derived in its use with his method of Evaluative Participation (E.P.). The E.P. is a method for determining the socio-economic levels of the community, and comprises several rating techniques for determining the social class position of individuals and families by the analysis of interviews secured from a representative cross-section of the residents of a community. See W. Lloyd Warner, Marcia Meeker, and Kenneth Eells, *Social Class in America: A Manual of Procedure for the Measure of Social Structure*, Chicago: Science Research Associates, 1949.

[2] W. Lloyd Warner and Paul S. Lunt, *The Social Life of a Modern Community*, New Haven: Yale University Press, 1946.

[3] W. Lloyd Warner and Associates, *Democracy in Jonesville*, New York: Harper and Brothers, 1949.

[4] Allison Davis and Burleigh Gardner, *Deep South*, Chicago: University of Chicago Press, 1941.

[5] Mozell C. Hill, "The All-Negro Society in Oklahoma." Unpublished Dissertation, University of Chicago, 1946.

* "Georgia Town" is a pseudonym for an actual community located in Southeast Georgia.

From *American Sociological Review*, Vol. 15, pp. 721-729. By permission.

Our approach involved the computation of I.S.C. scores for the entire population (12 years of age and over) and the use of these scores for converting the population into status levels (social classes) as suggested by Warner.[6] . . .

While we will not report directly upon the data collected by the E.P. method in this paper, preliminary analysis in collaboration with the I.S.C., as described below, indicates that there are five social levels in the community; and although various designations are used to name them by the residents of the town, we have used the terms first given common currency by Warner[7]—upper, upper middle, lower middle, upper lower, and lower lower. . . .

"Georgia Town" is a market center and a county seat in the "Cracker" culture area of southeast Georgia.[8] It has a population of approximately five thousand, of which thirty per cent is Negro. "Georgia Town" serves as the market center of a large rural area; in recent years the introduction of automobiles and all-weather roads has extended its trading area to the surrounding counties.

"Georgia Town" has both a recent history as a community and a long tradition as a continuous social unit. The social characteristics of the latter, which has been heuristically defined as a "Cracker" community[9] were marked by an open-country settlement with few institutional forms besides the church and family units. The areas was first settled in 1740. By 1790 it had been organized as a county by the Georgia State Legislature. Until 1830 "Georgia Town" was the location of one of the court sites at which the traveling court convened. In 1830 it was designated the county seat, and by 1880 the community was composed of a court house, a hotel, a general store, a jail, and six residences.

Since 1880 "Georgia Town" has grown slowly and steadily. It is located in an area that has become, in the last decade, an important agricultural center. The stimulus of government agricultural programs and the recent war has resulted in a marked decrease in the rural population and a corresponding increase in the size of the farm units, as well as an expansion in the mechanization of farm units.

"Georgia Town" is a representative community within the "Cracker" culture area. One of the special features of this cultural configuration is its bi-racial organization; another is the emphasis upon the family and the church. The area was settled in the main by family units, and due to

---

[6] Warner, Meeker and Eells, op. cit., p. 183. Warner was kind enough to furnish us with a copy of the manuscript prior to its publication. He called to our attention the need for an independent measure of the validity of the I.S.C. It should be pointed out, however, that Warner is in no way responsible for any errors in the initial report of our researches, though we owe him a debt of gratitude for the time and energy he has spent with us in explaining the theoretical and operational problems of Evaluative Participation. A separate paper is in preparation on this latter problem.

[7] W. L. Warner and Paul Lunt, op. cit.

[8] See Mozell C. Hill and Bevode C. McCall, "'Cracker Culture': A Preliminary Definition," Phylon, II (1950), 223-231.

[9] Ibid.

the lack of economic resources its cultural isolation was enhanced. Accordingly, during its early development the economic unit was the family farm which was nearly self-sufficient.

As "Georgia Town" has grown, social differentiation and stratification have become more pronounced. In recent years the importance of associations and church membership in status behavior has become more marked with the establishment of church missions by Protestants and Roman Catholics, and with the development of such associations as the Garden Club, the Country Club, the Kiwanis, the Lions, the Chamber of Commerce, the League of Women Voters, and others.

We were introduced to the community as employees of the Federal Government. An official of a Federal agency accompanied us to "Georgia Town" where we were introduced to certain key businessmen. This approach proved effective in terms of securing an entree and establishing rapport. Local county officials furnished us with an office in the County Court House and secured the use of school facilities for our field investigation.

After a four-month period of participant observation and free association interviewing we decided that the only feasible means of securing adequate data on the total community, within the time limits of the study, was to conduct a census. Since "Georgia Town" had no community directory or other listing of its citizens available to serve as a basis for computing I.S.C. scores, we were confronted with the task of constructing a census schedule for recording data on each individual in the community.

This schedule contained such general and standard items as age, sex, and marital status. We listed categories which would furnish the necessary data for computing I.S.C. scores: occupation, source of income, house-type, and dwelling area. Church membership and church preferences, membership in voluntary associations, frequency of attendance at churches and associations, education, and the skin color for Negro population were additional categories on the schedule. The schedules were distributed to the entire community with the aid of Professor David Hawk, his students at a nearby college, and graduate students at Atlanta University.

We secured census data on ninety-six per cent of the dwelling units in the community with the aid of a street map, marking each house and rating it on a seven-point scale.[10] We checked our survey of the dwelling units with an aerial photograph and found that the scope of our coverage of the "social community" was adequate.

It was necessary to employ several sophisticated informants in rating the dwelling areas. The best sources of information proved to be real estate salesmen, who drew boundary lines on a map and furnished us with pertinent descriptive characteristics of each area in terms of status. In addition, we secured the aid of old settlers who drove through the

[10] Warner, Meeker, and Eells, op. cit., pp. 143-150.

community classifying the areas. We were gratified by the internal consistency and agreement among the various informants, though two individuals had some difficulty in fixing the boundary lines between some of the higher status areas. We were then able to rate them along the seven-point scale,[11] and to enter dwelling area, house-type and source of income ratings on the schedule prior to the census.

We found it necessary to modify the occupational rating scale presented by Warner.[12] These changes were made in relation to the cultural setting of "Georgia Town" and reflect the middle-class proclivities among the whites in this market town. For example, along a seven-point scale we assigned a rating of three to radio engineers, health officials, foresters, florists and home demonstration agents, a rating of four to public health employees (non-professional) and college students. The latter refers to families in which the husband's occupation was listed as college student, and whose source of income was from Veterans' benefits and savings. Correspondingly, Veterans' Benefits, as a source of income, were assigned a rating of four. Under proprietors with a rating of four we added a category for traders; with a rating of four we included furniture and jewelry salesmen; with a rating of six we added ushers, convict guards and nightwatchmen. These ratings along with others were checked carefully against E.P. interview data.

The rating of sources of income proved to be a more difficult task in "Georgia Town." It was easy enough to secure a list of persons who supposedly had earned or inherited wealth, but there were so many inconsistencies and contradictions in our data that we found it necessary to employ Dun and Bradstreet as a cross-check for some businessmen and retired farmers. A similar problem was encountered in rating persons whose source of income was public or private relief. We had to consult county and private agency records to secure the names of families and individuals who were the recipients of relief. No obstacles were encountered with individuals and families whose sources of income were profits and fees, salaries, and wages.

After the I.S.C. scores were computed for 4,933 individuals in "Georgia Town," the distribution was converted into social class equivalents through the use of Warner's scale for predicting social class placement.[13] These data provided the frame for integrating and organizing social status materials for a clear-cut delineation of the status structure of the community; and in addition formed a basis for comparative analyses of the status structure of communities in the Southeast with those of other culture areas.

The social class composition of this bi-racial community is shown in

[11] *Ibid.*, pp. 151-154.
[12] *Ibid.*, pp. 140-141.
[13] *Ibid.*, p. 183. The I.S.C. was computed for the "head of household" and assigned to all other members of the "family unit." In computing class composition the entire study population was used inasmuch as there is variation in size of household at different social levels.

Table 1. The distribution of I.S.C. scores translated into social class equivalents reveals that of the 4,933 individuals scored, three per cent are in the upper class, and fourteen per cent are scored as upper middle. "Georgia Town," however, is predominately lower-middle and upper-lower class (27.6 per cent and 28.2 per cent, respectively) in socio-economic terms as well as in the employment of status symbols and behavior.

TABLE 1. THE SOCIAL CLASS DISTRIBUTION OF 4933 NEGROES AND WHITES
(12 YEARS OF AGE AND OVER) IN "GEORGIA TOWN," BY NUMBER AND PER CENT

Social Class	White		Negro		Total	
	Number	Per Cent	Number	Per Cent	Number	Per Cent
Upper	142	4.1	5	.3	147	3.0
Upper Middle	709	20.7	24	1.6	733	14.8
Lower Middle	1222	35.7	138	9.2	1360	27.6
Upper Lower	999	29.1	390	25.9	1389	28.2
Lower Lower	357	10.4	947	63.0	1304	26.4
Totals	3429	100.0	1504	100.0	4933	100.0

The lower-lower class in the total community is composed of 26.4 per cent of the residents. This is due to the wide discrepancy in class positions of the two caste groups. Sixty-three per cent, or 947 of the 1,504 Negroes scored, were rated lower-lower as compared to 10.4 per cent of the white population. Approximately fifty-six per cent of the white population is of middle-class status as compared with 10.8 per cent of the Negro residents. One hundred forty-two individuals in the white population were placed in the upper class while five Negroes (one family) possessed upper-class socio-economic characteristics.[14]

A comparison of the class structure of "Georgia Town" with those of "Yankee City" and "Jonesville" (Figures 1, 2 and 3) suggests several significant factors concerning the status structuring of individuals in modern American communities. The data of the three researches demonstrate well-defined status levels which make it possible for social scientists to locate, identify, interrelate and measure individuals in social interaction. The percentages of upper and upper-middle class persons in the three structures correspond; however, the percentage for the lower-lower class in "Jonesville" (12.5), compared with that for "Georgia Town" (26.4), points up a significant difference between "Midwest" and Southeastern communities. The square-shaped pyramidal structure of "Georgia Town" can be contrasted with the triangular shape of "Yankee City" and "Jonesville." However, the status distribution of individuals in "Georgia Town" is obscured by its rigid caste division, with its highly discriminated

[14] The high proportion of lower-class Negroes in bi-racially structured communities of the "Deep South" has been explained elsewhere. The reasons are apparent and need not be discussed here. These data simply indicate again, in bold relief, the inequalities inherent in a segregated economy and status system.

and unequal distributions of socio-economic and psychological rewards
—jobs, income, houses, living areas, educational opportunities, status
roles, social participation and prestige.

The status structure of Southern bi-racial communities, for example,
"Old City" with its unequal distribution of rights, privileges and duties,

1. Class Structure of "Georgia Town"
2. Class Structure of "Yankee City" as presented by W. Lloyd Warner and Associates. See
W. Lloyd Warner and Paul S. Lunt, *The Social Life of a Modern Community* (New Haven,
1941), p. 88.
3. Class Structure of "Jonesville" computed from Tables 18-19 in W. Lloyd Warner and
associates, *Democracy in Jonesville* (New York, 1949), p. 219.

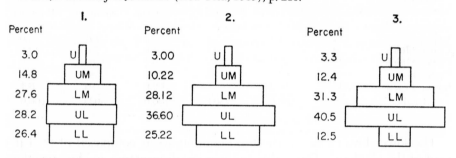

4. Relation Between the Caste/Class Structures of "Georgia Town."

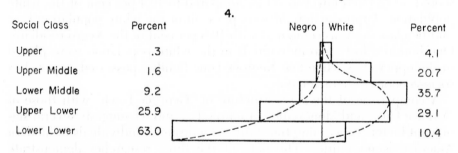

5. Relation Between the Caste/Class Structure of "Old City," as presented by W. Lloyd
Warner in the "Introduction" to *Deep South* (Chicago, 1941), p. 10.

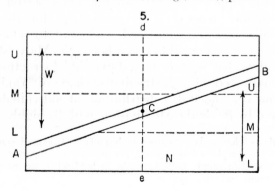

has been adequately described by Davis and Gardner and Warner.[15] For comparative purposes, Figures 4 and 5 are presented to demonstrate differences in our conceptualization of the class systems of the caste groups of "Georgia Town" and that of "Old City." Figure 4 emphasizes the middle-class orientation of the white population and the lower-class position of Negroes. It suggests the strivings of whites for socio-economic symbols. On the other hand, the graph for "Old City" reflects the stress as placed upon possession of differentials for power and prestige.

A comparison of Figures 4 and 5 indicates that the caste-lines in "Georgia Town" may not be as rigid as those of "Old City." Yet inter-caste mobility in both communities is held to an irreducible minimum. Moreover, Figure 4 suggests that in "Georgia Town" there may be a high degree of upward mobility, especially among the white residents. The data also suggest a greater amount of social and psychological space within which whites may operate than is true for Negroes.

6. Class Structure of Whites in "Georgia Town"
7. Class Structure of Negroes in "Georgia Town"
8. Class Structure of an All-Negro Society. See Mozell C. Hill, "The All-Negro Society in Oklahoma." Unpublished Ph.D. Dissertation, University of Chicago, 1946.

Figures 6, 7 and 8, which compare the class structures within the two caste groups of "Georgia Town" with the class structure of Negroes living in racially homogeneous communities in Oklahoma, point out a striking contrast. They emphasize the disproportionate number of lower-class Negroes *necessary* to maintain social balance and "order" in a racially segregated economy.

When the class structure of Negroes in "Georgia Town" is compared with that of the "all-Negro society of Oklahoma" [16] it is apparent that the latter is characterized by a more equalitarian structure, while the former tends to place individuals in a more unequal arrangement characterized by greater social differentiation. The status structure of the so-called "all-Negro society of Oklahoma" is composed of a small number of upper- and lower-class individuals. By far the majority of its population is middle class not only in socio-economic terms but also in behavior.

[15] See Davis and Gardner, *op. cit.*
[16] Hill, *op. cit.*

Superior socio-economic status of upper middle-class Negroes in "Georgia Town" and the maintenance of great social distance from lower-class Negroes may be due to the actions of the white caste in the selection of upper-class Negroes as a means of exerting informal pressures and maintaining social control in the Negro community. The position of upper- and upper-middle class Negroes, as the interview materials indicate, is insecure in both their relationships to the white caste and to lower class Negroes.

Table 2 shows the distribution of scores for Negroes and whites on each of the indices used in computing I.S.C. scores. The occupational and house-type ratings demonstrate consistent patterning that conforms to the distribution of the scores. These indices reveal a concentration of

TABLE 2. OCCUPATIONAL, SOURCE OF INCOME, HOUSE TYPE, DWELLING AREA, AND EDUCATIONAL RATINGS FOR NEGROES AND WHITES IN "GEORGIA TOWN," BY PER CENT

Rank	Occupation		Source of Income		House Type		Dwelling Area		Education	
	White	Negro	White	Negro	White	Negro	White	Negro	White	Negro
1	9.0	.5	.3	—	9.2	1.0	9.0	—	3.0	6.0
2	10.1	1.7	6.7	—	24.4	4.7	8.0	.1	25.6	4.2
3	21.4	3.5	22.3	7.1	17.0	1.2	15.0	40.1	7.3	5.0
4	32.0	2.7	30.1	4.7	12.8	12.0	23.0	1.7	39.3	10.4
5	10.6	13.7	38.5	81.7	19.0	10.5	14.1	25.0	8.5	7.8
6	12.9	13.4	.3	.5	13.3	29.1	12.6	9.5	15.0	42.6
7	4.0	64.5	1.8	6.0	4.3	41.5	18.3	23.6	2.3	24.0
Total	100.0	100.0	100.0	100.0	100.0	100.0	100.0	100.0	100.0	100.0

high scores for Negroes which places the greatest number at the bottom of the scale, while the white population converges at the center and toward the top. For example, 41.5 per cent of the houses occupied by Negroes in "Georgia Town" were rated seven, and are accordingly in a very poor state of repair; and only one per cent was rated excellent. In contrast, approximately 60 per cent of the houses occupied by whites are rated four and above, which indicates that the condition varies from good to excellent. The data on occupation present a similar picture. Sixty-four per cent of the occupations pursued by Negroes were rated seven (heavy labor, public relief, domestic service, farm labor, etc.) and approximately nine per cent were rated four and above (professional, proprietorial, clerical and kindred workers); whereas approximately seventy per cent of the occupations engaged in by whites were rated four and above, and only four per cent were rated at the bottom of the occupational scale.

The distribution of ratings for source of income does not demonstrate the different social levels as definitively as do occupational and house-type scales.[17] For example, 81.7 per cent of the Negroes are wage workers and are accordingly rated five on the scale; not one Negro family has earned or inherited wealth; and only six per cent are rated at the bottom of the scale. In a similar vein, source of income for the white community is not as differentiating as other indices.

The residential area factor, while an important symbol of status in "Georgia Town," does not conform in this community with the same degree of correspondence to the I.S.C. distribution of scores as do some of the other indices. Perhaps the absence of a large number of individuals with inherited and earned wealth limits residential selection. Moreover, the small number of Negroes in the middle and upper classes as well as rigid residential restriction limits the importance of the "area lived in" factor in the status structure. It is significant that no Negroes live in residential areas rated at the top of the scale and 41.5 per cent live in the most undesirable ("Black Bottom") districts. For the white community there is a more even distribution of individuals along the scale.

Education appears to be a differentiating index of social status in "Georgia Town." This distribution demonstrates the rather consistent patterning noted previously, with the concentration of Negroes at the bottom of the scale and the convergence of whites at the center and toward the top.[18] The relatively large percentage of whites rated five and below indicates the limited educational opportunities of the older whites in "cracker culture"; and the 25.6 per cent rated two reflects the presence of a small four-year college in the community. The significance of education in the Negro community as an index of status and upward mobility is suggested by the fact that a greater percentage of Negroes than whites were rated at the top of the educational scale, six per cent and three per cent, respectively.

Table 3, which compares the social class and educational levels of whites and Negroes in "Georgia Town," shows how effectively this index distinguishes the various status levels of the community. The data reveal the relations between education and social status; they demonstrate that college and professional education correlate highly with the upper-status levels, and correspondingly, that education limited to grammar schooling —the seventh grade and below—is associated with lower-status groups.

---

[17] Perhaps it should be pointed out that source of income in the market town of the Southeast is a more difficult index to determine for the groups in the upper and lower ranges. Inherited wealth and/or earned wealth can be located only in semi-confidential records such as those found in banks and tax offices. In addition, we found from our interview materials that information regarding source of income lacked the necessary internal consistency and, therefore, could not be relied upon with the same degree of confidence for validative materials as could occupation. Moreover, in recent years the trend has been toward increasing the confidential nature of handling records in public relief offices. This made it difficult for us to check the accuracy of the ratings on source of income for these three levels.

[18] Perhaps the Educational Index could be substituted for source of income in computing I.S.C. scores in future studies of Southeastern communities.

TABLE 3. SOCIAL CLASS AND EDUCATIONAL LEVEL OF WHITES
AND NEGROES IN "GEORGIA TOWN," BY PER CENT

Educational Level	Social Class									
	Upper		Upper Middle		Lower Middle		Upper Lower		Lower Negro	
	White	Negro	White	Negro	White	Negro	White	Negro	White	Negro
College, Graduate and Professional	67.6	100.0	54.5	65.0	32.7	25.0	7.5	2.9	0.8	1.1
High School Graduate	8.8	—	9.1	4.4	10.4	12.5	3.4	8.8	2.8	2.7
1-3 Years High School	18.6	—	30.7	4.4	41.5	11.5	46.5	14.7	29.4	9.6
Grammar School Graduate	4.0	—	2.8	4.4	5.1	10.4	13.4	10.5	20.6	6.5
4-7 Years Grammar School	1.0	—	2.3	17.4	9.6	28.1	26.7	47.4	34.7	51.0
0-3 Years Grammar School	—	—	0.6	4.4	0.7	12.5	2.5	15.7	11.7	29.1
Total	100.0	100.0	100.0	100.0	100.0	100.0	100.0	100.0	100.0	100.0

The amount of education appears to be more important concomitant of
high and low status levels among Negroes than is true for whites. This
suggests that education might be a more important index of class and
status mobility in the Negro community than is found in the white
society. In fact, education might be the mechanism and process for
levelling the social structure of these Southeastern bi-racial communities.

Several sociologists have suggested that skin color and physical features
are important factors in the status arrangement of Negroes.[19] Indeed,
some status analysts have attempted to test this hypothesis by correlating skin color with social participation. Negroes were rated in "Georgia
Town" according to skin color on a seven-point scale and these ratings
were grouped with their class positions.

Table 4 points out the status arrangement of Negroes by skin color. It

TABLE 4. SOCIAL CLASS AND SKIN COLOR OF NEGROES
IN "GEORGIA TOWN," BY PER CENT

Social Class	Skin Color						
	White	Light Yellow	Olive or Tan	Brown (Reddish)	Dark Brown	Very Dark Brown	Ebony	Total
Upper	20.0	80.0	—	—	—	—	—	100.0
Upper Middle	—	13.0	13.0	43.5	17.4	8.7	4.4	100.0
Lower Middle	.9	1.8	9.3	38.0	36.1	13.0	.9	100.0
Upper Lower	.3	.3	8.5	27.0	41.8	20.0	2.1	100.0
Lower Lower	—	.5	4.8	15.1	41.1	34.1	4.4	100.0

may be that selective factors are operating among Negroes in "Georgia
Town" in favor of darker-skinned individuals, for the total population
tends to range from light brown to very dark brown. Only a few are at
the extremes—white and ebony. Yet the data indicate that more white

[19] C. H. Parrish, "The Significance of Color in the Negro Community," Ph.D. Dissertation,
University of Chicago, 1944; W. Lloyd Warner, *Color and Human Nature*, Washington,
D.C.: American Council on Education, 1941; Horace Cayton and St. Clair Drake, *Black
Metropolis*, New York: Harcourt, Brace and Company, 1945.

and fair-skinned Negroes are concentrated in higher status levels than are darker ones. The data, however, should be considered as tentative, since numbers for the white and fair-skinned individuals are small. Thus the data, while not supporting the hypothesis, suggest that it is nevertheless a fruitful one, and needs to be tested further.

———————————Frank R. Westie and David H. Howard

Social Status Differentials and the Race Attitudes of Negroes

This paper reports some of the more salient findings of the second study of a projected multi-phase investigation of the relationship between social status differentials and attitudes in the realm of intergroup relations.

The first study,[1] the field-work for which was conducted in Indianapolis during 1950, involved the assessment of the attitudes of Whites of varying socio-economic status toward both Negroes and Whites of varying status. The present study, the data for which were gathered in Indianapolis during 1952, is to some extent a mirror-image of the first phase. Virtually all relevant variables are the same as in the first investigation. This time, however, we are concerned with the attitudes of Negroes toward Whites rather than with the attitudes of Whites toward Negroes.

The research dealing with the attitudes of minority group members toward the majority makes a rather thin chapter in the annals of sociological research, especially when compared to the volume of research on the other half of the intergroup relations picture.

The reasons for this apparent imbalance are fairly obvious. The intergroup relations area has been traditionally handled within a social pathology framework and this orientation has been conducive not only to the espousal of the values of the investigator, but has also lent itself to the assignment of blame and responsibility to particular individuals and groups for the society's failure to realize the investigator's values. Thus what is known in popular parlance as "the *Negro* problem" becomes in effect, in the parlance of social pathology, a "*White* problem"; the social norms which define in negative terms the attitudes and actions of Whites toward Negroes are seen (quite correctly, we might add) to have had their genesis and perpetuation in white society. Given this viewpoint, plus the fact that most investigators in this area have been concerned with amelioration of conflict and the more speedy realization of democratic ideals, it has been deemed efficient to concentrate our research efforts on the attitudes of the majority. The view has been, in

[1] Frank R. Westie, "Negro-White Status Differentials and Social Distance," *American Sociological Review*, 17 (October, 1952), pp. 550-558.

From *American Sociological Review*, Vol. 19, pp. 584-591. By permission.

effect, that the problem ultimately resides in the attitudes of the majority and that the cure lies in the changing of these attitudes.[2]

If, however, our purpose is to understand majority-minority relations, not as an instance of social pathology or as an extra-societal appendage, but rather as a part of the larger social system, then the attitudes of minority group members toward the majority become much more important than where the orientation is pathological. If minority-majority relationships are indeed an integral part of the system of social relationships which constitute our society, and if our purpose in studying them is to help fill the gaps in our knowledge of our society, then such relationships must be studied *as social relationships*, which means that they must be considered in their *reciprocal* aspects.[3]

Previous studies of the race attitudes of Negroes have been largely concerned with the attitudes of "Negroes in general" toward "Whites in general." The present study is concerned not only with the attitudes of Negroes toward Whites, but with attitudes of Negroes toward Negroes.[4] Moreover, the Negro respondents are given opportunity to respond to members of these two groups, not simply in terms of race, but also according to the within-group status of the attitude-object. By interviewing Negroes on different levels of the socio-economic hierarchy of the Negro community and assessing their attitudes toward whites and Negroes in occupations of divergent status, we establish the relationship between *social status differentials* and the race attitudes of Negroes. The term "social status differential" refers to the difference between the status of the respondent and status of the attitude object.

The instrument which was used in the study of Whites was employed in the present study of Negroes. Despite the fact that the members of another race were interviewed, it was not necessary to make any alterations in the scales, the attitude objects in the items, or in any other aspect of the instrument. This was due to the fact that the schedule calls for responses to both Whites and Negroes. Thus, the findings of the first study[5] (of Whites) are directly comparable to those of the present study.

The primary reason for including items calling for responses to Negroes as well as to Whites has to do with our technique of measuring prejudice.

---

[2] Whether attitudes are mere symptoms or in some sense causes, whether or not it is more efficient to treat attitudes rather than social conditions, are considerations which are not relevant to this paper; and, as far as we can tell, the findings contribute little to arguments on either side.

[3] We might add that it is precisely because most sociological investigators fail to consider such relationships in their reciprocal aspects that the larger part of their empirical research in this area is generally indistinguishable from the product of the psychologist. And until we relate this study to the first one, so are ours. Although the present article simply presents the findings regarding the attitudes of Negroes, these findings are being analyzed in relation to the findings regarding the attitudes of Whites in terms of Bogardus' concept of *social distance differentials*. See E. S. Bogardus, "Social Distance Differential," *Sociology and Social Research*, 32 (May-June, 1948), p. 882.

[4] The findings regarding the attitudes of Negroes toward Negroes are not presented in the present article.

[5] Westie, *op. cit.*, pp. 550-558.

This device, referred to as the *Summated Differences Technique*[6] yields a prejudice score which is a function of the difference in response to persons of the same occupation but of different races. For this reason we are able to measure prejudice toward Negroes at the same time as we get at prejudice toward Whites.

The instrument has been described at length in a previous article.[7] We need merely repeat here that the schedule includes four social distance scales which measure (1) *Residential Distance* (degree of residential proximity permitted), (2) *Position Distance* (degree of willingness to have the attitude-object occupy positions of power and prestige), (3) *Physical Distance* (the degree to which respondents are averse to physical contact with the attitude-object), and (4) *Interpersonal Distance* (the degree of proximity permitted in interpersonal interaction). The attitude-objects in the items of these scales are not simply "the Negro" or "a White man," but rather Whites and Negroes in eight different occupations.[8] In the present study we asked Negroes of varying status to respond to "Negro Doctor," "White Doctor," "Negro Ditch Digger," and "White Ditch Digger," *etc.*, in the various areas of social interaction implied by the titles of the scales.

The Samples

A sample of the Negro population of Indianapolis was interviewed during the summer of 1952. The universe from which the sample was drawn was defined to include all Negro males 21 years of age or over, who are heads of households and who live in blocks without Whites.

Since this study is focused upon the relationship between social status differentials and attitudes, it was necessary that our sample represent persons at the upper and lower reaches of the socio-economic ladder in sufficiently large numbers to permit statistical manipulation. This posed a major sampling problem. We were unable to draw area samples along socio-economic lines, as it was impossible to discover any clear-cut socio-economic status areas within the Negro community.[9] In Indianapolis, as elsewhere, Whites, rather than the Negro's income, determine where Negroes shall live, and the area of Negro residence so segregated tends to be uniformly low from the standpoint of socio-economic status. Although there is some variation in house type and dwelling area within the Negro community, the range of variation is small compared to the range in the White community; in the Negro community it is not uncommon to find living next door to one another persons who occupy positions at the opposite extremes of the occupational ladder.

[6] Frank R. Westie, "A Technique for the Measurement of Race Attitudes," *American Sociological Review*, 18 (February, 1953), pp. 73-78.

[7] *Ibid.*, pp. 73-78.

[8] The total range of occupations used was as follows: Doctor, Business Executive, Banker, Lawyer, Owner-Manager of a Small Store, Bookkeeper, Machine Operator, and Ditch Digger.

[9] From a map of Indianapolis prepared for the first phase in this research program, it was possible to outline the residential areas in which Negroes are concentrated.

Because of these characteristics of the Negro community, we decided to draw a single sample that would be sufficiently large to turn up a range of socio-economic types broad enough to permit establishing relationships between status differentials and attitudes. This sample was secured by assigning numbers to all blocks in the Negro community and then drawing a sample of blocks. A list of all households within the blocks was prepared from the Indianapolis City Directory. The households were then numbered and samples were drawn in proportion to the number of households in the block. Tables of random numbers were used in these drawings. Respondents were interviewed in the order drawn.

After a few dozen respondents had been interviewed, it became apparent that a single sample would not yield a sufficiently large number of persons of high socio-economic status unless this single sample were extended to prohibitive proportions. We decided, however, to continue interviewing until at least 50 persons of lower socio-economic status had been interviewed.[10]

In order to secure, within the limits of our budget, an adequate number of respondents of higher status, it was necessary to resort to an entirely different kind of sampling procedure from that employed for the lower group. The Upper sample was drawn by preparing lists of persons in the professions, higher status white-collar positions, and higher status business positions. All persons in these lists[11] had to qualify for placement in the first three ranks of the Warner scale.

[10] Socio-economic status classifications were made according to the occupational scale developed by W. L. Warner, M. Meeker, and E. Eels, Social Class in America, Chicago: Science Research Associates, Inc., 1949, Chapter 8. If a person's rank on this scale was 4 or more, he was considered to be of "lower" socio-economic status. Those with a score of 1 to 3 were assigned to the upper group for purposes of analysis. By the time 55 cases had been secured, we found that our quota of lower status persons had been achieved.

[11] The lists were prepared through interviews with business and professional persons in the Negro community. In addition to the list of business men and the list of higher-ranking white collar persons, separate lists were prepared for each of the following professions and white-collar occupations: Medicine, Dentistry, Social Work, Pharmacy, the Ministry (only persons with formal theological training), Law and Accountancy. A list of Negro teachers was secured from the Indianapolis Directory of Public School Teachers. From the standpoint of sampling accuracy, the list procedure is decidedly inferior to the area procedure used for the first sample. The following sources of error should be made explicit: (1) Upper status persons had greater chance of being included in the sample inasmuch as they were not excluded in the definition of the universe from which the "lower" sample was derived. Actually, however, only four persons in the first three ranks of the Warner scale turned up in the first sample. (2) In the construction of the lists it is quite possible that some occupations which qualify persons for the Upper sample are not listed. However, the percentage of such persons is probably small inasmuch as persons who contributed to the list were asked if they knew of persons of higher status who were not in any of the occupations enumerated. (3) Some of the individual lists themselves are probably not exhaustive. However, the Negro community itself is relatively small (population 65,000) and concentrated. Moreover, the proportion of persons of higher status is smaller than in the White community; the number of persons in any given profession is quite small. Thus, many professional persons who prepared lists of persons in their own profession were quite confident of the exhaustiveness and accuracy of their lists. At least two persons in each profession prepared lists of their own profession. Moreover, the judges were called upon to look for omissions in the lists of the other occupations. The professional persons were particularly helpful in filling gaps in the business and white-collar lists.

The interviews took place in the home of the respondent and all were conducted by the same interviewer—who is himself a Negro.

The Findings

The analyses seek answers to the following questions:

(1) What is the relationship between variations in the socio-economic status of Negroes and the social distance they accord Whites in general?

(2) What effect does the occupational status of the white person (as attitude-object) have upon the Negro's response to him?

(3) If the responses of Negroes are affected by the socio-economic status of the white to whom he responds, is this effect equal for different socio-economic levels of the Negro population?

(4) Are the responses of Negroes equally categorical (or non-categorical, as the case may be) in one kind of interaction as in another, or does the degree to which Negroes respond to "Whites as a type" depend on the kind of interaction involved?

Table 1 compares the Upper and Lower samples with respect to the average distance accorded Whites in eight occupations in the four interaction areas. The following general relationships are indicated:

(1) *There is an inverse relationship between the status of the Negro and the distance he would accord Whites: the higher the status of the Negro, the less the distance expressed toward Whites in general.* Thus, in Table 1, the Upper sample has a mean residential distance score of 2.56 toward White Doctor while the Lower sample has a score of 5.14, yielding a difference of 2.58. A qualification, however, is in order: In the Position Area we find that the Upper sample indicated greater distance than the Lower sample toward low status Whites. As one would expect, upper status persons are more averse than lower status persons to the idea of skilled and unskilled workers occupying positions of power and prestige in the community. It must also be added that, though the relationship outlined here holds in general, the Upper sample tends to express slightly more distance toward White Ditch Digger than does the Lower sample.

(2) *Least distance is expressed toward Whites of high status while greatest distance is accorded to the lowest status White.* We find, for example, that the Residential Distance accorded White Doctor by the Upper sample is only 2.56, while the distance toward White Ditch Digger is 6.32. This same trend can be discerned in all areas for both the Upper and Lower samples.

(3) *Upper status Negroes are less categorical in their responses to Whites than are lower status Negroes.* Table 1 reveals that the Upper and Lower samples differ in the degree to which increased status of the White operates to mitigate the distance accorded to Whites. In all areas of interaction, persons in the Lower sample vary less than the Upper sample in their responses to Whites of varying status. Where variations

TABLE 1. MEAN SOCIAL DISTANCE SCORES TOWARD WHITES BY SOCIO-ECONOMIC SAMPLES AND INTERACTION AREAS

Area [***]	Negro Sample	Distance Toward								Difference Between Doctor and Ditch Digger	N
		White Doctor	White Executive	White Banker	White Lawyer	White Owner-Manager	White Book-keeper	White Machine Operator	White Ditch Digger		
I	Upper	2.56[*]	3.10	2.98	2.93	3.34	3.37	4.24	6.32	3.76	41
	Lower	5.14	5.27	5.76	5.08	5.25	5.37	5.51	6.12	0.98	51
	Diff.[**]	2.58	2.17	2.78	2.15	1.91	2.00	1.27	-0.20		
II	Upper	5.83	4.59	4.85	3.85	8.85	8.73	10.59	13.41	9.56	41
	Lower	7.24	5.94	6.73	6.24	8.55	8.84	9.63	11.65	5.41	51
	Diff.[**]	1.41	1.35	1.88	2.39	-0.30	0.11	-0.96	-1.76		
III	Upper	5.63	5.51	5.39	5.32	5.73	5.44	5.76	6.71	1.08	41
	Lower	6.02	6.02	6.24	5.86	6.31	6.08	6.41	6.29	0.27	51
	Diff.[**]	0.39	0.51	0.85	0.54	0.58	0.64	0.65	-0.42		
IV	Upper	4.10	4.63	4.22	4.39	4.22	4.85	5.22	6.83	2.73	41
	Lower	5.78	6.24	5.73	5.63	6.37	6.20	6.18	6.86	1.08	51
	Diff.[**]	1.68	1.61	1.51	1.24	2.15	1.35	0.96	0.03		

[*] Lower scores indicate less distance.
[**] Difference between Upper and Lower Samples.
[***] I = Residential Area
II = Position Area
III = Physical Area
IV = Interpersonal Area

in the responses of lower status Negroes do occur, however, they tend to be in the direction of less distance toward higher status Whites. For the lower status respondents, the magnitude of the variations is so slight that they must be regarded as categorical in their responses to Whites except in the Position Area.

(4) *The responses of Negroes to Whites vary according to the area of interaction in which responses are elicited.* The data in Table 1 indicate that Negroes are not equally rigid in their responses to Whites in the various areas of interaction. The status of the White makes greatest difference to Negroes in the Position Area. Both high and low status Negroes would prefer to have Whites of high rather than low occupational status occupy positions of power and prestige in the community. Both upper and lower status Negroes are most rigid (that is, unaffected by variation in the White's occupational status) in the Physical Area, the variations here being unsystematic and statistically insignificant. The findings derived from this scale (which seeks to measure the degree to which respondents are averse to physical contacts with the attitude-object) indicate that Negroes do not respond in terms of conceptions of the relative cleanliness of the various categories of Whites.

Critical ratios were computed between average responses to Whites in occupation extremes, that is, between the mean distance expressed toward White Doctor and the mean distance expressed toward White Ditch Digger. Although these are *distance extremes* operationally defined in terms of actual distance expressed, one will agree that they tend to be status extremes as well. Lawyer rather than Doctor is used as the upper extreme in the case of Position Distance, because least distance was expressed toward Lawyer on this scale.

Table 2 presents the critical ratios of the differences between the

TABLE 2. COMPARISON OF MEAN DISTANCE SCORES TOWARD WHITES
IN OCCUPATION EXTREMES FOR UPPER AND LOWER SAMPLES
OF NEGRO RESPONDENTS

Area	Negro Sample	White Ditch Digger $\bar{X}_1$	White Doctor $\bar{X}_2$	$\bar{X}_1 - \bar{X}_2$	C.R. $(\bar{X}_1 - \bar{X}_2)$	N
I Residential	Upper	6.32	2.56	3.76	6.60	41
	Lower	6.12	5.14	0.98	1.44	51
II Position	Upper	13.41	3.85°	9.56	10.28	41
	Lower	11.65	6.24	5.41	5.30	51
III Physical	Upper	6.71	5.63	1.08	....°°	41
	Lower	6.29	6.02	0.27	....	51
IV Interpersonal	Upper	6.83	4.10	2.73	3.10	41
	Lower	6.86	5.78	1.08	1.44	51

° Lawyer used as occupation extreme in the Position Area.
°° Critical ratios were not computed for the Physical Area inasmuch as the differences are too small to be of statistical significance.

extreme means. For the upper sample on the Residential Scale the difference in mean distance scores between White Doctor and White Ditch Digger yields a critical ratio of 6.60, which is significant beyond the .01 level of probability. On the other hand, the critical ratio of 1.44 for the lower sample is not significant at the .05 level. On the Position Scale, the Upper sample's critical ratio of 10.28 and the Lower sample's critical ratio of 5.30 indicate significance beyond the .01 level. On the Interpersonal Scale the Upper sample has a critical ratio of 3.10 which is significant beyond the .01 level, while the 1.44 critical ratio for the lower sample is not significant at a satisfactory level. Critical ratios were not computed for the Physical Distance data inasmuch as the differences here appear *a priori* to be too small to be statistically significant.

Comparison of Negro Occupational Categories

In Table 3, which deals with Residential Distance, our respondents are classified into seven occupational categories.[12] This table reveals

TABLE 3. MEAN RESIDENTIAL DISTANCE SCORES TOWARD WHITES
BY OCCUPATIONAL RANK OF NEGRO RESPONDENTS

Negro Respondent's Occupational Rank	Distance Toward								Difference Between Doctor and Ditch Digger	N
	White Doctor	White Executive	White Banker	White Lawyer	White Owner-Manager	White Bookkeeper	White Machine Operator	White Ditch Digger		
1	2.00	2.53	2.47	2.80	3.33	3.40	4.80	7.00	5.00	15
2	2.48	3.29	2.86	2.71	2.90	3.00	3.52	6.00	3.52	21
3	4.60	4.00	5.00	4.20	5.20	4.80	5.60	5.60	1.00	5
4	5.17	3.33	4.67	4.67	3.17	4.50	4.83	5.33	0.16	6
5	5.14	6.29	5.00	5.29	5.29	5.29	4.71	5.71	0.57	7
6	5.20	4.53	6.40	4.73	5.00	5.53	5.00	6.20	1.00	15
7	5.09	5.96	5.87	5.35	5.96	5.52	6.26	6.39	1.30	23
Difference between 1 and 7	3.09	3.43	3.40	2.55	2.63	2.12	1.46	—0.61		
Total										92

findings similar to those observed in the sample comparisons. The number 1 category, which includes high ranking professional and white collar persons, expresses the least distance toward Whites in general, while the number 7 category, which is made up, for the most part, of unskilled workers and service persons, tends to express greatest distance. More-

[12] The seven point scale adapted from Alba Edwards by W. L. Warner was used for making the occupational classification of respondents. The lists of occupations included in each of the seven categories are too lengthy to be presented here. We can but remark on some of the occupations included in some of the categories along the continuum: Occupations included in Category 1 are of high status, e.g., doctor, lawyer, owner of a large business, big business executive. Categories 3 and 4 include, among others, those occupations associated with the label "white collar," while categories 6 and 7 include, among others, semi-skilled and unskilled workers, truck drivers, janitors, and service persons. The classifications were made on basis of rather detailed descriptions given by each respondent concerning his job activities. For explicit definitions of the categories used, see W. Lloyd Warner *et al.*, *op. cit.*, pp. 140-141.

over, as in the sample comparisons, high White status tends to mitigate distance as far as upper status Negroes are concerned, while the status of Whites tends to have relatively little effect on the responses of lower status Negroes. In the other three areas (for which tables are not presented here) the same kinds of relationships as described in the sample comparisons are apparent.

One will notice in Table 3 certain inconsistencies in the mean distance expressed by Occupational categories 3, 4, and 5. We suspected these inconsistencies to be due to the smallness of the N's of these three categories. In order to check on this possibility we grouped the seven categories into a three-fold system which would yield a larger N for the middle range. The grouping is as follows: (1, 2), (3, 4, 5), and (6, 7). When the data are grouped in this manner we find in Table 4, that the

TABLE 4. MEAN RESIDENTIAL SCORES TOWARD WHITES BY THREE-FOLD
GROUPING ON OCCUPATIONAL RANK OF NEGRO

Negro Respondent's Occupational Rank	Distance Toward								Difference Between Doctor and Ditch Digger	N
	White Doctor	White Executive	White Banker	White Lawyer	White Owner-Manager	White Book-keeper	White Machine Operator	White Ditch Digger		
Ranks 1 and 2	2.28	2.97	2.69	2.75	3.08	3.17	4.06	6.42	4.14	36
Ranks 3, 4, 5	5.00	4.67	4.89	4.78	4.56	4.89	5.00	5.56	0.56	18
Ranks 6 and 7	5.13	5.39	6.08	5.11	5.58	5.53	5.76	6.32	1.19	38
Difference between Ranks 1 and 2 and Ranks 6, 7	2.85	2.42	3.39	2.36	2.50	2.36	1.70	−0.10		
Total										92

relationships indicated by the sample comparisons emerge again, somewhat more clearly than where the seven-fold classification was used.

Although the purpose of this paper has been simply to present some of the empirical relationships indicated by this phase of the overall project, we realize that some readers may be curious concerning how the findings of the present study compare with the findings of the previous study of Whites. We can only point out here that the general relationships indicated by the present study are almost exactly similar to those found in the study of White respondents, although in the case of the White study the trends were more consistent and the response-differences between respondent categories somewhat larger.

Supplementary Bibliography

Morgan C. Brown, "The Status of Jobs and Occupations as Evaluated by an Urban Negro Sample." *American Sociological Review*, 1955, 20:561-566. Reprinted in Kimball Young and Raymond W. Mack, *Principles of Sociology: A*

Reader in Theory and Research, 2nd ed. N. Y.: American Book, 1962, pp. 310-316.

A research report documenting the differential perception of the occupational prestige hierarchy as a product of minority status.

St. Clair Drake and Horace R. Cayton, *Black Metropolis.* N. Y.: Harcourt, Brace, 1945.

A sociological profile of the segregated Negro community in Chicago, with an especially good treatment of class differences among Negroes.

E. Franklin Frazier, *Black Bourgeoisie.* Glencoe, Ill.: Free Press, 1957.

A penetrating study of the social adaptation of middle-class Negroes as they try to cope with the problem of being middle-class by some criteria but excluded from the middle of the social structure on racial grounds.

Erving Goffman, *The Presentation of Self in Everyday Life.* Garden City, N. Y.: Doubleday, 1959, a Doubleday Anchor Book.

An analytical essay on interaction laden with hypotheses pertinent to the understanding of minority role behavior.

Scott A. Greer, *Last Man In: Racial Access to Union Power.* Glencoe, Ill.: Free Press, 1959.

A report of research on labor union power structure and its functions for potential leadership from minority representatives.

IX Social Processes in Minority-Dominant Relations

Assimilation is the partial or total absorption of a minority person or group into the dominant group. Assimilation, then, is usually a one-way proposition, with very little reciprocity or exchange of values, traditions, or customs. The minority group discards its peculiar and foreign ways as the price of complete merger with and disappearance into the dominant social structure.

Acculturation is a related but somewhat different social process. There is an exchange of cultural artifacts, of food, words, music and, perhaps, of ideas, values, and customs relating to ceremonies. There are occasions when assimilation and acculturation go hand-in-hand. An example would be the Italian immigrant in the United States. Pizza, spaghetti, and other Italian dishes are now such a common part of the American cuisine that they can be found in supermarkets (often in frozen-food compartments). Yet the Italian-American has also assimilated. He is invisibly American, and retains few distinctive features which make him stand out in the society.

But assimilation and acculturation have no necessary association. It is not just that societies and subcultures and minority groups acculturate and assimilate; individuals do, too. The individual who acculturates without assimilating is a prime candidate for the status of "marginal man."

Marginality

A marginal man is on the periphery of two different cultures, but neither integrated into nor accepted by either one. The second-generation immigrant is often a marginal person. On the one hand, he wants to assimilate completely into the culture of the country in which he was born. Yet he retains many of the distinguishing marks of the old country be-

287

cause he was reared by first-generation immigrants who came to the new country after they were adults. In the neighborhood in which he was born, he is often an outcast, because the inhabitants see him as drifting away from the customs and traditions which they cherish. Yet at school or work he may be considered odd because of his foreign ways. Thus he knows a great deal about both cultures, but is not sufficiently *en rapport* to be totally acceptable to either.

Marginality clearly has its negative effect. There are problems of adjustment and readjustment which are rather obvious. However, not quite so easy to see are the positive effects of marginal status in society. Individuals who are greatly involved in their own culture, who are completely immersed and integrated into a well-defined structure of action, are often incapable of seeing basic problems which they live with every day. The marginal man, sitting on the fence, so to speak, apart from these activities, can often conceptualize such problems in new ways which may bring about fruitful changes. Some of the most insightful ideas expressed about the American culture have come from men marginal to it, not totally a part of it.

Socialization into Minority Roles

Minority group status is something which must be learned, and members of the dominant part of society co-operate in teaching it to the young offspring of minority group members. For the protection of their young, the parents themselves have to teach the proper roles for minority group members. They may teach any one of a combination of those discussed in the previous chapter.

To demonstrate at how early an age this socialization into minority status takes place, we may look at the findings from a study on the attitudes of race preference among white and Negro children aged four to seven. The researchers gave two sets of dolls to Negro children and two sets to white children. The first set of dolls was white, the second brown. They found that both the Negro and the white children showed a marked preference for the white dolls at the age of four.

Invasion and Succession

The concepts of "invasion" and "succession" are borrowed from plant ecology. A certain kind of plant life may occupy an area and dominate it, but this dominance may be threatened by the appearance ("invasion") of a new kind of plant life. If this new form of plant life is stronger and more dominant, it spreads and spreads, until finally it "succeeds" the former type of plant life, and takes over the area. Sociologists of urban life see certain parallels between this phenomenon and the residential mobility patterns in large cities.

One area of the city may be dominated by a certain ethnic group. Slowly, a new immigrant group "invades." The native group starts to move out of the area, and the vacancies fill up with more and more of the immigrant group. Finally, "succession" is achieved by the immigrant group. Often this pattern of invasion and succession is repeated by each new wave of immigrants from a new ethnic group.

The American Negro is almost universally placed into the role of invader and successor. He is almost never invaded and replaced by a new ethnic group.

The mere existence of the notion of "invasion" implies the homogeneous segregation of little ethnic and racial enclaves in various parts of a city. If the area is at all integrated and heterogeneous in ethnic composition, it makes no sense to speak of an invasion.

Segregation

Segregation can be either voluntary or externally enforced. It is usually some combination of the two. Even with the most aggressively assimilation-minded minorities, there is usually a "consciousness-of-kind" which is the product of their enforced segregation over a long period. They are often reluctant to cut all ties with the past. On the other hand, the most self-satisfied minorities, although deriving a large measure of gratification from their uniqueness, are continually confronted with the consequences of segregation.

Segregation of minority groups into tight residential communities serves as one of the most poignant reminders of the American dilemma. The Supreme Court decision of May, 1954, articulated the position that segregation which is enforced is inherently an unequal system.

The segregation of the minority group has definite advantages for the dominant population. By being concentrated into a single area, the minority is more vulnerable to quick and complete exploitation. Jewish villages were continually raided in the Middle Ages. Christians would ride into a Jewish community, rape, murder, and take off the most important Jew in the community for an exorbitant ransom.

The exploitation of the American Negro through tight residential segregation is more subtle and insidious. The white community and the real estate operators collectively force Negroes to remain in all-Negro communities. In Northern cities it is exceedingly difficult, if not impossible, for Negroes to purchase a home or to rent an apartment outside the boundaries of the all-Negro community. But since the rate of reproduction among Negroes is more than is required merely to replace the adult population, there is continual growth. Over time, the segregated area begins to bulge, and to spill over at the edges into the surrounding white communities. This is met with tremendous resistance, and succession is only accomplished after a considerable time.

Related Readings

Everett C. Hughes, in "Social Change and Status Protest: An Essay on the Marginal Man," says that it is in the nature of American society, with its mixtures of races, religions, and cultures and its emphasis on social mobility, to produce an extraordinary number of people who are marginal in some degree.

Several social processes in dominant-minority relations can be seen in "They Are Ready—If We Are," by Margaret Anderson. Some of the consequences of segregation are some of the problems of desegregation. The Negro child thrust into the newly desegregated school is cast suddenly into a marginal status, for much of the socialization he received to prepare him for a minority role is now irrelevant, or worse yet, hampers him. As Miss Anderson says, another generation will make an enormous difference in this situation because the present group of marginal children will be better equipped to prepare their own children for a new and different system of status.

—————————— Everett C. Hughes

Social Change and Status Protest.
An Essay on the Marginal Man

The phrase "marginal man" and the phenomenon it designates came formally into the study of society with the publication of Robert E. Park's essay, "Human Migration and the Marginal Man" in 1928. I call it an essay, for it has depth, breadth and richness of hypotheses, neither required nor expected in an ordinary scientific paper. Park planted seed enough to keep a generation of scientific cultivators busy.

While the phrase came with this publication, the essential idea is much older. Park refers to many others who had sensed the problem; notably Simmel, in his passages on the "stranger" in his *Soziologie* and Gilbert Murray, in his *Rise of the Greek Epic*. He takes Heinrich Heine as a living example of the thing about which he is talking. What Park did was to put the "marginal man" into a broader setting; to see him as a function of the break-up and mixing of cultures attendant upon migration and the great cultural revolutions. He turned a literary and poetic insight into a cluster of related scientific hypotheses. In doing so, he brought it down from the glamour of antiquity and the grandly historical

From *Phylon*, X, First Quarter, 1949, pp. 58-65.

to the level of the most modest European immigrant as well as the oft despised mulatto, and indeed even to all men in his remark that there are "periods of transition and crisis in the lives of most of us that are comparable with those which the immigrant experiences when he leaves home to seek his fortunes in a strange country."

The first part of Park's paper sketches broadly the relation of migration to cultures and social organization, leading up to its part in the break-up of the smaller traditional societies of which anthropologists have become the most expert students. The latter part focuses attention on the subjective aspects of migration and its effect upon human persons.

The first such effect he notes is "emancipation," the freeing of a man from customary expectations by travel and migration. Sometimes, we gather, the emancipated man is eager for new things; he explores and invents. In other cases, he may be painfully homesick for that which he left behind. Perhaps this homesickness is greatest when, as in the case of the Greek, that warm and sacred world for which he yearns no longer exists.

From the completely emancipated man, Park moves on to the "cultural hybrid";

> . . . a man living and sharing intimately in the cultural life and traditions of two distinct peoples; never quite willing to break, even if he were permitted to do so, with his past and his traditions, and not quite accepted, because of racial prejudice, in the new society in which he now sought to find a place.

The prototype of the "cultural hybrid" he found in the Jew emerging from the Ghetto. However, the person of mixed blood—to use the most misleading phrase of common talk about the races—is perhaps the most permanently and fatally condemned of all to the condition of marginality. And that fact, in so far as it is one, points to the true nature of the marginal position; for while the racial hybrid is ordinarily also a cultural hybrid, by virtue of the fact that both cultures and races develop their distinguishing marks in relative isolation, we have plenty of evidence in America that the racial hybrid need not be a cultural hybrid at all. The American Negro—whether of mixed blood or not—is not conspicuously a cultural hybrid. But he is a man with a status dilemma. And the more he, as an individual, acquires of those elements of American culture which bring to others the higher rewards of success, the greater is his dilemma.

In addition, the American Negro is a living contradiction of the canons of status in the American culture. The contradiction lies in the fact that a member of a group assigned a very humble and limited status bears other characteristics which ordinarily give or allow the individual to acquire higher status. The contradiction is objective, in that it appears to the eyes of others. The dilemma lies in the fact that he cannot accept the status to which Negroes are ordinarily assigned, but neither can he completely free himself from it. The dilemma, on the other hand, is essentially subjective. The Negro who passes as white no longer presents any contradiction to the eyes of others, but he still has the inner dilemma.

It is from the angle of status that I propose to analyze the phenomenon of marginality. Status is a term of society in that it refers specifically to a system of relations between people. But the definition of the status lies in a culture. In fact, one of the essential features of a person's status may be his identification with a culture.

Imagine a society in which the statuses are very well established. The rights and duties pertaining to each are well understood and generally beyond doubt and discussion. The ways by which an individual is assigned to and enters a given status are likewise well defined: by descent, sex, social learning and accomplishments of various kinds, arriving at a certain age, or by certain rites of passage, such as initiation and marriage. In such a case, one would expect—and the evidence on such societies seems to warrant it—that persons of a given status would exhibit a whole complex of social attributes, all of which seem naturally to pertain to that status. These attributes would be unconsciously woven into a seamless garment. Finally, everyone would know exactly who he is. His status identification would be clear and unquestioned by himself or others.

Imagine now the opposite—a society which is a complete free-for-all. Talents, both the virtuous and the nefarious, have full play. Everybody gets exactly what he has coming to him by virtue of his own efforts. It is a society without a hang-over from its past. If an enterprising lad of twenty were fittest to be head surgeon of a great hospital, he would be it. Make it more drastic; if a Jewish Negro girl of twenty, born in Russia and converted to the Witnesses of Jehovah were fittest to be head surgeon of Massachusetts General Hospital, she would be it. In such a society one could, in effect, say that status did not exist. Competition, of some purer sort than any we know, would determine without time-lag what each person would do and be. No such society ever existed. The ones we know are somewhere between this and the other people. Relatively, our society is nearer the free-for-all than have been most others we know of.

Free as is competition in our society, and strong as is the strain toward allowing talent and accomplishment free rein, there are many positions about which there is a halo of technically irrelevant, but socially expected characteristics. Thus the physician is still rather expected by most people to be a man. He is expected, further, to be of a certain age, and, often, to have certain ethnic and class characteristics. But in our mobile and changing society new kinds of persons continually acquire the technically and formally demanded skills or qualities of a profession, or other position. Whenever it happens, sociological news is made and a new and unexpected combination of social characteristics appears; thus, the woman senator, the Negro judge, a boy president of a university, a professor in the White House, Cinderella in the Rockefeller mansion. For certain positions there is a long period of training for inculcating the auxiliary characteristics of a status as well as the technical skills. Thus, a medical course is a long *rite de passage*. So is the seminary of the priesthood and the novitiate of a religious order. Essentially, the function of the novitiate is to guarantee that there shall be no *marginal* priests or monks. The marks of the world are to be washed off, so that the new-born priest shall be fully a priest, acting as such and judged as such by all other priests and by all the faithful.

Now it is not merely that the new people who come into positions lack certain expected characteristics, but that they positively belong to groups which themselves have a status definition which includes a combination of expected characteristics (such combinations are called stereotypes). The woman has certain traditional expected characteristics; she plays certain traditional roles. People are accustomed to act toward women in certain ways. Likewise, the Negro has a traditional role. The traditional roles of neither woman nor Negro include that of the physician. Hence, when either of them becomes a physician the question arises whether to treat her or him as physician or as woman or Negro. Likewise, on their part, there is the problem whether, in a given troublesome situation, to act completely as physician or in the other role. This is their dilemma. It arises from the fact that the culture has not yet provided a series of accepted definitions of behavior for the various situations which arise from the existence of this new kind of person. So long as the dilemma is present in the mind of the person, and so long as the existence of such a person appears a contradiction to others, just so long are the persons concerned in a marginal position.

Their marginality might presumably be reduced in several ways.

1. All such persons could give up the struggle, by retiring completely into the status with which they are most stubbornly identified by society. This people sometimes do. There are records of turning back to one's own people, culture or status which read like those of religious conversions, with conviction of sin, seeking and finding the light, doing penance and retiring into an exclusive world as into a cloistered religious order. Sometimes, however, such people become leaders of a cultural revival, which may be either religious or militant in temper.

People of the statuses threatened by marginal people generally favor this first solution—that of putting them back into their traditional places. Measures of repression and of exclusion are used to this end.

2. One of the statuses could disappear *as a status*. The word "woman" could cease to have social meaning, and become merely a biological designation without any status or role connotations. A few women have set this as the goal of the feminist movement. The word Negro would disappear—as it has tended to do in certain times and countries—in favor of a series of terms which would describe complexion and feature.

These terms, in a continuum from black to white or white to black, would be of use mainly to people who are careful about the color of their dresses and neckties and to the police, whose vocabulary for identifying complexions of wanted persons has always been meagre. In short, there would be no Negro group to which to belong.

3. Persons of marginal position might individually resign from the status which interferes with their other status aims. A woman who became a physician would simply not be a woman any more, although other people might remain identified with the status of women. A Negro would declare himself no longer a Negro. Such resignation is both subjectively and objectively difficult. The interplay of these two aspects of the difficulty constitutes a fascinating and sometimes tragic theme of human drama. The temptation to resign, and even to repudiate, is put heavily upon marginal people, as many a Negro can testify. If a Negro worker is somewhat accepted by white fellow workers in industry, they generally seem inwardly compelled to extract from him an admission that he is an exception among Negroes. If he is like them in the rest, why should he not be like them in their stereotypes also. It is a kind of betrayal to which we are all subject in some degree. When we yield, the cock crows thrice.

4. One or both of the statuses might, without disappearing, be so broadened and redefined as to reduce both the inner dilemma and the outward contradiction.

5. Another possible solution is elaboration of the social system to include a marginal group as an additional category of persons with their own identity and defined position. A number of people of similar marginal position may seek one another's company, and collectively strive to get a place for themselves. The Cape Coloured of South Africa, and the Eurasians of India are groups of this kind. In this country, the colored creoles of Louisiana, certain rural communities of light-colored people in both South and North, and the free Negroes in certain Southern communities in slavery times all attempted with some success to establish themselves as recognized groups, neither Negro nor white. During their time of success, they were exclusive of other persons who sought admittance to their ranks as every new member was a potential threat to their special status. They became, in fact, groups of kin-connected families; hence, something closer to Indian castes than anything else in America has been. But the strain toward keeping the American race system a simple dichotomy has worked against them. In recent times, when nearly everyone must have "papers" for relief, the draft, school, and the like, only the most "backwoodsy" of such groups can escape the fatal dichotomy.

The marginal groups just mentioned consist each of people who are marginal in the same way, and who consciously seek to fortify a common marginal position. Sometimes it happens that marginal people establish and live their lives in a marginal group, hardly knowing that they are doing so. There are whole segments of marginal society, with their marginal cultures among various ethnic and religious groups in this country, some of whom even developed a distinguishing speech. Large numbers of unmarried career women in American cities live in essential isolation from other women and with only formal contacts with men. In addition, there are other marginal groups who are not quite aware of their marginality, by virtue of living together a somewhat insulated life, but who are, furthermore, made up of people of the most diverse backgrounds; people who have in common, to start with, nothing but their marginality. These are to be found in cities and especially among young people. They are the American Bohemians.

All of these solutions appear as themes in the process of social and cultural adjustment and conflict. One can see in social movements— cultural, national, racial, feminist, class—all of these tendencies. The woman's movement has had its advocates of complete eradication of sex as a status determinant, its women who individually resigned from their sex and encouraged others to do so and those who have quietly or fervently gone back to and idealized the old roles. The main trend has been toward redefinition and broadening of the roles consonant wtih the status of women, and toward seeking also the integration of women into formerly exclusively male roles. One or another solution may be tried and given up. The internal politics of a social movement turns about choice of these solutions. If you will look inside any movement concerned with the status of a group of people and of their culture, you will find these conflicting tendencies. Shall it be a Negro Renaissance with return to Africa, individual passing, a fight for disappearance of Negro as a status identification, or some broadening and easing of the definition of the Negro status. I need not remind you of the many contingencies in such choices. In reality, a given solution is seldom adopted and stuck to to the exclusion of all others. There is a sort of dialectic of them as the pursuit of one changes the situation so as to bring another to the fore.

Up to this point, I have kept women and Negroes before you as illustrations of people with a status dilemma. American Negroes, product of migration and of the mixing of races and cultures that they are, are the kind of case to which the term marginal man has been conventionally applied. I have used the case of women to show that the phenomenon is not, in essence, one of racial and cultural mixing. It is one that may occur wherever there is sufficient social change going on to allow the emergence of people who are in a position of confusion of social identity, with its attendant conflicts of loyalty and frustration of personal and group aspirations. Migration and resulting cultural contact simply create the grand fields on which the battle of status is fought out among humans; a confusing and bloodier battle because its essence is that so many people are in doubt about which side they want to be on or may be allowed to be on.

In our own society the contact of cultures, races and religions, combines with social mobility, to produce an extraordinary number of people who are marginal in some degree, who have some conflict of identity in their own minds, who find some parts of the social world which they would like to enter closed to them, or open only at the expense of some treason to things and people they hold dear. American fiction has been full of such people, as it must be if it is to tell the story of America. Even English fiction of the nineteenth century abounds in such characters. Anthony Trollope's heroes and heroines are generally people who have more breeding than money, or more money than breeding. There are young men who can go into politics and stay in high society if they remain single or marry pots of money; but can be true to a half-promise to some poorer, dearer girl only by giving it all up and going to work for a living. Trollope's own story, told in his autobiography, is that of a boy who went to Harrow school so shabby and penniless that he was the butt of cruel jokes from masters and fellow pupils for the twelve years he was there.

In Trollope's England, marginal social position was almost entirely a matter of class mobility. There was little of ethnic difference in it. In America, marginality is thought of as resulting solely from the mixtures of cultures, races and religions. There may be more of the problem of class mobility in it, however, than Americans have been accustomed to admit.

In mentioning what you may think the trivial case of Trollope's young man who must choose between his career (class position) and his sweetheart, I incidentally introduced a crucial problem of marginality to which there is little allusion in the formal discussion of the subject, that of life or career contingencies in relation to status marginality.

I suppose a person is furthest from a marginal position if he is so placed that he can go clear through his life without status dilemma. Each of us lives part of his life in retrospect, part in the fleeting present, part in prospect. We see ourselves in a running perspective of the human life cycle. Each phase of our lives offers its own status definitions, rewards and punishments; each phase also has meaning as the preparation for the next. In Jules Romains' *Men of Good Will* there is a conscientious little boy who promises himself the indulgence of leisure after completion of self-appointed tasks of study repeated so and so many times. The tasks get greater and greater and the indulgence gets put off further and further as he grows up. In the end he becomes very like a case reported by the psychoanalyst, Abraham; that of an artist who promises himself a vacation as soon as he shall have produced a really worthy painting. He ends up, a sleepless wreck, in the hands of a psychiatrist. This is, in varying measure, the theme of life of all people who set high goals for themselves. It is the theme of balancing present and future.

Looking at this same problem from the standpoint of social organization, there are phases of life in which society is more open and more tolerant of diversity than others. Student life is traditionally such a phase.

People of various races, ethnic groups, class backgrounds, and of the two sexes mix in an adventuresome spirit of Bohemianism. The essence of Bohemianism is disregard of convention. Convention, in its turn, is in large part a set of definitions of status, hence of proper behavior. Student Bohemianism is a conventional relaxation of convention.

Now university life is two things, a *rite de passage* and a preparation for careers. In England, the two things are crystallized in two kinds of degrees. The Pass Degree is a *rite de passage* for sons of aristocrats and plutocrats; the Honors Degree, which requires work, is for people who have to make their way in the world, as most American students must do. But university life is here also a *rite of passage*, not merely from the status of adolescent to that of adult, but from one way of life to another and in many cases, from one culture or sub-culture to another.

The freedom of student life has always been tolerated by older adults on the assumption that it would, for each given individual, soon come to an end. We must then ask, both as social scientists and as persons with a life to lead, what are the hazards of passing from so free a phase of life into those which follow: of the transition from school to work, from irresponsible singleness to more or less responsible marriage, from young childless marriage to parenthood. Each of these has its hazards. Each of them generally brings one face to face with a stiffer set of status definitions, with greater mutual exclusiveness of social roles and consequently, with the greater possibility of status dilemma. This aspect of the problem of marginality has been very little studied. It is one of the crucial areas of study if we are really to advance our knowledge of modern society.

Before stopping, let us ask, with regard to social mobility and social change, the same question as we did earlier concerning the relation of migration to marginality. Are mobility and change necessary conditions of marginality, or are they, too, merely the favoring gale? Might there not be, in the most settled society, persons who are in protest against the roles assigned them; persons, even, who want to play some role for which there is no precedent or defined place in their culture? Need one have a woman's movement in order to have the individual woman who feels the masculine protest? Are all the inglorious village Miltons of unpoetic cultures so mute as those in Gray's Churchyard? I have often thought that the French-Canadian culture is so stable, not because of its isolation, but because there has been a whole continent for its free-thinkers and other rebels to escape into. I do not think we know the answer to these questions. But we have some clues. They suggest that the human individual does not always passively accept society's answer to the question, "Who am I?" with all its implications of present and future conduct. I suppose we might distinguish between that kind of protest which is merely a squirming within the harness, and that which is a questioning of the very terms and dimensions of the prevailing status definitions. At any rate, there is still much work to be done on the genesis of status protest; or, to put it the other way, on the processes by which the human biological individual is integrated—always in the presence and by the agency of other humans—into a status system.

───────Margaret Anderson

They Are Ready—if We Are

In this century, the chronicles of the Negro children in desegregated schools can bring stature or disgrace to the South, for this generation of Negro children is now in the process of becoming what it will be tomorrow. Its leaders, whether we approve or recognize them, are in today's classrooms.

As they enter our halls in increasing numbers, their potentialities will be suppressed or developed; so, too, their sense of values, attitudes and ideals. There is too much to be done, and too little time, to bewail all that has gone before.

Those who have the professional responsibility of helping to train young minds, and who feel a moral responsibility to respect the individuality of every child, find themselves asking: How can we begin to work with Negro children except by trying to develop an understanding of their problems, their hopes and aspirations, their expectations for the future?

And what better way is there to start than to ask the children themselves? Here, one finds himself wondering: Is there really so much difference between Negro children and white children that they must be studied differently?

We know they laugh uproariously. They push and shove, and play ball on the common. They wish on the stars. They feel sorry for children in other parts of the world; as, I know, the children in Uganda and Poland have felt sorry for them. They, too, delight in tinseled angels on Christmas trees. And they cry when hurt.

They have the same problems of growing up physically; of getting along with their parents, with other boys and girls; of succeeding in school, and fitting into an adult world; of understanding themselves.

Then how are they different?

The Negro child is different because he has problems which are the product of a social order not of his making. This social order is so impressed upon him that it is reflected in his way of life, and even in his speech and dress. It is now difficult to determine what is due to his innate capacities, and what is the result of environmental influences and opportunities.

New York Times Magazine, December 24, 1961, pp. 5, 27-28.

The Negro child therefore comes to us as an overburdened child. He comes overburdened in a hundred ways which make him old beyond his years. The road for him is three times as hard as for the average white child. At every turn there is an obstacle.

It might appear that the freedom he has gained to enter the white school would solve his problems automatically. On the contrary, this privilege creates additional problems he must face.

Listen to the children:

"We wondered if the teachers would like us," they said. "We wondered if the boys and girls would like us.***"

"Up there [meaning in the segregated elementary school], I understood what the teacher was saying. Down here, I just don't know what she's talking about.***"

"Up there, we sang. Down here, no one ever asked us. We'd like to show the other boys and girls what we can do."

"Well, I wondered if I would look to suit them, and what I should wear, and if I would have enough money, and whether I would pass. I know I don't have a chance unless I can get through high school."

In these spontaneous statements, the Negro child is telling us:

First, that he, too, desires acceptance. He has worried about being accepted in the white school by the students and by those in authority. He has entered frightened and insecure. His concern is for his physical safety, and for the knowledge that he will be treated kindly. Thrust into the new situation, he learns early to detect those who have empathy for his plight.

Secondly, he has become aware that his academic background is somehow different from that of the majority of white students, although many of them have come from very rural sections.

We know that, in the change-over from elementary school to high school, pupils have many adjustments to make. For the Negro child the shift is doubly hard if the transfer to the white school is made at the same time.

It appears also that there may be a wider difference in the training received by the Negro children and the white children in segregated elementary schools of the South than we would like to admit, in spite of the fact that they use the same textbooks, that many Southern communities are pouring more money into Negro elementary schools than into the white schools, and that their teachers hold degrees. "This," says a Negro teacher, "may be due to the difference between the Negro and white teacher-training institutions."

Be that as it may, the Negro child finds himself in the position of not only having to adjust to a different social environment but often to different academic standards. As a result, many have truancy problems, and the drop-out rate the first year is high. Some, in this period, choose to return to the segregated schools. Others overwork themselves to keep their grades up to standard.

Thirdly, the Negro child is telling us that he, too, wants recognition. He feels that he has something to offer. Perhaps it is a song, but this song to him may be more meaningful, for the time being, than a recitation from Shakespeare. And this song, which he wants to bring to others, for all we know may be nearer the true heart of music than could be offered by the most tutored of the tutored.

Lastly, he has become aware of his social and economic status, and he is concerned about his future.

"My parents never went to school. They want me to go."

"If I can just get through, I think the others in my family will come."

"I know you can't do anything unless you go to school."

He doesn't tell you that there is no one in his overcrowded two- or three-room home who can help him; that there are five or ten children and he has no private place to study; that there is not a reference book or even a daily newspaper, although there may be a television set in the house and a secondhand Cadillac in the yard.

"There's not much incentive for most of them," says a young Negro girl. "Their parents want to help, and they say they will, but so many just don't know how. How many Negro parents do you know who hold jobs that require higher training?"

"Family values are different," says a Negro teacher. "We've got to make them understand that notebook paper and books are more important than they think. It would be so easy if we could get this message home."

If the Negro child can finish the first year of high school, his chances of going on are increased. In this year he has proved himself worthy of the respect of his teachers and classmates. He begins to develop a feeling of belonging. A whole new world is opened to him.

We begin to observe that in an atmosphere free of tension he can learn and adjust to the new school; that he is adept at physical activities; that he is frequently good in study of languages; that he shows a keen interest in various forms of the arts.

Ordinarily, the Negro child is a happy child; and it takes so little to make him happy. He forgives easily. He generates enthusiasm. He endures. His verbal expression, which is often much deeper than his written expression, amazes observant teachers.

Some are truly gifted—just how gifted no one really knows. And, of course, there are those who learn very little, as is the case with some white children.

Meanwhile, the Negro child is absorbing a new way of life—a culture that emphasizes school attendance, obedience to law, faith in a parliament of nations, the acceptance of responsibilities that accompany freedom, a culture that values initiative, achievement, cleanliness.

"If we can just get this decade's Negro children through high school," the young Negro teacher goes on, "we are on our way. They will go on and do something. The ideals that are instilled now will be a part of their families'. In other words, we must grow up rather than be born."

But in this process of "growing up" the Negro student must still face two more obstacles, as if he must be tried not once but three times.

The Negro student who finishes high school and desires higher training now has the problem of getting into a college and, again, "getting through." Although he may have come twice as far academically as the average white student, considering where he was at the time he entered high school, he must again be compared and compete with the strongest students.

Then he must find a college which will accept him. This is no easy job in the South. And, in most instances, he must work his way, for few Negro parents can afford the expense of college.

Assuming he does well and finishes college, he is now faced with the third obstacle. He has the problem of getting a job which is equal to his training. Here the whole social and economic structure comes to bear against him.

But today's Negro high-school students have not yet learned firsthand of these later obstacles. Listen again to the children:

"I'm going to be a mechanic," says a burly one. "I've always liked to work with cars."

"I'll be a seamstress," says the wiry, quick one. "Already, I've won a prize for the best-made dress. Someday, I may just have a shop of my own."

"I'd like to be a beautician, and make people pretty."

"I'd like to be a teacher. Do you have to have algebra to be a teacher?"

"And I shall be a secretary and meet people . . ."

One, the serious one, who finds school easy, waits for the others to speak. "I haven't decided what I shall do. It is very important to me that I help other people," she says restlessly.

Oh, that we could wave a magic wand and make their dreams come true! These children ask so little compared to what this well-endowed nation has to offer its youth.

The Negro children with whom I have worked show an unusually high interest in people and groups. They express desires to engage in such occupations as teaching, business, social work, nursing—the service occupations.

In many ways, they show evidence of planning their careers more realistically, in view of their circumstances, than many white children. Whereas the average white child frequently is unable to conceive of not having the ability or the opportunity to do anything he desires, the Negro child learns to recognize his limitations and his opportunities the hard way.

The more talented and capable Negro students frequently seem in a hurry to get through school, as if they had some mission to perform. They have a hungry attitude toward learning. High school to them does not mean parties and proms and the happy frivolities of adolescence. It means "getting through" and "getting on." Some express it another way: "going into the service" or "going North."

This, to my mind, always seems sad. For the South is their home. Their forebears have served us well. It seems a pity that now their children should feel compelled to "move on" before we have helped them to develop the best they have.

This, of course, will take time. "Perhaps another generation," says a wise counselor.

Meanwhile, many of today's children, no doubt, will revert to the subservience of their parents. But each day more and more Negro students are breaking through the racial barriers, and in commendable ways.

Let me tell you the story of Donna.

Donna is an attractive Negro girl who stands tall among her classmates. She has completed four years of high school in three years.

One day, in the early fall, a group of nurses came to the school to explain to interested students the nurses' training program offered at their hospital. They were dressed in immaculate white uniforms and flowing navy capes.

The girls gathered and listened eagerly while the women in white described their profession. They emphasized the necessity of devotion to ideals and Christian principles, and a willingness to give a lifetime to others.

"It is hard," they said. "If you are not prepared to study and devote your life to others, you need not apply."

My girls listened attentively, including Donna. Ever since she was a young child she had said she wanted to be a nurse. Now she knew that there was more to becoming one than merely wishing. Occasionally, she glanced toward me.

When the nurses had finished, the students rushed forward to ask questions. All but Donna. She did not approach the visitors, but turned toward me.

"Will they take *me*?" She asked in a low voice.

"Donna," I said, "the good sister has sent word that although they have never had a Negro apply at their school, they have known for a long time that the day would come. They are prepared to accept your application. You must take the same test as the other girls, and the same score will be required of you."

A relieved expression came over her face. Then, suddenly, it seemed as if she would explode with happiness.

"Will you tell my mother?" she asked. "Will you tell my mother?"—as if a miracle had happened and her mother wouldn't believe it unless a teacher told her. That night I thanked God that I would be able to deliver this message of opportunity.

And in those moments there came to mind another day when I had looked into the tear-filled eyes of a 16-year-old Negro girl who had been subjected to the old accusation that Negroes have only "half a soul." I asked, "Do you think what you have gone through is really worth it?" She replied, "The only thing I know is that maybe it will be easier for someone else."

This was five years ago. I had lived to see the day when it *was* easier for someone else. Victoria had known all along that this was the way it would be.

Now, my Donna may fail her test—as, no doubt, many of the white girls may fail it. I do not know. The chemistry formulas do not come easily. She has worked late hours trying to master them.

But this much I do know: she has a good mind, and a gentle way, a kind heart. Surely the world has need of her talents.

The important thing is that Donna will now have the opportunity—even the opportunity to fail. This is tremendously important to today's Negro children. They do not mind failing as much as being denied the opportunity.

As Victoria knew, she must endure that others might have a chance, Donna knows that she must do her best to succeed. "And, oh, they try so very, very hard," says a compassionate teacher.

You see, the Donnas and the Victorias will be able to help *their* children. That alone will make all the difference.

❋   ❋   ❋

We need to listen to today's Negro children. Their dream, once considered only the white American dream, is now a universal one. The more we listen and help them, the less we will have to reckon with sit-ins, Freedom Riders, and frightful demonstrations tomorrow.

If we open our hearts to their problems and aspirations, perhaps together we can develop a new approach to living—a truly Christian approach which will bring stature to the South.

These, too, are our children. I have looked into their eyes, and I have felt their tears, and heard them speak. I do truly believe that, granted the opportunity, they are ready to help us refashion a very suspicious and untidy world. Hope is written all over their faces.

Supplementary Bibliography

Stuart Chase, *Roads to Agreement: Successful Methods in the Science of Human Relations.* N.Y.: Harper, 1951.
    A survey of modes of social organization based upon co-operation and of means of accommodating conflict.

Nathan Glazer and Davis McEntire, *Studies in Housing and Minority Groups;* Eunice and George Grier, *Privately Developed Interracial Housing;* Luigi Laurenti, *Property Values and Races;* Davis McEntire, *Residence and Race;* and Chester Rapkin and William G. Grigsby, *The Demand for Housing in Racially Mixed Areas.* Berkeley and Los Angeles: U. of California Press, 1960.

  Five volumes on invasion, succession, and the current status of the American Negro in the housing market.

Leo Kuper, Hilstan Watts, and Ronald Davies, *Durban: A Study in Racial Ecology.* London: Jonathan Cape, 1958.

  A good empirical study of the spatial distribution of races in a South African city.

Raymond W. Mack, "Ecological Patterns in an Industrial Shop." *Social Forces,* 1954, 32:351-356. Reprinted in Kimball Young and Raymond W. Mack, *Principles of Sociology: A Reader in Theory and Research,* 2nd ed. N. Y.: American Book, 1962, pp. 230-237.

  A description of a community in which ethnic segregation is projected from residential space to work space, with consequences for interaction and productivity.

Robert E. Park and H. A. Miller, *Old World Traits Transplanted.* N. Y.: Harper, 1921.

  A fine old discussion of the assimilation and acculturation of European immigrants in the United States.

X Functions of Institutionalized Discrimination

Because in Northern cities Negroes are generally forced to remain within specific residential boundaries, the rent which can be charged where demand outruns supply far exceeds what would otherwise be the "worth" of the property. Landlords in Negro slum areas partition large four-bedroom apartments, install kitchens in every room, and cram four large Negro families into this setting. Obviously, a few individuals can reap large profits from segregation. But this is only one of the consequences of institutionalized, or patterned and accepted, discrimination.

The existence of a group of people believed to be categorically inferior allows the members of the dominant population the luxury of feeling "better than someone else" without even the expenditure of energy. But even more, it provides a justification for keeping the "inferior" group in the dirty jobs in the society.

Color Caste

The word "caste" was originally used to describe the social-cultural-religious system of India. The society was divided into four major groups and thousands of subcastes, with a residual category called the "untouchables." The social element of this classification came from the resultant system of stratification and occupational assignment. One group was trained primarily for the military, another for merchant and trading occupations, another for the priesthood, and so on.

An important element of this classification system was the religious justification for its existence. A man born into the top caste (Brahmin, priesthood) could not move into a military position, and vice versa. In traditional India this was not a system of authoritarian imposition which the people objected to and resented. They regarded it as their religious

305

duty to maintain and uphold the system, and they themselves imposed negative sanctions on deviants.

The religious component of the Indian system has led some observers to the position that the term *caste* must be confined to this one peculiar situation in the world. However, there are certain caste-like features of many other systems of stratification in the world. The very fact that a Negro in the United States can no more change to white than an outcaste can change to Brahmin offers one point of comparison between religious caste in India and color caste in the United States.

Over half the adult male Negroes in the United States are engaged in service or unskilled labor, while only one-sixth of the white population is so employed. Negroes thus occupy a disproportionately large segment of the bottom of the occupational structure. This system is largely reinforced by the expectations of the majority. It is a quite common occurrence in all-white middle-class residential areas of the urban North to see Negro service workers arrive in droves at eight in the morning and leave at five in the afternoon. It is quite acceptable for some of these Negroes to live on the premises, to cook, clean house, and to take charge of the children.

But if a Negro is seen in such a neighborhood with a white shirt, tie, and brief case, apprehension will sweep through the area. The expectations have been violated. "Is there a Negro professional living in the area somewhere?" The Negro is in a service caste for many people, and they are comfortable only so long as Negroes wear overalls and a blue shirt, or an apron or work-dress.

Color Caste and the American Dilemma

There is a scarcity of highly desirable positions in a society. If these positions were open to all in free and open competition, the criteria for selection would have no automatic favoring of one "group" versus another. However, the more people that can be categorically dismissed from competition for these positions, the easier it is for the remaining group to achieve access.

Here is one of the more subtle of the consequences of this kind of competition. Those who do achieve can easily forget that they were not even in competition with the minority. They can believe that they were engaged in such competition, and that their own success indicates the validity of the low status which the minority group holds.

We see this often with middle-class executives from pleasant suburbs. Competent, well-scrubbed, middle-class Negroes who apply for executive positions are told that "this company" is not quite ready to take the step of hiring a Negro executive. "Perhaps in a few years, with time and education, this could occur." Thus the white executives are not in competition with the Negroes, since the latter are categorically excluded. Meanwhile the same white executives, insulated from the experience of having to execute the decisions for racial discrimination, come to believe that they were in free and open competition with Negroes, and believe that the Negroes failed to compete successfully. They thereby achieve the perfect rationalization of the stratification system extant in the society: "The minority group is where it is because it belongs there. It failed to achieve in 'free and open' competition."

In this manner, many Americans have solved (temporarily, at least) the "American dilemma." Instead of having the pang of conscience which Myrdal described, the dominant members come to believe that the minority deserves the place it occupies.

The Invariable Relevance of Race

The category Negro is invariably relevant in America. Suppose that a man from out of town plans to visit some friends in a new suburban community. The host and hostess plan a cocktail party and dinner in his honor, and invite several guests to meet him. They inform these guests that their friend is an M.D., has recently returned from a trip to West Germany, and is an ear specialist. The afternoon of the party and dinner, the guests arrive to meet the friend and are immediately introduced. They feel cheated, tricked, and hurt. The friend is a Negro, and *they were not told beforehand.*

The reason they feel cheated and tricked is that for them, the most important thing is not that this person is a friend, but that he is a Negro friend; not that he is an M.D., but a Negro M.D., not that he has been to Europe recently, but that he is a Negro who has been to Europe recently, and so on. His being a Negro cuts across everything he has done and everything he is. This is what is meant by invariable relevance.

One area where this is becoming less and less true is in major sports. Willie Mays is regarded as a great center fielder and a great hitter. But this is primarily because we have come to know Willie Mays in these terms, and only as an afterthought do we think of him as a great Negro center fielder. Such is not the case with Negro rookies; they are first of all Negro rookies.

Deerfield, Illinois, provides an even better example of the invariable relevance of race and the inability to see an individual behind a social type. Deerfield is a small, all-white, suburban community. Some builders bought property, planned to build houses on it, and to sell those houses to private individuals. Somehow, word leaked out that the builders also planned to sell a small percentage of the houses to Negroes. The plan was attacked by the residents of the community, both Christian and Jewish, as being a sneaky, underhanded plot. Why, they asked, wasn't this made public? Why, they asked, wasn't everyone told that the builders planned to sell to Negroes?

What moral, social, legal, and ethical obligation does a private member of a free-enterprise capitalistic society have to announce publicly his intentions to sell his property to a Negro? The residents of Deerfield (and they are not alone) seemed to feel that there is a considerable responsibility.

Most American citizens are free to consider the buying and selling of their property an essentially private matter. But for the Negro, things are different. Being a Negro is a public matter, of intense public concern, because race in American society is of invariable relevance.

Related Readings

Gerald D. Berreman documents a number of similarities between caste in India and the United States. In line with what we said in Chapter I concerning the value of discovering patterns in human relationships, Berreman contends that the customary emphasis on differences in the cultural content of various caste systems is less useful for an understanding of human behavior than a focus on the similarities in social structures and processes.

In "Caste, Economy, and Violence," Allison Davis shows how, in the American South, caste organizes the various institutional aspects of dominant-minority relations into a single integrated social system. Thus the appearance of intergroup conflict is evidence that the caste-like system is weakening enough for competition to arise between the races.

An example of such institutional integration as Davis discusses can be seen in Liston Pope's "Religion and the Class Structure." The class composition of religious denominations reinforces the societal stratification structure. The "American dilemma" is less a dilemma to the extent that Americans perceive no value conflict in worshiping at the altar of the brotherhood of man in segregated churches.

——————— Gerald D. Berreman

Caste in India and the United States [1]

. . . .

Many writers who have contributed to the vast literature on the caste system in India have emphasized its unique aspects and ignored or denied the qualities it shares with rigid systems of social stratification found in other societies. Others have claimed to find caste systems or caste groups in such widely scattered areas as Arabia, Polynesia, Africa, Guatemala, and Japan.[2] Some observers refer to Negro-white relations in the United States, and particularly in the South, as being those of caste,[3] a usage which others, including C. S. Johnson, Oliver C. Cox, and, more recently, G. E. Simpson and J. M. Yinger, have criticized. This paper will compare the relationship between "touchable," especially twice-born, and "untouchable" castes in India with that between Negroes and whites in the southern United States.

Caste can be defined so that it is applicable only to India, just as it is possible to define narrowly almost any sociocultural phenomenon. Indianists have traditionally held to specific, usually enumerative, definitions. Indeed, the caste system in India has several unique features, among which are its religious aspects, its complexity, and the degree to which the caste is a cohesive group that regulates the behavior of its members. Within India there is considerable variation in the characteristic of, and the relations among, the groups to which the term "caste" is applied.

However, caste can be accurately defined in broader terms. For many purposes similar social facts may be usefully categorized together, despite differences which, while not denied, are not crucial to the purposes at hand. For purposes of cross-cultural comparison this is necessary: for the study of social process, and with the aim of deriving generalizations, caste is a concept which might well be applied cross-culturally. For these

[1] Delivered in abbreviated form before the Fifty-eighth Annual Meeting of the American Anthropological Association in Mexico City, December, 1959, and based partly on research carried out in India under a Ford Foundation Foreign Area Training Fellowship during fifteen months of 1957-58 (reported in full in my "Kin, Caste, and Community in a Himalayan Hill Village" [unpublished Ph.D. dissertation, Cornell University, 1959]). I am indebted to Joel V. Berreman and Lloyd A. Fallers for their helpful comments.
[2] E. D. Chapple and C. S. Coon, *Principles of Anthropology* (New York: Henry Holt & Co., 1942), p. 437; S. F. Nadel, "Caste and Government in Primitive Society," *Journal of the Anthropological Society of Bombay*, New Series VIII (September, 1954), 9-22; M. M. Tumin, *Caste in a Peasant Society* (Princeton, N.J.: Princeton University Press, 1952); J. D. Donoghue, "An Eta Community in Japan: The Social Persistence of Outcaste Groups," *American Anthropologist*, LIX (December, 1957), 1000-1017.
[3] E.g., Allison Davis, Kingsley Davis, John Dollard, Buell Gallagher, Gunnar Myrdal, Kenneth Stampp, Lloyd Warner.

purposes a caste system may be defined as a *hierarchy of endogamous divisions in which membership is hereditary and permanent.* Here hierarchy includes inequality both in status and in access to goods and services. Interdependence of the subdivisions, restricted contacts among them, occupational specialization, and/or a degree of cultural distinctiveness might be added as criteria, although they appear to be correlates rather than defining characteristics.

This definition is perhaps best viewed as describing an ideal type at one end of a continuum along which systems of social stratification might be ranged. There can be little doubt that the systems in India and the southern United States would fall far toward the caste extreme of the continuum.[4] It now becomes necessary to look at the differences cited as crucial by those who object to use of the term "caste" in both societies. The objections raised by those interested in structure, relationships, and interaction will be discussed here; the objections of those interested in specific content will be ignored—not because the latter objections are less cogent, but because they are less relevant to the comparison of social systems.[5]

Johnson sees many similarities in the two systems but objects to identifying both as caste, since "a caste system is not only a separated system, it is a stable system in which changes are socially impossible; the fact that change cannot occur is accepted by all, or practically all, participants. . . . No expenditure of psychological or physical energy is necessary to maintain a caste system."[6] Simpson and Yinger agree with Johnson and further object that, in the United States, "we lack a set of religious principles justifying a rigid system of social stratification and causing it to be willingly accepted by those at all levels."[7] Cox lists a number of features of a caste system (i.e., caste in India) which distinguish it from an interracial situation (i.e., Negro-white relations in America), important among which are its "nonconflictive," "nonpathological," and "static" nature, coupled with absence of "aspiration and progressiveness."[8]

Central to these distinctions is that caste in India is passively accepted

[4] The Tira of Africa, for example, would not fall so far toward this extreme (cf. Nadel, *op. cit.*, pp. 18 ff.).

[5] As a matter of fact, ignorance of the details of content in the patterns of relations between whites and Negroes in the United States has prevented many Indianists from seeing very striking similarities. Two contrasting views of the cross-cultural applicability of the concept of caste have appeared since this paper was written: F. C. Bailey, "For a Sociology of India?" *Contributions to Indian Sociology*, No. 3 (July, 1959), 88-101, esp. 97-98; and E. R. Leach, "Introduction: What Should We Mean by Caste?" in *Aspects of Caste in South India, Ceylon and North-west Pakistan* ("Cambridge Papers in Social Anthropology," No. 2 [Cambridge: Cambridge University Press, 1959]), pp. 1-10.

[6] C. S. Johnson, *Growing Up in the Black Belt* (Washington, D.C.: American Council on Education, 1941), p. 326.

[7] G. E. Simpson and J. M. Yinger, *Racial and Cultural Minorities* (New York: Harper & Bros., 1953), p. 328.

[8] O. C. Cox, "Race and Caste: A Distinction," *American Journal of Sociology*, L (March, 1945), 360 (see also his *Caste, Class and Race* [Garden City, N.Y.: Doubleday & Co., 1948]).

and indorsed by all on the basis of religio-philosophical explanations which are universally subscribed to, while Negro-white relations in America are characterized by dissent, resentment, guilt, and conflict. But this contrast is invalid, resulting, as it does, from an idealized and unrealistic view of Indian caste, contrasted with a more realistic, pragmatic view of American race relations; Indian caste is viewed as it is supposed to work rather than as it does work; American race relations are seen as they do work rather than as they are supposed, by the privileged, to work. The traditional white southerner, asked to describe relations between the races, will describe the Negro as happy in his place, which he may quote science and Scripture to justify. This is similar to the explanations offered for the Indian system by the advantaged.

The point here is that ideal intercaste behavior and attitudes in India are much like those in America, while the actual interaction and attitudes are also similar. Commonly, ideal behavior and attitudes in India have been contrasted with real behavior and attitudes in America—a fact which has led to a false impression of difference. Similarly, comparisons of race relations in the rapidly changing urban or industrial South with caste relations in slowly changing rural or agrarian India lead to erroneous conclusions. Valid comparison can be made at either level, but must be with comparable data. The impact on intergroup relations of the social and economic changes which accompany urban life seems to be similar in both societies. Recent literature on village India and on the changing caste functions and caste relations in cities and industrial areas presents a realistic picture which goes far toward counteracting traditional stereotypes of Indian caste.[9]

In a study of caste functioning in Sirkanda, a hill village of northern Uttar Pradesh, India, I was struck by the similarity of relations between the twice-born and untouchable castes to race relations in the southern United States.[10] In both situations there is a genuine caste division, ac-

[9] See, for example, the following community studies: F. G. Bailey, *Caste and the Economic Frontier* (Manchester: University of Manchester Press, 1957); Berreman, *op. cit.*; S. C. Dube, *Indian Village* (Ithaca, N.Y.: Cornell University Press, 1955); Oscar Lewis, *Village Life in Northern India* (Urbana: University of Illinois Press, 1958); McKim Marriott (ed.), *Village India* (American Anthropological Association Memoir No. 83 [Chicago: University of Chicago Press, 1955]); M. E. Opler and R. D. Singh, "The Division of Labor in an Indian Village," in *A Reader in General Anthropolgy*, ed. C. S. Coon (New York: Henry Holt & Co., 1948), pp. 464-96; M. N. Srinivas *et al.*, *India's Villages* (Development Department, West Bengal: West Bengal Government Press, 1955). See also, for example, the following studies of caste in the contemporary setting: Bailey, *op. cit.*; N. K. Bose, "Some Aspects of Caste in Bengal," *American Journal of Folklore*, LXXI (July-September, 1958), 397-412; Leach, *op. cit.*; Arthur Niehoff, *Factory Workers in India* ("Milwaukee Public Museum Publications in Anthropology," No. 5 [1959]); M. N. Srinivas, "Caste in Modern India," *Journal of Asian Studies*, XVI (August, 1957), 529-48; and the several articles comprising the symposium on "Caste in India" contained in *Man in India*, XXXIX (April-June, 1959), 92-162.

[10] The following discussion is based not exclusively on the Sirkanda materials but on observations and literature in non-hill areas as well. The hill area presents some distinct regional variations in caste structure, important among which is the absence of intermediate castes—all are either twice-born or untouchable. This leads to a dichotomous situation, as in the United States, but one which differs in that there are important caste divisions on

cording to the definition above. In the two systems there are rigid rules of avoidance between castes, and certain types of contacts are defined as contaminating, while others are non-contaminating. The ideological justification for the rules differs in the two cultures, as do the definitions of the acts themselves; but these are cultural details. The tabooed contacts are symbolically rather than literally injurious as evidenced by the many inconsistencies in application of the rules.[11] Enforced deference, for example, is a prominent feature of both systems. Lack of deference from low castes is not contaminating, but it is promptly punished, for it implies equality. The essential similarity lies in the fact that the function of the rules in both cases is to maintain the caste system with institutionalized inequality as its fundamental feature. In the United States, color is a conspicuous mark of caste, while in India there are complex religious features which do not appear in America, but in both cases dwelling area, occupation, place of worship, and cultural behavior, and so on, are important symbols associated with caste status. The crucial fact is that caste status is determined, and therefore the systems are perpetuated, by birth: membership in them is ascribed and unalterable. Individuals in low castes are considered inherently inferior and are relegated to a disadvantaged position, regardless of their behavior. From the point of view of the social psychology of intergroup relations, this is probably the most important common and distinct feature of caste systems.

In both the United States and India, high castes maintain their superior position by exercising powerful sanctions, and they rationalize their status with elaborate philosophical, religious, psychological, or genetic explanations. The latter are not sufficient in themselves to maintain the systems, largely because they are incompletely accepted among those whose depressed position they are thought to justify. In both places castes are economically interdependent. In both there are great differences in power and privilege among, as well as class differences within, castes and elaborate barriers to free social intercourse among them.

Similarities in the two caste systems extend throughout the range of behavior and attitudes expressed in relations among groups. An important and conspicuous area of similarity is associated with competition for certain benefits or "gains" which are personally gratifying and/or socially valued and which by their nature or under the circumstances cannot be enjoyed by all equally. Competitive striving is, of course, not unique to caste organization; it is probably found to some extent in all societies. It

---

either side of the "pollution barrier" (cf. Bailey, op. cit., p. 8; Berreman, op. cit., pp. 389 ff.). Relations across this barrier do not differ greatly from similar relations among plains castes, although somewhat more informal contact is allowed—pollution comes about less easily—in the hills.

[11] The symbolic acts—the "etiquette" of caste relations—in India and in America are often remarkably similar. The symbolism in America is, of course, not primarily religious as much as it is in India, although the sacred aspects in India are often far from the minds of those engaging in the acts and are not infrequently unknown to them.

is subject to a variety of social controls resulting in a variety of forms of social stratification, one of which is a caste system as defined here. However, the genesis of caste systems is not here at issue.[12]

The caste system in India and in the United States has secured gains for the groups established at the top of the hierarchy. Their desire to retain their position for themselves and their children accounts for their efforts to perpetuate the system. John Dollard, in his discussion of "Southerntown," identifies their gains as economic, sexual, and in prestige.

In the economic field, low-caste dependence is maintained in India as in America by economic and physical sanctions. This assures not only greater high-caste income but a ready supply of free service and cheap labor from the low castes. It also guarantees the continuing availability of the other gains. In India it is the most explicitly recognized high-caste advantage.

The sexual gain for the southern white caste is defined by Dollard, quoting whom I will substitute "high caste" and "low caste" for "white" and "Negro," respectively. In this form his definition fits the Indian caste system equally well.

> In simplest terms, we mean by a "sexual gain" the fact that [high-caste] men, by virtue of their caste position, have access to two classes of women, those of the [high] and [low] castes. The same condition is somewhat true of the [low-caste] women, except that they are rather the objects of the gain than the choosers, though it is a fact that they have some degree of access to [high-caste] men as well as men of their own caste. [Low-caste] men and [high-caste] women, on the other hand, are limited to their own castes in sexual choices.[13]

This arrangement is maintained in the Indian caste system, as it is in America, by severe sanctions imposed upon any low-caste man who might venture to defy the code, by the toleration accorded high-caste men who have relations with low-caste women, and by the precautions which high-caste men take to protect their women from the low castes.

High-caste people gain, by virtue of their caste status alone, deference from others, constant reinforcement of a feeling of superiority, and a permanent scapegoat in the lower castes. Dollard has stated the implications of this gain in prestige, and, again substituting a caste designation for a racial one, his statement describes the Indian system perfectly:

> The gain here . . . consists in the fact that a member of the [high] caste has an automatic right to demand forms of behavior from [low-caste people] which serve to increase his own self-esteem.

[12] Cf. Nadel, op. cit.
[13] John Dollard, Caste and Class in a Southern Town ("Anchor Books" [Garden City, N.Y.: Doubleday & Co., 1957]), p. 135 (cf. Berreman, op. cit., pp. 470 ff.).

It must always be remembered that in the end this deference is demanded and not merely independently given.[14]

Ideally the high-caste person is paternalistic and authoritarian, while the low-caste person responds with deferential, submissive, subservient behavior. Gallagher might have been describing India rather than America when he noted: "By the attitudes of mingled fear, hostility, deprecation, discrimination, amused patronage, friendly domination, and rigid authoritarianism, the white caste generates opposite and complementary attitudes in the Negro caste." [15]

An additional high-caste gain in India is the religious tradition which gives people of high caste promise of greater rewards in the next life than those of low caste. People can increase their rewards in the next life by fulfilling their traditional caste duty. For high castes, this generally results in increasing the economic advantages and prestige acquired in this life, while it requires that the low castes subordinate their own economic gains and prestige in this life to the service and honor of high castes. Thus, for high-caste people, behavior leading to immediate rewards is consistent with ultimate rewards, while, for low-caste people, behavior required for the two rewards is contradictory.

These advantages are significant and recognized reasons for maintenance of the system by the privileged groups.[16] They are expressed in folklore, proverbs, and jokes; for instance, a story tells that, as the funeral procession of an old landlord passed two untouchable women going for water, one hand of the corpse fell from under the shroud and flopped about. One of the women turned to the other and remarked, "You see, Takur Singh is dead, but he still beckons to us." Other stories recount the avariciousness of Brahmins in their priestly role, the hardheartedness of landlords and the like.

The compensatory gains for low-caste people are cited more often by high-caste advocates of the system than by those alleged to enjoy them. They are gains common to authoritarian systems everywhere and are usually subject to the will of the dominant groups.

As noted above, India is frequently cited as an example of a society in which people of deprived and subject status are content with their lot, primarily justifying it by religion and philosophy. This is the characteristic of caste in India most often cited to distinguish it from hereditary

[14] Dollard, op. cit., p. 174. Nadel speaking of caste in general, has noted that "the lower caste are despised, not only unhappily under-privileged; they bear a stigma apart from being unfortunate. Conversely, the higher castes are not merely entitled to the possession of coveted privileges, but are also in some way exalted and endowed with a higher dignity" (Nadel, op. cit., p. 16).

[15] B. G. Gallagher, American Caste and the Negro College (New York: Columbia University Press, 1938), p. 109.

[16] Cf. Pauline M. Mahar, "Changing Caste Ideology in a North Indian Village" Journal of Social Issues, XIV (1958), 51-65, esp. pp. 55-56; Kailash K. Singh, "Inter-caste Tensions in Two Villages in North India" (unpublished Ph.D. dissertation, Cornell University, 1957), pp. 184-85; and M. N. Srinivas, "The Dominant Caste in Rampura," American Anthropologist, LXI (1959), 1-16, esp. p. 4.

systems elsewhere, notably in the southern United States. On the basis of my research and the literature, I maintain that this is not accurate and therefore not a valid distinction. Its prevalence is attributable in part, at least, to the vested interests of the advantaged and more articulate castes in the perpetuation of the caste system and the maintenance of a favorable view of it to outsiders. The same arguments and the same biases are frequently presented by apologists for the caste system of the southern United States.

In both systems there is a tendency to look to the past as a period of halcyon amity and to view conflict and resentment as resulting from outside disturbances of the earlier normal equilibrium. Alien ideas, or large-scale economic disturbances, or both, are often blamed for reform movements and rebellion. Such explanations may account for the national and regional reform movements which find their advocates and followers primarily among the educated and social elites; they do not account for the recurrent grass-roots attempts, long endemic in India, to raise caste status; for the state of mind which has often led to low-caste defections from Hinduism when the opportunity to do so without fear of major reprisals has presented itself; nor for the chronic resentment and tension which characterizes intercaste relations in even so remote a village as Sirkanda, the one in which I worked.

Among the low or untouchable castes in Sirkanda, there was a great deal of readily expressed resentment regarding their caste position. Specific complaints revolved around economic, prestige, and sexual impositions by the high castes. Although resentment was suppressed in the presence of people of the dominant high castes, it was readily expressed where there was no fear of detection or reprisal.[17] Low-caste people felt compelled to express village loyalties in public, but in private acts and attitudes caste loyalties were consistently and intensely dominant when the two conflicted.

Caste, as such, was not often seriously questioned in the village. Objections were characteristically directed not at "caste" but at "my position in the caste hierarchy."

In the multicaste system of India, abolition of the system evidently seems impossible from the point of view of any particular caste, and a change in its rank within the system is viewed by its members as the only plausible means of improving the situation. Moreover, abolition would destroy the caste as a group which is superior to at least some other groups, and, while it would give caste members an opportunity to mingle as equals with their superiors, it would also force them to mingle as equals with their inferiors. Abolition, even if it could be accomplished, would thus create an ambivalent situation for any particular caste in contrast to the clear-cut advantages of an improvement in rank.

[17] Elaborate precautions were often taken by informants to insure against any possibility that their expressions of feeling might become known to their caste superiors, which is very similar to behavior I have observed among Negroes of Montgomery, Alabama.

In the dual system of the southern United States where the high caste is clearly dominant, abolition of the caste division may be seen by the subordinate group as the only plausible remedy for their deprived position. Furthermore, they have nothing to lose but their inferior status, since there are no lower castes. There are, of course, Negroes and organized groups of Negroes, such as the black supremacist "Muslims" recently in the news in the United States, who want to invert the caste hierarchy; conversely, there are low-caste people in India who want to abolish the entire system. But these seem to be atypical viewpoints. The anticaste religions and reform movements which have from time to time appealed with some success to the lower castes in India, for example, Buddhism, Islam, Christianity, Skhism, have been unable, in practice, to remain casteless. This seems to be a point of real difference between Indian and American low-caste attitudes, for in America objection is more characteristically directed toward the system as such.[18]

In Sirkanda those low-caste people who spoke most piously against high-caste abuses were likely to be equally abusive to their caste inferiors. However, no low caste was encountered whose members did not seriously question its place in the hierarchy. A sizable literature is accumulating concerning castes which have sought to alter their status.[19] Such attempts were made in Sirkanda. A more common reaction to deprived status on the part of low-caste people was what Dollard calls "passive accommodation" coupled with occasional ingroup aggression.[20]

In both America and India there is a tendency for the person of low caste to "laugh it off" or to become resigned. In Sirkanda low-caste people could not avoid frequent contacts with their superiors, because of their proximity and relative numbers. Contacts were frequently informal, but status differences and the dangers of ritual pollution were not forgotten. An untouchable in this village who covered up his bitter resentment by playing the buffoon received favors denied to his more sullen caste fellows. The irresponsible, simple-minded untouchable is a widespread stereotype and one which he, like the Negro, has found useful. Similarly, sullen resignation, with the attendant stereotype of lazy shiftlessness, is a common response, typified in the southern Negro axiom, "Do what the man says." This, too, helps him avoid trouble, although it does little for the individual's self-respect. Aggression against the economically and numerically dominant high castes in Sirkanda was too dangerous to be a reasonable alternative. It was discussed by low-caste people in private but was rarely carried out. Even legitimate complaints to outside authority were avoided in view of the general belief that the

[18] Whether this difference in attitude is widely correlated with multiple, as compared to dual, caste systems, or is attributable to other differences in the Indian and American situations, can be established only by further comparative work.

[19] E.g., Opler and Singh, op. cit., p. 476; B. S. Cohn, "The Changing Status of a Depressed Caste," in Marriott (ed.), op. cit., pp. 53-77; and Bailey, op. cit., pp. 220-26.

[20] Dollard, op. cit., p. 253.

high-caste's wealth would insure an outcome unfavorable to the low castes—a belief well grounded in experience.

Since they harbored indignation and resentment, a number of rationalizations of their status were employed by low-caste people, apparently as mechanisms to lessen the sting of reality. Thus, they often attributed their caste status to relative wealth and numbers: "If we were wealthy and in the majority, we would make the high castes untouchable."

Three more explanations of their caste status were consistently offered by low-caste people. These had the effect of denying the legitimacy of their low-caste position:

1. Members of the entire caste (or subcaste) group would deny that they deserved the low status to which they had been assigned. One example:

> Englishmen and Muslims are untouchables because they have an alien religion and they eat beef. This is as it should be. We are Hindus and we do not eat beef, yet we, too, are treated as untouchables. This is not proper. We should be accorded higher status.

No group would admit to being lowest in the caste hierarchy.

2. People might grant that the caste of their clan, lineage, or family was of low status but deny that their particular group really belonged to it. I have not encountered a low-caste group which did not claim high-caste ancestry or origin. Thus a typical comment is:

> Yes, we are drummers by occupation, but our ancestor was a Brahmin who married a drummer woman. By rights, therefore, we should be Brahmins, but in such cases the high castes here go against the usual custom and assign the child the caste of his low-caste parent rather than of his father, from whom a person inherits everything else.

3. A person might grant that his own caste and even his lineage or family were of low status, but his explanation would excuse him from responsibility for it. Such explanations were supplied by Brahmins who, as the most privileged caste and the recipients of religiously motivated charity from all castes, have a vested interest in maintenance of the system and its acceptance by those at all levels. An individual's horoscope would describe him as having been of high caste and exemplary behavior in a previous life and therefore destined for even greater things in the present life. However, in performing some religiously meritorious act in his previous existence, he inadvertently sinned (e.g., he was a raja, tricked by dishonest servants who did not give to the Brahmin the charity he intended for them). As a result he had to be punished in this life with a low rebirth.

Thus, no one said, in effect, "I am of low status and so are my family members and my caste-fellows, and justly so, because of our misdeeds in previous lives." To do so would lead to a psychologically untenable position, though one advocated by high-caste people and by orthodox Hinduism. Rationalizations or beliefs such as these form a consistent pattern—they are not isolated instances. Neither are they unique to the village or culture reported here: the literature reveals similar beliefs elsewhere in North India.[21] They evidently indicate something less than enthusiastic acceptance of caste position and, meanwhile, they perhaps alleviate or divert resentment.

That people remain in an inferior position, therefore, does not mean that they do so willingly, or that they believe it is justified, or that they would not do anything in their power to change it, given the opportunity. Rationalizations of caste status which are consistent and convincing to those who are unaffected or who benefit from them seem much less so to those whose deprivation they are expected to justify or explain. Adherence to a religious principle may not significantly affect the attitudes and behavior to which logic would seem, or to which dogma attempts, to tie it. A comparison of the realities of caste attitudes and interaction in India and the United States suggests that no group of people is content to be low in a caste hierarchy—to live a life of inherited deprivation and subjection—regardless of the rationalizations offered them by their superiors or constructed by themselves. This is one of many points on which further cross-cultural comparison, and only cross-cultural comparison of caste behavior might be conclusive.

It should be evident that the range of similarities between caste in India and race relations in America, when viewed as relations among people, is wide and that the details are remarkably similar in view of the differences in cultural context. Without denying or belittling the differences, I would hold that the term "caste system" is applicable at the present time in the southern United States, if it is applicable anywhere outside of Hindu India, and that it can be usefully applied to societies with systems of hierarchical, endogamous subdivisions whose membership is hereditary and permanent, wherever they occur. By comparing caste situations, so defined, it should be possible to derive further insight, not only into caste in India, but into a widespread type of relations between groups—insight which is obscured if we insist upon treating Indian caste as entirely unique.

[21] Cf. E. T. Atkinson, *The Himalayan Districts of the North-Western Provinces of India* (Allahabad: North-Western Provinces and Oudh Press, 1886), III, 446; B. S. Cohn, "The Camars of Senapur: A Study of the Changing Status of a Depressed Caste" (unpublished Ph.D. dissertation, Cornell University, 1954), pp. 112 ff.; and D. N. Majumdar, *The Fortunes of Primitive Tribes* (Lucknow: Universal Publishers Ltd., 1944), p. 193.

═══════════Allison Davis

Caste, Economy, and Violence

. . . .

Caste in the deep South integrates into one system all aspects of white-Negro behavior: social, sexual, economic, political, educational, religious, legal, associational, and recreational. The basic subsystem—caste—is a rigid stratification, maintained by physical, social, and psychological punishments and rewards. Everywhere in the South, caste establishes and maintains an endogamous and socially separate system of white-Negro relationship in which by birth the Negroes are all of lower, and the whites all of higher, status. This social caste system is more rigid than that described in the classic literature on Hindu castes.

All white or colored institutions of the southern community, including the church, the school, and the courts, systematically organize and defend the caste system. The only institution which is not completely so organized is the economic. The purpose of this paper is to distinguish caste in the area[1] studied from social class and similar types of hierarchical relationships, to define the legal and customary sanctions of caste status, to describe the integration of the basic institutions into the largest system—that of color caste—and to state a theory of violence as a reaction to the breakdown of caste in the economic sphere.

I

Color caste in Old and Rural counties is a system of relationships which prevents intimate social participation between white and Negro persons. It is maintained by *endogamous* sanctions for each color group and by the associated negative sanctions upon *familial* or *clique* participation of whites with Negroes. Since caste in this society denies legal or customary recognition to sexual relationships between white and Negro people, no individual, white or Negro, can change his caste status by marriage.[2]

Nor can any person change his caste in Old and Rural counties by changing his occupation, or his religion, as is true in some other caste societies in the world. Even the absence in a "Negro" of the physical caste

---

[1] The counties specified in this article are those which were reported on in detail in Allison Davis, Burleigh B. Gardner, and Mary R. Gardner, *Deep South* (Chicago: University of Chicago Press, 1941).

[2] In the legal and customary rigidity of the endogamous control, the color-caste taboo here described appears to be more inviolable than the endogamous rule of most Hindu castes. See Professor Warner's survey of the evidence on this point in W. Lloyd Warner and Allison Davis, "A Comparative Study of American Caste," *Race Relations and the Race Problem,* ed. Edgar T. Thompson (Durham, N.C.: Duke University Press, 1939), pp. 219-29.

Reprinted by permission of *The American Journal of Sociology,* Vol. LI, July, 1945, pp. 7-15. Copyright, 1945, The University of Chicago. All rights reserved.

marks of pigmentation, conformation of the face, and hair form does not make him a member of the white caste. Caste status is determined by a legal and social definition of "blood" or kinship; it is therefore inherited from one's parents. If both of an individual's parents were not socially defined as "white," he is a "Negro" (lower caste), even if he is indistinguishable—as a physical type—from many of the upper-caste members. In the great majority of cases, however, a person's caste status can be defined at once by the inhabitants upon the basis of his skin color and hair form alone.

The basic caste marks of "blood" and physical appearance and the fundamental endogamous rule operate within the economic, occupational, educational, political, and social hierarchies so as to assure the great majority of whites a rank superior to Negroes. Thus the system of regulating marriage is strengthened by controls which subordinate Negroes to whites in all the institutions of the society and, consequently, establish a very strongly defined ranking of the two groups.

Social Class

The form which color-caste stratification has assumed in Old and Rural counties appears unusual to the comparative ethnologist, because it includes a system of social classes *within each caste*. The Negro or white person is born into a social class just as he is born into a color caste. As here conceived, caste and class are both systems for limiting and ranking social participation, but they differ in the degree to which they permit an individual to change from his birth rank. *Caste,* in the area studied, categorically prevents marriage or intimate social participation outside of one's color *birth group*. Within a color group, furthermore, *class* restricts marriage and participation to those individuals identified by symbols and behavior as of a similar kind and rank.

Unlike caste, however, class stratification allows an individual to change his birth rank and his group of intimate participants in his lifetime by changing his class-typed participation, behavior, and symbols. He may also marry outside his class.

As here conceived, therefore, and as defined in another study of this society,[3] a social class is the largest group of people whose members have intimate social access to each other. A class is composed of families and cliques. These units likewise are evaluated by the class members in a hierarchy of rank. The interrelationships between families and intimate cliques in such informal activities as visiting, dancing, receptions, teas, parties, fish-fries, and larger informal affairs constitute the structure of a social class. A person is a member of that social class within which most of his intimate participation occurs.

Not all the members of a color caste in Old and Rural counties, therefore, possess equal rank and similar ranges of participation. Within the Negro and white castes, all individuals are further stratified by their caste

[3] Davis, Gardner, and Gardner, *op. cit.,* chaps. iii-xi.

members into a social class hierarchy. Whereas there is a chance that they may move out of their class, there is no possibility, as the system now operates, that they may change their color-caste membership or participation. Through physical birthmarks an individual is assigned his caste position; whether he is white or Negro, he also dies in his birth caste.

Legal and Customary Sanctions of Caste

This system of defining white-Negro rank is not termed "caste" by the inhabitants. The white group refers to this complex of sanctions as "the color line," "white supremacy," "controlling the Negroes," "race superiority" and "race inferiority," and "keeping this a white man's country." Negroes use such protective euphemisms when talking to whites as "race relations" or "getting along with the white people"; in their own organizations they speak of "race prejudice," "the oppression of Negroes," and "racial injustice." In these expressions the natives refer to the societal controls which make whites superordinate as a group and Negroes subordinate. When these sanctions of rank are examined by the anthropologist, they are seen to have the essential characteristics of a caste system. They define the behavior of both whites and Negroes in such a way as to make their caste rank and prestige universally clear. They operate upon both groups. In all white-Negro relationships they restrict the behavior of both individuals; that is, a white person, as well as a Negro, has a well-defined caste role which he must accept. For learning and maintaining the appropriate caste behavior, an individual of either the Negro or the white group is rewarded by approval and acceptance from his caste; if he violates the controls, he is punished physically, economically, socially, or legally, depending upon the seriousness of the infraction.

Although both the white and the Negro society support the caste system, these sanctions assure high status and privileges to the white individual, and the opposite to the Negro, in all mixed relationships. The relative prestige of the castes is socially defined by color sanctions with respect to occupation, wages, public gatherings, politics, and education. It is this complex of privileges, socially and biologically evaluated, which establishes the superordinate rank of the white, and the subordinate rank of the Negro, group.

The caste controls range from the taboos upon Negro-white marriage and intimacy to those upon the most detailed points of Negro-white etiquette.[4] The basic sanctions in Old and Rural counties will be listed here in decreasing order of inviolability. Infringement by a Negro of any of these, even those concerning deference, is punished by death, whipping, expulsion from the county, or socioeconomic penalties. Whites, though seldom controlled by physical means, are stigmatized and economically punished by their own caste for violating any of these taboos.

Marriage between whites and Negroes is prohibited by a law which is

[4] Extensive illustration of the evidence gathered on caste sanctions is given in *ibid.*, chap. ii.

rigidly observed and enforced, thus supporting the cultural rule of endogamy. By law, also, the offspring of Negro-white unions must be defined as Negroes. Any individual with one Negro ancestor is therefore a Negro, no matter what number of white ancestors he may have had. "Blood" is thus defined so as to prevent mobility across caste lines. Associated with the rule of endogamy is the rule of separate group-seating of whites and Negroes in all public carriers and assemblages. This control is also legalized.

In maintaining the separate and endogamous nature of white-Negro relationships, the informal social controls are elaborately systematized, so as to prevent what the whites call "social equality." Not only are family and kinship relations legally and culturally interdicted between Negroes and whites but a white and a Negro may not visit as intimates. Thus clique relationships are likewise prevented between members of different color groups. With the taboo upon visiting are taboos upon eating or drinking together, dancing, playing cards, and upon all other types of intimacy. All these controls operate to support the endogamous restriction, by making intimate social access impossible.

When Negro-white sexual unions occur, they must therefore take place outside of the white, and usually of the Negro, family. Such unions are permitted only in the case of a white man and a Negro woman. In this area of sexual and social relationships, Negro-white unions are not regarded as establishing "social equality"; the same attitude is maintained with regard to association between Negro and white criminals, gamblers, or "low-life" persons. Although the white and Negro societies disapprove of all these types of association, the whites permit them because they are not a threat to the white family or social class system and are, therefore, not a violation of the endogamous ("legal marriage") caste taboo.

The socially separate, endogamous, superordinate-subordinate system of Negro-white relationships is further maintained by well-defined restrictions upon face-to-face participation. These controls establish an etiquette in all Negro-white contacts; they prescribe masterful or condescending behavior for the white and deferential behavior for the Negro. Caste etiquette varies slightly according to the class position of the white and Negro interacting in the face-to-face relationship; except in the case of the Negro-customer-white-salesman relationship, however, these modifications in etiquette never violate the masterful role of whites and the deferential role of Negroes. Even in this commercial relationship, white salesgirls in Old City address all upper-class colored women, except one, by their first names only.

Whites in this area must not shake hands with Negroes or address them as "Mr.," "Miss," or "Mrs." They address all Negroes either as "girl" or "boy" or by their first names. On the other hand, Negroes must address all whites honorifically. Even an upper-class Negro planter or physician will always address a lower-class white as "Mr.," "Mrs.," or "Miss," whereas whites will not address Negroes in this way, although they may address them as "Professor" or "Doctor." The few exceptions to these rules are limited to Negro domestics who may address their white employers by their first names plus the honorific form, such as "Miss Alice" or "Mr. John," and to some upper middle-class whites who occasionally address a Negro as "Mr." or "Mrs."

Deference to whites by Negroes also includes a conciliating and often whining tone in speaking, removal of the hat, and acquiescence to statements or demands by the white.[5] An absolute taboo prevails against any Negro's contradicting, cursing, or shouting angrily at any white. In the more isolated communities of the area, caste deference requires that a Negro shall not wear expensive "dressy" clothes on weekdays, shall not smoke cigars in the presence of whites, and shall drive his automobile to the side of the road at once to allow a white driver to pass.

The roles of deference for Negroes and of dominance for whites are supported by both physical and psychosocial punishments. In preventing what the whites call "social equality," caste etiquette ranks below only endogamy and social separateness in universality and inviolability. In certain contexts the smallest lapse in deference by a Negro may be punished by beating or death.

The whites place all Negroes into two categories: "good Negroes" and "bad Negroes." The former type meticulously observes the rules of deference; the latter type is low, "sullen," or "sassy" or "smart" toward whites. Negroes, however, use the term "good Negro" to refer to a Negro who is more deferential than the white society requires. Like the whites, they employ the term "bad Negro" to mean a Negro who openly violates caste etiquette, but there is usually an implication of social approval in the Negro usage.

The masterful role of whites and the deferential role of Negroes, learned and maintained as specific behavior patterns and reinforced by powerful sanctions, extend into every type of Negro-white relationship. They underlie the patriarchal "gift" pattern of white behavior toward Negroes in governmental, court, and economic relations and the begging, clowning, flattering, or subservient behavior of the Negroes. Within these caste-typed roles, Negroes and whites have their *modus vivendi*. The caste subordination of Negroes, which is enforced by the complex of legal, political, economic, educational, and social restrictions placed upon them, still allows the deferential Negro to attain certain limited rewards within his lower-caste status. The Negro "leader," minister, or school principal depends upon the patronage of whites to maintain Negro institutions like the school, or the church. The behavior of the effective Negro in this community is directed toward maneuvering the white into accepting more fully a patriarchal relationship to the Negro; both the Negro servant and the Negro leader thus attempt by flattery, cunning, and deference to compel the powerful white individual to act out his patriarchal role.

[5] Scratching the head and shuffling the feet, as if in indecision, are also deferential gestures of most Negroes in this area.

Caste Dogmas

The sanctions of endogamy, social separateness, and white mastery and Negro deference are likewise supported by dogmas in each color group. The most general dogmas of whites in Old and Rural counties concerning the reasons for the subordination of Negroes are that Negroes are inherently childish, primitively sexual, and, except for a few unusual individuals, incapable of intellectual and emotional maturity (socialization) on the level achieved by whites. These secular teachings are supported by the religious dogma that Negroes are inherently faithful, subservient, humble, and otherworldly. Within the Negro caste, the individual is taught that the whites as a group are superior in skills and power, extremely dangerous, all-powerful, and sinful. Negro ministers and leaders express this dogma as follows: Since whites are all-powerful, Negroes should avoid aggressive behavior toward the individuals and toward the white community as a whole; the successful accommodation of Negroes to whites requires their being deferential to whites and working conscientiously for them; Negroes have many invidious characteristics which account for white domination; and Negroes should develop their own Negro society more fully by "race loyalty" to Negro businesses, professional men, and leaders.[6]

Thus the dogmas of each caste positively sanction the separate, ranked, and endogamous relationship. Since the Christian dogma of the brotherhood of man and the democratic dogma of the inherent equality of all men before the law and state are also a part of Negro culture, however, the complete acceptance of caste dogma by Negroes includes only the inviolability of caste endogamy and social separateness. Although Negroes necessarily accept caste-ranking controls also, there is abundant evidence of psychological conflict over this categorical subordination.

The caste sanctions and teachings vary slightly according to age, sex, class, and rural-urban groups. For example, in Old and Rural counties, social separateness is less strictly enforced among very young children; also caste controls are more elaborate and severe in rural than in urban communities and in towns than in cities. Under all conditions, however, the basic restrictions upon marriage, public gatherings, social intimacy, and etiquette operate to maintain the superordinate-subordinate relationships of whites and Negroes and to make this ranking unchangeable and dependent upon birth.

Caste and Community Structure

All other systems of behavior within the society of Old and Rural counties are adjusted in some degree to the caste system. In formal organization, the caste sanctions are most rigidly applied in the political

---

[6] A detailed analysis of the operation of color-caste and class controls in the Negro church and associations in Old and Rural counties and in New Orleans has been prepared for the Carnegie Corporation by the writer, under the title, *The Negro Church and Associations in the Lower South: A Research Memorandum.*

and governmental systems, the organization and functioning of the courts, the educational system, the church and associations, and in organized recreation. In local government, only whites vote or hold state, county, or municipal offices. Only six Negroes in Old City had been allowed to register as voters in national elections; these registered Negroes admitted they did not vote, because they felt, as a leading Negro professional man said, that government was "the white man's business." In the rural counties, no Negro was registered. No Negroes were registered as voters in state or municipal elections, nor had any been a candidate for any county or municipal office since Reconstruction. The white officers in charge of registration and elections stated to one of the white interviewers that the whites prevented Negroes from registering as voters by intimidation and, if necessary, by violence.

In all law courts all judges, court officers, lawyers, and juries are white persons. Criminal cases involving a white and a Negro are almost invariably decided in favor of the white, even if he has been the attacker. Civil cases between Negroes and whites, involving damage to person or property, may be won by a Negro, especially if the white party to the suit is an insurance company or nonlocal corporation. Negroes very rarely sue local whites, however. Murder of a white by a Negro is always punished by death, whereas the murder of a Negro by a white is seldom punished by the courts. Attacks by Negroes upon Negroes usually are very slightly punished, even in the case of murder.

The educational and associational institutions of the community are all segmented into the white and Negro structures. Negro public schools are markedly inferior to white in teaching staff and in equipment; the per capita appropriation by the school board for Negroes is only a fraction of that for whites. The salaries of Negro teachers are lower than those for whites in parallel status. The churches and associations have either all-Negro or all-white membership; the only exceptions anywhere in the surrounding area are in certain labor unions in the building trades and in the Spiritualist and Sanctified churches. All other Protestant and Catholic churches exhibit a quite rigid form of segregation. The highest authority in the Episcopal church, the bishop, stated to a white interviewer the caste policy of his church as follows:

> I think that the only solution of the situation is for Negroes to develop independently of the whites. They must recognize the situation as it is and conform to it. They must work out their own destiny without attempting social equality.

The Catholic bishop likewise stated the acceptance of the caste structure of the community by his church:

> Actually we adapt ourselves to local conditions. Not only because the Negroes usually have a separate church but also because we feel it is better for them to have their own. They also prefer to have a separate church and request it.

Negro-white relationships, therefore, conform to a caste structure in the formal organizations of the society, as well as in the family, social clique, and more informal relationships. The only structure which does not exhibit this sharp dichotomy is the economic organization of the society. Although color-caste sanctions operate as occupational taboos to a high degree, the economic structure is not caste-segmented upon an all-or-none color basis, as are the political and religious structures. That is, economic status does not follow color status with the well-nigh perfect correlation formed in regard to political and legal status.

II

In certain fields, notably in storekeeping, contracting, farming, and professional service to colored persons, the economic system is still sufficiently "free" in competition to prevent the rigid application of caste taboos. Although a large proportion of colored proprietors and contractors, lacking adequate capital, have been unable to compete successfully, the economic system has maintained a small group of colored persons of relatively high status. It has thus prevented the full development of caste —that development in which *all* members of the lower caste are legally, or by virtue of unbreakable custom, below *all* members of the upper caste in wages, occupational status, and the value of property owned.

The evidence establishes the following relationship between the systems of color caste and of economic stratification in the area studied. In general, the economic status of Negroes is inferior to that of whites; nevertheless, economic behavior openly conflicts with caste dogma at times, such as when white landlords accept Negro farm tenants in preference to white. The distribution of economic status is strongly bimodal for color; nevertheless, both Negroes and whites occupy every sort of occupational status—from landlord to day laborer. The same distribution is observed for economic status as measured by landownership, amount of cotton produced, and fertility of soil cultivated.

A study of income, savings, property ownership, and occupations has revealed the marked statistical tendency of economic and occupational status to follow caste lines; together with an actually wide intra-caste spread of economic status. With regard to the first system of behavior, that is, the economic-class stratification *within* each color caste, the chief determinants are considered to be the laws and customs of a "freely competitive" economy, the differential control and fertility of land, the differential availability of credit, and powerful economic-class dogmas and antagonisms.

The second characteristic of economic stratification, namely, the great preponderance in higher economic status of whites over Negroes, is related to the operation of the direct primary caste sanctions, which enable the white landlord to subordinate the Negro tenant even more effectively than the white tenant by law, by custom, and, if necessary, by force. The primary caste controls likewise assure the white landlord a marked competitive advantage over the Negro landlord with regard to the purchase of land, the command of credit, and the securing of tenants. In the urban society, moreover, direct caste sanctions operate to exclude Negroes from practically all preferred occupational status.

The crucial observation remains, however, that some few Negroes enjoy higher economic symbols and rank than many whites. This skew in the relationship between color caste and economic status is observed as a conflict between economic behavior patterns in a competitive system and caste patterns, deriving from a system of social stratification based upon marks of color and "blood." The criteria of status in the two systems are essentially different. A Negro landlord enjoys the economic functions and symbols of a person in the higher positions of the economic hierarchy: he may even have a white tenant working for him. But in social relationships, even with his white tenant, he is lower caste. The existence of these two systems is historically demonstrated by the position of free Negroes in the period of slavery. Most free Negroes actually possessed higher economic status than the chattel slaves and than some "poor whites." Like the slaves, however, they were lower caste, that is, members of a socially separate, endogamous, and subordinated group.

In so far as the present economic system has prevented the full extension of the caste system, it appears to have been operating upon two principles: that of the sanctity of private property and that of free competition. This latter aspect of the national economic and legal structures gives rise to the presence in Old County of nonlocal factories and sawmills. These manufacturing firms hire labor as cheaply as they can get it, with the result that in industries where white workers have not been able to establish caste taboos, colored workers are employed to do much the same type of labor as whites. They may even be preferred to white workers, because they can be hired for a lower wage.

These nonlocal industries not only tend to disrupt caste relations in labor but they put into the hands of colored workers money which the local white storekeepers are extremely anxious to obtain. Since money has the highest value in the economic system, it causes white middle- and lower-class storekeepers to wait upon colored patrons deferentially. Money thereby increases the difficulties of adjusting caste, which seems to be essentially a structure of pastoral and agricultural societies, to a manufacturing and commercial economy. This money economy likewise leads the group of entrepreneurs and middlemen to whom it has given rise—the most powerful group in the production of cotton because they control credit and therefore production—to be unmindful whether they buy cotton from a colored or white farmer, whether they sell food, automobiles, and clothes to one or the other, whether they allow nonlocal industries to subordinate the lower economic group of whites to the lower group of colored workers. They care principally about increasing their money. Even the local white farmowners prefer colored tenants to white, because they can obtain higher profits from the former. From the point of view of the white lower group, such behavior is a violation of caste. It indicates a fundamental conflict between the economic system and the caste dogma.

In the second place, the principle of the sanctity of private property has generally operated to prevent the expropriation of colored owners. Even during the period of slavery, free colored persons were allowed to own property in Old City and in the state generally. This right was not taken from them during the twenty years immediately preceding the Civil War, when the legislature severely restricted their behavior in other respects. At the close of the Civil War, the same reactionary legislature which passed the so-called "Black Code" in Mississippi, providing "apprentice" laws, *granted* to freedmen the right to own property in incorporated towns and cities. Since that time, colored owners have not been expropriated, except in isolated cases of terrorization. To expropriate colored property owners would be to violate the most fundamental principle of the economic system and to establish a precedent for the expropriation of other subordinated groups, such as the lower economic group of white people, Jews, Italians, and "foreign" ethnic groups of all kinds.

It is necessary to point out, however, that the modification of the caste system in the interests of the profits of the upper and middle economic groups of white people by no means amounts to an abrogation of caste in economic relationships. The economic interests of these groups would also demand that cheaper colored labor should be employed in the "white-collar" jobs in business offices, governmental offices, stores, and banks. In this field, however, the interests of the employer group conflict not only with those of the lower economic group of whites but also with those of the more literate and aggressive middle group of whites. A white store which employed colored clerks, for example, would be boycotted by both these groups. The taboo upon the employment of colored workers in such fields is the result of the political power and the purchasing power of the white middle and lower groups. As a result of these taboos in the field of "white-collar" work, the educated colored person occupies a well-nigh hopeless position in Old County.

The superior political power of the middle and lower groups of white people consequent upon the disfranchisement of the colored population, has enabled them to establish a caste barrier to the employment of colored clerical workers in municipal, state, and federal governmental offices. The inability of these white groups to extend caste taboos so as to prevent colored persons from owning real estate and from competing with white skilled and unskilled labor may be attributed to the fact that the rights of private property and of a free labor market for the planter and the manufacturer are still sacred legal rights in Old County.

A more detailed knowledge of the caste system as it exists in economic settings which differ from the old plantation economy of Old County would enable one to define the degree of subordination of the lower caste according to the type of economy. A tentative hypothesis might be advanced that the physical terrorization of colored people is most common in those areas where their general economic status is highest. In the "newer" agricultural, oil-producing, and manufacturing sections of Mississippi and of the South in general, where relatively large groups of colored people are economically superordinate to relatively large groups of white people, open racial conflict and terrorization seem to be at their height. Such conflict results from the fact that in many economic symbols, such as clothes, automobiles, and houses, a relatively large number of colored people are superior to many of the poorer whites. The white society, as a whole, often resorts to terrorization to reassert the dogma of caste and to indicate that in physical and legal power over the life and limb of colored people, at least, the caste sanctions are effective.

In the Mississippi Delta, where white and colored farm tenants are competing at an increasing rate, and in a mill-town society, a sawmill society, or an oil-mining society, where similar competition exists, most of the white men *work* for a living, as contrasted with the white planters in Old County—and work in daily contact with colored men, even though the former may be termed "supervisors." Here, where most white men, dressed in overalls or work clothes, are almost as poor as the colored workers and occupy approximately the same occupational level, it is most difficult to maintain the caste lines with the rigidity and authority which the dogma demands. In such a community, therefore, the white population continually must resort to terrorization in order to impress the colored group with the fact that *economic* equality, or even superiority on the part of the latter, is not *real* equality or superordination; in other words, that caste exists all along the line, as the myth demands, and that actually *any* white man, no matter how poor or illiterate, is superordinate to any colored man, and must be treated with the appropriate deference.

In the old plantation areas in South Carolina, Alabama, and Mississippi, on the other hand, where almost all the colored people are families of poverty-stricken tenants and almost all the white people are families of owners or large landlords, caste is almost "perfect" economically and socially, and therefore relatively little terrorization of the lower caste is needed to support it. In fine, where caste is most fully extended there is little need for violence, because the colored people are thoroughly subordinated economically, occupationally, and socially. When the castes are in economic competition as laborers and tenants, however, violence and conflict seem to be at their height.

—————————Liston Pope

Religion and the Class Structure

. . . .

Community Studies

There have been a number of close studies of social stratification in particular American communities in the last twenty-five years, and they yield more precise information concerning religion and the class structure than can be deduced from public opinion polls. Their findings are too varied in detail (this is their great merit) to permit summary here, but generalizations based on them would include the following:

Social stratification

1. Every American community, from the most rural to the most urban, from Plainville through Middletown to Metropolis, has some pronounced pattern of social stratification, and religious institutions and practices are always very closely associated with this pattern. The number of classes, or layers, varies from community to community; Old City in the Deep South differs in important respects from Yankee City in New England; not all social hierarchies call their bottom class, as do the residents of Plainville, "people who live like the animals." However much details may differ, the stratification is found in all American communities, and religion is always one of its salient features.

2. Differentiation within Protestantism corresponds fairly closely to class divisions. Individual Protestant churches tend to be "class churches," with members drawn principally from one class group. Even where membership cuts across class lines, control of the church and its policies is generally in the hands of officials drawn from one class, usually the middle class.

Protestant denominations in their total outreach touch nearly all sections of the population. But each denomination tends also to be associated with a particular social status. Such denominations as the Congregational, Episcopal, and Presbyterian are generally associated in local communities with the middle and upper classes; the Methodist, Baptist, and Disciples of Christ denominations are more typically associated with the middle classes. The Lutheran denominations are harder to classify, because of their closer association with farmers, with particular ethnic backgrounds, and with skilled workers.

Though all of these major denominations have adherents from the lower classes, the religious expression of the latter has increasingly taken place in the last quarter-century through the new Pentecostal and holiness sects, which represent on the one hand a protest (couched in religious form) against social exclusion and on the other a compensatory method

Reprinted by permission of *The Annals of the American Academy of Political and Social Science*, Vol. 256, March, 1948, pp. 84-91.

(also in religious form) for regaining status and for redefining class lines in religious terms. Some of these sect groups are already beginning to repeat the age-old transition toward establishment as respected churches, moving up the social scale (in terms of the class status of their adherents) as they do so. Christianity itself began among the poor, who accepted it less because they were poor than because they were marginal; most of its branches have long since permeated the higher classes of their societies and have relatively neglected the poor.

Ethnic division

3. Internal differentiation in the Catholic Church tends to follow ethnic lines more largely than economic lines.[9] Ethnic divisions cut across the organization of Catholic parishes by geographical districts, though the latter have often themselves reflected the residential propinquity of immigrants from a particular country. Thus the local Catholic churches in a community may include a French Catholic church, a Polish Catholic church, an Irish Catholic church, and the like.

"Nationality churches" are found in Protestantism also, but they tend to be exceptional and to be associated more clearly with social (and often spatial) isolation than is the case in Catholicism. There is a great deal of evidence that nationality churches, whether Protestant or Catholic, are gradually losing their peculiar ethnic connections. As the number of foreign born has declined, sermons in English have been introduced to supplement—or to replace—the mother tongue.

The institution has found it very difficult to bridge effectively the cultural gap between its older and younger members. Of most importance, intermarriage is increasingly modifying ethnic divisions in urban centers, though some groups (especially the Jewish, Italian, and Polish) remain more endogamous than others; such intermarriage, however, "is not general and indiscriminate but is channeled by religious barriers; and groups with the same religions tend to intermarry." [10] Religious divisions may therefore become even more important indices of stratification in the future. Meanwhile, the nationality church continues to serve as a cohesive force, at least for its older members, and at the same time it helps to insulate them against disruptive and assimilative influences.

4. Differentiation within Judaism corresponds to a combination of ethnic and class pressures, with the latter probably stronger in the large. Higher-class and better-educated Jews tend to leave Orthodox synagogues and to join Conservative or Reform congregations, or to become secularized. Studies of this alignment are inadequate, but the general trend

[9] See John W. McConnell, *The Evolution of Social Classes,* Washington, 1942; Elin Anderson, *We Americans: A Study of Cleavage in an American City,* Cambridge, Mass., 1938; W. Lloyd Warner and Leo Srole, *The Social Systems of American Ethnic Groups,* New Haven, 1945.

[10] Ruby Jo Reeves Kennedy, "Single or Triple Melting-Pot? Intermarriage Trends in New Haven, 1870-1940," *American Journal of Sociology,* Vol. 49, No. 4 (Jan. 1944), pp. 331-39.

appears clear. This trend has not prevailed, incidentally, among the Jews of Great Britain.

Church of the middle class

5. Religious organizations decline in influence at both extreme ends of the social scale, among the most privileged (though there is some contrary evidence) and among the most disadvantaged. In this very general sense, the churches are associated especially with the middle classes.

Negro Stratification

A few statistics will summarize the relation of Negro churchmen to the white religious institutions.[11] Of the more than 14 million Negroes in the United States, about 6.8 million belong to some church. Of these, about 300 thousand are Catholics; two-thirds of the Negro Catholics are in segregated or separate churches. Of the 6.5 million Negro Protestants, about half a million belong to the predominantly white denominations. While Negroes are integrated into denominational affairs to varying degree in higher ecclesiastical bodies (synods, presbyteries, general conferences, and so forth), there is almost no mixing of whites and Negroes at the level of the individual congregation. According to unpublished studies by Frank Loescher, Dwight Culver, and others, less than 1 per cent of the white congregations have any Negro members (and each of these generally has only two or three), and less than one-half of 1 per cent of the Negro Protestants who belong to "white denominations" worship regularly with white persons.

The remaning six million Negro churchmen belong to all-Negro denominations. Nearly all of them are Methodists or Baptists. There are social classes within the Negro community, though the criteria differ from those operative in the white community. Religion tends to be associated with Negro class divisions in a particular context, however, much as it does among whites.[12]

Dynamics of Religion and Class

There has been a long debate over whether religion or class is primary in social structure and change, with the other as a function or a secondary manifestation. Max Weber and Karl Marx represent extreme views; Bergson appears to be more nearly correct in the light of evidence accumulated recently.[13] Religion, despite the close association of its institutions with the class structure, is neither simply a product nor a cause, a sanction nor an enemy, of social stratification. It may be either or both, as it has been in various societies at various times.

There is little evidence that religion will operate in the near future to

[11] For further details, see the articles by John LaFarge and by the present writer in *Survey Graphic*, Vol. 36, No. 1 (Jan. 1947), pp. 59 and 61.
[12] V. E. Daniel, "Ritual and Stratification in Chicago Negro Churches," *American Sociological Review*, Vol. 7, No. 3 (June 1942), pp. 352-61.
[13] Henri Bergson, *The Two Sources of Morality and Religion* (New York, 1935).

change American class structure appreciably. Several opinion polls have shown ministers to be discontent with many aspects of social organization in this country, and church leaders—of all faiths—are more concerned about racial patterns in America than ever before. (There is less concern about class lines than about race barriers.) But unless a drastic transformation comes about in the churches, they will probably continue for the most part to adapt to class divisions—and even to intensify them—as they have done in the past.

Supplementary Bibliography

Allison Davis, Burleigh B. Gardner, and Mary R. Gardner, *Deep South: A Social-Anthropological Study of Caste and Class.* Chicago: U. of Chicago Press, 1941.
  A noted field study of color-caste in a city in Southern United States.

Oliver Cromwell Cox, "Race and Caste: A Distinction." *American Journal of Sociology,* 1945, 50:360.
  A statement by the leading exponent of the idea that race relations are not like caste relations and should not be analyzed as if they were.

Fred Greene, *The Far East.* N. Y.: Rinehart, 1957.
  A description of Oriental social organization emphasizing the powerful inertia of tradition.

Raymond W. Mack, Raymond J. Murphy, and Seymour Yellin, "The Protestant Ethic, Level of Aspiration, and Social Mobility: An Empirical Test." *American Sociological Review,* 1956, 21:295-300. Reprinted in Kimball Young and Raymond W. Mack, *Principles of Sociology: A Reader in Theory and Research,* 2nd ed. N. Y.: American Book, 1962, pp. 181-187.
  An attempt to answer the question of whether religious subcultures in the United States override the national culture in determining mobility attitudes and behavior.

Richard D. Schwartz, "Functional Alternatives to Inequality." *American Sociological Review,* 1955, 20:424-430.
  A discussion of the idea of social stratification as fundamentally a consequence of the division of labor.

XI The Implications of Ethnocentrism

Social scientists search for patterns of human behavior in an attempt to discover the universal elements of social systems. Most social and cultural elements are conditional upon other factors, which may or may not be present. One such universal, however, which borders on the unconditional is the tendency for groups to regard themselves and their own ways as superior to the personnel and ways of other groups. This tendency to judge other groups and cultures by the standards prevalent in one's own group is called *ethnocentrism.*

The Functions of Ethnocentrism

Ethnocentrism is a quality which cuts across all groups, all shapes, sizes, and colors; all nationalities, religious groups, and gangs; all universities, families, and treaty alliances.

This self-seen superiority has a very definite function. It provides an excellent basis for maintaining the stability of the group as a unit. It keeps individual members from wanting to leave the group, because no one would want to join an inferior group.

In-group Virtues as Out-group Vices

Ethnocentrism is at work when dominant groups reject minority performances regardless of their nature and content. There is some justification for the minority person's feeling that "you can't win."

There is a disproportionately small number of Negroes in the professions of medicine and law. Members of the dominant white majority cite this fact as evidence for the characterization of Negroes as lazy, indolent, irresponsible, and ignorant. These are clearly vices. There is a disproportionately large number of Jews in the professions of medicine and law. But is this regarded as a virtue? To the contrary, members of the dominant Christian majority cite this as evidence for the characterization of Jews as pushy, clannish, and aggressive. Whatever the minority (or out-group) does, the dominant in-group can look on it as an objectionable characteristic. Abe Lincoln worked hard into the night to teach himself many things. This is the virtue of being industrious, having a purpose, and attaining it. He is highly respected as a national hero. But medical student Abe Cohen works hard into the night, and he is another pushy Jew.

Will Rogers was an easy-going, lovable guy who took life as it came and never let things upset him. He too became a national hero of sorts. But the same sauntering gait from Negro Willie Rogers is condemned as lack of motivation. As Robert K. Merton phrases it, "In-group virtues are out-group vices."

The Costs of Ethnocentrism

There are other functions of ethnocentrism which have negative consequences for the in-group. There is the exclusion from membership of out-group people who might greatly benefit the group in the achievement of its goals. There is the unjust treatment of outsiders merely because they have been defined as different. The ethnocentric group member can then rationalize this injustice on the grounds that the outsider doesn't deserve the same kind of treatment as a member of his own group.

Sports teams provide a good illustration. Twenty years ago many athletic units, both professional and college, would not think of using a Negro athlete. His "moral inferiority" and the "reaction" of team members were often cited as the primary reasons. Slowly Negroes began to gain acceptance in the sports world. The teams which first hired Negroes, in fact, tended to achieve a greater measure of success than those who did not—perhaps because they were recruiting from a larger pool of talent than those teams which automatically overlooked 10 percent of the population.

It would be a mistake to take the example from the sports world as though it stood alone, with no relation to other endeavors. There is some unknown amount of brain power and creativity squandered in the cotton fields of the Mississippi Delta, in the Gary steel mills, and in the factories of Detroit and Chicago. The corporations of the land which say over and over again that "we aren't quite ready for a Negro executive yet" may be turning away an idea-man who would help them meet their competition. Medical school sections of great universities who turn away Jewish applicant after Jewish applicant because they have reached their quota can be seen in the same light. Ethnocentrism has its positive function of group solidarity but the social costs are often high.

Related Readings

In his *Folkways*, William Graham Sumner illustrated ethnocentrism and drew attention to the manner in which it contributed to the survival of the group. Even though, as Sumner contends, ethnocentrism promotes social control, it entails measurable costs for the group, as William R. Catton, Jr., and Sung Chick Hong demonstrate in "The Relation of Apparent Minority Ethnocentrism to Majority Antipathy." Taking into account the effects of a third variable, which they call "Social Dominance G," they show that to some extent majority antipathy can be explained by apparent minority ethnocentrism.

Ruby Jo Reeves Kennedy, in "Single or Triple Melting-pot?" offers evidence of the strength of ethnocentrism among religious groups in New Haven. Although the assimilation process in America shows husbands and wives merging previously distinct national heritages, the three major religious boundaries remain to inhibit the thesis of America as a melting pot.

Persuasive data on the power of group norms is presented by Solomon E. Asch in "Opinions and Social Pressure." One reason that ethnocentrism can operate as chauvinism and that racial and ethnic discrimination can flourish in contravention to the values of a democratic society resides in the human impulse to conform to the norms of the group.

——————————William Graham Sumner

On Ethnocentrism and the Accommodation of Conflict

· ·

12. *Tradition and its restraints.* It is evident that the "ways" of the older and more experienced members of a society deserve great authority in any primitive group. We find that this rational authority leads to customs of deference and to etiquette in favor of the old. The old in turn cling stubbornly to tradition and to the example of their own predecessors. Thus tradition and custom become intertwined and are a strong coercion which directs the society upon fixed lines, and strangles liberty. Children see their parents always yield to the same custom and obey the same persons. They see that the elders are allowed to do all the talking, and that if an outsider enters, he is saluted by those who are at home accord-

From Sumner, William Graham, *Folkways:* Boston: Ginn, 1906, pp. 11-18.

ing to rank and in fixed order. All this becomes rule for children, and helps to give to all primitive customs their stereotyped formality. "The fixed ways of looking at things which are inculcated by education and tribal discipline are the precipitate of an old cultural development, and in their continued operation they are the moral anchor of the Indian, although they are also the fetters which restrain his individual will." [1]

13. *The Concept of "primitive society"; we-group and others-group.* The conception of "primitive society" which we ought to form is that of small groups scattered over a territory. The size of the groups is determined by the conditions of the struggle for existence. The internal organization of each group corresponds to its size. A group of groups may have some relation to each other (kin, neighborhood, alliance, connubium and commercium) which draws them together and differentiates them from others. Thus a differentiation arises between ourselves, the we-group, or in-group, and everybody else, or the others-groups, out-groups. The insiders in a we-group are in a relation of peace, order, law, government, and industry, to each other. Their relation to all outsiders, or others-groups, is one of war and plunder, except so far as agreements have modified it. If a group is exogamic, the women in it were born abroad somewhere. Other foreigners who might be found in it are adopted persons, guest friends, and slaves.

14. *Sentiments in the in-group and towards the out-group.* The relation of comradeship and peace in the we-group and that of hostility and war towards others-groups are correlative to each other. The exigencies of war with outsiders are what make peace inside, lest internal discord should weaken the we-group for war. These exigencies also make government and law in the in-group, in order to prevent quarrels and enforce discipline. Thus war and peace have reacted on each other and developed each other, one within the group, the other in the intergroup relation. The closer the neighbors, and the stronger they are, the intenser is the warfare, and then the intenser is the internal organization and discipline of each. Sentiments are produced to correspond. Loyalty to the group, sacrifice for it, hatred and contempt for outsiders, brotherhood within, warlikeness without,—all grow together, common products of the same situation. These relations and sentiments constitute a social philosophy. It is sanctified by connection with religion. Men of an others-group are outsiders with whose ancestors the ancestors of the we-group waged war. The ghosts of the latter will see with pleasure their descendants keep up the fight, and will help them. Virtue consists in killing, plundering, and enslaving outsiders.

15. *Ethnocentrism* is the technical name for this view of things in which one's own group is the center of everything, and all others are scaled and rated with reference to it. Folkways correspond to it to cover both the inner and the outer relation. Each group nourishes its own pride and vanity, boasts itself superior, exalts its own divinities, and looks with

[1] *Globus*, LXXXVII, 128.

contempt on outsiders. Each group thinks its own folkways the only right ones, and if it observes that other groups have other folkways, these excite its scorn. Opprobrious epithets are derived from these differences. "Pig-eater," "cow-eater," "uncircumcised," "jabberers," are epithets of contempt and abomination. The Tupis called the Portuguese by a derisive epithet descriptive of birds which have feathers around their feet, on account of trousers.[2] For our present purpose the most important fact is that ethno-centrism leads a people to exaggerate and intensify everything in their own folkways which is peculiar and which differentiates them from others. It therefore strengthens the folkways.

16. *Illustrations of ethnocentrism.* The Papuans on New Guinea are broken up into village units which are kept separate by hostility, canni-balism, head hunting, and divergences of language and religion. Each village is integrated by its own language, religion, and interests. A group of villages is sometimes united into a limited unity by connubium. A wife taken inside of this group unit has full status; one taken outside of it has not. The petty group units are peace groups within and are hostile to all outsiders.[3] The Mbayas of South America believed that their deity had bidden them live by making war on others, taking their wives and prop-erty, and killing their men.[4]

17. When Caribs were asked whence they came, they answered, "We alone are people." [5] The meaning of the name Kiowa is "real or principal people." [6] The Lapps call themselves "men," or "human beings." [7] The Greenland Eskimo think that Europeans have been sent to Greenland to learn virtue and good manners from the Greenlanders. Their highest form of praise for a European is that he is, or soon will be, as good as a Green-lander.[8] The Tunguses call themselves "men." [9] As a rule it is found that nature peoples call themselves "men." Others are something else—perhaps not defined—but not real men. In myths the origin of their own tribe is that of the real human race. They do not account for the others. The Ainos derive their name from that of the first man, whom they worship as a god. Evidently the name of the god is derived from the tribe name.[10] When the tribal name has another sense, it is always boastful or proud. The Ovambo name is a corruption of the name of the tribe for themselves, which means "the wealth." Amongst the most remarkable people in the world for ethnocentrism are the Seri of Lower California. They observe an attitude of suspicion and hostility to all outsiders, and strictly forbid marriage with outsiders.

18. The Jews divided all mankind into themselves and Gentiles. They

[2] Martius, *Ethnog. Brasil.*, 51.
[3] Krieger, *New Guinea*, 192.
[4] Tylor, *Anthropology*, 225.
[5] Martius, *Ethnog. Brasil.*, 51.
[6] *Bur. Eth.*, XIV, 1078.
[7] Wiklund, *Om Lapparna i Sverige*, 5.
[8] Fries, *Grönland*, 139.
[9] Hiekisch, *Tungusen*, 48.
[10] Hitchcock in *U.S. Nat. Mus.*, 1890, 432.

were the "chosen people." The Greeks and Romans called all outsiders
"barbarians." In Euripides' tragedy of *Iphigenia in Aulis* Iphigenia says
that it is fitting that Greeks should rule over barbarians, but not contrariwise, because Greeks are free, and barbarians are slaves. The Arabs regarded themselves as the noblest nation and all others as more or less
barbarous.[11] In 1896, the Chinese minister of education and his counselors
edited a manual in which this statement occurs: "How grand and glorious
is the Empire of China, the middle kingdom! She is the largest and richest
in the world. The grandest men in the world have all come from the
middle empire." [12] In all the literature of all the states equivalent statements occur, although they are not so naïvely expressed. In Russian books
and newspapers the civilizing mission of Russia is talked about, just as,
in the books and journals of France, Germany, and the United States, the
civilizing mission of those countries is assumed and referred to as well
understood. Each state now regards itself as the leader of civilization, the
best, the freest, and the wisest, and all others as inferior. Within a few
years our own man-on-the-curbstone has learned to class all foreigners of
the Latin peoples as "dagos," and "dago" has become an epithet of
contempt. These are all cases of ethnocentrism.

19. *Patriotism* is a sentiment which belongs to modern states. It stands
in antithesis to the mediaeval notion of catholicity. Patriotism is loyalty
to the civic group to which one belongs by birth or other group bond.
It is a sentiment of fellowship and cooperation in all the hopes, work, and
suffering of the group. Mediaeval catholicity would have made all Christians an in-group and would have set them in hostility to all Moham-
medans and other non-Christians. It never could be realized. When the
great modern states took form and assumed control of societal interests,
group sentiment was produced in connection with those states. Men
responded willingly to a demand for support and help from an institution
which could and did serve interests. The state drew to itself the loyalty
which had been given to men (lords), and it became the object of that
group vanity and antagonism which had been ethnocentric. For the
modern man patriotism has become one of the first of duties and one of
the noblest of sentiments. It is what he owes to the state for what the
state does for him, and the state is, for the modern man a cluster of civic
institutions from which he draws security and conditions of welfare. The
masses are always patriotic. For them the old ethnocentric jealousy,
vanity, truculency, and ambition are the strongest elements in patriotism.
Such sentiments are easily awakened in a crowd. They are sure to be
popular. Wider knowledge always proves that they are not based on facts.
That we are good and others are bad is never true. By history, literature,
travel, and science men are made cosmopolitan. The selected classes of
all states become associated; they intermarry. The differentiation by states
loses importance. All states give the same security and conditions of wel-

[11] Von Kremer, *Kulturgesch. d. Orients*, II, 236.
[12] Bishop, *Korea*, 438.

fare to all. The standards of civic institutions are the same, or tend to become such, and it is a matter of pride in each state to offer civic status and opportunities equal to the best. Every group of any kind whatsoever demands that each of its members shall help defend group interests. Every group stigmatizes any one who fails in zeal, labor, and sacrifices for group interests. Thus the sentiment of loyalty to the group, or the group head, which was so strong in the Middle Ages, is kept up, as far as possible, in regard to modern states and governments. The group force is also employed to enforce the obligations of devotion to group interests. It follows that judgments are precluded and criticism is silenced.

20. *Chauvinism.* That patriotism may degenerate into a vice is shown by the invention of a name for the vice: chauvinism. It is a name for boastful and truculent group self-assertion. It overrules personal judgment and character, and puts the whole group at the mercy of the clique which is ruling at the moment. It produces the dominance of watchwords and phrases which take the place of reason and conscience in determining conduct. The patriotic bias is a recognized perversion of thought and judgment against which our education should guard us.

21. *The struggle for existence and the competition of life; antagonistic cooperation.* The struggle for existence must be carried on under life conditions and in connection with the competition of life. The life conditions consist in variable elements of the environment, the supply of materials necessary to support life, the difficulty of exploiting them, the state of the arts, and the circumstances of physiography, climate, meteorology, etc., which favor life or the contrary. The struggle for existence is a process in which an individual and nature are the parties. The individual is engaged in a process by which he wins from his environment what he needs to support his existence. In the competition of life the parties are men and other organisms. The men strive with each other, or with the flora and fauna with which they are associated. The competition of life is the rivalry, antagonism, and mutual displacement in which the individual is involved with other organisms by his efforts to carry on the struggle for existence for himself. It is, therefore, the competition of life which is the societal element, and which produces societal organization. The number present and in competition is another of the life conditions. At a time and place the life conditions are the same for a number of human beings who are present, and the problems of life policy are the same. This is another reason why the attempts to satisfy interest become mass phenomena and result in folkways. The individual and social elements are always in interplay with each other if there are a number present. If one is trying to carry on the struggle for existence with nature, the fact that others are doing the same in the same environment is an essential condition for him. Then arises an alternative. He and the others may so interfere with each other that all shall fail, or they may combine, and by cooperation raise their efforts against nature to a higher power. This latter method is industrial organization. The crisis which produces it is constantly renewed, and

men are forced to raise the organization to greater complexity and more comprehensive power, without limit. Interests are the relations of action and reaction between the individual and the life conditions, through which relations the evolution of the individual is produced. That evolution, so long as it goes on prosperously, is well living, and it results in the self-realization of the individual, for we may think of each one as capable of fulfilling some career and attaining to some character and state of power by the developing of predispositions which he possesses. It would be an error, however, to suppose that all nature is a chaos of warfare and competition. Combination and cooperation are so fundamentally necessary that even very low life forms are found in symbiosis for mutual dependence and assistance. A combination can exist where each of its members would perish. Competition and combination are two forms of life association which alternate through the whole organic and superorganic domains. The neglect of this fact leads to many socialistic fallacies. Combination is of the essence of organization, and organization is the great device for increased power by a number of unequal and dissimilar units brought into association for a common purpose. McGee[13] says of the desert of Papagueria, in southwestern Arizona, that "a large part of the plants and animals of the desert dwell together in harmony and mutual helpfulness (which he shows in detail); for their energies are directed not so much against one another as against the rigorous environmental conditions growing out of dearth of water. This communality does not involve loss of individuality, . . . indeed the plants and animals are characterized by an individuality greater than that displayed in regions in which perpetuity of the species depends less closely on the persistence of individuals." Hence he speaks of the "solidarity of life" in the desert. "The saguaro is a monstrosity in fact as well as in appearance,—a product of miscegenation between plant and animal, probably depending for its form of life history, if not for its very existence, on its commensals." [14] The Seri protect pelicans from themselves by a partial taboo, which is not understood. It seems that they could not respect a breeding time, or establish a closed season, yet they have such an appetite for the birds and their eggs that they would speedily exterminate them if there were no restraint. This combination has been well called antagonistic cooperation. It consists in the combination of two persons or groups to satisfy a great common interest while minor antagonisms of interest which exist between them are suppressed. The plants and animals of the desert are rivals for what water there is, but they combine as if with an intelligent purpose to attain to a maximum of life under the conditions. There are many cases of animals who cooperate in the same way. Our farmers put crows and robins under a protective taboo because the birds destroy insects. The birds also destroy grain and fruits, but this is tolerated on account of their services. Madame Pommerol says of the inhabitants of Sahara that the

[13] *Amer. Anthrop.*, VIII, 365.
[14] Cf. also *Bur. Eth.*, XVII (Part I), 190*.

people of the towns and the nomads are enemies by caste and race, but allies in interest. The nomads need refuge and shelter. The townspeople need messengers and transportation. Hence ties of contract, quarrels, fights, raids, vengeances, and reconciliations for the sake of common enterprises of plunder.[15] Antagonistic cooperation is the most productive form of combination in high civilization. It is a high action of the reason to overlook lesser antagonisms in order to work together for great interests. Political parties are constantly forced to do it. In the art of the statesman it is a constant policy. The difference between great parties and factions in any parliamentary system is of the first importance; that difference consists in the fact that parties can suppress minor differences, and combine for what they think most essential to public welfare, while factions divide and subdivide on petty differences. Inasmuch as the suppression of minor differences means a suppression of the emotional element, while the other policy encourages the narrow issues in regard to which feeling is always most intense, the former policy allows for less play to feeling and passion.

[15] *Une Femme chez les Sahariennes,* 105.

——————————— William R. Catton, Jr., and Sung Chick Hong

The Relation of Apparent Minority Ethnocentrism to Majority Antipathy

. . . . , ...

Ethnocentrism, according to Sumner, "leads a people to exaggerate and intensify everything in their own folkways which is peculiar and which differentiates them from others." [1] This tends to strengthen the folkways, he argued. It was Sumner's belief, in other words, that ethnocentrism is functional.

What does ethnocentrism cost, though? If ethnocentrism is functional in promoting social control within the group, is it dysfunctional in relations between groups? Lundberg has suggested that it may be: "Conspicuous (i.e., more than usual) ethnocentrism on the part of any group in a community is likely to incur a certain hostility on the part of other groups regardless of particular racial, religious or other characteristics." [2] A similar view has been stated by Sorokin: "When and where each group in a multigroup society has its values different from those of the other minority groups and from those of the majority, when there is no common

[1] William Graham Sumner, *Folkways,* Boston: Ginn and Co., 1906, p. 13.
[2] George A. Lundberg, "Some Neglected Aspects of the 'Minorities' Problem," *Modern Age,* 2 (Summer, 1958), pp. 290-291.

Reprinted from *American Sociological Review,* Vol. 27, No. 2, April, 1962, pp. 178-191. By permission.

fund of values, . . . there will be an abundance of antagonism between the different minority groups and between these and the majority group." [3]

To contend that hostility by one group may be evoked by ethnocentric behavior on the part of another group in a multigroup society is less conventional than to study the *prejudices* of the hostile group.[4] In sociology, as Rose and Rose have pointed out, current theories and factual studies of prejudice find the causes of prejudice elsewhere than in the minority group itself. "This is amazing when it is considered that the everyday explanation always locates the causes in the minority group." [5] The present paper should not be construed as an endorsement of the "everyday explanation for prejudice," and it does not proceed from the assumptions of "the man in the street" regarding the virtues or the faults of particular minorities. It does, however, report data which bear upon the hypothesis that *majority hostility is associated with the appearance of ethnocentrism in minorities.*

That such hypotheses are not more common in the sociological literature is due, Furfey believes, to a humanitarian philosophy which pervades the thinking of social pathologists.[6] The humanitarian sociologist seems to be reluctant to give any appearance of "blaming" minorities for the majority hostility they experience. Somehow, the assumption of majority pathology is more palatable.

There may, however, be an additional reason for this predilection in theories of hostility between groups. Difficulties in definition and measurement of the relevant variables may be a barrier to consideration of the hypothesis that majority hostility toward a number of minorities varies in proportion to their respective degree of ethnocentrism. How can we measure the extent to which the behavior of a given minority is ethnocentric? Such data are not readily available either in census volumes, voting records, or the usual public opinion survey reports.

[3] Pitirim A. Sorokin, "Comments on William F. Albright's 'Some Functions of Organized Minorities,' " in Lyman Bryson, *et al.*, editors, *Approaches to National Unity*, New York: Harper and Brothers, 1945, p. 274.

[4] Lewis A. Coser, *The Functions of Social Conflict*, Glencoe, Ill.: The Free Press, 1956, p. 45.

[5] Arnold Rose and Caroline Rose, *America Divided*, New York: Alfred A. Knopf, 1948, p. 304. On the other hand, Williams, speaking of conflict between groups differentiated on the basis of religion, says, "Conflict . . . can emerge even if everyone involved is initially devoid of stereotypes, ignorance, standardized modes of scapegoating, or diffuse unfulfilled needs for aggression." Robin M. Williams, Jr., "Religion, Value Orientations, and Intergroup Conflict," in Eleanor E. Maccoby, Theodore M. Newcomb, and Eugene L. Hartley, *Readings in Social Psychology* (3rd ed.), New York: Henry Holt and Co., 1958, p. 647. Simpson and Yinger cite several instances in which efforts to reduce prejudice and discrimination involve changing some of the behavior of minorities. They note that suggestions to proceed in this way may be greeted with derision by minority-group members, and are unlikely to be taken seriously when offered gratuitously by a member of the dominant group who may thus explain away his own responsibilities. See George E. Simpson and J. Milton Yinger, *Racial and Cultural Minorities* (Rev. ed.), New York: Harper and Brothers, 1958, pp. 800-804.

[6] Paul H. Furfey, "Sociological Science and the Problem of Values," Ch. 6 in Llewellyn Gross, editor, *Symposium on Sociological Theory*, Evanston, Ill.: Row, Peterson, 1959, p. 523.

The Measurement of Apparent Ethnocentrism

It is the opinion of the present authors that such measurement problems are amenable to solution at least in a preliminary way by a straightforward application of psychometric techniques. If N different specimens of handwriting can be scaled by m judges on a continuum of neatness, or if N different dessert dishes can be scaled by m judges on a continuum of delectability, or if N different statements of attitude toward desegregation can be scaled by m judges on a continuum of favorability, there is nothing in principle to preclude the use of routine scaling procedures to place N minority groups on a continuum of apparent ethnocentrism, using the ratings of m judges.

The judgments rendered are, of course, *responses* by the judges to the stimuli being scaled. It is conventional in most psychometric work to regard the scale scores derived from these judgments as measures of some specified attribute of the stimuli, not as measures of some characteristic of the judges. Usually it is not necessary to make a point of this. Inanimate stimuli cannot object to this assumption. In applying psychometric techniques to the problem of scaling human minorities along a continuum of apparent ethnocentrism, however, the researcher virtually invites criticism from spokesmen for one or more of the minorities in question if he adopts this conventional assumption. It will be contended that he is *not* measuring the minorities, but is only measuring the judges' stereotyped attitudes toward those minorities. In answer, the researcher will naturally point to the large body of careful methodological research showing that the ordering of stimuli on a continuum can be independent of the judges' own attitudes.[7] He may also ask his critics to share the burden of proof and to demonstrate, rather than simply to argue, that his scale scores are *only* a function of the judges' prejudices and not at all a function of actual minority attributes.

If, then, the same N minority groups can be scaled in terms of apparent ethnocentrism and also in terms of the degree of antipathy they incur in their relations with the majority, the correlation between these two scaled variables can be found, and the hypothesis stated above can be tested. In statistical terms that hypothesis becomes: The correlation between the degree of ethnocentrism imputed by a set of (majority) judges to a minority group and the degree of social amicability felt by them toward the minority will be significantly different from zero and negative in sign. That is, the higher a minority group in apparent ethnocentrism, the lower its acceptability to the majority.

Five hundred and fifty-seven students at the University of Washington participated as judges in the present study during December, 1958. This group of judges included persons registered in classes in anthropology, architecture, business, economics, education, mathematics, psychology,

---

[7] For a summary of these studies, see Allen L. Edwards, *Techniques of Attitude Scale Construction*, New York: Appleton-Century-Crofts, 1957, pp. 106-119.

sociology, and speech. Evening-class (extension) students were chosen in preference to day-class (resident) students because it was assumed that the former were less isolated than day students from the larger community and might therefore be able to make more realistic judgments regarding the minorities to be scaled.

The scaling for the present study was carried out in the following manner. In their classrooms the student judges were given questionnaires which began with one of five (randomly assigned) descriptions of the behavior of a fictitious minority called "Ethnians." Approximately one-fifth of the judges were given a description of highly *ethnocentric* Ethnians, which read as follows:

> Suppose you moved into a new community and found that a group of Ethnians lived there too. Suppose that these Ethnians were very strongly convinced that they were superior to all other people. They constantly tried to prove their superiority by citing examples of members of their group who were famous in the arts, sciences, business, and politics. Most of them clung to holidays, habits, and public practices that were very different from the rest of the community. They regarded it as a great loss of purity if one of their children married a non-Ethnian. They formed separate charity organizations solely to help their own members. They showed great loyalty to their own group in all matters and tended to regard almost all criticisms as a sign of hatred on the part of the larger community. This led them to react to non-Ethnians with very strong dislike and antagonism.

On the same page, the judges were asked: "Does the behavior of these Ethnians remind you of any groups you know? If so, list the first three groups that come to mind." Responses to this question were used as a basis for selecting a sub-set of so-called "unprejudiced" judges as will be explained later.

Later on in the questionnaire, the judges were asked to rate on a ten-point numerical scale how ethnocentric they thought each of the following minorities was (in comparison with the description of the Ethnians):

   a. American Indians
   b. Americans of Chinese background
   c. Americans of Catholic background
   d. Americans of French background
   e. Americans of German background
   f. Americans of Greek background
   g. Americans of Irish background
   h. Americans of Italian background
   i. Americans of Japanese background
   j. Americans of Jewish background
   k. Americans of Mexican background
   l. Americans of Negro background
   m. Americans of Filipino background
   n. Americans of Polish background

    o. Americans of Puerto Rican background
    p. Americans of Russian background
    q. Americans of Swedish background
    r. "Your own group"

Means of their judgments were taken as measures of the relative ethno-centrism apparently exhibited by these eighteen groups. The validity of this measure will be discussed after the rest of the questionnaire procedure has been explained. It is important to emphasize here that we were not concerned with individual judgments, but with the mean of the collective judgments toward a particular minority. Persons who filled out our questionnaire are to be regarded as *measuring devices*, not as subjects. Our "subjects" are the eighteen minorities listed in the questionnaire. Questions of sampling and problems of statistical inference, which may occur to the reader when our findings are reported below, should be addressed primarily to this sample of eighteen from a universe of all minorities, and only secondarily to the "universe" represented by the "sample" of evening-class students who performed this psychometric task.[8]

Several pages later in the questionnaire, judges were given a social distance scale to fill out. This scale asked the following questions with regard to each of the eighteen minorities: (1) "Would you like working beside a member of the following groups?" (2) "Would you like to have members of any of the following groups go to the same public schools as teenage boys and girls of your own group?" (3) "Would you like to have members of any of the following groups live in your neighborhood?" (4)"Now think of all these groups as next-door neighbors. Is there any you would like to have as *next-door* neighbors?" (5) "Is there any on the list that, in general, you would like to invite into your home for a social evening?" (6) "Is there any group in the list that, in general, you would like to have date teenage boys and girls of your own group?" (7) "Suppose you were thinking of getting married. Is there any on the list that you would be willing to marry?" It was assumed that these seven questions represent successive levels of intimacy of relationship, and this part of each judge's questionnaire was scored by assigning to each minority the number designating the highest level of intimacy to which that judge was willing to admit that minority. The mean of these "social nearness" scores was computed for each of the eighteen minorities.

Finally, the questionnaire included an anti-Semitism scale taken from an earlier study by Morse and Allport.[9] This scale was filled out by all judges and was used as an additional screening device for selecting a sub-set of "pure" (unprejudiced) judges.

[8] It would, of course, be of some interest to compare the present sets of scale scores with other sets obtained from judges recruited in other regions of the country, and it is hoped that such replications of this study will be carried out.
[9] See Nancy C. Morse and F. H. Allport, "The Causality of Anti-Semitism: An Investigation of Seven Hypotheses," *Journal of Psychology*, 34 (October, 1952), pp. 197-233.

It should be noted that all of the judges answered the social distance scale, whereas only about one-fifth of the judges were asked to rate the eighteen minorities for apparent ethnocentrism. Likewise, another random one-fifth rated the minorities for extent of apparent disproportionate political influence, another one-fifth for extent of apparent allegiance to a foreign power, another one-fifth for extent of apparent monopolistic holding of high-status jobs, and the last one-fifth for extent of apparent undue special privileges and immunities.[10]

[10] The descriptions of Ethnian behavior with which the eighteen minorities were compared by the respective sub-sets of judges all began with the sentence, "Suppose you moved into a new community and found that a small group of Ethnians lived there too." Thereafter they read as follows:

Disproportionate Political Influence—"Suppose that these Ethnians were especially active in politics. An unusually large number of them, considering the small size of their group, were office holders, and the Ethnians were very strongly inclined to vote for only those candidates who were Ethnians. Any politician running for office had to get his picture into the papers with a group of Ethnians if he was to have a chance of being elected. Likewise, appointments to offices controlled by Ethnians would go to Ethnians in more than proportionate numbers. The rest of the community usually felt that Ethnian office holders were much more concerned about the welfare of Ethnians than of the whole community. Certain types of legislation hardly came up for consideration because it was well known to the legislators that such bills would be offensive to the Ethnian group."

Allegiance to a Foreign Power—"Suppose that these Ethnians retained a very strong attachment to Ethnia, their foreign homeland. The local Ethnians always celebrated the national holidays of Ethnia and paid little attention to holidays of the larger community. The picture of a prominent leader of Ethnia was proudly displayed in many Ethnian homes in this community. They were also very active in helping Ethnia. For example, they carried on extensive and highly publicized money-raising 'drives' for the benefit of Ethnia not only among their own members but in the community as a whole. The Ethnians maintained a very skillful and efficient organization to gain favorable publicity for Ethnia, and brought strong pressure to bear on public policy regarding Ethnia. In other words, the Ethnians seemed to pay their primary loyalty to Ethnia rather than to their local community."

Monopolistic Holding of High-Status Jobs—"Suppose it is found that Ethnians had much better jobs and more money than the average. The Ethnians lived in the larger homes in the more desirable neighborhood in the community. The Ethnians claim that this is merely the result of the Ethnians' superior abilities. Other people in the community, however, feel that the prominence of the Ethnians is due to the favoritism of Ethnians for their own group through appointments and other influences they exert. In any event, it is a fact that Ethnians are over-represented in high-status occupations like medicine, law, music, and politics. It is also assumed throughout the community that one's chances of getting a top job, or important business contracts, or important managerial positions are higher if one is an Ethnian than if not."

Undue Special Privileges and Immunities—"Suppose that these Ethnians were always trying to gain certain special privileges. This made them, for example, exempt from public criticisms of the type which other groups had to put up with. That is, the Ethnians had special organizations to protect Ethnians against criticism or attacks which other members of the community had to put up with as a matter of course and without any special protection. Thus, the Ethnians would make organized protest about books, movies, and speeches, which unfavorably criticized them. These Ethnians would try to suppress such criticism through censorship, boycott, or other influence in the publishing or communication industries. Even the police would sometimes hesitate to arrest an Ethnian for disorderly public behavior because of fear that Ethnians would complain about it as persecution, and would bring pressure to bear on higher officials to reprove the offending policemen."

The Findings

Mean "social nearness" ratings and mean ethnocentrism ratings were converted to standard scores (see Table 1) and then plotted against each other in Figure 1. Each circle in this scattergram represents a minority group, and its lateral position indicates the relative ethnocentrism im-

TABLE 1. SCALE SCORES DERIVED FROM VARIOUS SETS OF RATINGS OF 18 MINORITIES BY VARIOUS SETS OF JUDGES

	All Judges							"Pure" Judges		"Prejudiced" Judges
	Ethno.	Pol. Infl.	For. All.	Ec. Mon.	Spec. Priv.	G	Social Nearness	Ethno.	Social Nearness	Ethno.
Amer. Indian	— .11	—1.30	—1.58	—1.56	— .55	—1.11	—1.09	.33	—1.16	— .26
Chinese	.55	— .81	.54	— .44	— .61	— .58	— .57	.68	— .60	.50
Catholic	1.69	2.48	.68	1.71	2.18	2.05	.34	1.83	.14	1.60
French	—1.78	— .25	— .72	.10	.58	.25	1.07	—1.70	1.08	—1.78
German	—1.05	.29	— .03	.76	.71	.67	1.12	—1.22	1.11	— .99
Greek	.28	.56	.54	— .17	— .08	— .20	.36	.23	.37	.29
Irish	— .47	.66	.58	.26	.82	.56	1.08	— .37	1.03	— .51
Italian	.34	.73	1.06	.54	.44	.53	.54	.03	.60	.42
Japanese	.67	— .59	1.37	— .23	— .42	— .37	— .56	.63	— .62	.67
Jewish	2.72	1.40	1.86	2.36	.29	1.37	— .34	2.03	— .06	2.89
Mexican	.20	— .97	— .28	—1.17	—1.61	—1.34	—1.41	.08	—1.42	— .39
Negro	— .27	.19	—2.36	— .90	—1.56	—1.02	—1.79	.48	—1.87	.10
Filipino	— .29	—1.07	— .47	.97	—1.02	—1.02	— .96	.18	— .89	.46
Polish	— .70	.43	— .17	— .35	— .06	— .11	.74	— .60	.80	— .72
Puerto Rican	.27	—1.00	.10	—1.15	—1.32	—1.21	—1.47	.66	—1.40	.12
Russian	— .30	— .46	.01	— .10	.00	.12	.72	— .81	.72	.12
Swedish	.81	.15	.10	.29	.56	.39	1.16	—1.12	1.14	— .69
"Your own group"	— .92	1.47	—1.06	1.07	1.55	1.35	1.22	—1.41	1.09	— .74
N of judges	108	112	116	114	107	. . .	557	23	131	85

Scores in each column except the column headed "G" represent the departure of a given minority's mean rating from the mean of all means in the column, with the column standard deviation taken as the unit. The "G" scores are weighted sums based on corresponding scores in columns two, four, and five.

puted to that minority by a random one-fifth of our judges while its vertical position represents the relative social nearness allowed that minority by all of our judges.

It can be seen by visual inspection of Figure 1 that—for the sample of eighteen minorities—the two variables are *not related as stipulated by our hypothesis*. It is clear, however, that the two variables are *not simply uncorrelated*. Above the mean on the "social nearness" scale they are correlated negatively, consistent with the hypothesis, but below the social nearness mean the correlation is positive. In short, the relationship appears to be curvilinear over the range represented by these eighteen minorities.

In Figure 2, the same two variables are again related to each other, but the measurements here are based on the mean judgments of so-called "pure" respondents. These were defined as follows: judges who were white, Protestant, scoring below the median on the anti-Semitism scale, and not mentioning Jews when asked to list three groups of whom they were reminded by the description of the fictitious Ethnians. Within this group of "pure" judges, it was felt, the variance in the measures obtained for the eighteen minorities could not be readily attributed simply to the "prejudices" of the judges, since we have screened out the "prejudiced" judges before computing the means on which Figure 2 is based. The most striking feature of this scattergram is its general similarity to Figure 1. The same curvilinear relationship stands out, and when the "pure" measures of apparent ethnocentrism are correlated with the measures obtained from so-called "prejudiced" judges, we find a correlation of .879, signifi-

1. Correlation of Social Nearness with Ethnocentrism Imputed to Each of 18 Minorities by All Judges
2. Correlation of Social Nearness with Ethnocentrism Imputed to Each of 18 Minorities by White, Protestant, Non-stereotyping, Non-anti-semitic Judges

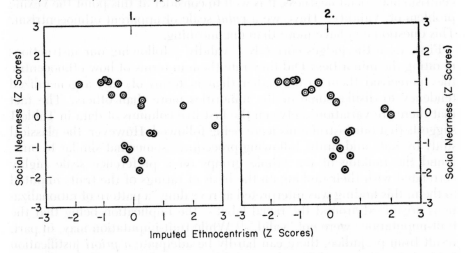

3. Correlation of Social Nearness with "Social Dominance G" Imputed to Each of 18 Minorities by All Judges
4. Correlation of Residual Social Nearness with Ethnocentrism Imputed to Each of 18 Minorities

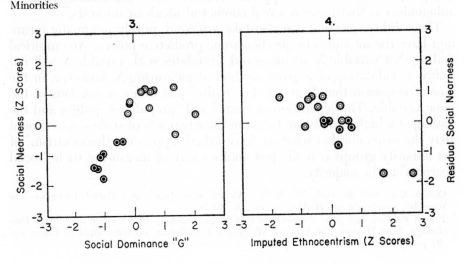

cant beyond the .01 level. That the screening of our judges in this fashion makes so little difference in the relative ethnocentrism scores of the eighteen rated minorities is evidence in support of our contention that minority groups can be psychometrically scaled like any other kind of stimuli. In the present instance we have scaled them on a continuum of apparent ethnocentrism. As in other studies, scaling other kinds of stimuli, the attitudes of our judges showed little interference with the judging task.

The Question of Validity

While the remainder of this paper is concerned with exploring the implications of this curvilinear relationship between apparent ethnocentrism and social nearness, it is well to consider at this point the vexing problem of "validity." Have we a *valid* scale of apparent ethnocentrism? This question can have more than one meaning.

First, were the judges correctly ("validly") following our instructions in rating the minorities? Did they rate them in terms of how ethnocentric they perceived them to be, rather than in terms of, say, a generalized tendency to dislike some of the minorities more than others? The fact that there are variations between the first five columns of data in Table 1 suggests that our instructions *were* being followed. However, the classical study by Katz and Braly, following procedures somewhat similar to ours, found the ranking of ten ethnic groups on a preference scale highly correlated with their ranking on the basis of ratings of the traits imputed to them; this finding was interpreted as revealing "a pattern of rationalizations organized around the racial label"—the implication being that the trait-imputations were not "valid." [11] While trait-imputation may, in part, result from prejudice, there can hardly be adequate *a priori* justification for ignoring the possibility that prejudice may also, in part, result from trait-imputation. Parsons, for one, has argued that scapegoating of one group by another "rarely appears without *some* 'reasonable' basis of antagonism in that there is a real conflict of ideals or interests." [12]

The validity question can also take a second, purely pragmatic meaning: have the measures in question some predictive power? An empirical finding that variable X, as measured, correlates with variable Y will not suffice as validation of a given method of measuring X, however, in the face of suspicion that X and Y are "really" just different versions of the same variable. The separation of "pure" and "prejudiced" judges and the finding of a high correlation between their two sets of scale scores should allay the suspicion that what we have called "apparent ethnocentrism" of the minority groups is really just another way of measuring their "social nearness" to the majority.

[11] Daniel Katz and Kenneth W. Braly, "Verbal Stereotypes and Racial Prejudice," in Maccoby, Newcomb, and Hartley, *op. cit.*, pp. 40-46.

[12] Talcott Parsons, *Religious Perspectives of College Teaching in Sociology and Social Psychology*, New Haven: The Edward W. Hagen Foundation, no date; cited in Coser, *op. cit.*, p. 40.

Closely related to this is a third interpretation of the validity question: does the chosen method of measuring variable X correlate with another (accepted) method of measuring the same variable? Guilford has stated that judges' ratings can rarely be validated in this manner. The usual practice, in fact, has been to use such ratings themselves "as the outside criterion against which to check the validity of a new test of ability or of personality." In thus validating newly constructed tests or scales, the "validity" of ratings is *assumed*.[13] If one feels reluctant to make that assumption in connection with the present study, it is the reluctance rather than the conventional assumption which needs to be examined and explained.

Finally, the question of validity can be taken to mean: do our measures of *apparent* ethnocentrism correlate with actual ethnocentric behavior by the minorities in question? It may not be necessary, of course, for a minority to be "actually" ethnocentric in order to appear ethnocentric. If apparent ethnocentrism evokes hostility it may do so regardless of the extent to which appearance reflects "reality." Nevertheless, it is meaningful to ask: do judges' ratings of the apparent ethnocentrism of a number of minority groups have any relationship to observable behavior by those minorities of a sort that can be labelled ethnocentric? It is precisely the unavailability of data on the "actual" ethnocentrism of a sufficient number of minorities which has led us to employ the psychometric method, but it is interesting to relate this method to some meager data that are available.

Rosen, in partial explanation of their different rates of social mobility, compared six racial and ethnic groups in regard to the "achievement syndrome," consisting of achievement motivation, achievement values, and vocational aspiration. Controlling for social class, significant differences were found among the six groups. It is not implausible to suppose that groups which differ on the achievement syndrome may also differ on "actual" as well as apparent ethnocentrism. It should be recalled that our judges rated the various minorities *in comparison with* fictitious Ethnians, whose description as highly ethnocentric people included the statement that "They constantly tried to prove their superiority by citing examples of members of their group who were famous in the arts, sciences, business, and politics." Thus our operational definition of apparent ethnocentrism is closely related, in content, to the achievement syndrome. Four of our minorities correspond with four of the six studied by Rosen, and there is about as close rank-order agreement between our measure of their apparent ethnocentrism and his measures of their achievement orientation as there is among his measures of the various components of that syndrome.[14]

Our description of ethnocentric behavior among Ethnians also included

[13] J. P. Guilford, *Psychometric Methods*, New York: McGraw-Hill, 1936, p. 279.
[14] Bernard C. Rosen, "Race, Ethnicity, and the Achievement Syndrome," *American Sociological Review*, 24 (February, 1959), pp. 47-60.

the statement, "They regarded it as a great loss of purity if one of their children married a non-Ethnian." Empirical intermarriage data, then, might offer some partial validation of our psychometric measure of apparent ethnocentrism. Heiss, in a study of religious intermarriage in Midtown Manhattan, provides data on 1167 marriages.[15] In our Table 1, Jews and Catholics, respectively, have the highest and next highest average rating for apparent ethnocentrism. If avoidance of intermarriage is a *major* ingredient in "actual" ethnocentrism, then we should expect to find (if apparent and "actual" ethnocentrism correspond) a very high degree of such avoidance among Jews, a rather high degree among Catholics, and rather less among others, i.e., Protestants. According to the data reported by Heiss, 18.4 per cent of his Jewish respondents were intermarried, compared with 21.4 per cent of the Catholic respondents and 33.9 per cent of the Protestant respondents. By themselves, however, these figures tell us nothing of the *avoidance* of intermarriage. Depending on marginal proportions, such figures *could* result from non-assortative mating in a mixed population. The Heiss data also show that among the 1167 spouses of his respondents, 86.1 per cent were non-Jewish, 48.1 per cent were non-Catholic, and 67.2 per cent were non-Protestant. These figures represent maximum potential intermarriage rates for Jews, Catholics, and Protestants, respectively, if marriage were unselective within this marriage "pool." By subtracting the actual intermarriage rate from the maximum potential rate, and dividing the difference by the maximum potential, we get an index that varies between zero and unity and denotes the proportion of possible intermarriages not contracted by respondents of a given faith. For Jews this index is .79, for Catholics it is .56, and for Protestants it is .48. Thus the rank order of "intermarriage avoidance" among these three groups corresponds with the rank order of apparent ethnocentrism.

With these very meager data, then, it can be suggested that apparent ethnocentrism as measured in the present study probably corresponds to some extent with actual ethnocentric behavior by the various minority groups. Even if this were not so it would remain a legitimate sociological problem to investigate the consequences of a group's *appearing* ethnocentric.

The Search for Explanation

On two counts the curvilinear relationship between apparent ethnocentrism and social nearness demands explanation. First, if it is true that the bulk of the sociological literature on minority-majority relations neglects minority behavior as a factor in the development of majority hostility, any finding that indicates these two variables are *not unrelated* would merit further investigation regardless of the shape of their relationship. But in addition, a curvilinear relationship is especially interesting

[15] Jerold S. Heiss, "Premarital Characteristics of the Religiously Intermarried in an Urban Area," *American Sociological Review*, 25 (February, 1960), p. 49.

because it suggests that a third variable may be interacting somehow with the two in question.

In quest of this third variable it was helpful to consider an analogous relationship between two variables in another science. Recalling that the volume of a given quantity of water decreases as it cools, down to 4° C., after which it increases again until the freezing point is reached, the reader can perhaps visualize a graph on which density is plotted against temperature. The relationship would be curvilinear, with the maximum density occurring at 4° C. Physics textbooks refer to "the anomalous expansion of water" in the temperature range on either side of this point,[16] and the anomaly has helped reveal a great deal about the molecular structure of water and processes in the change of that structure. It appears that the otherwise natural tendency for density to increase continuously with decreasing temperature is "masked by expansion due to the formation of . . . polymerised molecules"[17] (H_6O_3 or H_4O_2 instead of H_2O). Throughout the range of temperature at which water exists in a liquid state, two opposing processes appear to be affecting its density: the density of water tends to decrease as a result of thermal expansion as temperature *rises;* the density of water tends to decrease as a result of polymerization as temperature *falls.* The two processes are continuous and just happen to balance each other at 4° C.

Perhaps, analogously, there is a "masking" effect in the relationship between social nearness and apparent minority ethnocentrism. Our hypothesis asserts that as apparent ethnocentrism rises social nearness will decrease (negative correlation). This is true over the upper half of the range which we have observed on the social nearness scale. Is it "masked" in the lower half of the observed range by an opposite relationship of social nearness to a third variable? Our search for an explanation for our curvilinear finding is thus directed toward some attribute *other than ethnocentrism* which, while not necessarily correlated with ethnocentrism, at least does vary in a sample of minorities showing varied apparent ethnocentrism, and thus *can* be positively correlated with social nearness.

It was possible to construct such a variable with data obtained from three other sub-sets of judges in the present study. Lundberg had originally hypothesized that majority hostility would be aroused not only by ethnocentric minorities but also by minorities (1) that were disproportionately influential politically, (2) that held a monopoly of high-status jobs, or (3) that enjoyed undue special privileges and immunities.[18] Our

[16] See, for example, Francis Weston Sears and Mark W. Zemansky, *University Physics* (2nd ed.), Reading, Mass.: Addison-Wesley Publishing Co., 1955, p. 266.

[17] P. C. L. Thorne and E. R. Roberts, *Inorganic Chemistry* (4th ed.), New York: Nordeman Publishing Co., 1943, p. 398. It is worth noting, incidentally, that whereas density is a physical property of water, its anomalous relation to temperature (another *physical* variable) has to be explained *chemically.* This is a case in point against the kind of disciplinary boundary rigidity on which Durkheim insisted. See Emile Durkheim, *Rules of the Sociological Method,* Glencoe, Ill.: The Free Press, 1950, pp. 110-111.

[18] Lundberg, *op. cit.,* pp. 290-291.

eighteen minorities were rated on each of these variables by one-fifth of the judges (see Table 1 for the resulting scale scores). In each case, however, the variable that was hypothesized to be provocative of majority hostility turned out instead to be *positively* correlated with social nearness (two of the three correlations being significant at the .05 level).[19] It was decided, therefore, to capitalize on this rejection of three of Lundberg's hypotheses by combining these three variables into a general measure of "social dominance." Intercorrelations between the three were computed (see Table 2). From these intercorrelations it was possible to

TABLE 2. INTERCORRELATIONS, G-FACTOR SATURATIONS, AND G-FACTOR
REGRESSION WEIGHTS OF 3 VARIABLES FOR 18 MINORITIES

	Economic Monopoly	Political Influence	Special Privilege
Economic monopoly	....	.885	.799
Political influence	.885	....	.797
Special privilege	.799	.797	....
r_{ig}	.942	.849	.940
Regression weight	.433	.158	.421

solve for the "saturations" of the three variables with a Spearman *general factor*. From these saturations, regression weights were obtained which enabled the three variables to be combined into a "Social Dominance G" score for each minority.[20]

In Figure 3 it can be readily seen that there is a high positive correlation between "Social Dominance G" and social nearness for our sample of eighteen minorities. For all eighteen minorities this correlation is .710, significant at the .01 level. It is *possible*, therefore, that the hypothesized negative correlation between apparent ethnocentrism and social nearness is indeed partly "masked" by this third variable. To see that it is not only possible but also *likely*, consider the way the minorities cluster together in all three scattergrams. In each case the seven minorities which rate lowest on social nearness can be seen to stand out as a more or less separate cluster. Which minorities are these? They happen to be the ones which would be popularly designated as "colored."

[19] For a more detailed account of the rejection of these other hypotheses, see Sung Chick Hong, "Majority Perception of Minority Behavior and Its Relationship to Hostility Toward Ethnic Minorities: A Test of George A. Lundberg's Hypotheses," unpublished Ph.D. thesis, Seattle: University of Washington Library, 1959.

[20] See Godfrey Thomson, *The Factorial Analysis of Human Ability* (5th ed.), New York: Houghton Mifflin, 1951, Ch. 1, 4, and 15. These computations were possible only for the measures obtained from the unscreened sets of judges. Measures obtained from the "pure" judges resulted in a "Heywood case" wherein one variable has a G-factor saturation greater than unity. It seems probable that this absurdity resulted in the present instance from the instability introduced into our measures when means based on *reduced numbers* of judges were calculated. For scaling the three variables in question, there were only 28, 25, and 27 "pure" judges respectively.

Let us examine this cluster of seven minorities separately from the other eleven. (To facilitate this they have been set off in the three scattergrams with a shaded center dot in their respective circles; the other eleven groups each have white center dots in their respective circles.)

When we restrict the range to include the seven "colored" minorities only, the correlation between "Social Dominance G" and social nearness remains high; it is .780 which is significant at the .05 level. Ordinarily, of course, to restrict the range of a variable tends to reduce its correlation with another variable; in the present instance that did not happen. Among the other eleven groups, however, the correlation is −.266, not significantly different from zero.

By contrast, the correlation between apparent ethnocentrism and social nearness breaks down in just the reverse fashion. Among the seven "colored" groups it is not significantly different from zero (being only .449), whereas among the remaining eleven groups the correlation is in accord with our hypothesis, −.918, significant at the .01 level.

It can be said, then, that the *positive* correlation between "Social Dominance G" and social nearness (which is found to hold over the entire range observed in this study) is *predominant* for the seven low-status "colored" minorities, while the *negative* correlation between apparent ethnocentrism and social nearness is *predominant* for the remaining eleven (higher-status) minorities. The effect of apparent ethnocentrism on social nearness is "masked" over that part of the observed range where "Social Dominance G" is most strongly related to social nearness, and vice versa.

What is the relationship between social nearness and apparent ethnocentrism when the "masking" effect of "Social Dominance G" is removed? From inspection of Figure 3 it can be seen that the regression of social nearness on "Social Dominance G" can be fairly well approximated by a linear equation in which the intercept is zero and the slope is unity. Thus, by the simple expedient of subtracting the "Social Dominance G" scores from the social nearness scores in Table 1, we can obtain a set of "residual social nearness" scores. Their variation measures the variation in social nearness not "accounted for" by variation in "Social Dominance G." By plotting these residual social nearness scores against the apparent ethnocentrism scores, we can learn the shape of the "unmasked" relation between social nearness and apparent ethnocentrism. This is shown in Figure 4. It is clearly negative in slope over the entire range and is approximately linear.

Conclusions

It would not be quite correct to say that these operations have now confirmed the hypothesis with which this study began. Rather, through the serendipitous discovery of the "masking" phenomenon, we have been able to modify the hypothesis. Our data seem to show that *after social dominance has been taken into account,* the appearance of ethnocentrism in minorities is a *further* factor in the development of majority hostility. Further research is still needed, of course, to determine more fully to what extent *apparent* ethnocentrism depends on actual ethnocentric behavior among minorities. In view of the high correlation between scale scores obtained from "pure" judges and from "prejudiced" judges in the present study, it would hardly seem prudent to dismiss "apparent ethnocentrism" from further sociological consideration by *assuming* it to be unrelated to "real" ethnocentric behavior.

If the present study were to be replicated with another sample of N "minorities" (e.g., a set of occupational categories such as "lawyers," "bricklayers," "surgeons," "truckdrivers," "optometrists," etc.), we predict that social nearness would be found to be negatively correlated with apparent ethnocentrism among those groups rated high in "Social Dominance G" but positively correlated among those groups rated low in "Social Dominance G." Such a prediction is based on the hypothesis that the racial (or "color") distinction on which we based our partitioning of the scattergrams in the present study was not an intrinsic dichotomy but was only a convenient index of the equilibrium point between two opposing influences (analogous to the 4° C. point of maximum water density). With another sample of minorities—occupationally rather than ethnically distinguished from each other[21]—the equilibrium point (represented by the bend in the curve in Figure 1) might be displaced upward or downward, just as with "heavy water" (deuterium oxide) maximum density occurs at 11.6° instead of 4° C. Except for such displacement, however, it is our expectation that the variables would again exhibit a similar relationship, with two opposing processes "masking" each other. We expect that the "unmasked" relationship between social nearness and apparent ethnocentrism would again be negative and approximately linear, as in Figure 4.

If such replications of this study continued to produce this pattern of findings, it seems to us that this would have important implications for certain social action organizations. The results of the study reported in the present paper support the statement that however functional ethnocentrism may be within the group, for a group to appear ethnocentric entails measurable costs in intergroup relations. Socially dominant groups do not escape this dilemma but rather are particularly subject to being penalized for the appearance of ethnocentric behavior. Perhaps groups which are patently subject to discrimination (i.e., are not dominant) are thus in a position to strive for better treatment without thereby seeming ethnocentric to the same degree as groups which are already well off and seeking to consolidate or increase their advantages.

The minority "defense agencies" often seem to base their policies

---

[21] In the present sample of minorities we have confounded at least the following three attributes: race or color, nationality, and religion. By careful inspection of the scattergrams herein presented, the reader can perhaps make tentative inferences as to the manner in which each of these attributes may separately influence the relations between apparent ethnocentrism, "Social Dominance G," and social nearness.

(quite understandably) on the assumption that the roots of prejudice lie in majority pathology or majority ignorance. A favorite technique for striving for better treatment for a minority is to publicize its virtues and accomplishments, to prove that it is not inferior to the majority at whose hands it suffers discrimination.[22] However true such publicity may be, the present study suggests that its impact on majority attitudes may often be just the opposite of what is intended. If such publicity creates the impression that the minority being defended is ethnocentric, this impression might actually aggravate majority antipathy. The further possibility that such publicity might tend to increase the "actual" ethnocentrism of the minority in question, as well as its apparent ethnocentrism, deserves investigation too. The "self-fulfilling prophecy" may cut both ways.

[22] Of the research on intergroup relations "a high proportion has been concerned with the causes of prejudice and discrimination, relatively little with the strategies that are effective, in specific situations, in reducing them. There is great need for more of the latter." Simpson and Yinger, *op. cit.*, p. 806.

─────────Ruby Jo Reeves Kennedy

Single or Triple Melting-Pot?
Intermarriage Trends in New Haven, 1870-1940

· ·

Most authorities on population problems agree that intermarriage is the surest means of assimilation and the most infallible index of its occurrence. America has long been described as a great and bottomless melting-pot into which have been thrown peoples from all parts of the world. Boiling and seething there together, they will, it is believed, ultimately lose all distinguishable marks of their diverse backgrounds; and some fine day American society will become one homogeneous group—a single amalgam blended of the many and varied types brought to our shores by the great waves of immigration of the past century. "Here individuals of all nations are melted into a new race of man, whose labours and posterity will one day cause great changes in the world." [1] This blending-together, this ironing-out of cultural disparities, is, in the final stages, to be accomplished through intermarriage.

Speculations concerning the actual amount of intermarriage which has already taken place are mostly impressionistic, for too few statistical studies have been made to warrant valid generalizations.

The present study set out to investigate what has actually been happening with reference to intermarriage in New Haven, Connecticut, for

[1] J. Hector de Crèvecœur, *Letters from an American Farmer* (London, 1782), quoted in C. Wittke, *We Who Built America* (New York: Prentice-Hall, 1940), p. 42.

Reprinted by permission of *The American Journal of Sociology*, Vol. XLIX, January, 1944, pp. 331-339. Copyright, 1944, The University of Chicago. All rights reserved.

the last seventy years. Records of 9,044 marriages in New Haven were examined; and those of 1870, 1900, 1930, and 1940 were isolated for detailed scrutiny. Marriages increased from 920 in 1870 to 1,770 in 1900, to 2,538 in 1930, and to 3,816 in 1940. Our fundamental interest is in discovering whether general intermarriage or stratified intermarriage is taking place, that is, whether intermarriage is producing a complete mixture or several layers of mixture. In short, is American society really a single melting-pot or one with two or more separate compartments, each producing a special blend of its own?

Full investigation of this highly important problem involves the answering of a series of questions, so that no possibly significant factor may be neglected. These questions and their best order of treatment, in our opinion, are as follows:

1. To what extent do individuals marry within their own culture group? [2] Which groups seem least and which most inclined to in-marriage? Is ethnic endogamy becoming more or less prevalent with the passage of time? What variations appear between the several ethnic groups in this regard? Do the sexes differ in their behavior on any of these points?

2. When out-marriage does occur, is group preference discernible? That is, when individuals of any ethnic group marry out, do they demonstrate pronounced likes and dislikes for specified other groups? What reasons can be discovered for these preferences?

3. How does religious affiliation influence tendencies toward in- or out-marriage?

Taking up the first set of questions, we find that ethnic endogamy has been customary in New Haven for the last threescore and ten years. The partners in more than two-thirds (69.23 per cent) of all couples during this period were of the same national derivation. The in-marriage rate, however, though high throughout, shows a steady decline from 91.20 per cent in 1870 to 75.93 per cent in 1900, to 65.80 in 1930, and to 63.64 per cent in 1940. The slackening rate of decrease after 1930 may indicate that a relatively permanent pattern of ethnic endogamy has now been established.

Although in-marriage has declined, it still continues to be an important determinant in the selection of mates, as is indicated by its high rate in 1940. Moreover, through the years the tendency toward in-marriage has remained stronger and more persistent in some groups than in others. Seven white ethnic stocks figure importantly in the composition of New Haven's population.[3] Five of these—Jews, Italians, British-Americans,

---

[2] Interracial marriages (Negro-white) are negligible, constituting less than one-tenth of 1 per cent of the total cases: none in 1870 and 1900, 2 in 1930, 3 in 1940.

[3] In 1930, of a total population of 163,000: Italians, 50,000; Irish, 35,000; Jews, 25,000; British-Americans, 20,000; Germans, 10,000; Poles, 6,000; Scandinavians, 3,500. Negroes number 5,300.

Irish, and Poles—have steadily maintained high in-marriage rates, while two—Germans and Scandinavians—have shown pronounced tendencies toward exogamy (see Table 1).

The in-marriage rates of males and females during this seventy-year period have been remarkably similar. The decline has been virtually the same for both—from 91.74 in 1870 to 63.12 per cent in 1940 for grooms, and from 90.65 in 1870 to 63.66 per cent in 1940 for brides. However, sex differentials do appear among some of the ethnic groups. British-American, Jewish, and Italian brides have shown a stronger tendency than their male counterparts to marry within the group, whereas the contrary is true of the Irish and Poles. Among Germans and Scandinavians no sex differences appear in the in-marriage rates (see Table 1).

TABLE 1. PERCENTAGE DISTRIBUTION OF IN-MARRIAGE BY NATIONAL
ORIGIN GROUPS, 1870, 1900, 1930, 1940

	Total	1870	1900	1930	1940	Males 1870-1940	Females 1870-1940
Jewish	94.72	100.00	98.92	95.00	93.70	94.14	97.93
Italian	85.12	....	97.71	86.71	81.89	78.92	84.96
British-American	67.50	92.31	72.00	58.82	54.56	63.12	68.59
Irish	64.53	93.05	74.75	74.25	45.06	69.41	60.59
Polish	57.71	....	100.00	68.04	52.78	61.43	53.80
German	47.44	86.67	55.26	39.84	27.19	45.24	45.66
Scandinavian	42.65	40.00	82.76	33.73	18.46	41.51	41.90
Total	69.23	91.20	75.93	65.80	63.64	....	....
Male	69.41	91.74	75.45	65.85	63.12	....	....
Female	69.44	90.65	76.41	65.75	63.66	....	....

This leads us to the second set of queries posed at the beginning of this paper, i.e., those having to do with group preferences in out-marriage. We find that the five largest nationality groups in New Haven represent a triple division on religious grounds: Jewish, Protestant (British-American, German, and Scandinavian), and Catholic (Irish, Italian, and Polish). Whether single or multiple mixture is occurring in New Haven may be discovered by an analysis of preferential marriage groups chosen by persons marrying "out." Thus if Irish, Italians, and Poles (all mainly Catholic nationalities) marry mostly among these same three groups, while British-Americans, Germans, and Scandinavians (all mainly Protestant nationalities) marry mostly among themselves, then we shall have good proof that assimilation through intermarriage is occurring along three vertical lines—Jewish, Catholic, and Protestant—and not generally and indiscriminately. We shall, in other words, be able to state that, *while strict endogamy is loosening, religious endogamy is persisting and the future cleavages will be along religious lines rather than along nationality lines as in the past.* If this is the case, then the traditional "single-melting-pot" idea must be abandoned, and a new conception, which we term the "triple-melting-pot" theory of American assimilation, will take its place as the true expression of what is happening to the various nationality groups in the United States. This is the hypothesis which we believe the present paper proves true.

Intermarriage is indeed of the triple-melting-pot variety in New Haven. In 1870, 99.11 per cent; in 1900, 90.86 per cent; in 1930, 78.19 per cent; and in 1940, 79.72 per cent of the British-Americans, Germans, and Scandinavians intermarried among themselves. Likewise, in 1870, 95.35 per cent; in 1900, 85.78 per cent; in 1930, 82.05 per cent; and in 1940, 83.71 per cent of the Irish, Italians, and Poles chose mates from among themselves. The Jews are the most endogamous of all groups except Negroes. In the rare instances when they do marry out, they prefer British-Americans, Germans, and Scandinavians (non-Catholics) to Irish, Italians, and Poles (Catholics) (see Table 2).

TABLE 2. PERCENTAGE DISTRIBUTION OF INTERMARRIAGE ACCORDING
TO RELIGIOUS SIMILARITY AND DISSIMILARITY, 1870-1940

Year	British-American, Scandinavian, German	Italian, Irish, Polish	Jewish
1870:			
Protestant	99.11	4.65	
Catholic	0.89	95.35	
Jewish			100.00
1900:			
Protestant	90.86	14.22	1.18
Catholic	8.00	85.78	
Jewish	0.14		98.82
1930:			
Protestant	78.19	17.68	1.70
Catholic	21.36	82.05	1.29
Jewish	0.45	0.27	97.01
1940:			
Protestant	79.72	11.52	3.62
Catholic	18.80	83.71	2.06
Jewish	1.48	4.77	94.32

The fact that the intermarriage rate among Irish, Italians, and Poles in 1870 and 1900 was lower than that among the three non-Catholic groups was owing to the virtual absence of Italians and Poles in New Haven in those years. Since the Irish constituted virtually all the Catholics in the city in 1870 and 1900, any non-Irish mates they chose were, perforce, Protestants. In later years the rate of endogamy within the three Catholic groups exceeded that within the three non-Catholic groups (1930—Protestants, 78.19 per cent, Catholics, 82.05 per cent; 1940— Protestants, 79.12 per cent, Catholics, 83.71 per cent). This would seem to indicate the apparent eagerness of the Irish to secure Catholic mates even at the cost of marrying into recently arrived groups with relatively low social prestige.

Wessel says that the scarcity of marriages between Irish and Italians in Stamford, Connecticut, is owing to the lower social status of the latter group; and on the basis of this explanation she remarks: "We find elsewhere that continued residence in America is necessary to wipe out cultural differences. It may indeed wipe out religious differences too." [4] Our material causes us to believe that the latter is not happening in New Haven. Cultural lines may fade, but religious barriers are holding fast. As the Italians have gained residential tenure (and economic prestige) in this city, their marriages with the Irish have rapidly increased, rising from 7.8 per cent in 1900 to 10.4 per cent in 1930 and to 19.8 per cent in 1940.

In New Haven there has also been an increase, though not so marked, in Irish-Polish marriages, from 2.83 per cent in 1930 to 5.88 per cent in 1940. We regard the lower rate of Irish-Polish as compared with Irish-Italian marriages as owing primarily to the greater number of Italians. The relatively lower economic status of the Poles may also be a factor.

While, as has been shown, the Irish, Italians, and Poles show a pronounced tendency to intermarry among themselves, a fair number of them marry into other groups (see Table 2). The same is true of the British-Americans, Germans, and Scandinavians. Noteworthy is the fact, however, that in both instances the rate of marriage outside the religious boundary has remained relatively unchanged for the last decade; if anything, there has been a slight movement in the other direction.

This indication of the correctness of our hypothesis led us next to examine the specific groups with whom intermarriage occurred. If out-groups preferences are based upon religious similarities, as we have suggested, then certain marked likes and dislikes should appear in the vari-

TABLE 3. RANK-ORDER DISTRIBUTION OF EXPECTED AND ACTUAL
PREFERENTIAL MARRIAGE GROUPS, 1870, 1900, 1930, 1940

	Irish	British-American	German	Scandinavian	Italian	Polish
Expected	Ir, It, P, G, Br-A, Sc	Br-A, G, Sc, Ir, It, P	G, Br-A, Sc, Ir, It, P	Sc, Br-A, G, Ir, It, P	It, Ir, P, G, Br-A, Sc	P, It, Ir, G, Br-A, Sc
Actual 1870	Ir, Br-A, G, Sc	Br-A, G, Ir, Sc	G, Br-A, Ir	Sc, Br-A, Ir	It	....
1900	Ir, Br-A, G, Sc	Br-A, Ir, G, Sc	G, Br-A, Ir, Sc	Sc, Br-A, G, Ir	It, Ir, G	P
1930	Ir, Br-A, G, It, Sc, P	Br-A, Ir, G, Sc, It, P	G, Br-A, Ir, Sc, It, P	Sc, Br-A, G, Ir	It, Ir, Br-A, G, P, Sc	P, Br-A, It, Ir, G
1940	Ir, Br-A, It, G, P, Sc	Br-A, Ir, G, It, P, Sc	Br-A, G, Ir, It, P, Sc	Br-A, Sc, Ir, P, It, G	It, Br-A, Ir, P, G	P, It, Br-A, G, Ir

ous intermarriage rates. Table 3 compares the "expected" preferences and the actual preferences (in rank order) for each year and each group.

This table, by itself, would seem to throw doubt upon our hypothesis that religious preference rules out-marriage choice. The Irish, for in-

[4] B. B. Wessel, *An Ethnic Survey of Woonsocket, Rhode Island* (Chicago: University of Chicago Press, 1931), p. 150.

stance, next to marrying themselves, should have preferred Italians and Poles, who are predominately Catholic. Instead, through the years they have given second preference to British-Americans and have also favored Germans over Poles, who are Catholic almost without exception. Therefore, in the case of the Irish we raise this query: Why so many marriages with British-Americans and Germans and so few with Poles? Again, British-Americans deviated from expectation in several instances, particularly in their marked tendency to choose Irish as marriage mates.

Seeking explanations for these and the other irregularities disclosed in Table 3, we analyzed all marriages according to the type of ceremony used to sanction them (see Table 4).

TABLE 4. PERCENTAGE DISTRIBUTION OF PREDOMINANT TYPE
OF CEREMONY FOR IN- AND OUT-MARRIAGES OF THE
SIX MAJOR GROUPS, 1870, 1900, 1930, 1940

YEAR	PER CENT CATHOLIC			PER CENT NON-CATHOLIC			PER CENT HEBREW
	Irish	Italian	Polish	British-American	German	Scandinavian	Jewish
	In-marriage						
1870	93.18	....	....	98.94	86.54	100.00	100.00
1900	93.01	90.93	100.00	100.00	88.89	100.00	100.00
1930	90.90	80.76	69.84	91.56	83.67	92.85	99.58
1940	94.78	85.04	75.00	79.83	83.86	100.00	75.96
	Out-marriage						
1870	55.00	....	....	94.12	73.33	66.67	....
1900	54.33	33.33	....	78.72	79.80	90.00	....
1930	67.77	56.25	58.06	57.34	60.81	83.63	77.77
1940	71.41	62.44	54.41	56.43	57.82	83.01	35.71

Catholic nuptials have sanctioned the majority of Italian, Irish, and Polish in-marriages from 1870 to 1940, while non-Catholic (Protestant or civil) ceremonies have predominated among the in-marriages of British-Americans, Germans, and Scandinavians. Virtually all the Jewish in-marriages from 1870 to 1930 were solemnized by rabbis (see Table 4). The drop from 99.58 per cent in 1930 to 75.96 per cent in 1940 of Jewish services for Jewish in-marriages is almost entirely owing to civil ceremonies. This may indicate a marked movement away from the synagogue and its traditional ritual among the Jews. But our material emphatically does not suggest an appreciable decrease in Jewish endogamy. Table 4 also shows that Catholic ceremonies predominate in the out-marriages of Poles, Italians, and Irish and are increasing in the latter two groups. Likewise, more than half of the out-marriages of the British-Americans, Germans, and Scandinavians since 1870 have been sanctioned by non-Catholic services. It is clear, thus, that religion is an important factor in marriage, whether endogamous or exogamous.

While it is true that Italians, Irish, and Poles often marry British-Americans, Germans, and Scandinavians, the majority of such unions are sanctioned by Catholic nuptials. Thus the Irish, in choosing more British-American and German than Italian and Polish spouses, are not giving up Catholicism at all but are bringing over increasingly large proportions of these non-Catholics to their church (in the case of the British-Americans from 48.14 per cent in 1900 to 73.52 per cent in 1940). "Bringing over" is what really happens, for the non-Catholic partners to such unions must promise that offspring born to them will be brought up in the Catholic faith. While the person immediately involved need not actually become a convert, he does so vicariously, through his children.

It would seem that marriage with either British-Americans or Germans is more desirable to the Irish than marriage with Italians or Poles because the former two groups are older, more firmly established residents of New Haven, and enjoy greater social status and economic security than the more recently arrived immigrants. Especially desirable, it would appear, is marriage with the British-Americans, because they, though not the largest group in the city,[5] represent the ideal of assimilation sought by all other ethnic groups. Therefore the Irish, by marrying British-Americans in Catholic ceremonies, accomplish the twofold purpose of blending into the dominant culture group and at the same time preserving their own religious heritage as typified by the use of Catholic nuptials. Marriage with Italians and Poles, on the other hand, satisfies only the second of these desires.

The pattern of Irish preferential out-groups continued unchanged until 1930, when Italians slipped in ahead of Scandinavians; while in 1940 Italians moved up again ahead of Germans, and Poles superseded Scandinavians. This breakdown of an old pattern seems to indicate the willingness of the Irish to marry Italians and Poles (Catholics) in preference to Germans and Scandinavians, but not in preference to British-Americans, who represent the epitome of "real American" culture. Still, even in this case, the Irish win the better of a compromise by bringing over to their church as many as possible of these non-Catholics, a practice which is increasing with the passage of time (see Table 5).

The Italians and Poles also would probably prefer British-American, German, and Scandinavian spouses if such marriages did not involve giving up Catholicism. But, being of recent immigrant origin, still bearing many foreign characteristics, and standing very low on the scale of social status, they are far less successful than the Irish in bringing over the older, Protestant groups to their church in marriage. The Italians and Poles have much less to offer in the way of social prestige and economic security than the Irish, and their general standard of living is still considerably lower than that of the older groups.

The Irish, however, have advanced swiftly since their arrival as starving émigrés in the middle of the last century. As a matter of fact, were it not for their firm adherence to Catholicism, the Irish would long ago have merged into and become a part of the dominant culture group.

[5] With their 20,000 members they are the third largest group in the city.

TABLE 5. PERCENTAGE DISTRIBUTION OF OUT-MARRIAGES ACCORDING TO TYPE OF RELIGIOUS CEREMONY, 1870, 1900, 1930, 1940

GROUPS	Catholic				Non-Catholic			
	1870	1900	1930	1940	1870	1900	1930	1940
Irish with:								
Italian		100.00	72.73	78.72			27.27	21.28
Polish			83.33	71.42			16.67	28.58
British-American	11.11	48.14	69.30	73.52	88.89	51.86	30.70	26.48
German	100.00	44.45	65.21	75.60		55.55	34.79	24.40
Scandinavian	100.00		14.30	16.67		100.00	85.70	83.33
Jewish								
Italian with:								
Polish			50.00	75.61			50.00	24.39
British-American			26.32	50.68		100.00	73.68	49.32
German	100.00		58.34	47.85		100.00	41.66	52.15
Scandinavian				50.00			100.00	50.00
Jewish								
Polish with:								
British-American			37.50	36.58			62.50	63.42
German			100.00	62.50				37.50
Scandinavian				25.00				75.00
Jewish								
British-American with:								
German		12.20	32.69	31.95	100.00	87.80	67.31	68.05
Scandinavian			18.51	11.11	100.00	100.00	81.49	88.89
Jewish								
German with:								
Scandinavian			33.33	8.33			66.67	91.67
Jewish								100.00
Scandinavian with:								
Jewish								

GROUPS	Jewish				Non-Jewish			
	1870	1900	1930	1940	1870	1900	1930	1940
Jewish with:								
Irish				33.33			100.00	66.67
Italian			100.00					100.00
Polish			100.00					100.00
British-American		100.00	100.00	50.00				50.00
German			100.00	100.00				
Scandinavian								

Many authorities have recognized and stressed the effect of Catholicism upon the character and degree of Irish assimilation.

Woofter says that prejudice "has shifted from Germans to Irish, from Scandinavians to South Europeans. The despised alien of yesterday becomes the 100 per cent American of today and joins the native-born in scorn of freshly arrived nationals." [6] Part of the Irishmen's rapid absorption of American culture was undoubtedly due to the fact that they, unlike all other non-British immigrants, encountered no language difficulty, for, as one authority says, "ignorance of our language is an important barrier to assimilation. . . . Generally speaking, adherence to a foreign language within a country tends to cocoon an ethnic group and keep it alien." [7]

On the other hand, it is understandable that the southern and eastern

[6] T. J. Woofter, *Races and Ethnic Groups in American Life* (New York: McGraw-Hill Book Co., 1933), p. 207.

[7] W. S. Smith, *Americans in the Making* (New York: D. Appleton-Century Co., 1939), pp. 147-48.

European immigrants, with recent peasant backgrounds and strange languages, as well as Catholic religion, do not make very eligible or desirable marriage partners for the groups already long settled and well established in New Haven. There is, in other words, nothing much in their favor from the viewpoint of the British-Americans. However, their Catholicism does appeal to the Irish and to some extent to the Germans, a minority of whom are Catholic themselves. We can note the consequence of this situation in the fact that, until 1940, Italians selected Irish mates in preference to any other outsiders. In that year, however, they married more British-Americans than Irish (see Table 3). Nevertheless, although the proportion of Catholic nuptials sanctioning marriages of Italians with British-Americans increased from 26.32 per cent in 1930 to 50.68 per cent in 1940, these are far lower than the corresponding proportions of Catholic weddings in unions of Irish and British-Americans, which reached 69.30 per cent in 1930 and 73.52 per cent in 1940 (see Table 5). Therefore, it looks as though the Italians are not only less influential than the Irish in "bringing over" British-Americans to their church but also more willing to surrender on this point and participate in non-Catholic ceremonies. It may be a matter of temporarily slighting religious conviction in favor of assimilation, as the Irish were probably doing back in 1900, when less than half (48.14 per cent) of their unions with British-Americans were sanctioned by Catholic nuptials. Perhaps, as the Italians advance economically, become more Americanized, and therefore more eligible marriage partners, they, too, will be in a stronger position to demand Catholic services of their non-Catholic mates. The increasing rate of Catholic services for Italian out-marriages (from 56.25 per cent in 1930 to 62.44 per cent in 1940) indicates that this trend is already under way (see Table 4). Decreasing Italian-German and Italian-Scandinavian marriages and increasing Italian-Polish unions suggest that the Italians, like the Irish, probably prefer Catholic to non-Catholic mates, even though they will often sacrifice this desire for the sake of marriage with British-Americans.

Not until 1930 did Poles marry non-Poles in any appreciable numbers. In that year their preferential marriage groups were British-Americans, Irish, and Italians; in 1940, unions with Italians exceeded those with British-Americans, while the Irish dropped below the Germans. The increase of Polish-Italian marriages may be attributed to the similarity of the two groups in religion, economic status, and length of residence in America. The Irish, however, differ from the Poles in all respects excepting religion. The fact that Catholic nuptials sanction fewer in- as well as out-marriages among the Poles than in the case of either the Irish or the Italians may be interpreted as indicating weaker allegiance to Catholicism on the part of the Poles. If this is true, then it seems quite probable, as their economic and social status in New Haven improves, that they will show a stronger tendency to intermarry with British-Americans, Germans, and Scandinavians than either the Irish or the

Italians, who are evidently much more insistent upon Catholic wedding services.

Although there is a strong—and a slightly increasing—tendency for British-Americans, Scandinavians, and Germans to marry among themselves, an examination of the specific groups with whom they intermarry raises this question: Why do they marry so many Irish, Italians, and Poles? British-Americans have consistently given first and second preference in out-marriage to Irish and Germans, respectively, since 1870; while Scandinavians held third place until 1940, when they were superseded by Italians and Poles (see Table 3). The preferential groups of the Germans and Scandinavians have been virtually the same as those of the British-Americans (see Table 3).

British-Americans, Germans, Scandinavians, and Irish are the oldest, the economically most progressive, and the socially most prominent groups in New Haven's population. S. Koenig in a recent study of ethnic groups in Connecticut industry comments:

> The analysis demonstrates quite definitely the superior position held by certain groups, notably the British-Americans, in Connecticut industry. The latter clearly predominate in the most remunerative fields and position. The groups from northern and western Europe, namely, the Irish, Swedes, and Germans, and to some extent, the French-Canadians, as a rule, tend to gravitate towards jobs generally offering greater security and higher remuneration. On the other hand, the groups who originally came from eastern and southern Europe, namely, the Poles, Lithuanians, Ukrainians, and Italians, tend to be in fields usually requiring less skill and to occupy positions offering less security, remuneration, and status. . . . In general, it may be said, that aside from the British-Americans, who undoubtedly appear as the leaders in industry, those groups which have been here longest or have become more acculturated have reached a higher level in the occupational ladder, at least insofar as industry is concerned.[8]

New Haven was one of the six cities included in Koenig's survey. Thus, on economic and social grounds, it would be surprising indeed were British-Americans, German, and Scandinavians not to intermarry with the Irish, whose only important point of divergence from themselves is religion. The increasing tendency of the older groups to marry Italians is probably owing in a large part to sheer numerical pressure, since the Italians constitute a third of New Haven's population. The British-Americans who marry Italians probably do not represent the most prosperous and socially secure members of this group. Evidence for this statement is found in another New Haven study which revealed that in both 1930 and 1940 Italians showed a marked tendency to "neighborhood" marriage, i.e., to choose their mates from within five, ten, and twenty blocks.[9]

[8] "Ethnic Groups in Connecticut Industry," *Social Forces*, Vol. XX, No. 1 (October, 1941).
[9] R. J. R. Kennedy, "Residential Propinquity and Ethnic Endogamy," *American Journal of Sociology*, XLVIII, No. 5 (March 1, 1943), 580-84.

This is attributable in part to their high in-marriage rate, for the Italians cluster in a certain few sections of the city. But premarital residential propinquity also characterized Italian out-marriages, as is shown in the fact that in 74.6 per cent of such unions both parties lived within twenty blocks, and 49.2 per cent within ten blocks of each other before marriage. Since the predominantly Italian-populated sections are among the poorest and most congested in the city and residentially least desirable, we are justified in inferring that the British-Americans, Germans, and Scandinavians who dwell there have an economic status similar to that of their Italian neighbors.

Returning now to the queries posed earlier in this paper, we may summarize thus:

1. The increasing intermarriage in New Haven is not general and indiscriminate but is channeled by religious barriers; and groups with the same religions tend to intermarry. Thus, Irish, Italians, and Poles intermarry mostly among themselves, and British-Americans, Germans, and Scandinavians do likewise, while Jews seldom marry Gentiles.

2. When marriage crosses religious barriers, as it often does, religion still plays a dominant role, especially among Catholics. The high frequency of Catholic nuptials sanctioning the out-marriages of Irish, Italians, and Poles implies that their choice of spouses is determined largely by the willingness of their non-Catholic mates to be brought over to the church. Indeed, Catholic nuptials are increasing in marriages of Catholics with non-Catholics.

On the basis of the evidence disclosed in this analysis of marriage records, our main conclusion is, therefore, that assortative mating rather than random intermarriage has been occurring in New Haven since 1870 and that assimilation in this city is of a stratified character. The "melting-pot, general-mixture" idea popularized by Zangwill and supported by others has failed to materialize in this particular community. Religious differences function as the chief basis of stratification.

———— Solomon E. Asch

Opinions and Social Pressure

That social influences shape every person's practices, judgments and beliefs is a truism to which anyone will readily assent. A child masters his "native" dialect down to the finest nuances; a member of a tribe of cannibals accepts cannibalism as altogether fitting and proper. All the social sciences take their departure from the observation of the profound effects that groups exert on their members. For psychologists, group pressure

From *Scientific American*, November, 1955, pp. 18, 31-35. Reprinted with permission.

upon the minds of individuals raises a host of questions they would like
to investigate in detail.

How, and to what extent, do social forces constrain people's opinions
and attitudes? This question is especially pertinent in our day. The same
epoch that has witnessed the unprecedented technical extension of communication has also brought into existence the deliberate manipulation
of opinion and the "engineering of consent." There are many good reasons why, as citizens and as scientists, we should be concerned with
studying the ways in which human beings form their opinions and the
role that social conditions play.

Studies of these questions began with the interest in hypnosis aroused
by the French physician Jean Martin Charcot (a teacher of Sigmund
Freud) toward the end of the 19th century. Charcot believed that only
hysterical patients could be fully hypnotized, but this view was soon
challenged by two other physicians, Hyppolyte Bernheim and A. A.
Liébault, who demonstrated that they could put most people under the
hypnotic spell. Bernheim proposed that hypnosis was but an extreme
form of a normal psychological process which became known as "suggestibility." It was shown that monotonous reiteration of instructions
could induce in normal persons in the waking state involuntary bodily
changes such as swaying or rigidity of the arms, and sensations such as
warmth and odor.

It was not long before social thinkers seized upon these discoveries as
a basis for explaining numerous social phenomena, from the spread of
opinion to the formation of crowds and the following of leaders. The
sociologist Gabriel Tarde summed it all up in the aphorism: "Social man
is a somnambulist."

When the new discipline of social psychology was born at the beginning of this century, its first experiments were essentially adaptations of
the suggestion demonstration. The technique generally followed a simple
plan. The subjects, usually college students, were asked to give their
opinions or preferences concerning various matters; some time later they
were again asked to state their choices, but now they were also informed
of the opinions held by authorities or large groups of their peers on the
same matters. (Often the alleged consensus was fictitious.) Most of these
studies had substantially the same result: confronted with opinions contrary to their own, many subjects apparently shifted their judgments in
the direction of the views of the majorities or the experts. The late
psychologist Edward L. Thorndike reported that he had succeeded in
modifying the esthetic preferences of adults by this procedure. Other
psychologists reported that people's evaluations of the merit of a literary
passage could be raised or lowered by ascribing the passage to different
authors. Apparently the sheer weight of numbers or authority sufficed
to change opinions, even when no arguments for the opinions themselves
were provided.

Now the very ease of success in these experiments arouses suspicion.

Did the subjects actually change their opinions, or were the experimental victories scored only on paper? On grounds of common sense, one must question whether opinions are generally as watery as these studies indicate. There is some reason to wonder whether it was not the investigators who, in their enthusiasm for a theory, were suggestible, and whether the ostensibly gullible subjects were not providing answers which they thought good subjects were expected to give.

1. Subjects were shown two cards. One bore a standard line. The other bore three lines, one of which was the same length as the standard. The subjects were asked to choose this line.

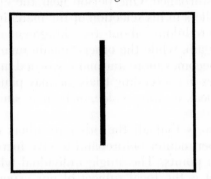 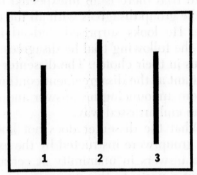

The investigations were guided by certain underlying assumptions, which today are common currency and account for much that is thought and said about the operations of propaganda and public opinion. The assumptions are that people submit uncritically and painlessly to external manipulation by suggestion or prestige, and that any given idea or value can be "sold" or "unsold" without reference to its merits. We should be skeptical, however, of the supposition that the power of social pressure necessarily implies uncritical submission to it: independence and the capacity to rise above group passion are also open to human beings. Further, one may question on psychological grounds whether it is possible as a rule to change a person's judgment of a situation or an object without first changing his knowledge or assumptions about it.

In what follows I shall describe some experiments in an investigation of the effects of group pressure which was carried out recently with the help of a number of my associates. The tests not only demonstrate the operations of group pressure upon individuals but also illustrate a new kind of attack on the problem and some of the more subtle questions that it raises.

A group of seven to nine young men, all college students, are assembled in a classroom for a "psychological experiment" in visual judgment. The experimenter informs them that they will be comparing the lengths of lines. He shows two large white cards. On one is a single vertical black line—the standard whose length is to be matched. On the other card are three vertical lines of various lengths. The subjects are to choose the one that is of the same length as the line on the other card. One of the three actually is of the same length; the other two are substantially different, the difference ranging from three quarters of an inch to an inch and three quarters.

The experiment opens uneventfully. The subjects announce their answers in the order in which they have been seated in the room, and on the first round every person chooses the same matching line. Then a second set of cards is exposed; again the group is unanimous. The members appear ready to endure politely another boring experiment. On the third trial there is an unexpected disturbance. One person near the end of the group disagrees with all the others in his selection of the matching line. He looks surprised, indeed incredulous, about the disagreement. On the following trial he disagrees again, while the others remain unanimous in their choice. The dissenter becomes more and more worried and hesitant as the disagreement continues in succeeding trials; he may pause before announcing his answer and speak in a low voice, or he may smile in an embarrassed way.

What the dissenter does not know is that all the other members of the group were instructed by the experimenter beforehand to give incorrect answers in unanimity at certain points. The single individual who is not a party to this prearrangement is the focal subject of our experiment. He is placed in a position in which, while he is actually giving the correct answers, he finds himself unexpectedly in a minority of one, opposed by a unanimous and arbitrary majority with respect to a clear and simple fact. Upon him we have brought to bear two opposed forces: the evidence of his senses and the unanimous opinion of a group of his peers. Also, he must declare his judgments in public, before a majority which has also stated its position publicly.

The instructed majority occasionally reports correctly in order to reduce the possibility that the naive subject will suspect collusion against him. (In only a few cases did the subject actually show suspicion; when this happened, the experiment was stopped and the results were not counted.) There are 18 trials in each series, and on 12 of these the majority responds erroneously.

How do people respond to group pressure in this situation? I shall report first the statistical results of a series in which a total of 123 subjects from three institutions of higher learning (not including my own, Swarthmore College) were placed in the minority situation described above.

Two alternatives were open to the subject: he could act independently, repudiating the majority, or he could go along with the majority, repudiating the evidence of his senses. Of the 123 put to the test, a considerable percentage yielded to the majority. Whereas in ordinary circumstances individuals matching the lines will make mistakes less than 1 per cent of the time, under group pressure the minority subjects swung to acceptance of the misleading majority's wrong judgments in 36.8 per cent of the selections.

Of course individuals differed in response. At one extreme, about one quarter of the subjects were completely independent and never agreed with the erroneous judgments of the majority. At the other extreme, some individuals went with the majority nearly all the time. The performances of individuals in this experiment tend to be highly consistent. Those who strike out on the path of independence do not, as a rule, succumb to the majority even over an extended series of trials, while those who choose the path of compliance are unable to free themselves as the ordeal is prolonged.

The reasons for the startling individual differences have not yet been investigated in detail. At this point we can only report some tentative generalizations from talks with the subjects, each of whom was interviewed at the end of the experiment. Among the independent individuals were many who held fast because of staunch confidence in their own judgment. The most significant fact about them was not absence of responsiveness to the majority but a capacity to recover from doubt and to reestablish their equilibrium. Others who acted independently came to believe that the majority was correct in its answers, but they continued their dissent on the simple ground that it was their obligation to call the play as they saw it.

Among the extremely yielding persons we found a group who quickly reached the conclusion: "I am wrong, they are right." Others yielded in order "not to spoil your results." Many of the individuals who went along suspected that the majority were "sheep" following the first responder, or that the majority were victims of an optical illusion; nevertheless, these suspicions failed to free them at the moment of decision. More disquieting were the reactions of subjects who construed their difference from the majority as a sign of some general deficiency in themselves, which at all costs they must hide. On this basis they desperately tried to merge with the majority, not realizing the longer-range consequences to themselves. All the yielding subjects underestimated the frequency with which they conformed.

Which aspect of the influence of a majority is more important—the size of the majority or its unanimity? The experiment was modified to examine this question. In one series the size of the opposition was varied from one to 15 persons. The results showed a clear trend. When a subject was confronted with only a single individual who contradicted his answers, he was swayed little: he continued to answer independently and correctly in nearly all trials. When the opposition was increased to two, the pressure became substantial: minority subjects now accepted the wrong answer 13.6 per cent of the time. Under the pressure of a majority of three, the subjects' errors jumped to 31.8 per cent. But further increases in the size of the majority apparently did not increase the weight of the pressure substantially. Clearly the size of the opposition is important only up to a point.

Disturbance of the majority's unanimity had a striking effect. In this experiment the subject was given the support of a truthful partner—either another individual who did not know of the prearranged agreement among the rest of the group, or a person who was instructed to give correct answers throughout.

The presence of a supporting partner depleted the majority of much of its power. Its pressure on the dissenting individual was reduced to one fourth: that is, subjects answered incorrectly only one fourth as often as under the pressure of a unanimous majority. The weakest persons did not yield as readily. Most interesting were the reactions to the partner. Generally the feeling toward him was one of warmth and closeness; he was credited with inspiring confidence. However, the subjects repudiated the suggestion that the partner decided them to be independent.

Was the partner's effect a consequence of his dissent, or was it related to his accuracy? We now introduced into the experimental group a person who was instructed to dissent from the majority but also to disagree with the subject. In some experiments the majority was always to choose the worst of the comparison lines and the instructed dissenter to pick the line that was closer to the length of the standard one; in others the majority was consistently intermediate and the dissenter most in error. In this manner we were able to study the relative influence of "compromising" and "extremist" dissenters.

Again the results are clear. When a moderate dissenter is present, the effect of the majority on the subject decreases by approximately one third, and extremes of yielding disappear. Moreover, most of the errors the subjects do make are moderate, rather than flagrant. In short, the dissenter largely controls the choice of errors. To this extent the subjects broke away from the majority even while bending to it.

On the other hand, when the dissenter always chose the line that was more flagrantly different from the standard, the results were of quite a different kind. The extremist dissenter produced a remarkable freeing of the subjects; their errors dropped to only 9 per cent. Furthermore, all the errors were of the moderate variety. We were able to conclude that dissent *per se* increased independence and moderated the errors that occurred, and that the direction of dissent exerted consistent effects.

In all the foregoing experiments each subject was observed only in a single setting. We now turned to studying the effects upon a given individual of a change in the situation to which he was exposed. The first experiment examined the consequences of losing or gaining a partner. The instructed partner began by answering correctly on the first six trials. With his support the subject usually resisted pressure from the majority: 18 of 27 subjects were completely independent. But after six trials the partner joined the majority. As soon as he did so, there was an abrupt rise in the subjects' errors. Their submission to the majority was just about as frequent as when the minority subject was opposed by a unanimous majority throughout.

It was surprising to find that the experience of having had a partner and of having braved the majority opposition with him had failed to strengthen the individuals' independence. Questioning at the conclusion of the experiment suggested that we had overlooked an important circumstance; namely, the strong specific effect of "desertion" by the partner to the other side. We therefore changed the conditions so that the partner would simply leave the group at the proper point. (To allay suspicion it was announced in advance that he had an appointment with the dean.) In this form of the experiment, the partner's effect outlasted his presence. The errors increased after his departure, but less markedly than after a partner switched to the majority.

In a variant of this procedure the trials began with the majority unanimously giving correct answers. Then they gradually broke away until on the sixth trial the naive subject was alone and the group unanimously against him. As long as the subject had anyone on his side, he was almost invariably independent, but as soon as he found himself alone, the tendency to conform to the majority rose abruptly.

As might be expected, an individual's resistance to group pressure in these experiments depends to a considerable degree on how wrong the majority is. We varied the discrepancy between the standard line and the other lines systematically, with the hope of reaching a point where the error of the majority would be so glaring that every subject would repudiate it and choose independently. In this we regretfully did not succeed. Even when the difference between the lines was seven inches, there were still some who yielded to the error of the majority.

The study provides clear answers to a few relatively simple questions, and it raises many others that await investigation. We would like to know the degree of consistency of persons in situations which differ in content and structure. If consistency of independence or conformity in behavior is shown to be a fact, how is it functionally related to qualities of character and personality? In what ways is independence related to sociological or cultural conditions? Are leaders more independent than other people, or are they adept at following their followers? These and many other questions may perhaps be answerable by investigations of the type described here.

Life in society requires consensus as an indispensable condition. But consensus, to be productive, requires that each individual contribute independently out of his experience and insight. When consensus comes under the dominance of conformity, the social process is polluted and the individual at the same time surrenders the powers on which his functioning as a feeling and thinking being depends. That we have found the tendency to conformity in our society so strong that reasonably intelligent and well-meaning young people are willing to call white black is a matter of concern. It raises questions about our ways of education and about the values that guide our conduct.

Yet anyone inclined to draw too pessimistic conclusions from this report would do well to remind himself that the capacities for independence are not to be underestimated. He may also draw some consolation from a further observation: those who participated in this challenging experiment agreed nearly without exception that independence was preferable to conformity.

Supplementary Bibliography

Howard S. Becker, "The Professional Dance Band Musician and His Audience." *American Journal of Sociology,* 1951, 57:136-144.
> A striking illustration of ethnocentrism in an occupational subculture, in which employer, employee, and consumer have distinct and conflicting definitions of the goals and norms of the occupation.

Donald T. Campbell and Robert A. LeVine, "A Proposal for Cooperative Cross-cultural Research on Ethnocentrism." *The Journal of Conflict Resolution,* 1961, 5:82-108.
> A review of the evidence concerning the universality of ethnocentrism and of outgroup stereotypes, with an interview outline for cross-cultural research on ethnocentrism.

Ruby Jo Reeves Kennedy, "Single or Triple Melting-Pot? Intermarriage in New Haven, 1870-1950." *American Journal of Sociology,* 1952, 58:56-59.
> An extension of an earlier study (for which the cut-off date was 1940) reporting a pattern of ethnic endogamy in which Catholicism, Protestantism, and Judaism serve as the bulwarks.

Clyde Kluckhohn and D. Leighton, *The Navaho.* Cambridge: Harvard U. Press, 1947.
> A brilliant anthropological portrait of a people who, like others, consider themselves "The People."

XII The Accommodation of Intergroup Conflict

Competition between groups can take different forms. At one extreme, there can be open conflict and the explicit attempt to eliminate the other group. Or there can be pluralistic competition, in which all groups party to the conflict agree to let all groups survive in peaceful competition.

Factors in the Incidence of Intergroup Conflict

Competition is only one necessary condition for conflict. Another major factor in the incidence of conflict is visibility: the ability to identify the members of the out-group. The "others" must have some distinguishing feature. This is why competing football teams wear different-colored jerseys, and warplanes carry insignia. In the Middle Ages, Jews were forced to wear armbands and to live in a restricted area of a community called a "ghetto." We have seen how concentration in the population, or segregation, adds to the visibility of a minority, as does cultural difference. The physiognomic visibility of most Negroes makes it unnecessary for them to wear an artificial mark.

A second factor in the incidence of conflict is contact between the two hostile groups. There can be no conflict without contact. In this sense, complete and total segregation of competing groups from each other would eliminate the possibility of conflict. (Mothers know this when they say, "If you and Webster can't play together nicely, you'll each have to stay in your own yard." Total segregation: no conflict. However, the elimination of contact as a means of avoiding conflict is usually unworkable in the case of minorities, not only because of the complicated interdependence of the modern world, but because dominant people ordinarily have a vested interest in contact with the minority population. When you explain that one solution to race relations problems in the United States means no bus driver this morning, no waiter this afternoon, and no garbage collection tomorrow, many people decide that total segregation is by no means the best answer to the reduction of intergroup conflict.

The Reduction of Conflict

One solution to intergroup conflict is the appearance of a third group which is the common enemy of both of the originally competing groups. In time of war, Negroes and Jews are seen as fellow Americans instead of out-groups. But few would pose war as a desirable solution to conflict.

The various minority groups in any given society have different kinds of responses to conflict situations. Some choose to retaliate in kind, with as much aggressive strength as they can muster. Others choose to try to assimilate, to emulate the members of the dominant majority as best they can in an effort to gain acceptance. Total assimilation is another avenue to the elimination of conflict.

Contact is a double-edged sword. We noted that contact is necessary for conflict. But contact can also be highly conducive to the reduction of conflict. One of the more common bits of folk wisdom is that the solution to the race question lies in increased contact. This is not necessarily true. There is certainly more contact between the races in the South than in the North, yet few would argue that the relations between the races are better in the South.

The answer to this tricky question of contact and conflict now seems to be fairly well documented by social science research. Intergroup conflict is reduced when there is contact between equal-status members of the two groups. That is, it does no good for a lower- or working-class Negro to have intimate personal contact with a middle- or upper-class white. This goes on very frequently in the kitchens and basements of the country, with no lessening of intergroup conflict. To be sure, the personal association with the individual cook may be warm and friendly, but the view of the group remains—indeed, may be reinforced by contact with individuals who act as evidence to confirm the stereotype of the race.

To destroy such stereotypes calls for contact of a very specific kind: middle-class whites must closely associate with middle-class Negroes in jobs where both enjoy the same kinds of rights and privileges. The differences between them become quite small when viewed in this framework, and they begin to see it that way, too.

Conclusion

Competition, visibility, and contact are prerequisites to intergroup conflict. All three are basic elements of the American social and cultural system. While conflict is not a necessary consequence of these factors, it is impossible to ensure the absence of conflict when all three are present.

Some whites resolve the American dilemma for themselves by coming to the rationalized position that the stratification system is a consequence of a just, a free, and an open competitive system. Negroes, according to this position, get what they deserve and deserve what they get: the bottom rung. But the free and open character of the social system is an illusion developed out of lack of personal exposure to the decision to discriminate.

Until we can learn to live in accordance with our own democratic and Judaeo-Christian ideals, we shall live with conflict engendered by an ascribed status system of color-caste within an open system encouraging each and all to achieve to the limit of his capacities.

Related Readings

Muzafer Sherif's "Experiments in Group Conflict" show that the possibility of accommodating intergroup conflict is greatly enhanced by joint striving toward shared goals.

It is neither permissive nor repressive measures as such which engender conflict. Rather, quite in keeping with theories of status inconsistency, marginality, and the low tolerance of human beings for role ambiguity, it is inconsistency or vacillation in government policies which has led to violence. A carefully calculated policy of abiding by the law and avoiding violence is reported by Claude Sitton in "Atlanta's Example: Good Sense and Dignity."

However, it is foolhardy to assume that conflict can be avoided and that community decisions will be made on a rational basis simply as a result of giving people scientifically determined facts. As Joseph D. Lohman and Dietrich C. Rietzes emphasize in their "Note on Race Relations in Mass Society," the significance of public opinion rests partly in the fact that behavior in modern society is increasingly influenced by deliberately organized interest groups. An individual's propensity to racial and ethnic prejudice may be less crucial information than the definition of the situation supplied for him through social organization.

══════════════Muzafer Sherif

Experiments in Group Conflict

Conflict between groups—whether between boys' gangs, social classes, "races" or nations—has no simple cause, nor is mankind yet in sight of a cure. It is often rooted deep in personal, social, economic, religious and historical forces. Nevertheless it is possible to identify certain general factors which have a crucial influence on the attitude of any group toward others. Social scientists have long sought to bring these factors to light by studying what might be called the "natural history" of groups and group relations. Intergroup conflict and harmony is not a subject that lends itself easily to laboratory experiments. But in recent years there has been a beginning of attempts to investigate the problem under controlled yet lifelike conditions, and I shall report here the results of a program of experimental studies of groups which I started in 1948. Among the persons working with me were Marvin B. Sussman, Robert Huntington, O. J. Harvey, B. Jack White, William R. Hood and Carolyn W. Sherif. The experiments were conducted in 1949, 1953 and 1954; this article gives a composite of the findings.

We wanted to conduct our study with groups of the informal type, where group organization and attitudes would evolve naturally and spontaneously, without formal direction or external pressures. For this purpose we conceived that an isolated summer camp would make a good experimental setting, and that decision led us to choose as subjects boys about 11 or 12 years old, who would find camping natural and fascinating. Since our aim was to study the development of group relations among these boys under carefully controlled conditions, with as little interference as possible from personal neuroses, background influences or prior experiences, we selected normal boys of homogeneous background who did not know one another before they came to the camp.

They were picked by a long and thorough procedure. We interviewed each boy's family, teachers and school officials, studied his school and medical records, obtained his scores on personality tests and observed him in his classes and at play with his schoolmates. With all this information we were able to assure ourselves that the boys chosen were of like kind and background: all were healthy, socially well-adjusted, somewhat above average in intelligence and from stable, white, Protestant, middle-class homes.

None of the boys was aware that he was part of an experiment on group relations. The investigators appeared as a regular camp staff—camp

From *Scientific American*, November, 1956, pp. 32, 54-58. Reprinted with permission.

directors, counselors and so on. The boys met one another for the first time in buses that took them to the camp, and so far as they knew it was a normal summer of camping. To keep the situation as lifelike as possible, we conducted all our experiments within the framework of regular camp activities and games. We set up projects which were so interesting and attractive that the boys plunged into them enthusiastically without suspecting that they might be test situations. Unobtrusively we made records of their behavior, even using "candid" cameras and microphones when feasible.

We began by observing how the boys became a coherent group. The first of our camps was conducted in the hills of northern Connecticut in the summer of 1949. When the boys arrived, they were all housed at first in one large bunkhouse. As was to be expected, they quickly formed particular friendships and chose buddies. We had deliberately put all the boys together in this expectation, because we wanted to see what would happen later after the boys were separated into different groups. Our object was to reduce the factor of personal attraction in the formation of groups. In a few days we divided the boys into two groups and put them in different cabins. Before doing so, we asked each boy informally who his best friends were, and then took pains to place the "best friends" in different groups so far as possible. (The pain of separation was assuaged by allowing each group to go at once on a hike and camp-out.)

As everyone knows, a group of strangers brought together in some common activity soon acquires an informal and spontaneous kind of organization. It comes to look upon some members as leaders, divides up duties, adopts unwritten norms of behavior, develops an *esprit de corps*. Our boys followed this pattern as they shared a series of experiences. In each group the boys pooled their efforts, organized duties and divided up tasks in work and play. Different individuals assumed different responsibilities. One boy excelled in cooking. Another led in athletics. Others, though not outstanding in any one skill, could be counted on to pitch in and do their level best in anything the group attempted. One or two seemed to disrupt activities, to start teasing at the wrong moment or offer useless suggestions. A few boys consistently had good suggestions and showed ability to coordinate the efforts of others in carrying them through. Within a few days one person had proved himself more resourceful and skillful than the rest. Thus, rather quickly, a leader and lieutenants emerged. Some boys sifted toward the bottom of the heap, while others jockeyed for higher positions.

We watched these developments closely and rated the boys' relative positions in the group, not only on the basis of our own observations but also by informal sounding of the boys' opinions as to who got things started, who got things done, who could be counted on to support group activities.

As the group became an organization, the boys coined nicknames. The big, blond, hardy leader of one group was dubbed "Baby Face" by his admiring followers. A boy with a rather long head became "Lemon Head." Each group developed its own jargon, special jokes, secrets and special ways of performing tasks. One group, after killing a snake near a place where it had gone to swim, named the place "Moccasin Creek" and thereafter preferred this swimming hole to any other, though there were better ones nearby.

Wayward members who failed to do things "right" or who did not contribute their bit to the common effort found themselves receiving the "silent treatment," ridicule or even threats. Each group selected symbols and a name, and they had these put on their caps and T-shirts. The 1954 camp was conducted in Oklahoma, near a famous hideaway of Jesse James called Robber's Cave. The two groups of boys at this camp named themselves the Rattlers and the Eagles.

Our conclusions on every phase of the study were based on a variety of observations, rather than on any single method. For example, we devised a game to test the boys' evaluations of one another. Before an important baseball game, we set up a target board for the boys to throw at, on the pretense of making practice for the game more interesting. There were no marks on the front of the board for the boys to judge objectively how close the ball came to a bull's-eye, but, unknown to them, the board was wired to flashing lights behind so that an observer could see exactly where the ball hit. We found that the boys consistently overestimated

1. Friendship choices of campers for others in their own cabin are shown for Red Devils (*white*) and Bulldogs (*black*). At first a low percentage of friendships were in the cabin group (*left*). After five days, most friendship choices were within the group (*right*).
2. During conflict between the two groups in the Robber's Cave experiment there were few friendships between cabins (*left*). After cooperation toward common goals had restored good feelings, the number of friendships between groups rose significantly (*right*).
3. Negative Ratings of each group by the other were common during the period of conflict (*left*) but decreased when harmony was restored (*right*). The graphs show percent who thought that *all* (rather than *some* or *none*) of the other group were cheaters, sneaks, etc.

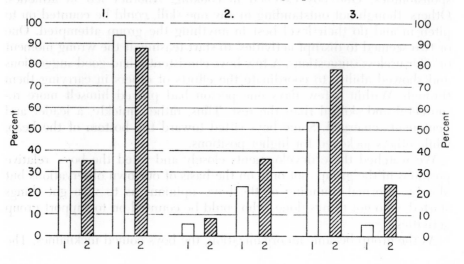

the performances by the most highly regarded members of their group and underestimated the scores of those of low social standing.

The attitudes of group members were even more dramatically illustrated during a cook-out in the woods. The staff supplied the boys with unprepared food and let them cook it themselves. One boy promptly started to build a fire, asking for help in getting wood. Another attacked the raw hamburger to make patties. Others prepared a place to put buns, relishes and the like. Two mixed soft drinks from flavoring and sugar. One boy who stood around without helping was told by the others to "get to it." Shortly the fire was blazing and the cook had hamburgers sizzling. Two boys distributed them as rapidly as they became edible. Soon it was time for the watermelon. A low-ranking member of the group took a knife and started toward the melon. Some of the boys protested. The most highly regarded boy in the group took over the knife, saying, "You guys who yell the loudest get yours last."

When the two groups in the camp had developed group organization and spirit, we proceeded to the experimental studies of intergroup relations. The groups had had no previous encounters; indeed, in the 1954 camp at Robber's Cave the two groups came in separate buses and were kept apart while each acquired a group feeling.

Our working hypothesis was that when two groups have conflicting aims—i.e., when one can achieve its ends only at the expense of the other —their members will become hostile to each other even though the groups are composed of normal well-adjusted individuals. There is a corollary to this assumption which we shall consider later. To produce friction between the groups of boys we arranged a tournament of games: baseball, touch football, a tug-of-war, a treasure hunt and so on. The tournament started in a spirit of good sportsmanship. But as it progressed good feeling soon evaporated. The members of each group began to call their rivals "stinkers," "sneaks" and "cheaters." They refused to have anything more to do with individuals in the opposing group. The boys in the 1949 camp turned against buddies whom they had chosen as "best friends" when they first arrived at the camp. A large proportion of the boys in each group gave negative ratings to all the boys in the other. The rival groups made threatening posters and planned raids, collecting secret hoards of green apples for ammunition. In the Robber's Cave camp the Eagles, after a defeat in a tournament game, burned a banner left behind by the Rattlers; the next morning the Rattlers seized the Eagles' flag when they arrived on the athletic field. From that time on name-calling, scuffles and raids were the rule of the day.

Within each group, of course, solidarity increased. There were changes: one group deposed its leader because he could not "take it" in the contests with the adversary; another group overnight made something of a hero of a big boy who had previously been regarded as a bully. But morale and cooperativeness within the group became stronger. It is noteworthy that this heightening of cooperativeness and generally democratic behavior did not carry over to the group's relations with other groups.

We now turned to the other side of the problem: How can two groups in conflict be brought into harmony? We first undertook to test the theory that pleasant social contacts between members of conflicting groups will reduce friction between them. In the 1954 camp we brought the hostile Rattlers and Eagles together for social events: going to the movies, eating in the same dining room and so on. But far from reducing conflict, these situations only served as opportunities for the rival groups to berate and attack each other. In the dining-hall line they shoved each other aside, and the group that lost the contest for the head of the line shouted "Ladies first!" at the winner. They threw paper, food and vile names at each other at the tables. An Eagle bumped by a Rattler was admonished by his fellow Eagles to brush "the dirt" off his clothes.

We then returned to the corollary of our assumption about the creation of conflict. Just as competition generates friction, working in a common endeavor should promote harmony. It seemed to us, considering group relations in the everyday world, that where harmony between groups is established, the most decisive factor is the existence of "superordinate" goals which have a compelling appeal for both but which neither could achieve without the other. To test this hypothesis experimentally, we created a series of urgent, and natural, situations which challenged our boys.

One was a breakdown in the water supply. Water came to our camp in pipes from a tank about a mile away. We arranged to interrupt it and then called the boys together to inform them of the crisis. Both groups promptly volunteered to search the water line for the trouble. They worked together harmoniously, and before the end of the afternoon they had located and corrected the difficulty.

A similar opportunity offered itself when the boys requested a movie. We told them that the camp could not afford to rent one. The two groups then got together, figured out how much each group would have to contribute, chose the film by a vote and enjoyed the showing together.

One day the two groups went on an outing at a lake some distance away. A large truck was to go to town for food. But when everyone was hungry and ready to eat, it developed that the truck would not start (we had taken care of that). The boys got a rope—the same rope they had used in their acrimonious tug-of-war—and all pulled together to start the truck.

These joint efforts did not immediately dispel hostility. At first the groups returned to the old bickering and name-calling as soon as the job in hand was finished. But gradually the series of cooperative acts reduced friction and conflict. The members of the two groups began to feel more friendly to each other. For example, a Rattler whom the Eagles disliked for his sharp tongue and skill in defeating them became a "good egg."

The boys stopped shoving in the meal line. They no longer called each other names, and sat together at the table. New friendships developed between individuals in the two groups.

In the end the groups were actively seeking opportunities to mingle, to entertain and "treat" each other. They decided to hold a joint campfire. They took turns presenting skits and songs. Members of both groups requested that they go home together on the same bus, rather than on the separate buses in which they had come. On the way the bus stopped for refreshments. One group still had five dollars which they had won as a prize in a contest. They decided to spend this sum on refreshments. On their own initiative they invited their former rivals to be their guests for malted milks.

Our interviews with the boys confirmed this change. From choosing their "best friends" almost exclusively in their own group, many of them shifted to listing boys in the other group as best friends [see . . . chart . . .]. They were glad to have a second chance to rate boys in the other group, some of them remarking that they had changed their minds since the first rating made after the tournament. Indeed they had. The new ratings were largely favorable [see chart . . .].

Efforts to reduce friction and prejudice between groups in our society have usually followed rather different methods. Much attention has been given to bringing members of hostile groups together socially, to communicating accurate and favorable information about one group to the other, and to bringing the leaders of groups together to enlist their influence. But as everyone knows, such measures sometimes reduce intergroup tensions and sometimes do not. Social contacts, as our experiments demonstrated, may only serve as occasions for intensifying conflict. Favorable information about a disliked group may be ignored or reinterpreted to fit stereotyped notions about the group. Leaders cannot act without regard for the prevailing temper in their own groups.

What our limited experiments have shown is that the possibilities for achieving harmony are greatly enhanced when groups are brought together to work toward common ends. Then favorable information about a disliked group is seen in a new light, and leaders are in a position to take bolder steps toward cooperation. In short, hostility gives way when groups pull together to achieve overriding goals which are real and compelling to all concerned.

——————————Claude Sitton

Atlanta's Example: Good Sense and Dignity

"Regardless of our personal feelings or past habits, we are living in a changing world," says William B. Hartsfield, who recently stepped down after more than two decades as Mayor of Atlanta. "To progress, Atlanta must be part of that world."

His words help to explain why this city—the commercial, industrial and transportation capital of the Southeast—is today setting an example for its Deep South neighbors in making the racial adjustments dictated by necessity.

The millennium has by no means arrived for the Negroes who account for two out of five of the central city's 496,000 residents or one out of five of the more than 1,000,000 persons in its metropolitan area. Their gains in such fields as public-school desegregation and equal job opportunities have been token at best. Only eight Negro students, for example, now attend four previously all-white high schools.

No important advance has come without pressure. Sometimes it has been exerted by the Negroes, who wield considerable political and economic power. Sometimes it has stemmed from the Federal Government. On other occasions, it has come from the city's white liberals or from a combination of these three forces.

The result is the virtual end of segregation by law—but not by custom. Few Negroes have exercised their newly won rights. Some have been discouraged by the actions and attitudes of whites. The reluctance of many others can be attributed to the apathy bred by a substandard cultural and economic status, the fear rooted in past experience and the inability to overcome the subtle inhibitions built into the social system through the years.

Nevertheless, the advances made by Atlanta are far greater than the most optimistic observer would have predicted ten years ago. There has been no defiance of the Federal courts. In fact, Atlanta waged one of the most determined fights yet seen in the region against a rurally dominated state government over the issue of local option in public-school desegregation. Nor has there been any attempt to prolong resistance to demands for change made outside the courts once it became clear that to do so would be futile, dangerous or both.

Once a concession has been agreed upon, a majority of the city's professional, civic and business men have sought to persuade the white community that it should be made gracefully. Officials have asserted time

New York Times Magazine, May 6, 1962, pp. 22, 123, 128.

and again that they would brook no disorder. And the threats of mob rule evoked by desegregation elsewhere in the South have never arisen here.

As a result, civic leaders from more than a dozen other Southern cities have come here in recent months to learn whether Atlanta's experience might be helpful in resolving racial difficulties in their communities. One leading Atlantan—by no means a liberal—recalls that he told one such visitor that it often proved helpful to invite Negroes to lunch to discuss interracial problems.

"You mean to say you actually sit down and eat with them?" came the startled reply.

"Oh, sure. You don't even notice the difference after just a few minutes."

The reasons that underlie this shifting social pattern are many and complex. Racial change has posed a problem for Atlanta since Gen. William Tecumseh Sherman's legions freed its slaves and put the city to the torch in 1864. Twenty-five years later, Henry W. Grady, editor of The Atlanta Constitution, told the merchants of Boston:

"The problem of race * * * is so bound up in our honorable obligation to the world that we would not disentangle it if we could. * * * I would rather see my people render back this question rightly solved than to see them gather all the spoils over which faction has contended since Catiline conspired and Caesar fought."

For the city's Negroes, the years from 1906—when a four-day race riot brought death to ten Negroes and two whites—to 1946 might well be called "the lean forty" from the standpoint of civil rights. Their goals were no more ambitious than to obtain streets, sidewalks and sewers, schools and funds with which to operate them, police and fire protection.

Moreover, there was the sporadic reign of terror carried on by the Ku Klux Klan. The hooded knights never controlled the city. But their floggings, cross-burnings and parades struck fear into the hearts of Negroes and the few nonconformist whites.

Even then, however, the picture had its brighter aspects. A group of Northern whites arrived only a year after Sherman's departure to establish educational institutions. These grew into the complex of six predominantly Negro colleges and universities found in the city today. As a result, a well-trained group of business and professional leaders emerged in the Negro community.

Barred from the counting-houses and law offices of Peachtree Street, Negroes established their own business and commercial colony along Auburn Avenue. There was the Citizens Trust Company, which weathered the Great Depression while banks throughout the nation were failing. Next door was The Atlanta Daily World, for a time the only Negro daily newspaper in America. Fortunes were made and the city's Negro community became, and remains today, one of the most wealthy—perhaps the wealthiest—in the nation.

Residents recall that the late John Wesley Dobbs, a prominent political leader and father of Mattiwilda Dobbs, the operatic soprano, often sang the avenue's praises in a speech that has become something of a classic.

"It takes sugar to sweeten things," Dobbs would say, "and as you know it takes money to buy sugar. The acquisition of this kind of wealth along Auburn Avenue has caused us to call it 'Sweet Auburn.' Sweet Auburn Avenue, ladies and gentlemen, is not a slum street; it's not over behind the railroad tracks. It runs straight into Peachtree Street. When you go up Sweet Auburn, you're going to town, that's all."

Because of Auburn Avenue's economic weight, good race relations became good business for some influential whites. After the Federal courts struck down Georgia's white primary law in 1946, they became good politics as well. There was little opposition, then or now, to Negro registration in Atlanta. And because the Democratic nomination was tantamount to election, participation by Negroes in the primary brought a realignment of the political balance of power. "The lean forty" was coming to an end.

A year after the primary breakthrough, the city's aldermen approved the hiring of Negro policemen for Negro neighborhoods. A more sizable share of expenditures for public facilities began flowing into those neighborhoods. Other changes followed. But none involved a major breach in the wall of segregation.

Then came the 1954 Supreme Court decision against the public-school segregation. Negroes' grudging acceptance of the status quo here and throughout the South dissipated almost overnight. The pressure on white Atlanta grew in depth and intensity.

Slowly, then with increasing rapidity, racial barriers began to fall, though not equally in every field. Public golf courses were desegregated under a Federal court order. The city library's main branch began admitting Negroes after it became apparent that legal action was inevitable otherwise. A test case, described as "more or less friendly," ended Jim Crow seating in public transportation.

The Freedom Riders rolled through Atlanta without incident en route to a riotous greeting in Alabama. A Federal court order opened a restaurant in the old municipal air terminal to Negroes, and when its jet-age replacement went into operation not a vestige of discrimination could be found in its waiting rooms, cocktail lounges, rest rooms or restaurants.

Restrictions have been removed in the legitimate theatre and desegregated groups attend functions in the municipal auditorium. When the city's new A. A. A. baseball team, the Atlanta Crackers, opened the season at Ponce de Leon Park, there was no segregation on the playing field or in the stands.

The Metropolitan Opera performed last week before a racially mixed Atlanta audience for the first time. Downtown movie theatres have indicated that they will make the change after the opera leaves town. And the issue of hotel desegregation is under negotiation.

In some other areas, progress has been slower. Lunch counters in drug, department and variety stores ended segregation only after eighteen months of sporadic sit-in demonstrations, scores of arrests, picketing and a highly effective boycott. Negro physicians and dentists still are generally barred from the city's public hospital, although one doctor has been admitted to practice.

Public-school desegregation which took place peacefully last August, has been the most significant advance in psychological terms. It also shows most clearly the reasons for Atlanta's measure of success—and the shortcomings of its achievement.

Throughout this period of difficult change, most white Atlantans have shown calmness, common sense and respect for the law. Possibly typical of their attitude were the remarks Chief of Police Herbert T. Jenkins addressed to his men as they began special training in preparation for school desegregation.

"I am prepared to yield to the judgment of the Supreme Court," he said. "Why? As law-enforcement officers, there is no other position we can honestly take."

A significant factor in Atlanta's success has been the willingness of many whites—city officials and private citizens—to risk public displeasure while working to assure a peaceful change-over. The city's two white daily newspapers, The Atlanta Journal and The Atlanta Constitution, its clergymen and a group of housewives—the last organized under the name of HOPE (Help Our Public Education)—pioneered in a drive to keep the schools open even if doing so meant the end of segregation.

It has been said that self-interest is the touchstone of social change and the city's white business leaders soon came to see the danger inherent in a refusal to compromise. They had a powerful influence in assisting not only Atlanta but Georgia to escape from the trap of massive resistance.

Negro leaders, too, played an important role in averting a number of crises. They have, if anything, erred on the side of patience. This is particularly true of the business men in the seats of power along Auburn Avenue and West Hunter Street.

Yet, for all its symbolic importance, school desegregation remains no more than a token, although education officials have indicated that substantial extension of the process will take place next fall. A report to the Greater Atlanta Council on Human Relations, an interracial group, describes the treatment received at times by the eight Negro pupils:

"No doubt there are other junior and senior transfer students in the Atlanta schools who do not eat lunch with their classmates. There may be others who have had various articles, including food, thrown at them. There may be others who cannot recall a single instance of association with a classmate outside of school. There may be others who have 'thought up things to say when people speak to me' but never had a chance to say them. We do not happen to know about them."

Negroes are proud of the strides made by the city toward equal opportunity for all—proud, but not satisfied. They are fully aware that future progress, as has been true of that in the past, depends more on their own efforts than on white beneficence. This is the impression left by such leaders as Mrs. Grace Towns Hamilton, who for seventeen years headed the Atlanta Urban League's work. Her husband is registrar of Morehouse College.

The Hamilton's small, modern house looks out on a view somewhat symbolic of the distance that Atlanta has come—and that it yet has to go. On the heights near by stand the buildings of the Atlanta University complex and a few of the fine old homes of some of the more wealthy Negroes. The valley below is a tangle of slums. Across it to the east rises the skyline of the white business district, gleaming prosperously in the afternoon sun.

Mrs. Hamilton has praise for some of the city's white leaders. "But the thing that I resent is that we, the deprived people, must be eternally grateful for the crumbs that are thrown. This galls me."

The whites know that new demands will be made upon them in the days ahead. But this shakes their confidence in the future not one whit. The new Mayor, Ivan Allen Jr., past president of the Chamber of Commerce and a former office-supply company executive, slaps his desk for emphasis as he declares:

"I don't think there's any doubt that we are going to have stresses and strains on the racial problem for a long time to come. But we will continue to meet these problems as they come up and we will try to treat them with good sense and dignity and thus find a solution to them."

Cities—even Southern cities—have such varied social, political and economic structures that few valid parallels can be drawn between them in the field of race relations. However, Atlanta's neighbors might find something of value in its pattern of change. The significance does not lie so much in the extent of the progress made here as in the fact that Atlanta has achieved this change with relatively little disruption or lasting bitterness. It has demonstrated an ability to learn from its own mistakes and those of others. It has produced leadership capable of applying those lessons. And its whites and Negroes have created a working relationship which promises to serve them well in dealing with the demands for more substantial adjustments likely to come in the future.

In a small law office in the heart of the business district sits the man who played perhaps the key role in this social drama, former Mayor

Hartsfield. He believes Atlanta's booming economic growth, if nothing else, should convince other Southern cities that it provides a stimulating example.

"We've accepted what is world opinion," he says. "We're not consumed with hatred of each other. We are free to use our talents and energies to grow and to attract industry.

"The leaders in these other cities can see the difference in the approaches of Atlanta and Little Rock to the problem, but they're afraid to speak out. They've got to assume leadership.

"Hate never built anything. There's nothing to be gained from hate but stagnation. Let's forget about fighting and go to work."

——————————Joseph D. Lohman and Dietrich C. Reitzes

Note on Race Relations in Mass Society

. . . .

The basic sciences slowly and continuously feed their findings and generalizations into the world of practical affairs, but in recent years crises in technology and social relations have been making extraordinary and urgent demands upon scientific knowledge. One such crisis is that precipitated by racial contacts.

Racial relations are no longer a domestic problem which can be solved at national leisure. They have developed into a problem which greatly affects our relations with other countries. The weaknesses in our domestic race relations provide an extremely effective propaganda tool for the Communists in undermining America's status in those parts of the world which are predominantly nonwhite. This, of course, is the greater portion of the world.

Tragically enough, much of the current research in race relations is of limited usefulness in the face of the "American dilemma." We are in need of more adequate generalizations if our basic knowledge about racial relations is to be employed to implement democratic values.

The shortcomings of our knowledge about racial relations center in two basic and interrelated notions about human behavior in modern society. One is that any specific social relation as such can be theorized *in vacuo;* thus, that *special theories* are appropriate and necessary to an explanation of the behavior of individuals in situations of racial contact.

The other notion is that human behavior in such situations is, for the most part, definitively structured by the attitudes of individuals as such. In consequence collective manifestations of racial relations are interpreted from the perspective of the individuals who constitute the group. And hence the corollary has been adduced that all changes in race rela-

Reprinted by permission of *The American Journal of Sociology*, Vol. LVIII, November, 1952, pp. 240-246. Copyright, 1952, The University of Chicago. All rights reserved.

tions are brought about through the manipulation of individual attitudes. It is the theme of this paper that these subtle and far-reaching assumptions are questionable and that, moreover, they are limiting much of the current social research.

The behavior of individuals in situations involving contact with members of other racial and ethnic stocks must be regarded as a specific aspect of general human behavior, and, correspondingly, the understanding and analysis of such human behavior are dependent upon the adequacy of our more general theories of human nature and society. They must be related to the social structure inside of which behavior is taking place.

Modern society is increasingly characterized by the fact that individuals participate in specific social situations not as singular and unchanging entities but by playing specifically differentiated roles (i.e., as homeowners, workers, shoppers, merchants, etc.). Such role-playing comes less and less frequently under definitions provided by traditional folkways and mores. It is increasingly structured and defined by the demands and requirements of organizations set up for the purpose of realizing specific objectives. For the most part, the interests of individuals as homeowners, workers, or merchants are now realized within the framework of such institutions.

Mannheim has stressed this aspect of modern society in observing that individuals

> are compelled to renounce their private interests and to subordinate themselves to the interests of the larger social units. . . . The attitude produced by competitive action between antagonistic individuals is transformed into a new attitude of group solidarity *though the groups from which it derives are not all inclusive.* . . . The individual today . . . is gradually realizing that by resigning partial advantages he helps to save his own *interests.* . . . Today the individual thinks not in terms of the welfare of the community or mankind as a whole but in terms of that of his own particular groups.[1]

In recent years greater attention has been focused on the fact that we no longer live in a society that is meaningful or understandable in terms of traditional "practices" or established routines of social etiquette. In our time the human community has come to represent, for the most part, great impersonal aggregations of individuals. We live in what has been referred to as "mass society." The term centers attention upon those aspects of current collective life which give it a new meaning and emphasis. It refers to organizations of people who are not held together by informal understandings, beliefs, or practices. However, the immensity of their numbers introduces wide differences of background and opinion; even of disagreements and overt conflict. The groupings are increasingly deliberate, in response to specific needs, and are acting toward the realization of specific interests. The increasing evidence of dependence

[1] Karl Mannheim, *Man and Society* (New York: Harcourt, Brace & Co., 1940), pp. 69-70.

in modern society upon such deliberately organized groups has been noted by Mannheim:

> [The] stage of spontaneity . . . of groups does not last very long, as in mass society it has to be succeeded by a stage of *strict organization;* for, of the achievements of modern mass society only those can endure which are sponsored by definite organization.[2]

The activities of such deliberately organized groups are necessarily centered in specific interests of individuals and hence are seldom, if ever, inclusive of the whole range of interest and activity of even a single individual. It follows, as Mannheim points out, that "mass society tends to produce the most self-contradictory behavior not only in society but also in the personal life of the individual."[3]

Thus, two observations can be made regarding the nature of modern society. First, that there are a decreasing number of homogeneous, social, or cultural units of which it can be said that their membership directly mirrors, and hence is the individual counterpart of, such collectivities. On the other hand, we observe social life as exhibiting a constant condition of flux, mobility, and change, giving society the appearance of a shapeless mass, whose form and organization are achieved through deliberate and calculated association. It is within the framework of these social developments that the specific phenomena of racial relations should be examined.

In this view of the matter, a view of race relations which centers upon the concept of individual attitudes is severely limited. While there are some situations in which the behavior of persons toward others can be explained individual *qua* individual, in terms of specific attitudes, in the major and significant areas of social life—namely, jobs, business, and the community—this conception is not adequate. Thus most situations of racial contact are defined by the collectively defined interests of the individuals concerned and do not merely manifest their private feelings toward other races, for example, Negroes.

Thus, the residential neighborhood is the special locale in which individuals attempt to realize such specific interests as personal and social deference and the protection of property values; in the commercial districts and in neighborhood shopping centers, it is profits, value received, and convenience; and, on the job, it is wages, security, and working conditions. In terms of these several kinds of interests, the activities of individuals are mobilized and collectively shaped in modern mass society. Of necessity, these interests bring individuals together in organizations and cause the members to reflect in themselves, as individuals, the *raison d'être* of the collectivities. These deliberately organized groups structure and define the situations for the individual and offer him ready and avail-

[2] *Ibid.*, p. 134.
[3] *Ibid.*, p. 60.

able definitions of behavior. Individual behavior is, for all practical purposes, made a fiction. Hence a distinctly personal attitude toward minority groups may be of little consequence in explaining an individual's behavior.

The reality is the social fact: the key to the situation and the individual's action is the collectivity, and in our time the collectivity is increasingly of the nature of a deliberately organized interest group. The collectivity even supplies the individual with a well-formulated rationale which makes meaningful and even personally justifies his activity; for example, in the acceptance and rejection of minority groups. Thus it is more frequently the policy, strategy, and tactics of deliberately organized interest groups, rather than the folkways, rather than the individual dimensions of personal prejudices or racial amity, which control behavior in specific situations.

It is important to point out, however, that the organizational or collective influences do not work merely as external pressure or force. In the process of accepting collective definition of the situation as to race as in other respects, the individual creates certain self-conceptions, taking over and internalizing roles which are in accordance with the definition of the situation as provided by the collectivity. Since these roles become personal possessions, a part of the self, they are, in effect, principles of conduct for the individual, an authority in their own right. But they do not necessarily reflect general racial attitudes and are frequently even at variance with generalized sentiments and feelings about specific racial groups. They can and do vary with an individual's behavior toward the same object in situations which involve a different self-interest and thus a different self-conception. For example, a person may have a "general attitude" of dislike toward Negroes. But, under certain circumstances, in his role as "property owner," he may join with others to use violence in preventing a Negro from moving into his neighborhood.

However, the same person at the same time may be mobilized and disciplined at his job by his labor union's definition of the situation. In his role as a "union steward," he may even be sympathetic with a Negro who had been insulted by the refusal of a white girl to dance with him at a union dance. Yet he is not necessarily aware of the apparent contradiction. Indeed, his experience is a common one, for it is a distortion of the reality to refer his behavior to some generalized attitude or frame of mind. The question of consistency, which arises when an explanation is sought in individual psychology, is irrelevant in the above context.

What often are characterized as attitudes or tendencies to act are better understood as social myths. These myths, or false beliefs, are, of course, of considerable social significance, since they are an instrumental aspect of the recruitment of individuals in deliberately organized groups. The myths which he adopts and reiterates enable the individual to justify discrimination, both to himself and to others. This is particularly important in a democratic country like the United States, where the individual feels compelled to conform to the ethical tradition expressed in the "American creed."

Since these myths have no basis in fact, they are subject to challenge and exposure. But the destruction of a myth, however, does not necessarily have an effect on behavior, since myths function, in the main, to rationalize actions and are not usually themselves the basis for action. If a myth becomes suspect, it does not follow that a new myth will replace it.

A number of the current racial myths are so ubiquitous and so much taken for granted that they are like the very air we breathe. Their significance in the mobilization of individuals is self-evident, but it is an oversimplification to treat them conceptually as attitudes.

The following are of special current significance in race relations:

1. The myth that acts of racial discrimination are caused by the belief that other races are inferior. This myth is reflected in the other correlative that formal education will bring about changes in racial practices and that logic and information can improve race relations.
2. The myth of "separate but equal"; that absolute equality can be achieved under a system of segregation.
3. The myth that it is impossible to accomplish any change in the tradition-bound South.
4. The myth that we cannot legislate beliefs; that we must conquer individual bigotry and prejudice before we can change the shape of race relations. These notions are the basis for the myth that law cannot be effective in the area of racial relations; we cannot legislate morals.
5. The myth that there is a rank order of rational change; that certain relations must be modified first and others only later.
6. The myth that violence is inevitable if ever and whenever changes in race relations are effected.
7. The myth that in time of crisis we must make progress slowly. It follows that the democratic struggle over the globe can be fought independent of, and without reference to, the local struggle.

The significance of these myths for our research is that behavior is hardly to be understood by studying merely the individual and his generalized attitudes or verbalisms. The individual must be studied in terms of his identification with collectivities, and the terms and conditions of his participation in them, and so the collective framework must be identified and understood before his behavior may be understood. Hence it is of the utmost importance that our studies be oriented toward the collective life, which in our time is characterized by the emergence of the formal and deliberately organized group.

This point of view is the product of the empirical experience and research in various law-enforcement agencies, in a number of situations of community tension, and in a detailed study of segregation in Washington, D.C., which was published in the report, "Segregation in the Nation's Capital." [4]

The Washington study particularly points to the necessity of analyzing racial segregation and discrimination in terms of organizational structure. As it developed, it became increasingly clear that an explanation of the pattern of racial segregation could be found neither in the individual attitudes of the people in Washington nor in the frequently expressed statement that Washington is a "southern city." However, the dynamics of the situation became evident when approached in the perspective of the organizational power structure of Washington.

This power structure applied with like relevance and force to other aspects of race relations in Washington. The racial employment practices of governmental agencies are of three kinds: (a) exclusion of Negroes from employment in any job categories (but Negroes are acceptable for the most menial work which whites will not accept); (b) segregation, Negroes being employed in other than menial ranks, but only in the lower routine jobs and in separately established units; and (c) integration, jobs being open, in principle at least, to Negroes at all levels on equal terms.

There is a tremendous circulation of government employees among the several agencies in Washington, but a person in one agency may be exposed to a quite different pattern of race relations in another agency, if transferred to it. This is the common experience of Washington governmental employees. Moreover, while top-policy directives for the several agencies are the same, actual practices among the agencies differ according to function, internal bureaucratic traditions, and the interpretation of organizational motif by key personnel. The rationalization that differences in practice reflect the disposition of the working force to accept or reject the Negro were widespread, but the evidence that wholesale reorganization from within, or internal redirectives by authoritative personnel, could, overnight, change the policy in an agency was equally ubiquitous.[5]

The same considerations apply in other areas of Washington's social life, public accommodation, housing, and private employment. In each of these critical points of racial contact evidence is plentiful that the terms and conditions of such contact are a function of the interaction of organized collectivities. It becomes increasingly clear that it is irrelevant and an oversimplification to regard bigotry or intolerance or the individual's disposition to accept or reject Negroes as such as the controlling conditions.

The Washington study encompassed the entire community, with a

---

[4] Joseph D. Lohman *et al.*, "Segregation in the Nation's Capital" (Washington, D.C.: National Committee on Segregation in the Nation's Capital, November, 1948). (Mimeographed.)
[5] William C. Bradbury, Jr., *Discrimination in Employment in the Federal Government*, Part V, *Segregation in Washington* (Washington, D.C.: National Committee on Segregation in the Nation's Capital, November, 1948).

corresponding emphasis upon its organization and structure. Another study designed to throw light upon Negro-white interaction in three situations involving white industrial workers was conducted in Chicago. They were (1) the residential neighborhood; (2) the industrial work situation; and (3) neighborhood shopping centers.[6]

The subjects of the study were selected so as to fulfil these requirements, respectively: (1) residence in a neighborhood area of Chicago which was known to be strongly opposed to the acceptance of Negroes; (2) membership in an industrial union which had a clear-cut and definitely implemented policy of equality of whites and Negroes (Negroes in this union were admitted without reservation as to race and were elected to and held office as union stewards and executive board members; at the time of the study the position of vice-president was held by a Negro); and (3) the white individuals did most of their shopping in stores which served Negroes on the basis of complete equality.

In all three situations it was discovered that the individual's generalized feelings and attitudes toward Negroes were inadequate to explain actual behavior. Such generalized feelings were systematically repressed and subordinated in the face of more specific interests. Thus, in the work situation, the specific interests of wages, working conditions, and job security were identified with the union, and hence the union's position on racial questions was in control. On the other hand, in the neighborhood, such interests as personal and social deference as well as protection of property values were identified with the objectives of the local improvement association. Consequently, the civic organizations' position of completely rejecting Negroes as potential neighbors were determinative.

It is of particular interest to note that there was no statistical correlation between acceptance or rejection of Negroes on the job and acceptance or rejection of Negroes in the neighborhood. That is, there was no evidence to support the common belief that persons who show a high degree of acceptance of Negroes on the job will necessarily show a low degree of rejection of Negroes in their home communities.

These findings have been operationally validated in a number of situations where programs have been inaugurated dealing with outbreaks in race violence. Two situations which were given considerable attention by the newspapers were the following.

In 1949 the Department of the Interior was challenged on its policy of nonsegregation in the public swimming pools of Washington. The immediate result was violence at the Anacostia pool. As a result the pool was closed for the remainder of the 1949 season. Throughout the winter of 1949-50 there was widespread discussion in Washington about the announced policy of the department to again open all the pools without segregation. In April, 1950, the *Washington Post*, in an editorial, stated:

[6] Dietrich C. Reitzes, "Collective Factors in Race Relations" (unpublished Ph.D. thesis, University of Chicago, March, 1950).

Secretary Chapman has taken an arbitrary stand, in our opinion, by insisting that the six swimming pools under control of the Interior Department be operated on a nonsegregated basis. . . . The Interior Department could not keep the pools closed all summer without producing a justified explosion in the community. Nor could it operate all of them on a nonsegregated basis without provoking new racial tension and risking worse disorders than occurred last year. The Department has done its duty in laying down the general principle of nonsegregation, and it can continue to make its influence felt by requiring a gradual approach to that objective. But it cannot take an adamant and extreme stand without injuring the cause that it seeks to promote.

Better race relations are not fostered by dictation in such matters to local committees, nor by the sudden enforcement of rules that are certain to incite interracial animosities. In the absence of agreement, the best thing the Department can do is to turn the pools over to the board for operation in accord with its more realistic policy.

In the meantime, however, the National Capital Parks had conducted a training program of its personnel impressing upon the personnel their duty to follow the official policy.[7] Particularly in the case of the police, their professional status was stressed. No direct attempt was made to change their individual feelings about Negroes. The results can best be judged from another editorial of the *Washington Post* which appeared in September, 1950:

The completion of the first full year of nonsegregated swimming at the six Washington pools controlled by the Interior Department affords an appropriate opportunity for sober reexamination of what has been an overheated community issue. Total attendance at the six pools during the summer months of 1950 was 235,533; of this number, about 90,000 swimmers were colored and about 146,000 were white. No disturbance or unhappy incident of any kind occurred in the course of the season.

The orderliness of the program is attributable in large part, of course, to the care and intelligence with which it was administered by National Capital Parks. Adequate police protection was provided, and the police officers assigned to this duty were trained specifically to deal with its problems; in this connection the Metropolitan Police, who took extraordinary care to see that order was maintained in the areas around the pools, deserve a share of the credit. The record demonstrates conclusively that nonsegregated swimming can be handled safely and harmoniously in Washington provided the leadership is sympathetic and sensible. Trouble is likely to arise only if, as was the case in 1949, some organized group attempts to foment it.

The lesson of the summer's experience, in our judgment, is that nonsegregated swimming is here to stay; that it can be conducted safely and harmoniously under level-headed leadership; and that along these lines in-

[7] The program of consultation and instruction was undertaken by the senior author at the invitation of the Department of Interior, under which agency the National Capital Parks function.

creased swimming facilities should be made available for use next summer. The experience is a credit to the community's good sense. It is a credit especially to the church and civic groups which worked to prevent trouble and to prepare the community for orderly acceptance of the new practice. The outcome is all the more gratifying to *The Washington Post* because last spring we shared the widespread fear that the community was not yet ready to accept nonsegregated swimming without a recurrence of violence.

Similarly, after a serious racial disturbance in Chicago in 1949, known as the Peoria Street Incident, the police lieutenants and sergeants of Chicago were trained in the proper handling of racial disturbances. The results of the course are reflected in the following letter sent by the Chicago Commission on Human Relations to the mayor of Chicago:

About 8:00 P.M. on Sunday evening April 16, 1950 an accident occurred at 63rd Street and Carpenter involving two automobiles, one driven by a Negro woman and the other occupied by a white couple. The occupants of both automobiles reportedly settled matters amicably between themselves. It appeared that both were equally at fault. However, a crowd quickly gathered, tension rose and fighting began among the bystanders with sides quickly taken along racial lines. The area around 63rd and Carpenter is very mixed,—63rd Street has for a long time been a dividing line for the Southward movement of Negroes in the Ogden Park community. There are a number of bars along the street, and there have been interracial incidents in this area in previous times.

Police officers from the Englewood station arrived at the scene quickly. The sergeant in charge sensed the potential danger and unhesitatingly requested reinforcements to help clear the streets. . . . This operation was swift and effective. Commission representatives went immediately to the scene, and by the time they reached there, which was less than 20 minutes, the area was found completely under control with no crowds gathered and with no visible sign of tension.

This was the first interracial incident on the streets where a crowd gathered and fighting occurred since your statement of City policy of November 30 which called for immediate dispersal of any such crowds. It is also the first incident since the conclusion of the Training Program in Human Relations given by Professor Lohman to the Captains and Lieutenants of the Police Department. We can state flatly that the operation on 63rd and Carpenter completely fulfilled your instructions as to police policy and also carried out the basic principles of dispersal which were presented by Professor Lohman.

We believe you should feel a genuine sense of pride in the performance of the Police Department in this incident, which prevented any disorder on a larger scale by the swiftness of the action in handling it. We feel that you should be also pleased because this police operation took place in the Englewood community where tensions between racial elements of the community are at an intensified level.

The Commission on Human Relations commends highly this fine example of adequate and efficient police work.

In both the Chicago and the Washington incidents the situations were radically redefined after a sharpening and clarification of public policy and of the role of the law-enforcement agencies in the implementation of it. Considerable apprehension had existed, and with good reason, as to the role of the police and their disposition to countenance acts of violence in opposition to Negroes.

In the absence of a clearly stated and unambiguous policy, further complicated by an absence of a definition of the professional role of the police in such incidents, other organized and conflicting interests take control. This ultimately produces violence. After a program of training of the police, which stressed their role and responsibility in the maintenance of law and order without reference to their personal feelings and beliefs, a new collective fact emerged and took control. The training of the police was not designed to effect changes in their personal attitudes and prejudices but solely to redefine and set forth their role as professional law-enforcement agents in the implementing of public policy.

The performance of the police showed marked differences in these varying collectively defined situations. And similarly, the public's conduct reflects the definition provided by authoritative and unambiguous statements of policy.

It would be a mistake to assume that significant changes have taken place in the racial attitudes, so called, of the individual policemen in Washington or Chicago. Similarly, it is idle to attempt to explain the seemingly contradictory racial behavior of government employees, or urban industrial workers, in terms of their personal feelings and sentiments. In modern mass society the group continues as the essential reality in human behavior, but the relevant and controlling collectivities are, increasingly, deliberately organized interest groups.

Supplementary Bibliography

Eleanor E. Maccoby, Theodore M. Newcomb, and Eugene L. Hartley, *Readings in Social Psychology*, 3rd ed. N. Y.: Holt, 1958.
  Contains a number of pertinent pieces, including an excellent article by Robin M. Williams, Jr., "Religion, Value Orientations, and Intergroup Conflict."

Raymond W. Mack and Richard C. Snyder, "The Analysis of Social Conflict: Toward an Overview and Synthesis." *The Journal of Conflict Resolution*, 1957, 1: 212-248.
  An attempt to derive propositions and hypotheses from previous research and writing on conflict.

John P. Roche and Milton M. Gordon, "Can Morality Be Legislated?" *New York Times Magazine*, May 22, 1955, pp. 10, 42, 44, 49. Reprinted in Kimball Young and Raymond W. Mack, *Principles of Sociology: A Reader in Theory and Research*, 2nd ed. N. Y.: American Book, 1962, pp. 337-342.